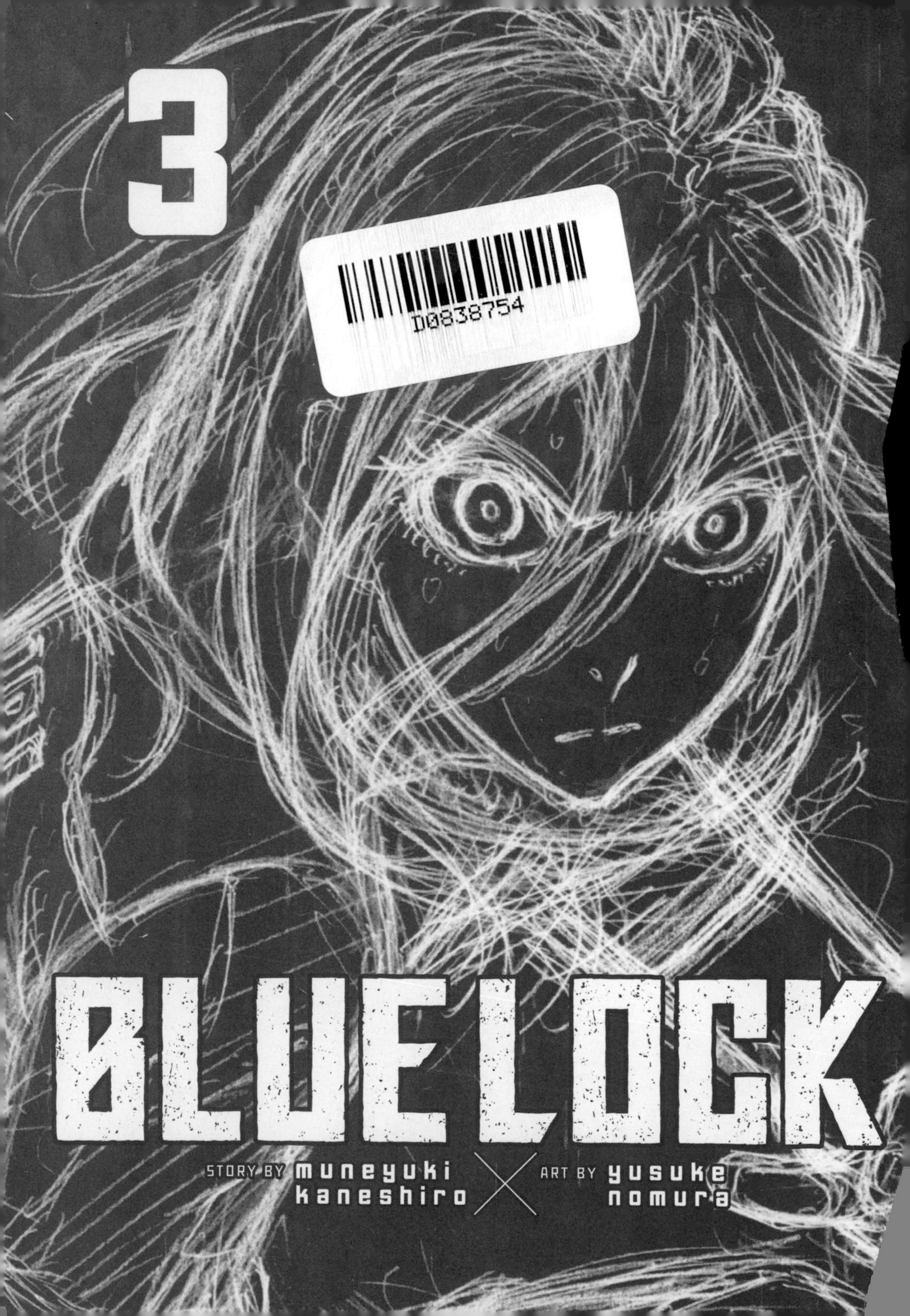
3
BLUE LOCK
STORY BY muneyuki kaneshiro
ART BY yusuke nomura

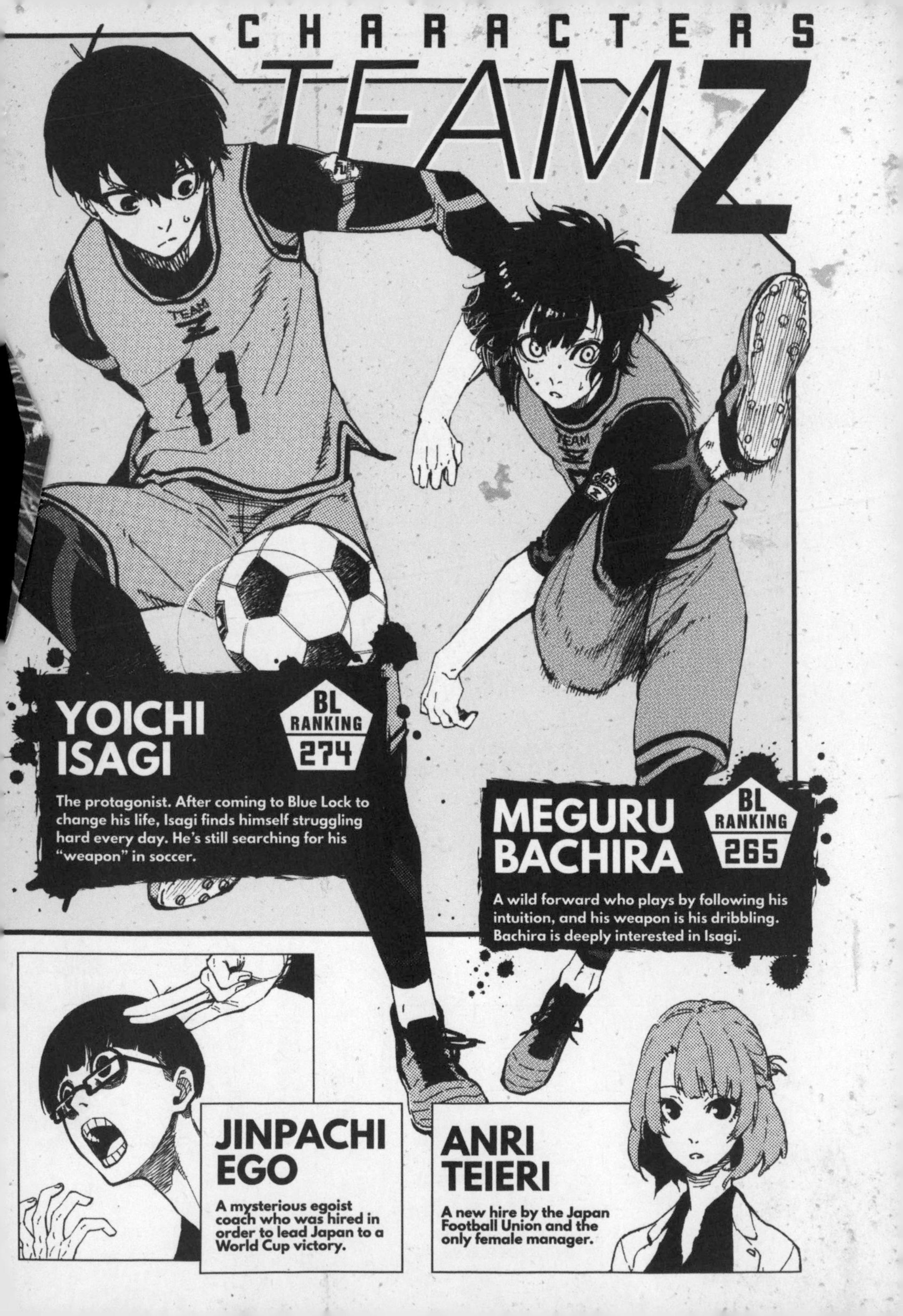
CHARACTERS
TEAM Z
YOICHI ISAGI
BL RANKING 274
The protagonist. After coming to Blue Lock to change his life, Isagi finds himself struggling hard every day. He's still searching for his "weapon" in soccer.
MEGURU BACHIRA
BL RANKING 265
A wild forward who plays by following his intuition, and his weapon is his dribbling. Bachira is deeply interested in Isagi.
JINPACHI EGO
A mysterious egoist coach who was hired in order to lead Japan to a World Cup victory.
ANRI TEIERI
A new hire by the Japan Football Union and the only female manager.

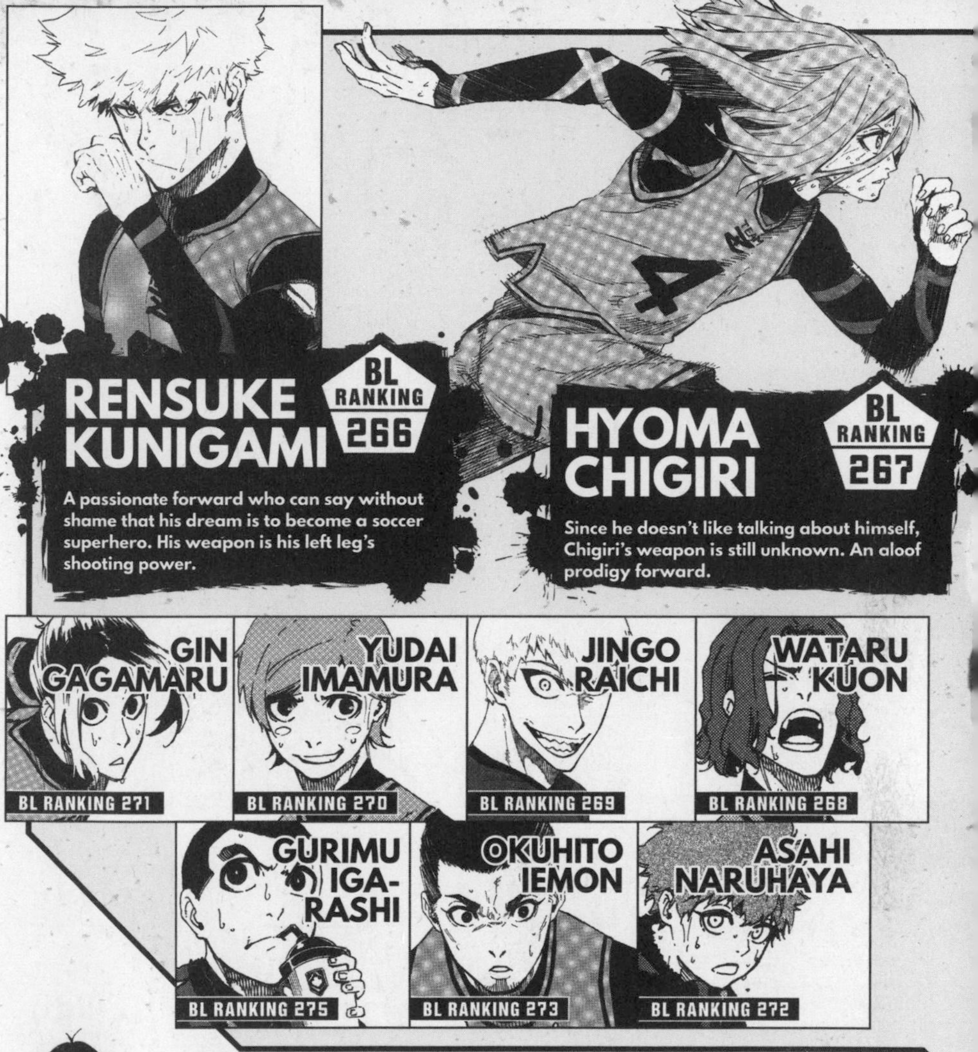
HYOMA CHIGIRI
BL RANKING 267
Since he doesn't like talking about himself, Chigiri's weapon is still unknown. An aloof prodigy forward.
RENSUKE KUNIGAMI
BL RANKING 266
A passionate forward who can say without shame that his dream is to become a soccer superhero. His weapon is his left leg's shooting power.
WATARU KUON
BL RANKING 268
JINGO RAICHI
BL RANKING 269
YUDAI IMAMURA
BL RANKING 270
GIN GAGAMARU
BL RANKING 271
ASAHI NARUHAYA
BL RANKING 272
OKUHITO IEMON
BL RANKING 273
GURIMU IGA-RASHI
BL RANKING 275

WING 5

HERE ARE THE RESULTS AFTER THE FOURTH MATCH!

	TEAM	POINTS	POINT DIFF.
1	V	3	+8
2	W	3	+3
3	X	3	+1
4	Z	3	-3
5	Y	0	-9

	V	W	X	Y	Z
V				○ 8-0	
W			○ 4-1		
X		● 1-4			○ 5-1
Y	● 0-8				● 1-2
Z			● 1-5	○ 2-1	

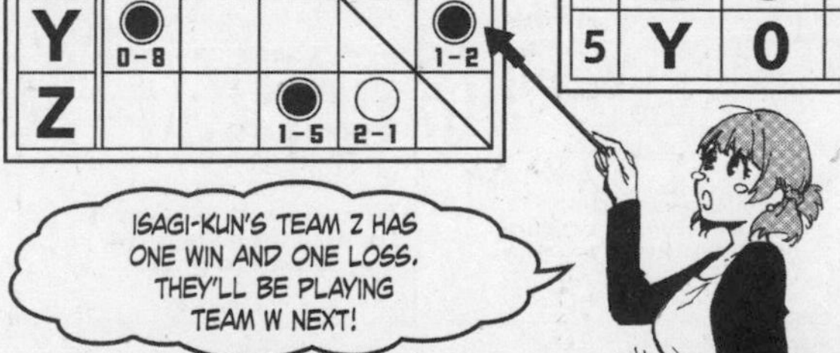
ISAGI-KUN'S TEAM Z HAS ONE WIN AND ONE LOSS. THEY'LL BE PLAYING TEAM W NEXT!

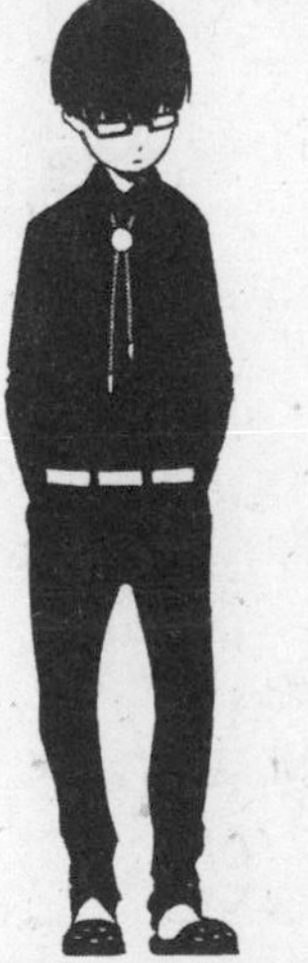

CONTENTS

CHAPTER 14: RESOLVE

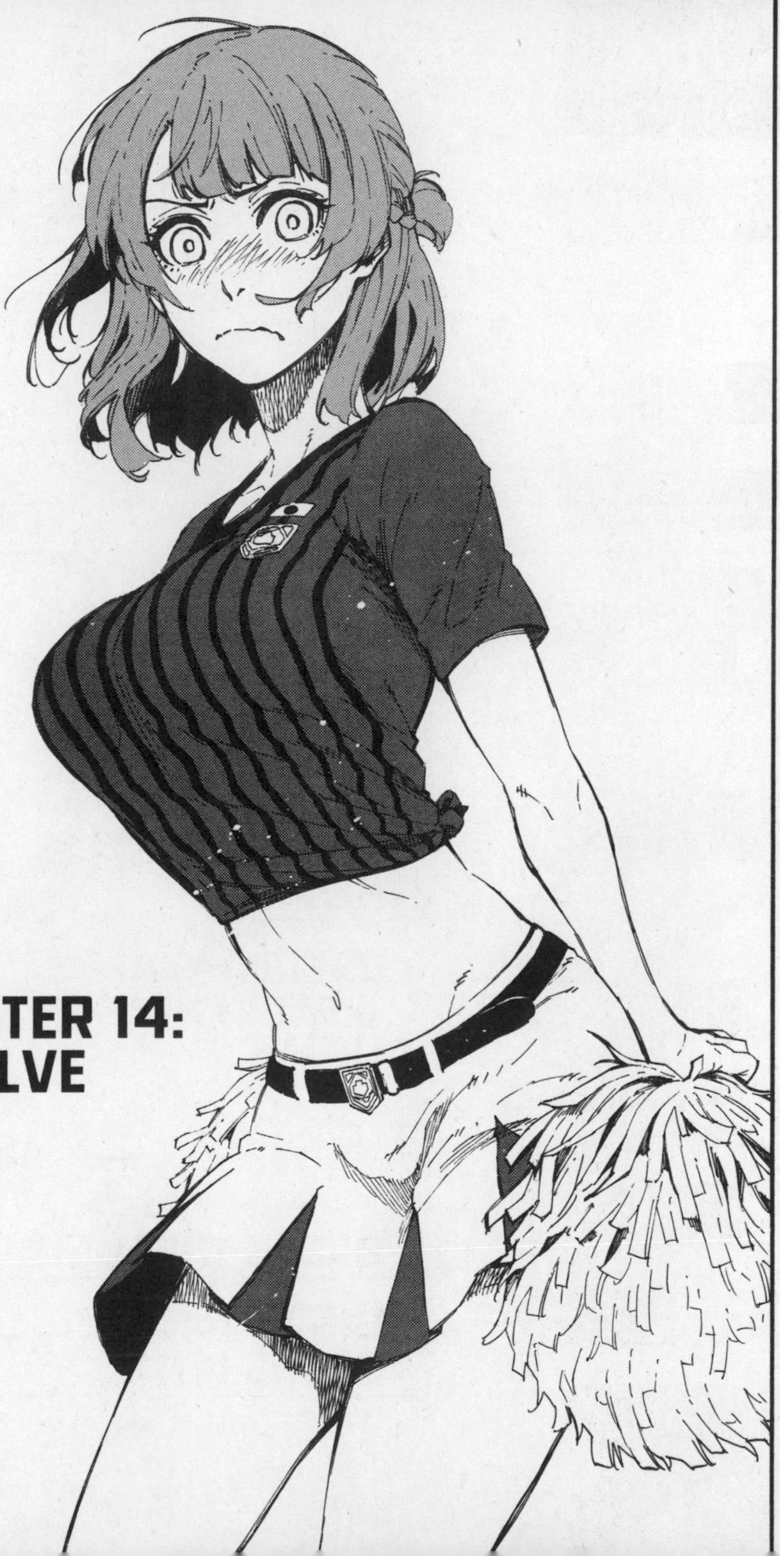

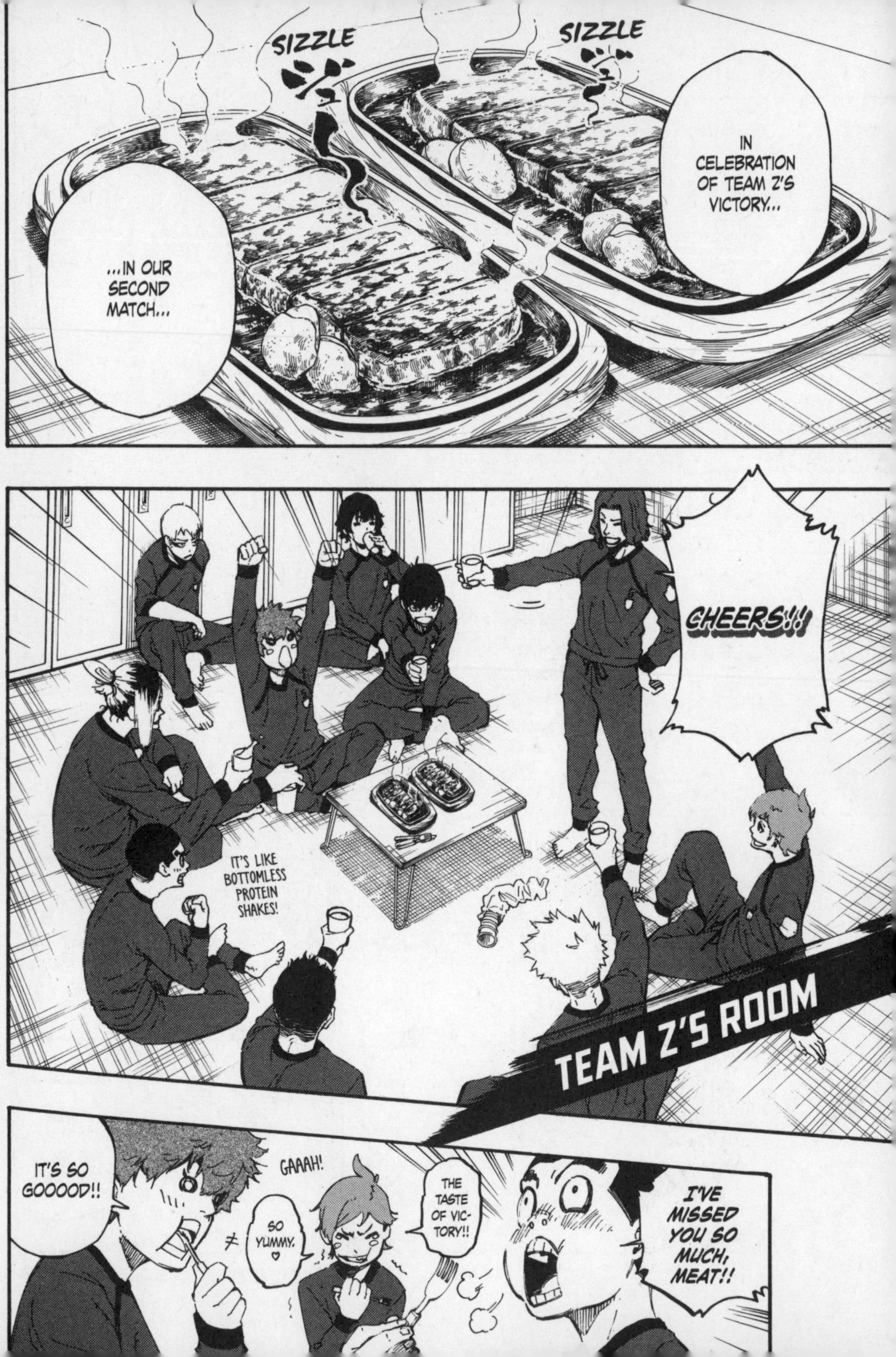
SIZZLE
IN CELEBRATION OF TEAM Z'S VICTORY...
SIZZLE
...IN OUR SECOND MATCH...
CHEERS!!!
IT'S LIKE BOTTOMLESS PROTEIN SHAKES!
TEAM Z'S ROOM
I'VE MISSED YOU SO MUCH, MEAT!!
THE TASTE OF VIC-TORY!!
SO YUMMY. ♡
GAAAH!
IT'S SO GOOOOD!!

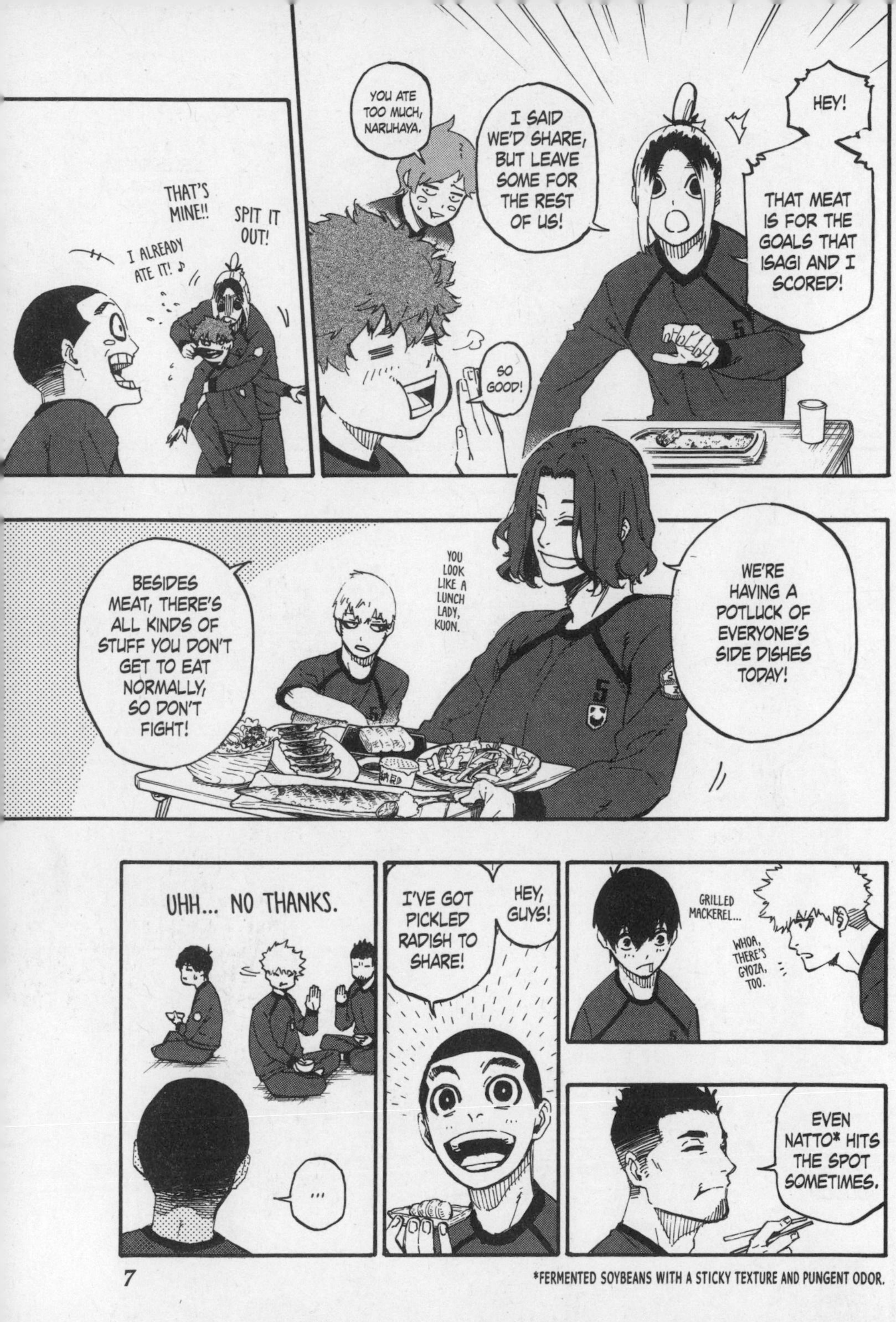
HEY!
THAT MEAT IS FOR THE GOALS THAT ISAGI AND I SCORED!
I SAID WE'D SHARE, BUT LEAVE SOME FOR THE REST OF US!
YOU ATE TOO MUCH, NARUHAYA.
SO GOOD!
SPIT IT OUT!
THAT'S MINE!!
I ALREADY ATE IT! ♪
WE'RE HAVING A POTLUCK OF EVERYONE'S SIDE DISHES TODAY!
YOU LOOK LIKE A LUNCH LADY, KUON.
BESIDES MEAT, THERE'S ALL KINDS OF STUFF YOU DON'T GET TO EAT NORMALLY, SO DON'T FIGHT!
GRILLED MACKEREL...
WHOA, THERE'S GYOZA, TOO.
EVEN NATTO* HITS THE SPOT SOMETIMES.
HEY, GUYS!
I'VE GOT PICKLED RADISH TO SHARE!
UHH... NO THANKS.
...

*FERMENTED SOYBEANS WITH A STICKY TEXTURE AND PUNGENT ODOR.

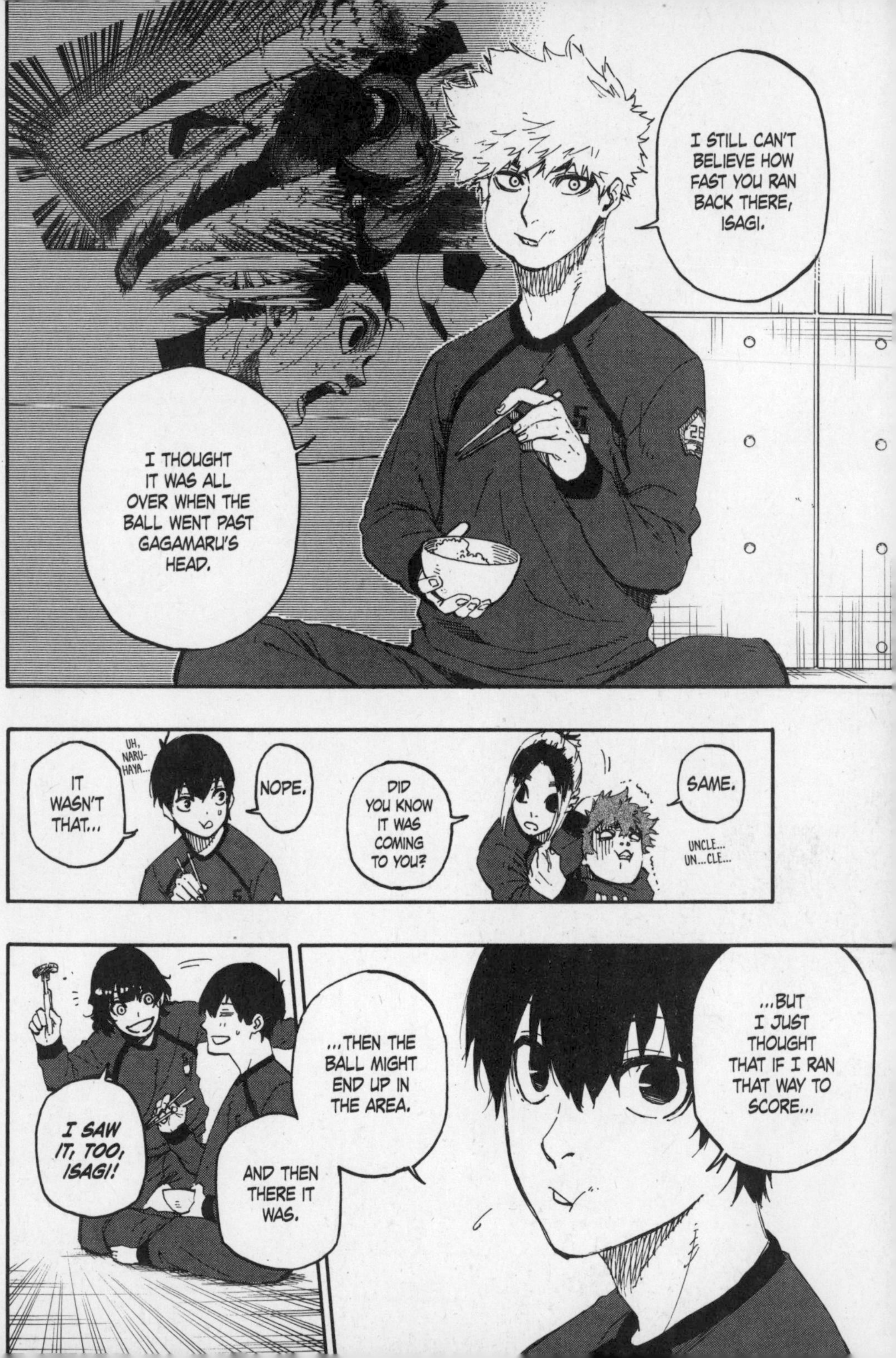
I STILL CAN'T BELIEVE HOW FAST YOU RAN BACK THERE, ISAGI.
I THOUGHT IT WAS ALL OVER WHEN THE BALL WENT PAST GAGAMARU'S HEAD.
SAME.
UNCLE... UN...CLE...
DID YOU KNOW IT WAS COMING TO YOU?
NOPE.
UH, NARU-HAYA...
IT WASN'T THAT...
...BUT I JUST THOUGHT THAT IF I RAN THAT WAY TO SCORE...
...THEN THE BALL MIGHT END UP IN THE AREA.
AND THEN THERE IT WAS.
I SAW IT, TOO, ISAGI!

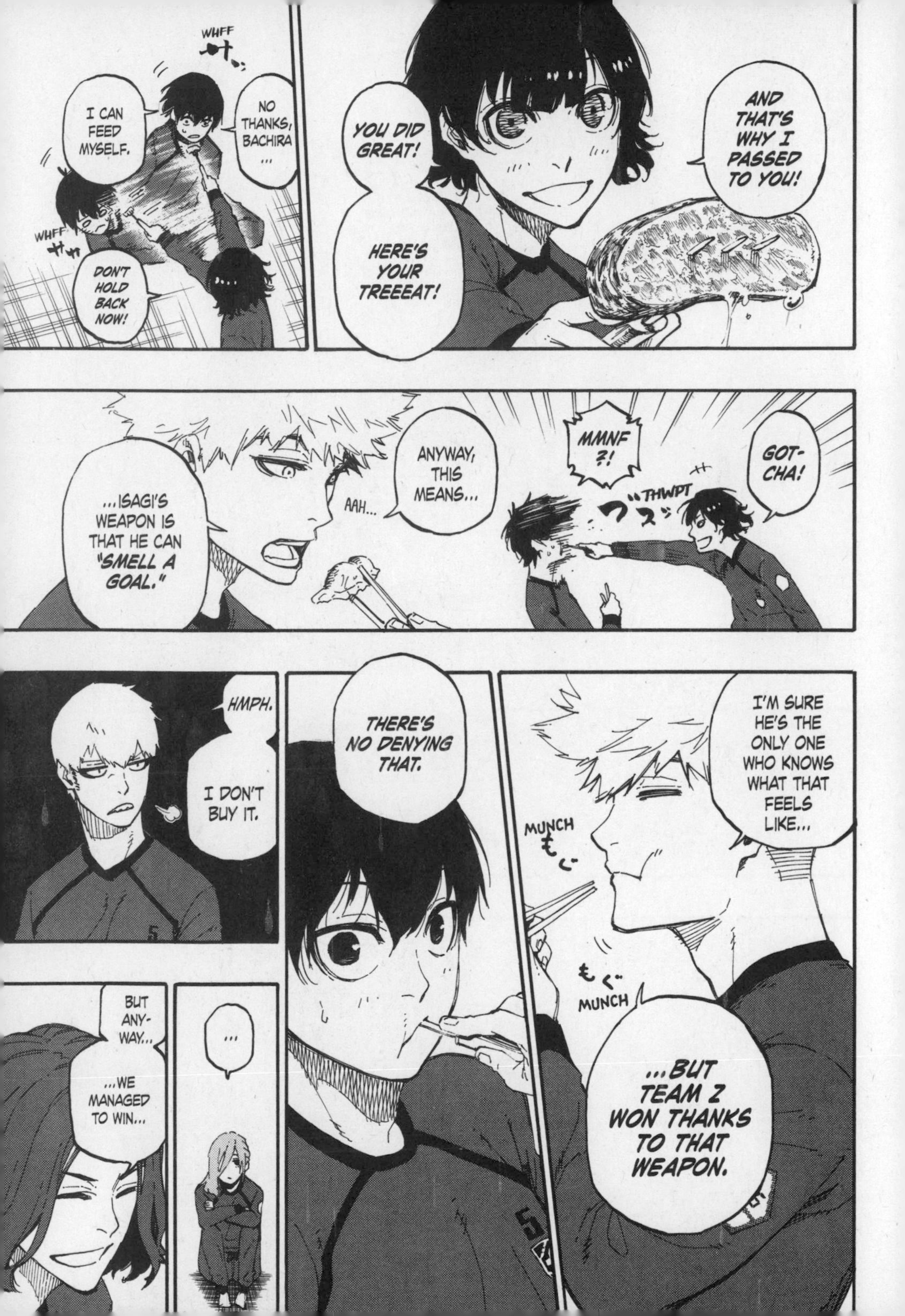
AND THAT'S WHY I PASSED TO YOU!
YOU DID GREAT!
HERE'S YOUR TREEEAT!
WHFF
NO THANKS, BACHIRA ...
I CAN FEED MYSELF.
WHFF
DON'T HOLD BACK NOW!
GOT-CHA!
MMNF ?!
THWPT
ANYWAY, THIS MEANS...
AAH...
...ISAGI'S WEAPON IS THAT HE CAN "SMELL A GOAL."
I'M SURE HE'S THE ONLY ONE WHO KNOWS WHAT THAT FEELS LIKE...
MUNCH
MUNCH
...BUT TEAM Z WON THANKS TO THAT WEAPON.
THERE'S NO DENYING THAT.
HMPH.
I DON'T BUY IT.
...
BUT ANY-WAY...
...WE MANAGED TO WIN...

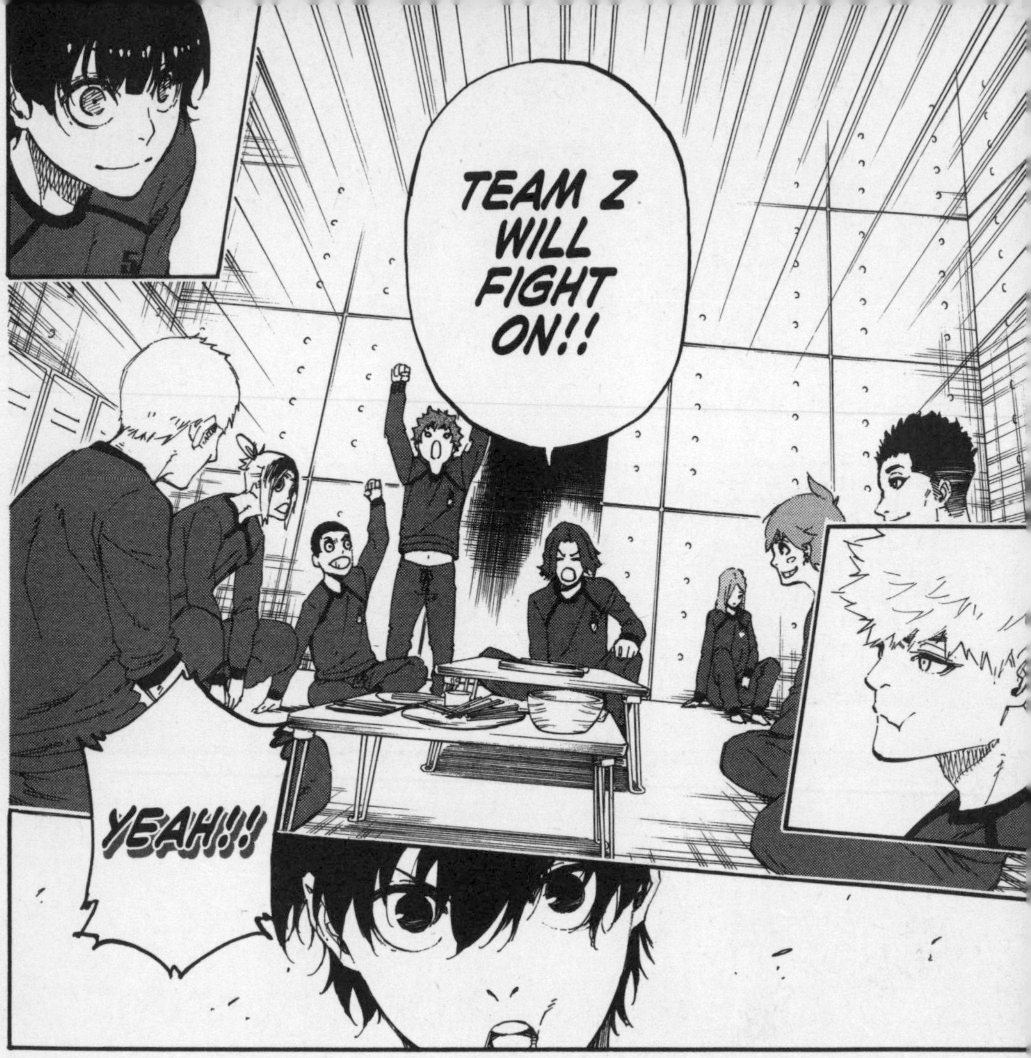
TEAM Z WILL FIGHT ON!!
YEAH!!!

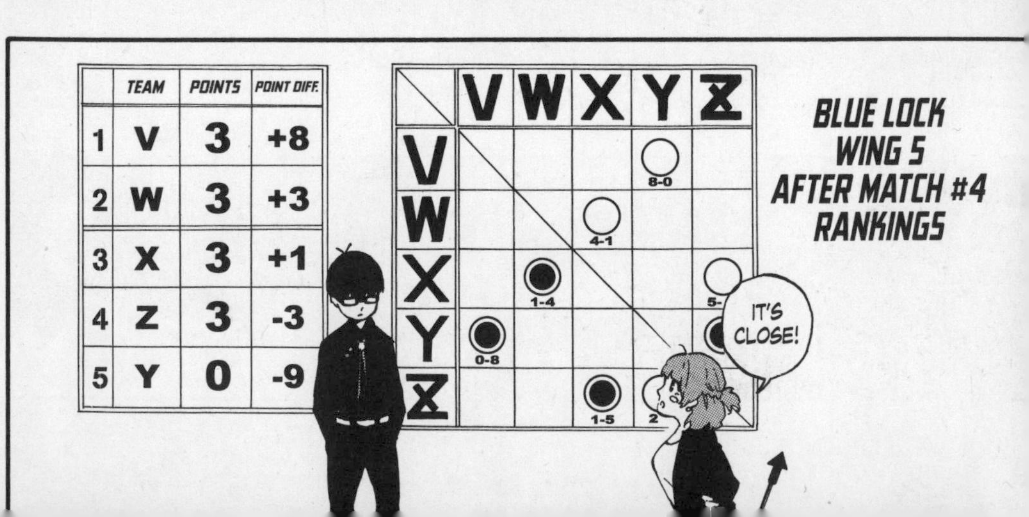
BLUE LOCK WING 5 AFTER MATCH #4 RANKINGS
IT'S CLOSE!

	TEAM	POINTS	POINT DIFF.
1	V	3	+8
2	W	3	+3
3	X	3	+1
4	Z	3	-3
5	Y	0	-9

	V	W	X	Y	Z
V				○ 8-0	
W			○ 4-1		
X		● 1-4			○ 5-
Y	● 0-8				●
Z			● 1-5	○ 2	

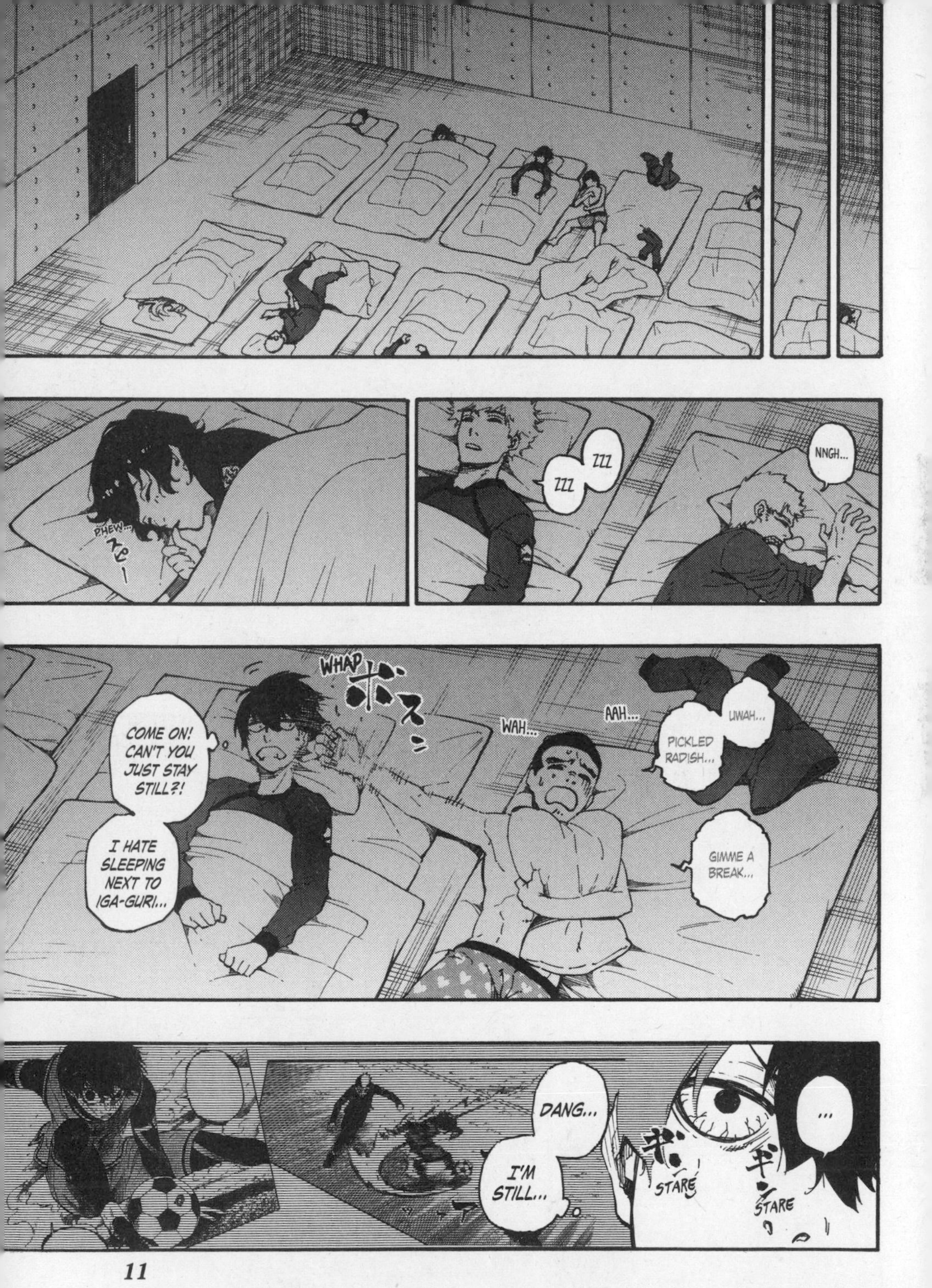
NNGH...
ZZZ
ZZZ
PHEW... スピー
UWAH... PICKLED RADISH...
AAH...
WAH...
GIMME A BREAK...
WHAP ボスン
COME ON! CAN'T YOU JUST STAY STILL?!
I HATE SLEEPING NEXT TO IGA-GURI...
...
STARE ギン
STARE ギン
DANG...
I'M STILL...

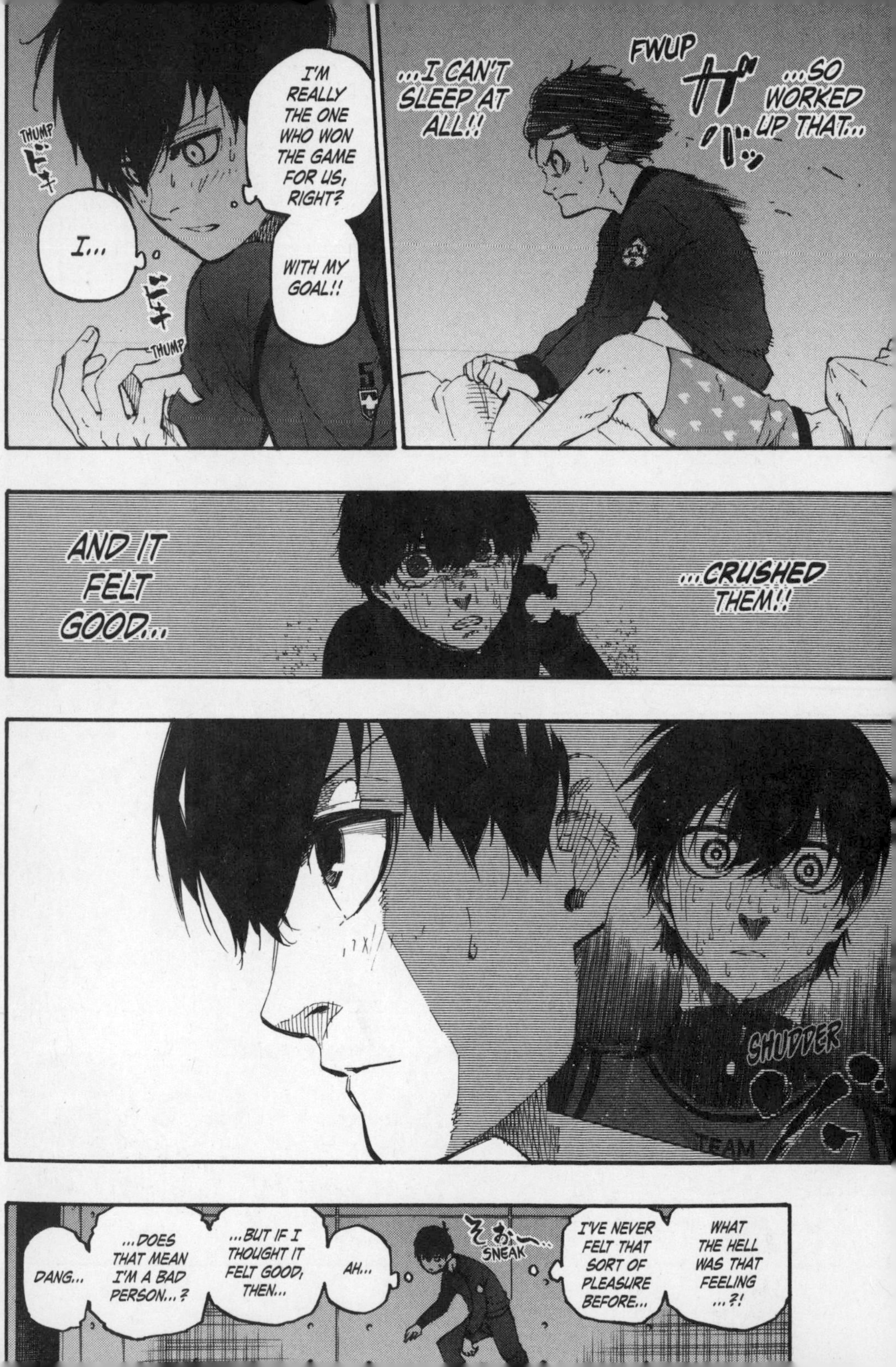
FWUP
...SO WORKED UP THAT...
...I CAN'T SLEEP AT ALL!!
I'M REALLY THE ONE WHO WON THE GAME FOR US, RIGHT?
WITH MY GOAL!!
THUMP
I...
THUMP
...CRUSHED THEM!!
AND IT FELT GOOD...
SHUDDER
TEAM
WHAT THE HELL WAS THAT FEELING ...?!
I'VE NEVER FELT THAT SORT OF PLEASURE BEFORE...
SNEAK
AH...
...BUT IF I THOUGHT IT FELT GOOD, THEN...
...DOES THAT MEAN I'M A BAD PERSON...?
DANG...

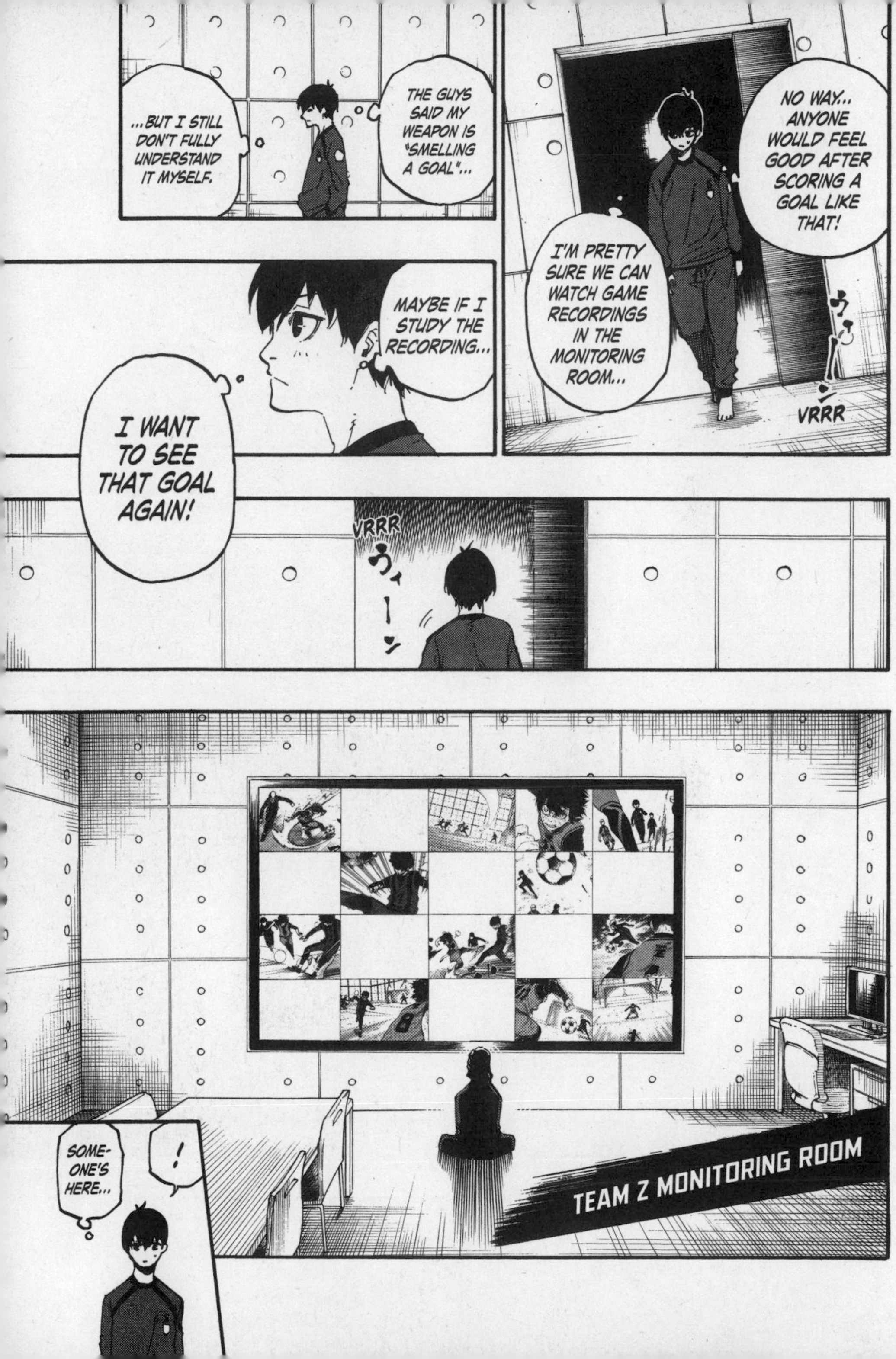
NO WAY... ANYONE WOULD FEEL GOOD AFTER SCORING A GOAL LIKE THAT!
I'M PRETTY SURE WE CAN WATCH GAME RECORDINGS IN THE MONITORING ROOM...
VRRR
THE GUYS SAID MY WEAPON IS "SMELLING A GOAL"...
...BUT I STILL DON'T FULLY UNDERSTAND IT MYSELF.
MAYBE IF I STUDY THE RECORDING...
I WANT TO SEE THAT GOAL AGAIN!
VRRR
ウィーン
TEAM Z MONITORING ROOM
!
SOME-ONE'S HERE...

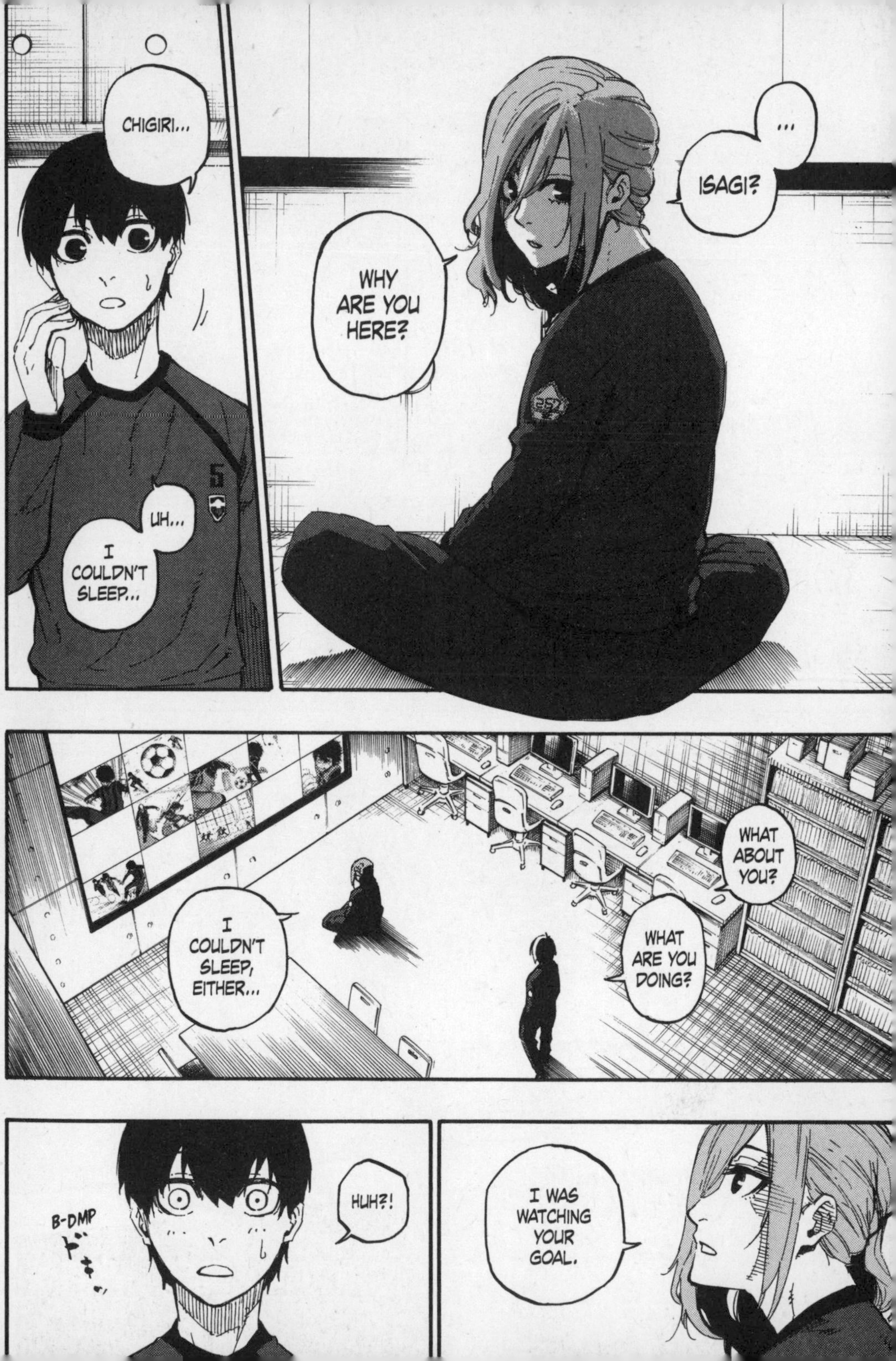
...
ISAGI?
WHY ARE YOU HERE?
CHIGIRI...
UH...
I COULDN'T SLEEP...
WHAT ABOUT YOU?
WHAT ARE YOU DOING?
I COULDN'T SLEEP, EITHER...
I WAS WATCHING YOUR GOAL.
HUH?!
B-DMP
ドキ

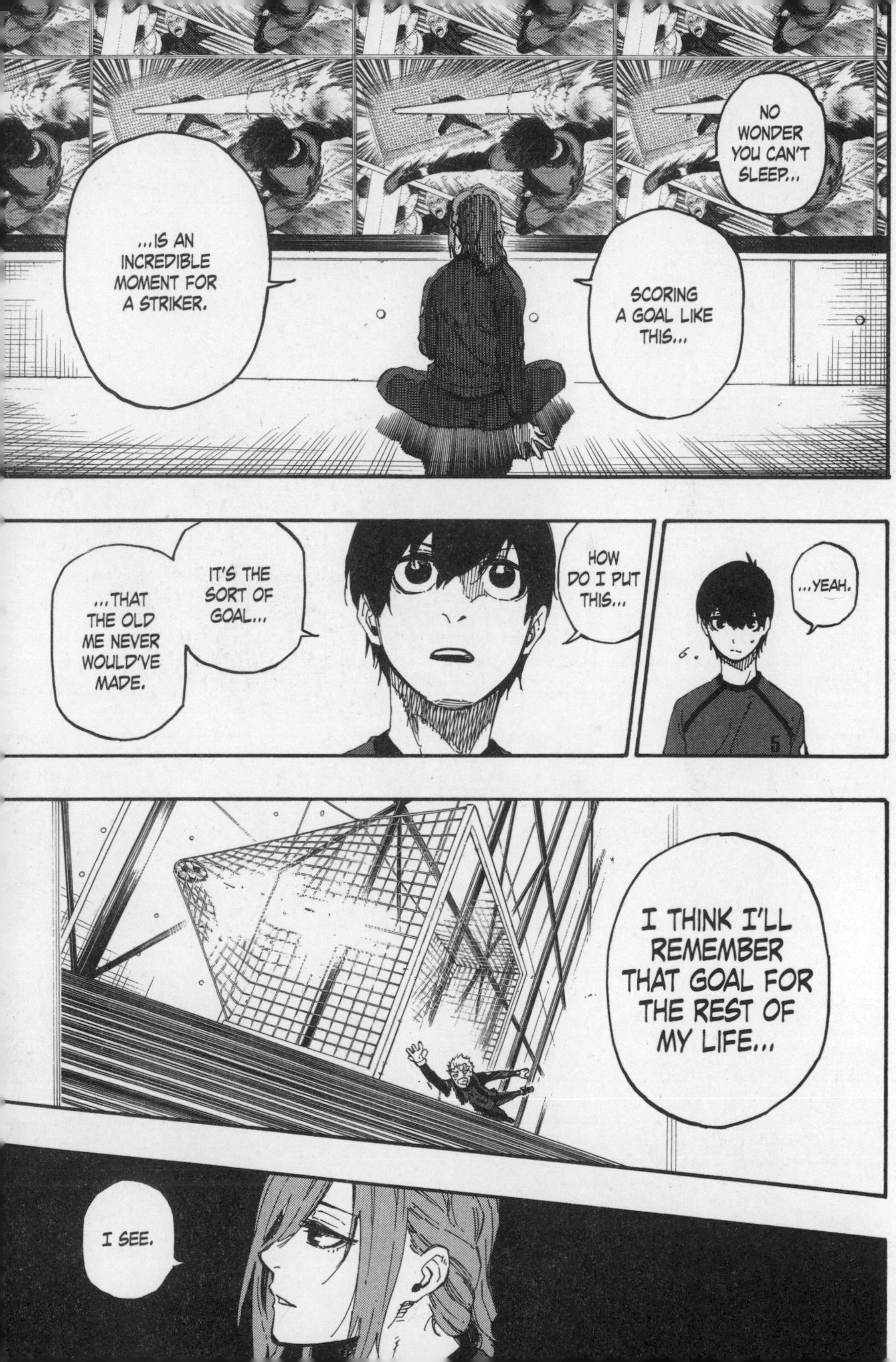
NO WONDER YOU CAN'T SLEEP...
SCORING A GOAL LIKE THIS...
...IS AN INCREDIBLE MOMENT FOR A STRIKER.
...YEAH.
HOW DO I PUT THIS...
IT'S THE SORT OF GOAL...
...THAT THE OLD ME NEVER WOULD'VE MADE.
I THINK I'LL REMEMBER THAT GOAL FOR THE REST OF MY LIFE...
I SEE.

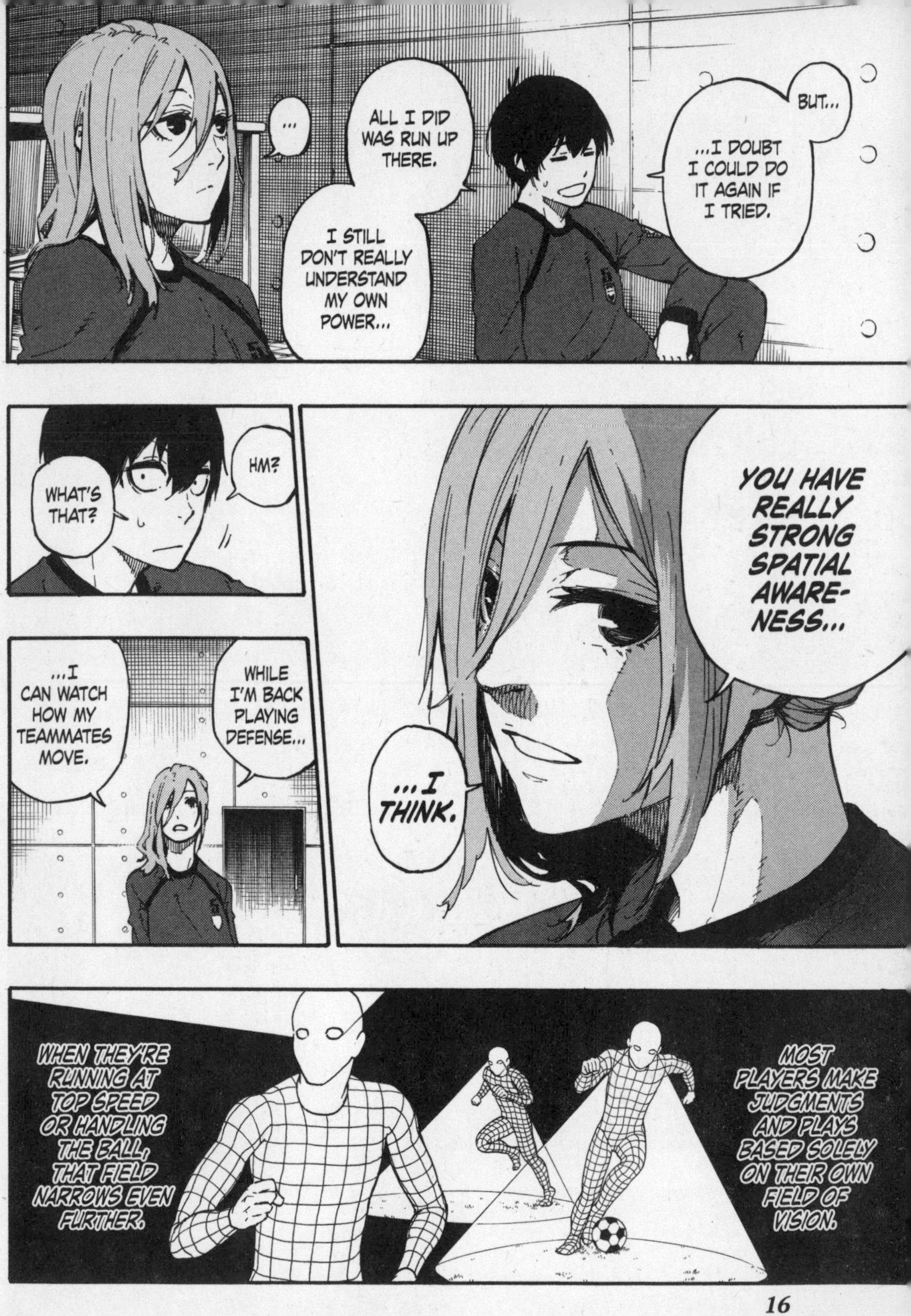
BUT...
...I DOUBT I COULD DO IT AGAIN IF I TRIED.
ALL I DID WAS RUN UP THERE.
I STILL DON'T REALLY UNDERSTAND MY OWN POWER...
...
YOU HAVE REALLY STRONG SPATIAL AWARE-NESS...
...I THINK.
HM?
WHAT'S THAT?
WHILE I'M BACK PLAYING DEFENSE...
...I CAN WATCH HOW MY TEAMMATES MOVE.
MOST PLAYERS MAKE JUDGMENTS AND PLAYS BASED SOLELY ON THEIR OWN FIELD OF VISION.
WHEN THEY'RE RUNNING AT TOP SPEED OR HANDLING THE BALL, THAT FIELD NARROWS EVEN FURTHER.

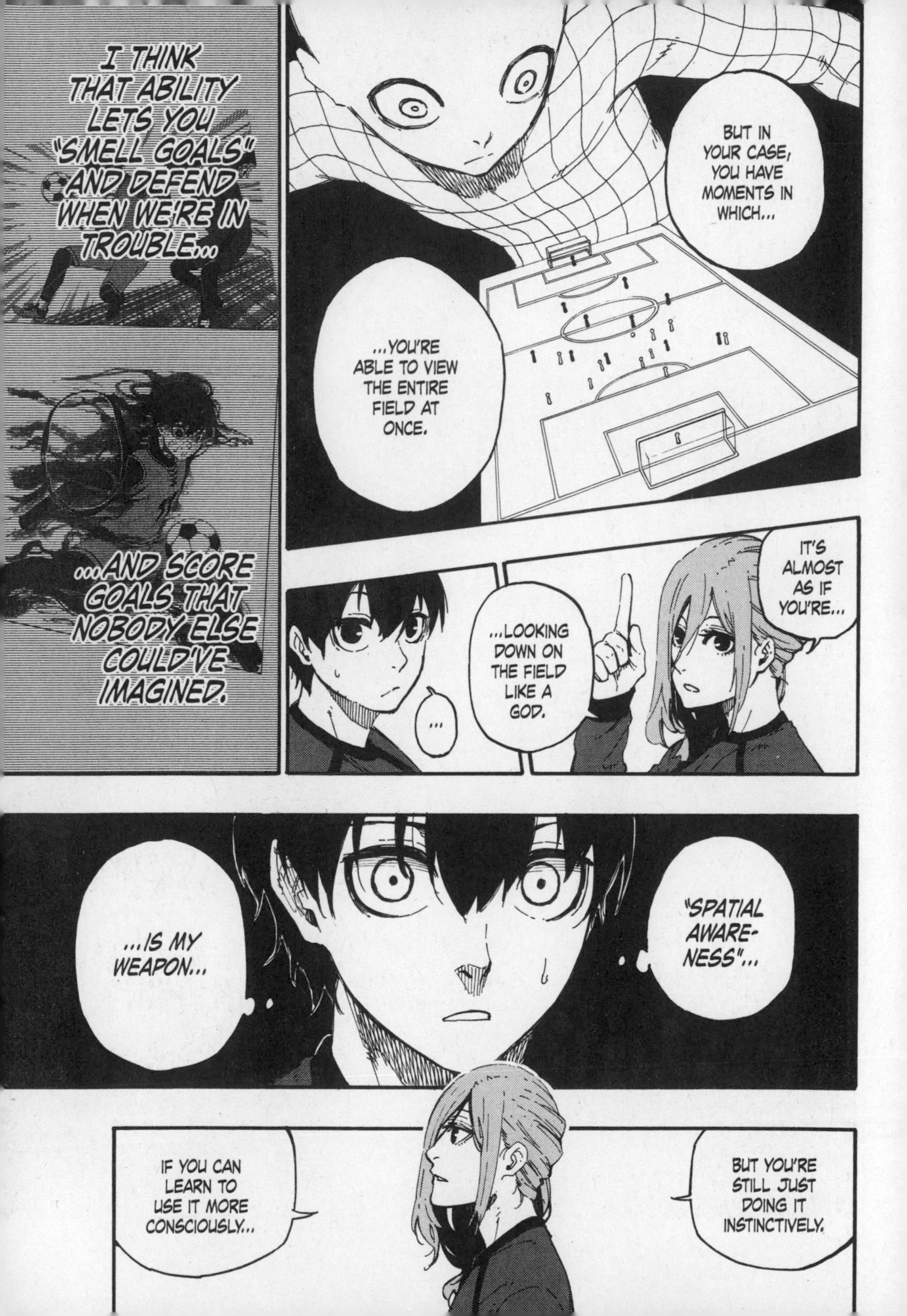
BUT IN YOUR CASE, YOU HAVE MOMENTS IN WHICH...
...YOU'RE ABLE TO VIEW THE ENTIRE FIELD AT ONCE.
IT'S ALMOST AS IF YOU'RE...
...LOOKING DOWN ON THE FIELD LIKE A GOD.
...
I THINK THAT ABILITY LETS YOU "SMELL GOALS" AND DEFEND WHEN WE'RE IN TROUBLE...
...AND SCORE GOALS THAT NOBODY ELSE COULD'VE IMAGINED.
"SPATIAL AWARE-NESS"...
...IS MY WEAPON...
BUT YOU'RE STILL JUST DOING IT INSTINCTIVELY.
IF YOU CAN LEARN TO USE IT MORE CONSCIOUSLY...

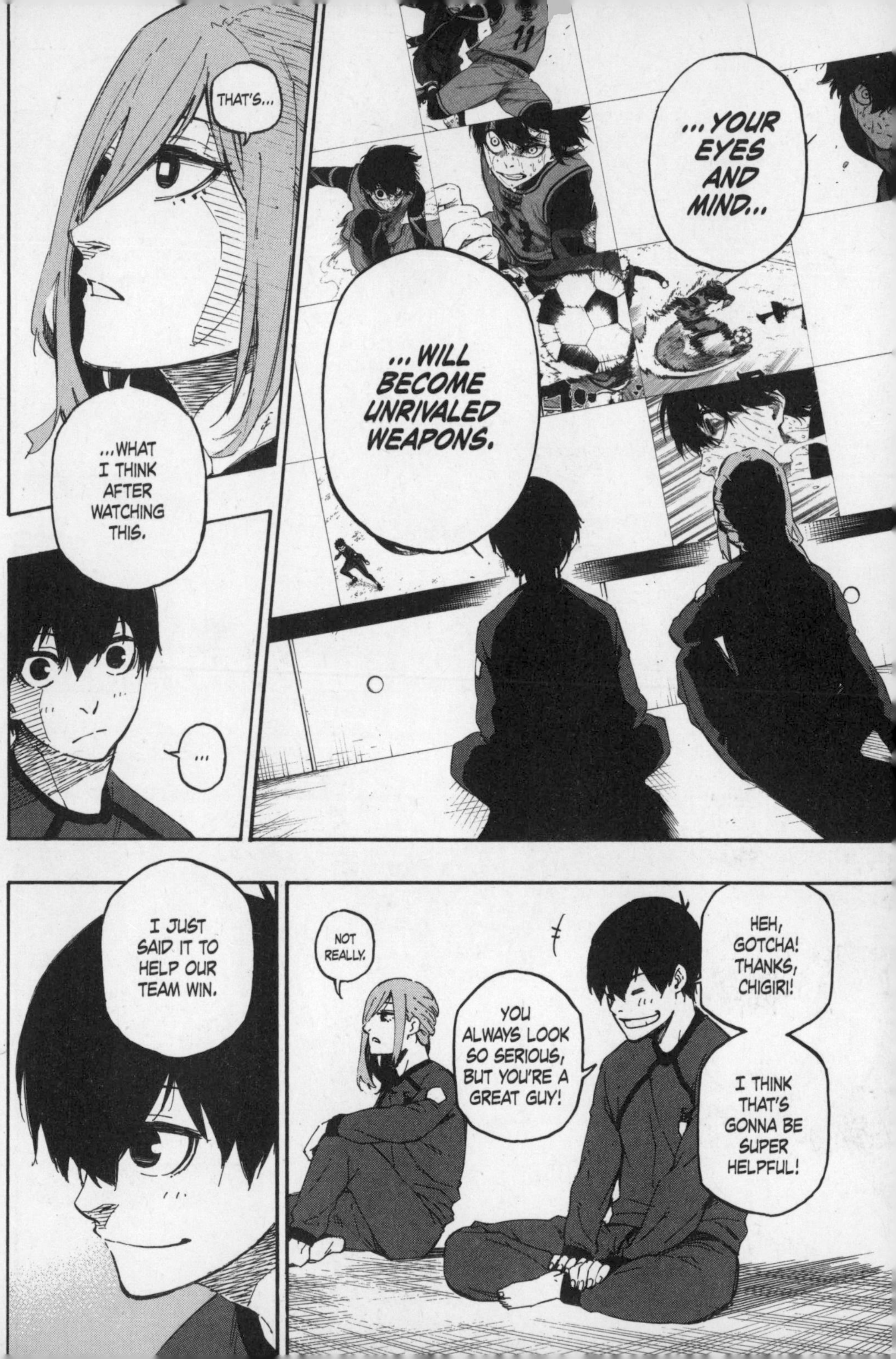
...YOUR EYES AND MIND...
...WILL BECOME UNRIVALED WEAPONS.
THAT'S...
...WHAT I THINK AFTER WATCHING THIS.
...
HEH, GOTCHA! THANKS, CHIGIRI!
I THINK THAT'S GONNA BE SUPER HELPFUL!
YOU ALWAYS LOOK SO SERIOUS, BUT YOU'RE A GREAT GUY!
NOT REALLY.
I JUST SAID IT TO HELP OUR TEAM WIN.

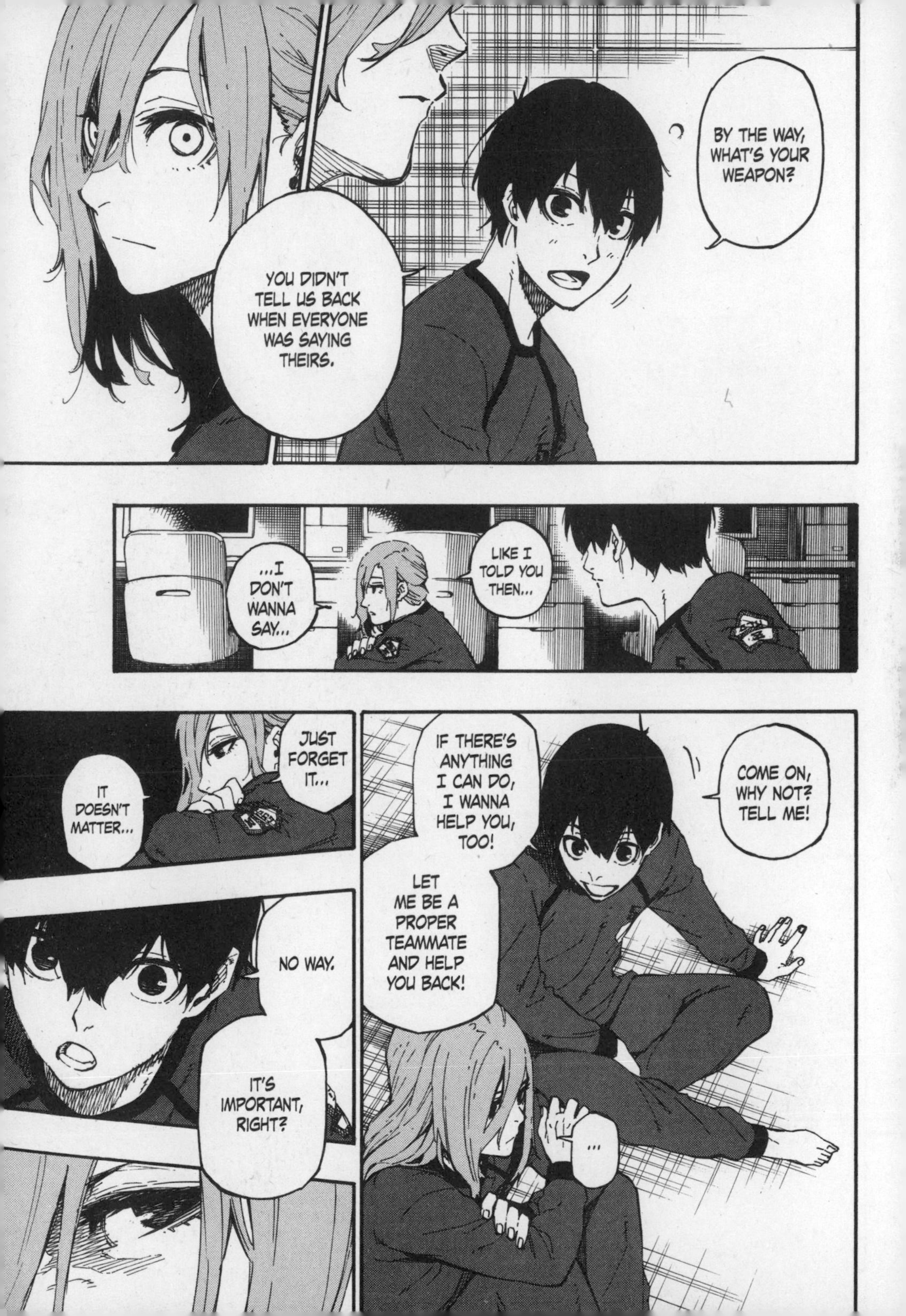
BY THE WAY, WHAT'S YOUR WEAPON?
YOU DIDN'T TELL US BACK WHEN EVERYONE WAS SAYING THEIRS.
LIKE I TOLD YOU THEN...
...I DON'T WANNA SAY...
COME ON, WHY NOT? TELL ME!
IF THERE'S ANYTHING I CAN DO, I WANNA HELP YOU, TOO!
LET ME BE A PROPER TEAMMATE AND HELP YOU BACK!
...
JUST FORGET IT...
IT DOESN'T MATTER...
NO WAY.
IT'S IMPORTANT, RIGHT?

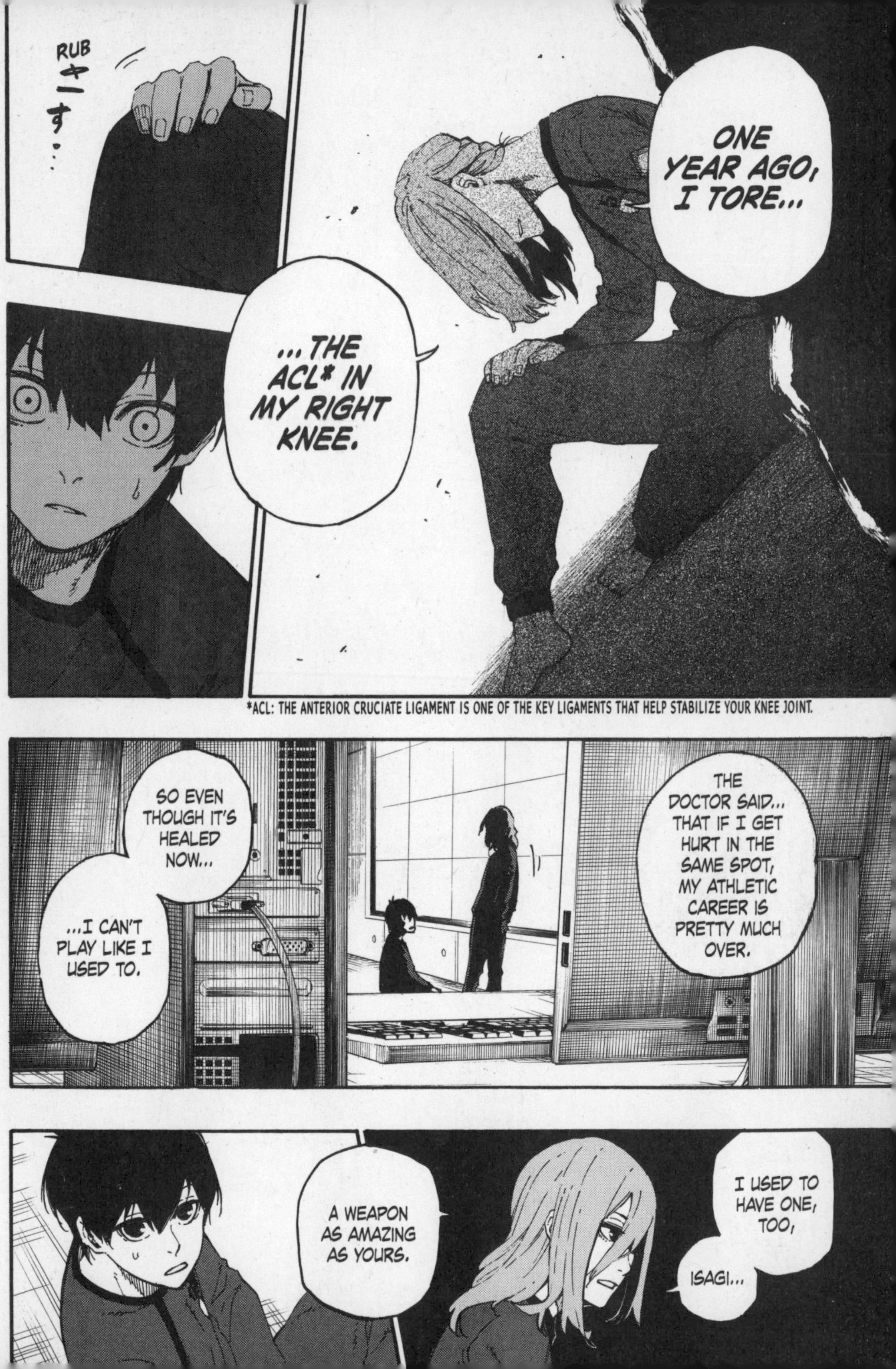
ONE YEAR AGO, I TORE...
...THE ACL* IN MY RIGHT KNEE.
RUB
THE DOCTOR SAID... THAT IF I GET HURT IN THE SAME SPOT, MY ATHLETIC CAREER IS PRETTY MUCH OVER.
SO EVEN THOUGH IT'S HEALED NOW...
...I CAN'T PLAY LIKE I USED TO.
I USED TO HAVE ONE, TOO,
ISAGI...
A WEAPON AS AMAZING AS YOURS.

*ACL: THE ANTERIOR CRUCIATE LIGAMENT IS ONE OF THE KEY LIGAMENTS THAT HELP STABILIZE YOUR KNEE JOINT.

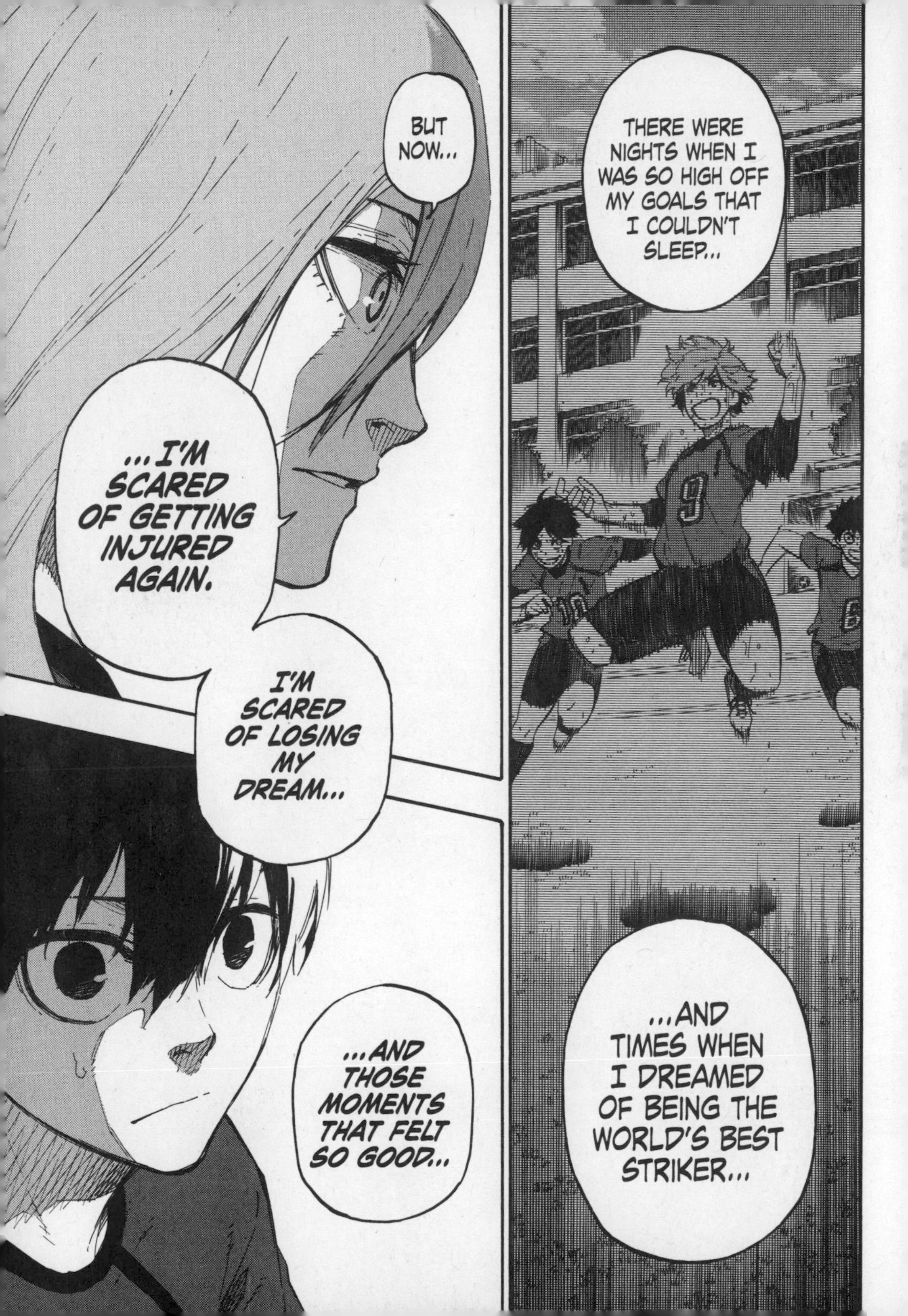
THERE WERE NIGHTS WHEN I WAS SO HIGH OFF MY GOALS THAT I COULDN'T SLEEP...
...AND TIMES WHEN I DREAMED OF BEING THE WORLD'S BEST STRIKER...
BUT NOW...
...I'M SCARED OF GETTING INJURED AGAIN.
I'M SCARED OF LOSING MY DREAM...
...AND THOSE MOMENTS THAT FELT SO GOOD...

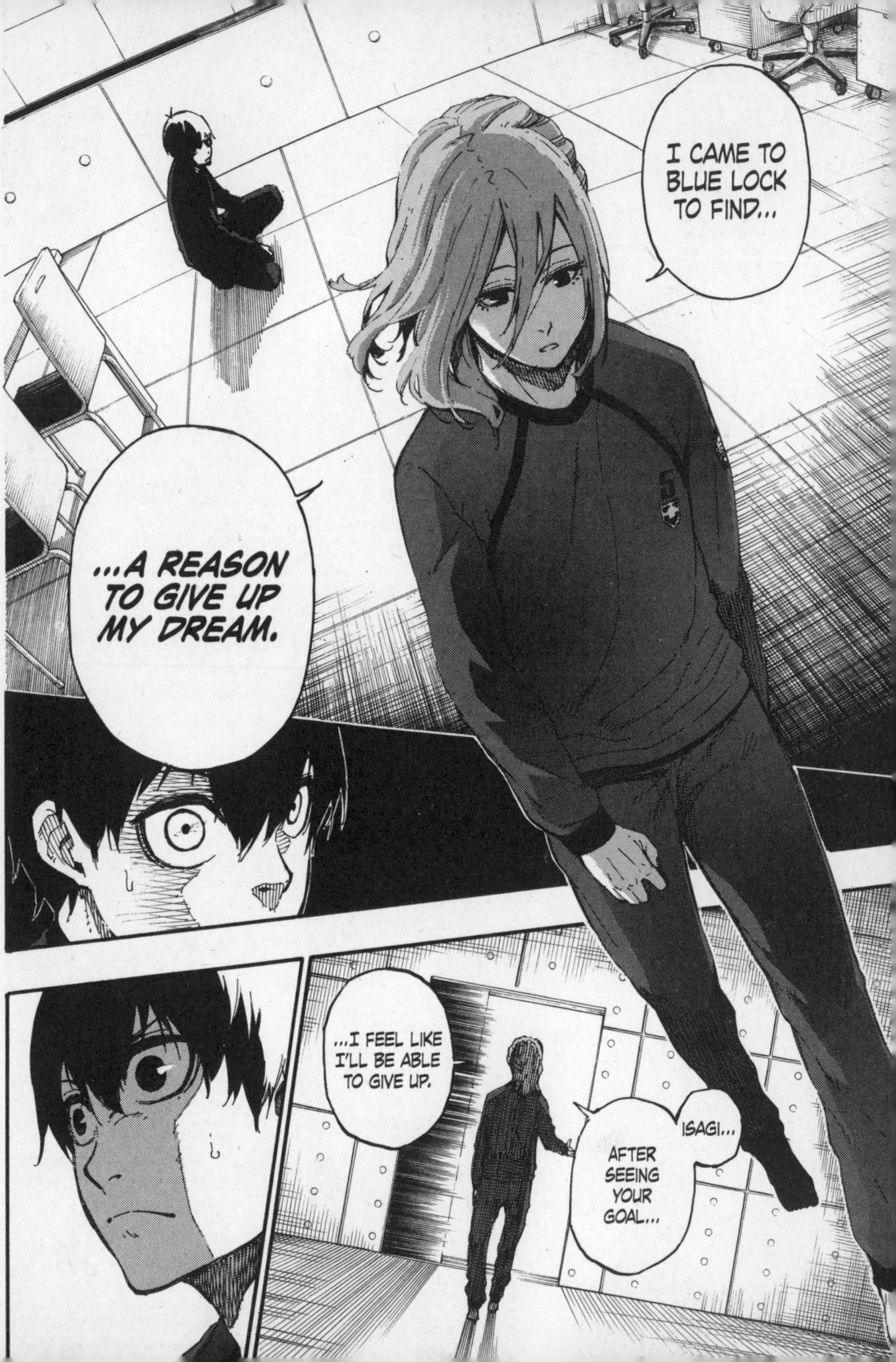
I CAME TO BLUE LOCK TO FIND...
...A REASON TO GIVE UP MY DREAM.
ISAGI...
AFTER SEEING YOUR GOAL...
...I FEEL LIKE I'LL BE ABLE TO GIVE UP.

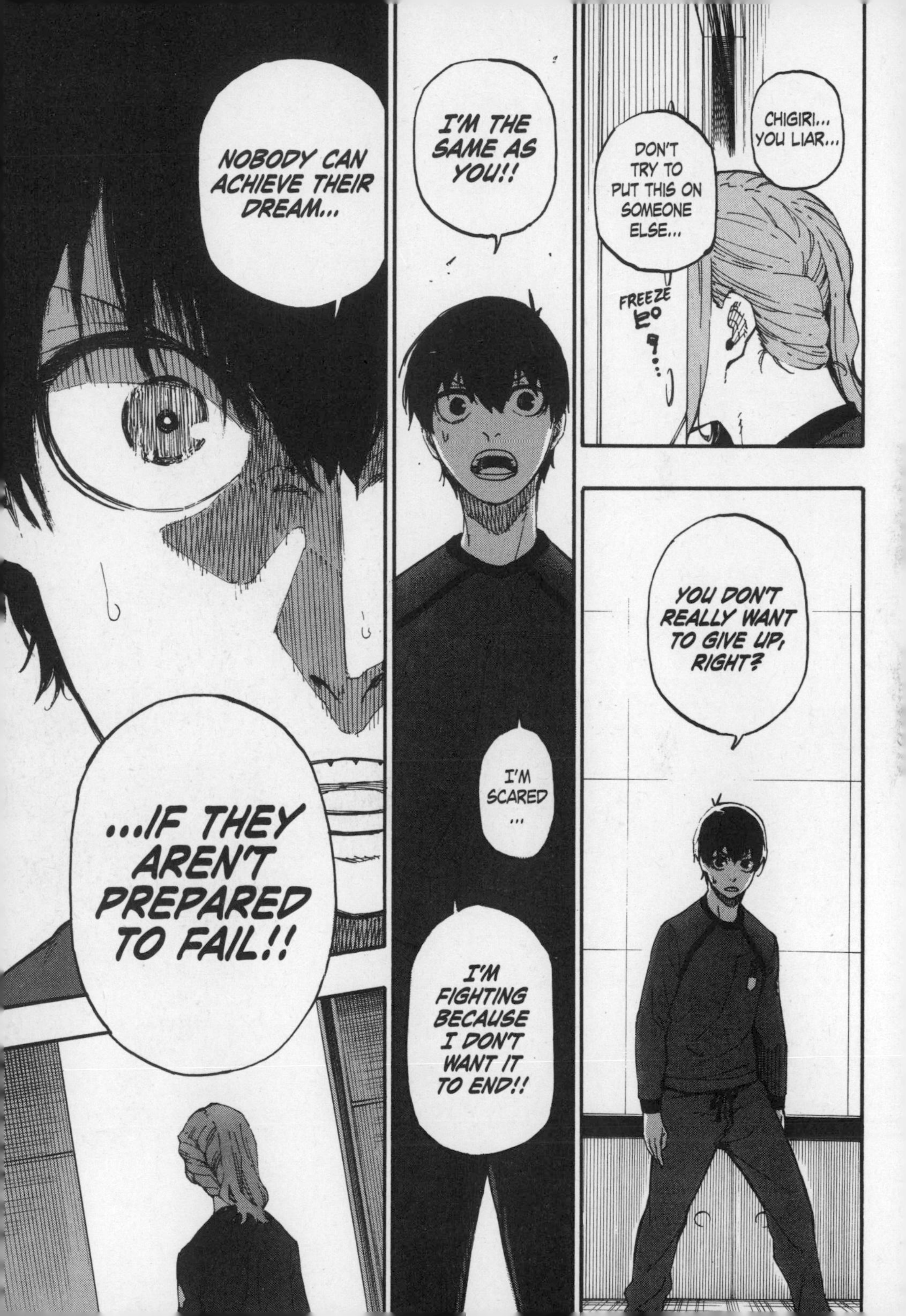
CHIGIRI... YOU LIAR...
DON'T TRY TO PUT THIS ON SOMEONE ELSE...
FREEZE
YOU DON'T REALLY WANT TO GIVE UP, RIGHT?
I'M THE SAME AS YOU!!
I'M SCARED ...
I'M FIGHTING BECAUSE I DON'T WANT IT TO END!!
NOBODY CAN ACHIEVE THEIR DREAM...
...IF THEY AREN'T PREPARED TO FAIL!!

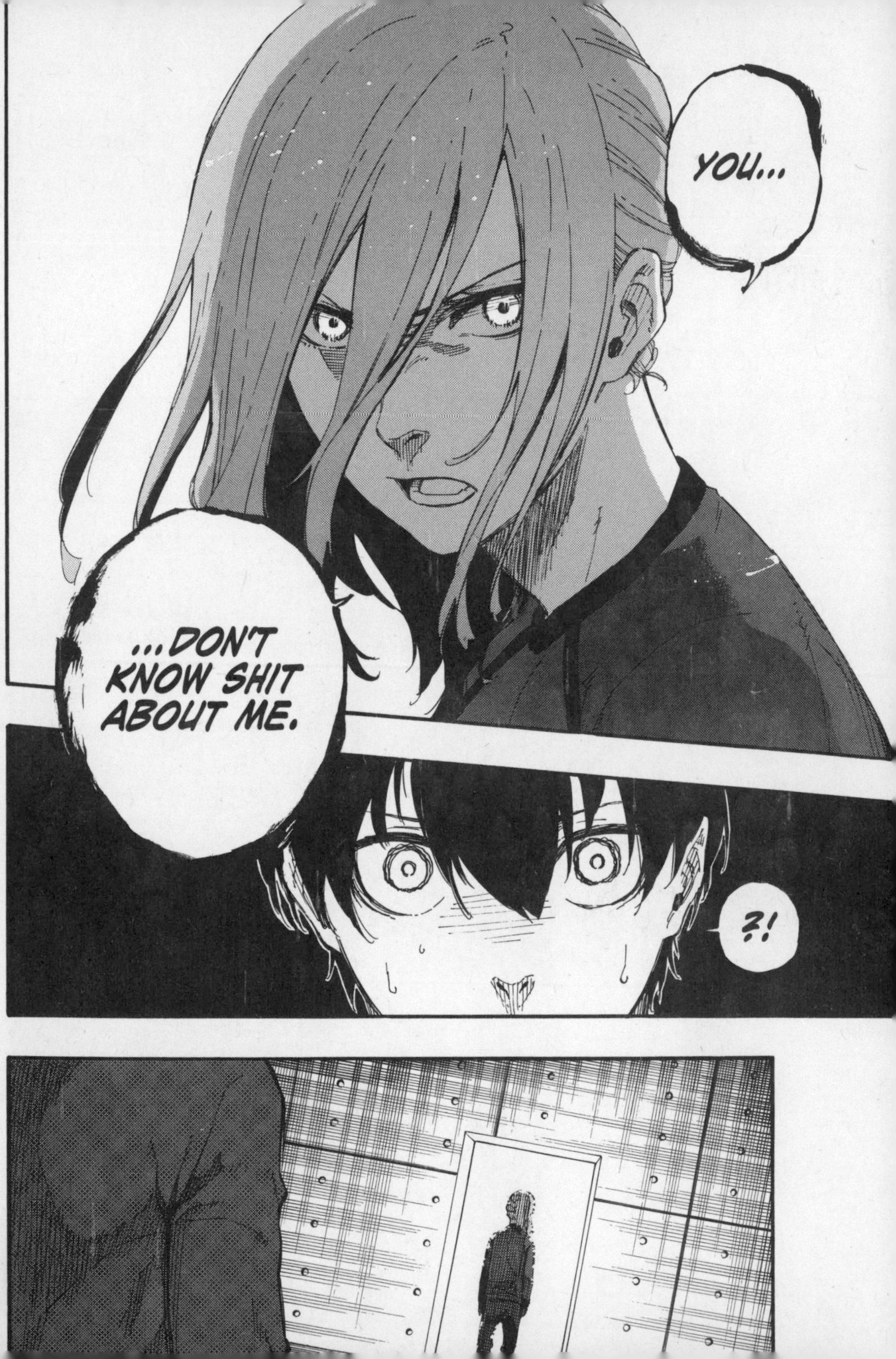
YOU...
...DON'T KNOW SHIT ABOUT ME.
?!

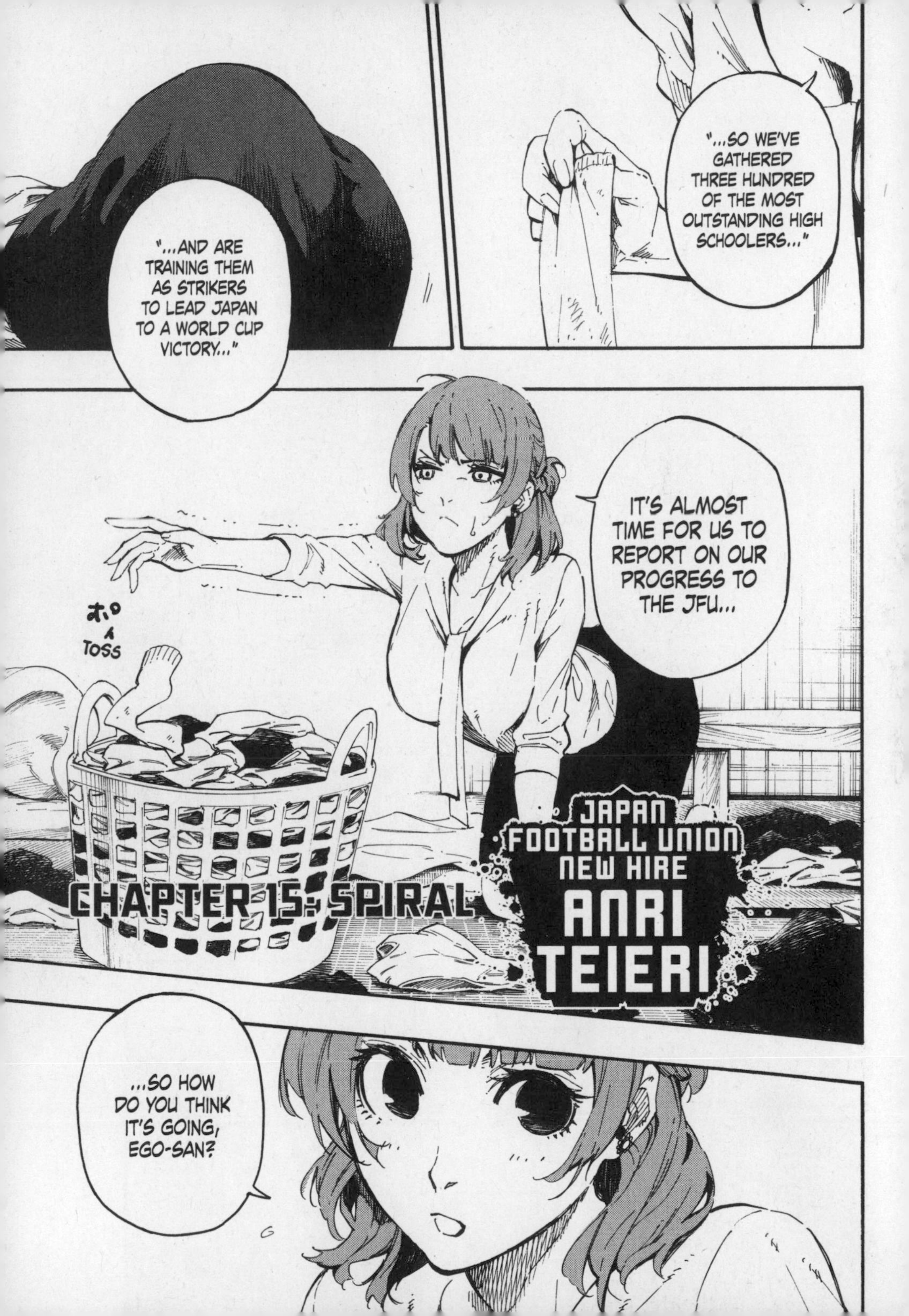
"...SO WE'VE GATHERED THREE HUNDRED OF THE MOST OUTSTANDING HIGH SCHOOLERS..."
"...AND ARE TRAINING THEM AS STRIKERS TO LEAD JAPAN TO A WORLD CUP VICTORY..."
IT'S ALMOST TIME FOR US TO REPORT ON OUR PROGRESS TO THE JFU...
TOSS
JAPAN FOOTBALL UNION NEW HIRE
ANRI TEIERI
CHAPTER 15: SPIRAL
...SO HOW DO YOU THINK IT'S GOING, EGO-SAN?

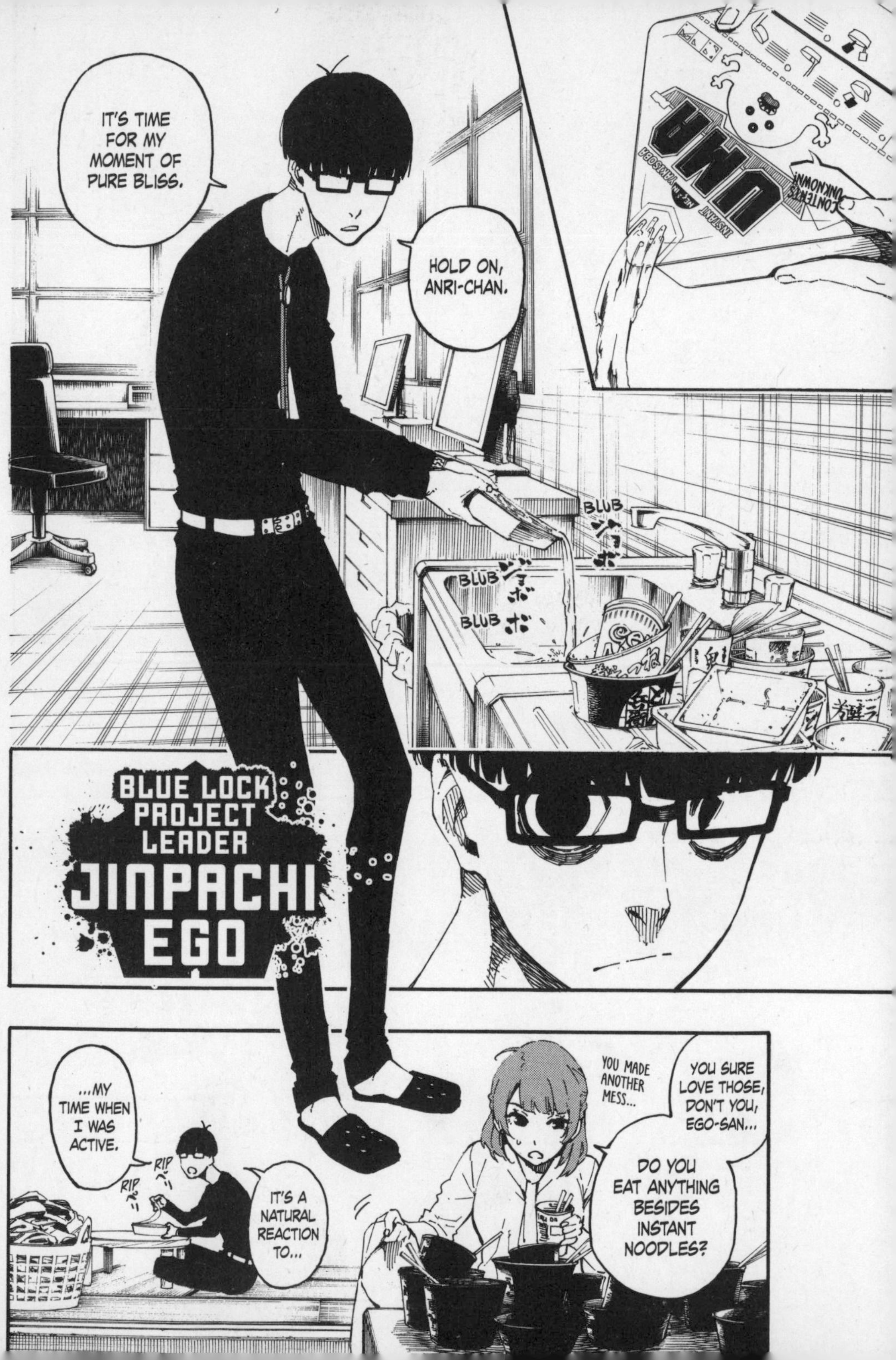
UMA
CONTENTS UNKNOWN!
HOLD ON, ANRI-CHAN.
IT'S TIME FOR MY MOMENT OF PURE BLISS.
BLUB
BLUB
BLUB
BLUE LOCK PROJECT LEADER
JINPACHI EGO
YOU SURE LOVE THOSE, DON'T YOU, EGO-SAN...
YOU MADE ANOTHER MESS...
DO YOU EAT ANYTHING BESIDES INSTANT NOODLES?
IT'S A NATURAL REACTION TO...
RIP
RIP
...MY TIME WHEN I WAS ACTIVE.

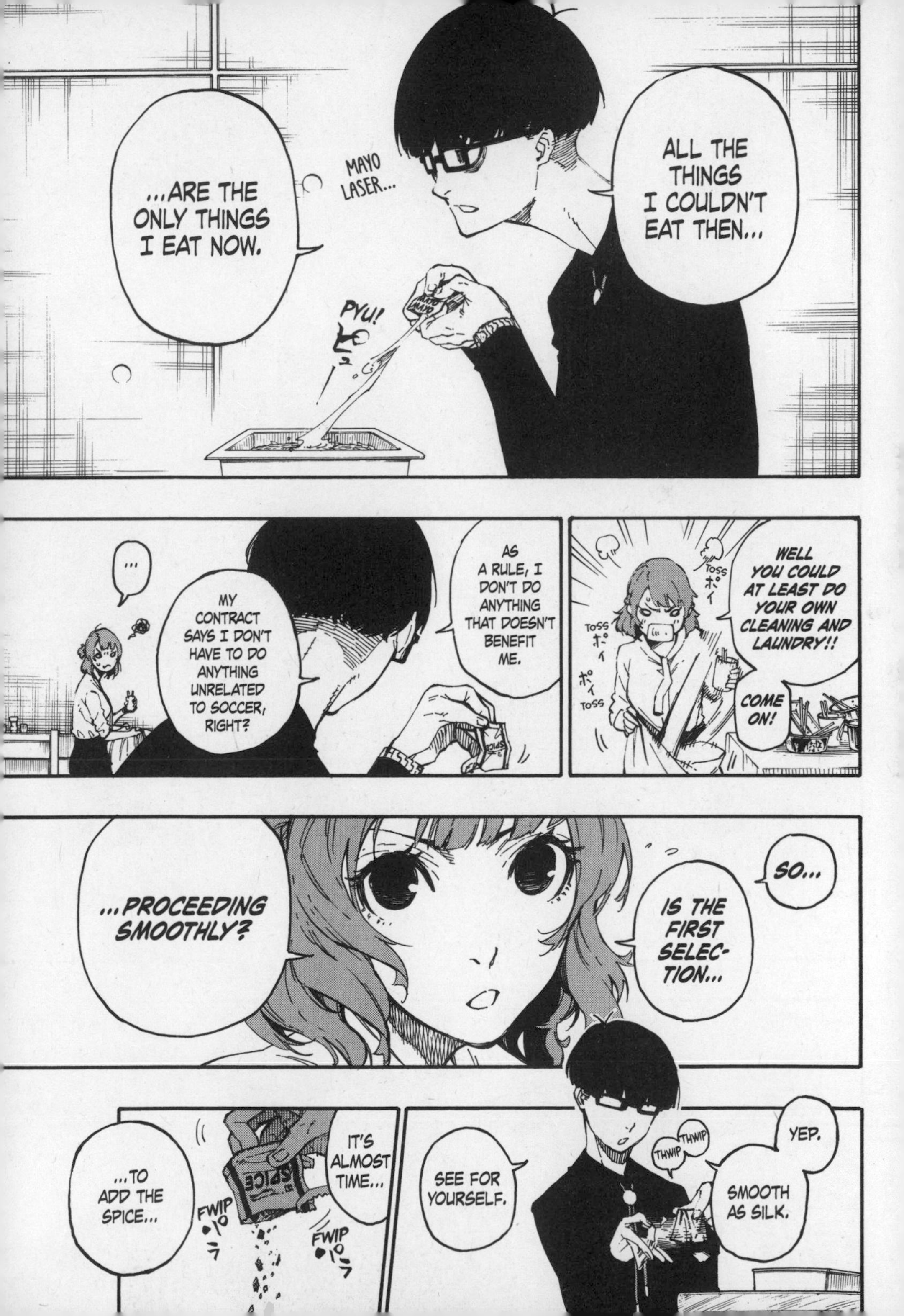
ALL THE THINGS I COULDN'T EAT THEN...
MAYO LASER...
...ARE THE ONLY THINGS I EAT NOW.
PYU!
WELL YOU COULD AT LEAST DO YOUR OWN CLEANING AND LAUNDRY!!
TOSS
TOSS
TOSS
COME ON!
AS A RULE, I DON'T DO ANYTHING THAT DOESN'T BENEFIT ME.
MY CONTRACT SAYS I DON'T HAVE TO DO ANYTHING UNRELATED TO SOCCER, RIGHT?
...
SO...
IS THE FIRST SELECTION...
...PROCEEDING SMOOTHLY?
YEP.
THWIP
THWIP
SMOOTH AS SILK.
SEE FOR YOURSELF.
IT'S ALMOST TIME...
FWIP
FWIP
...TO ADD THE SPICE...

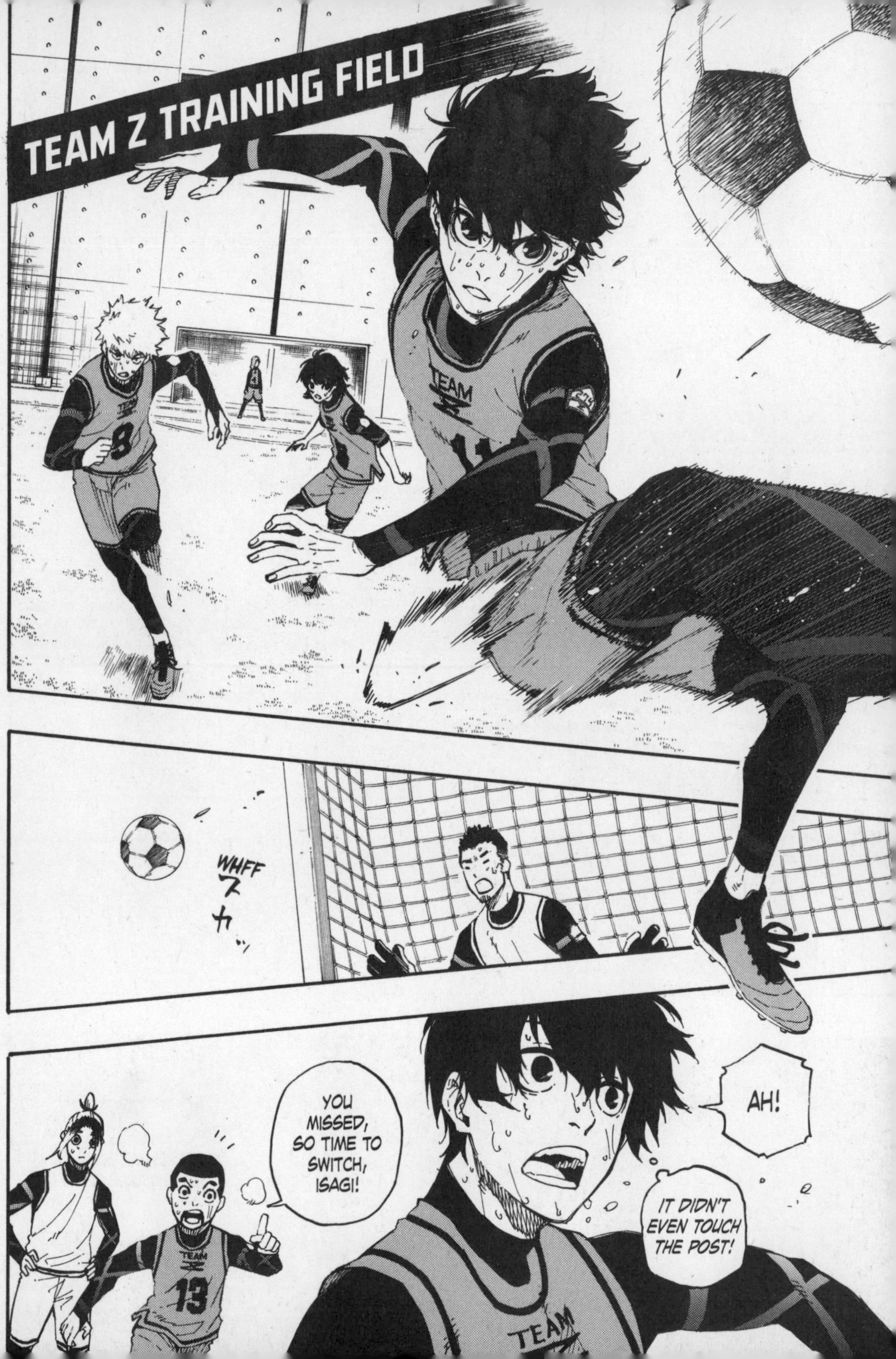
TEAM Z TRAINING FIELD
WHFF
AH!
YOU MISSED, SO TIME TO SWITCH, ISAGI!
IT DIDN'T EVEN TOUCH THE POST!

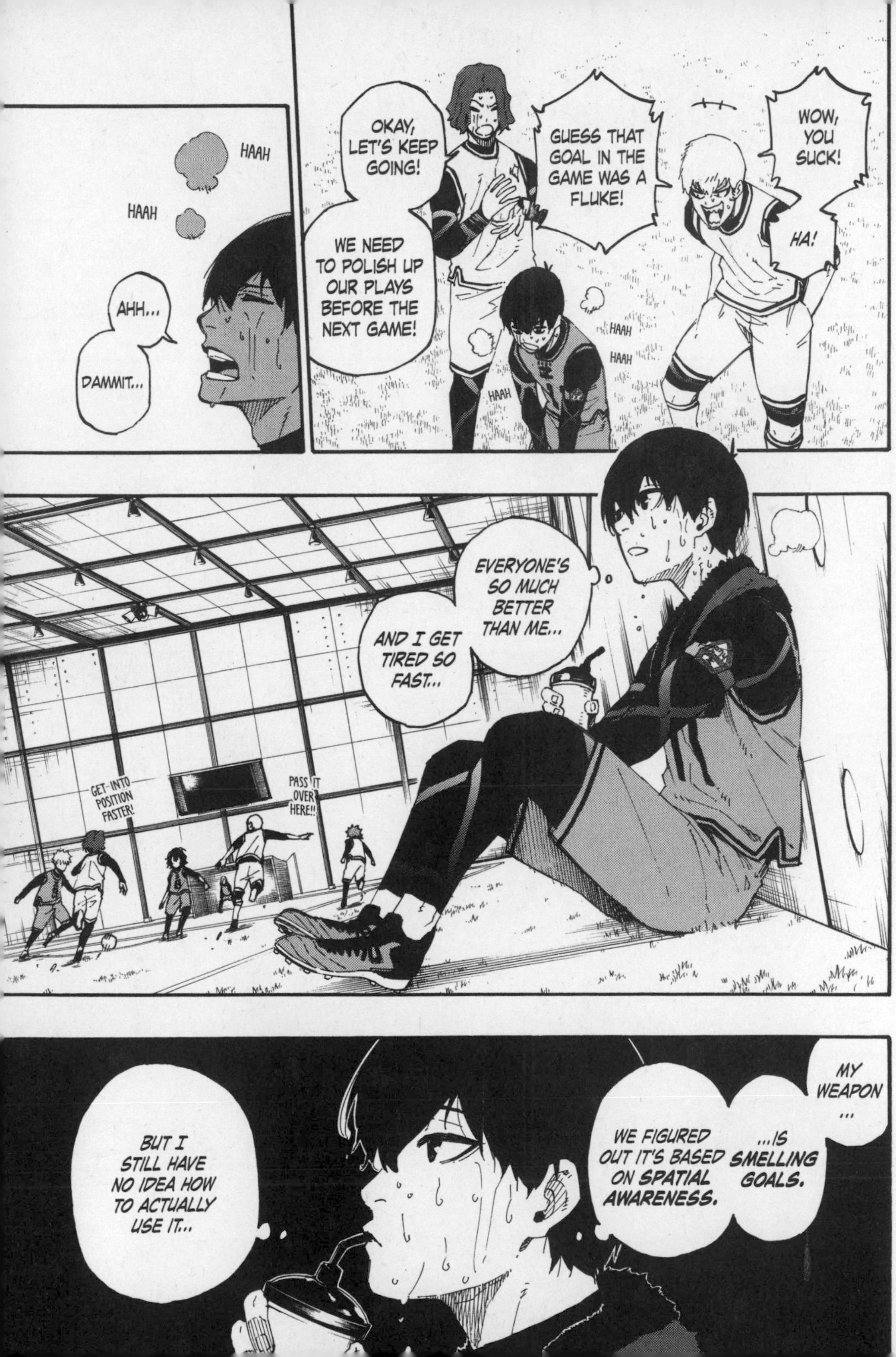
WOW, YOU SUCK!
HA!
GUESS THAT GOAL IN THE GAME WAS A FLUKE!
OKAY, LET'S KEEP GOING!
WE NEED TO POLISH UP OUR PLAYS BEFORE THE NEXT GAME!
HAAH
HAAH
HAAH
HAAH
HAAH
AHH...
DAMMIT...
EVERYONE'S SO MUCH BETTER THAN ME...
AND I GET TIRED SO FAST...
PASS IT OVER HERE!!
GET INTO POSITION FASTER!
MY WEAPON ...
...IS SMELLING GOALS.
WE FIGURED OUT IT'S BASED ON SPATIAL AWARENESS.
BUT I STILL HAVE NO IDEA HOW TO ACTUALLY USE IT...

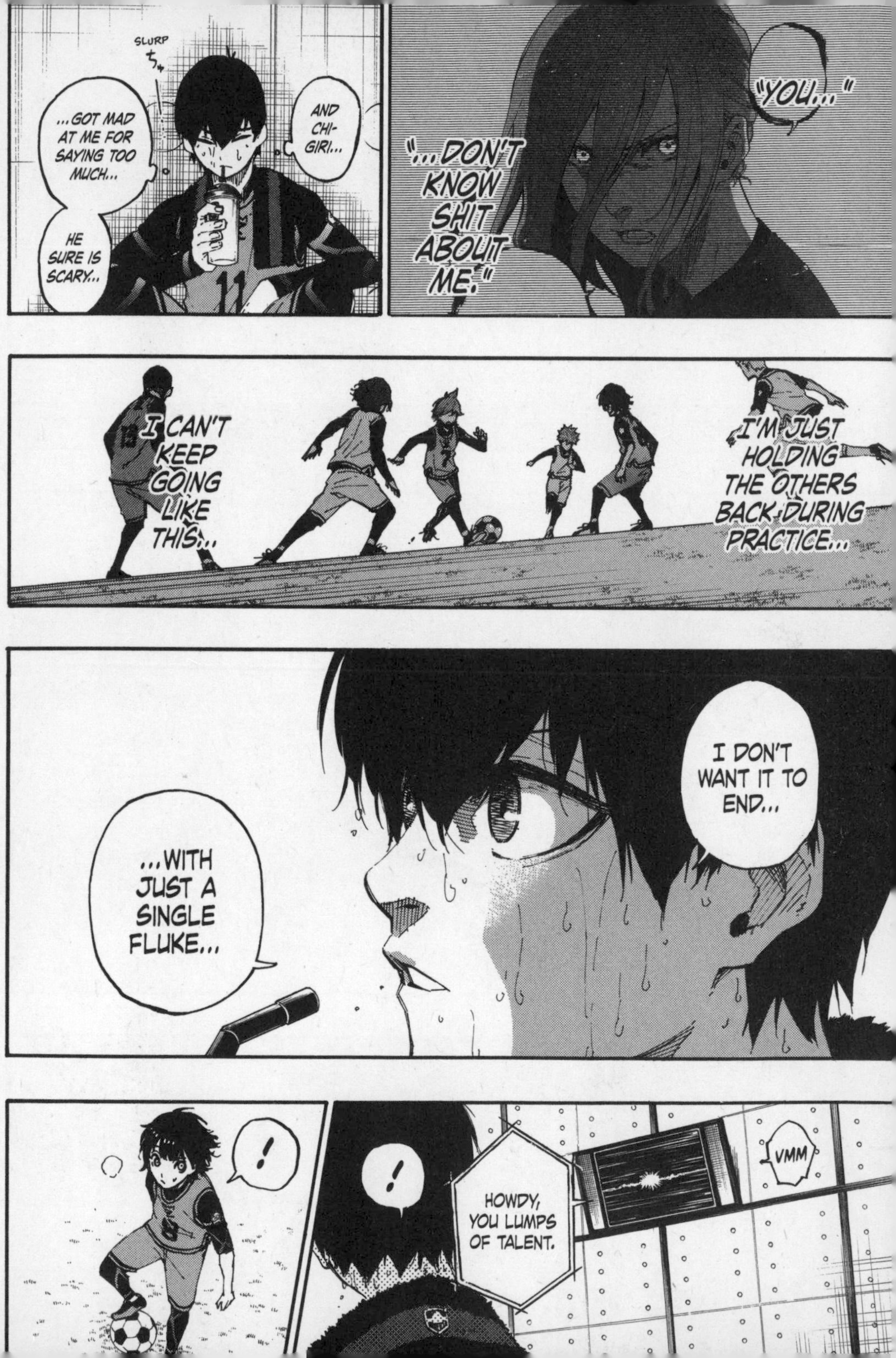
"YOU..."
"...DON'T KNOW SHIT ABOUT ME."
SLURP
AND CHI-GIRI...
...GOT MAD AT ME FOR SAYING TOO MUCH...
HE SURE IS SCARY...
I'M JUST HOLDING THE OTHERS BACK DURING PRACTICE...
I CAN'T KEEP GOING LIKE THIS...
I DON'T WANT IT TO END...
...WITH JUST A SINGLE FLUKE...
VMM
HOWDY, YOU LUMPS OF TALENT.
!
!

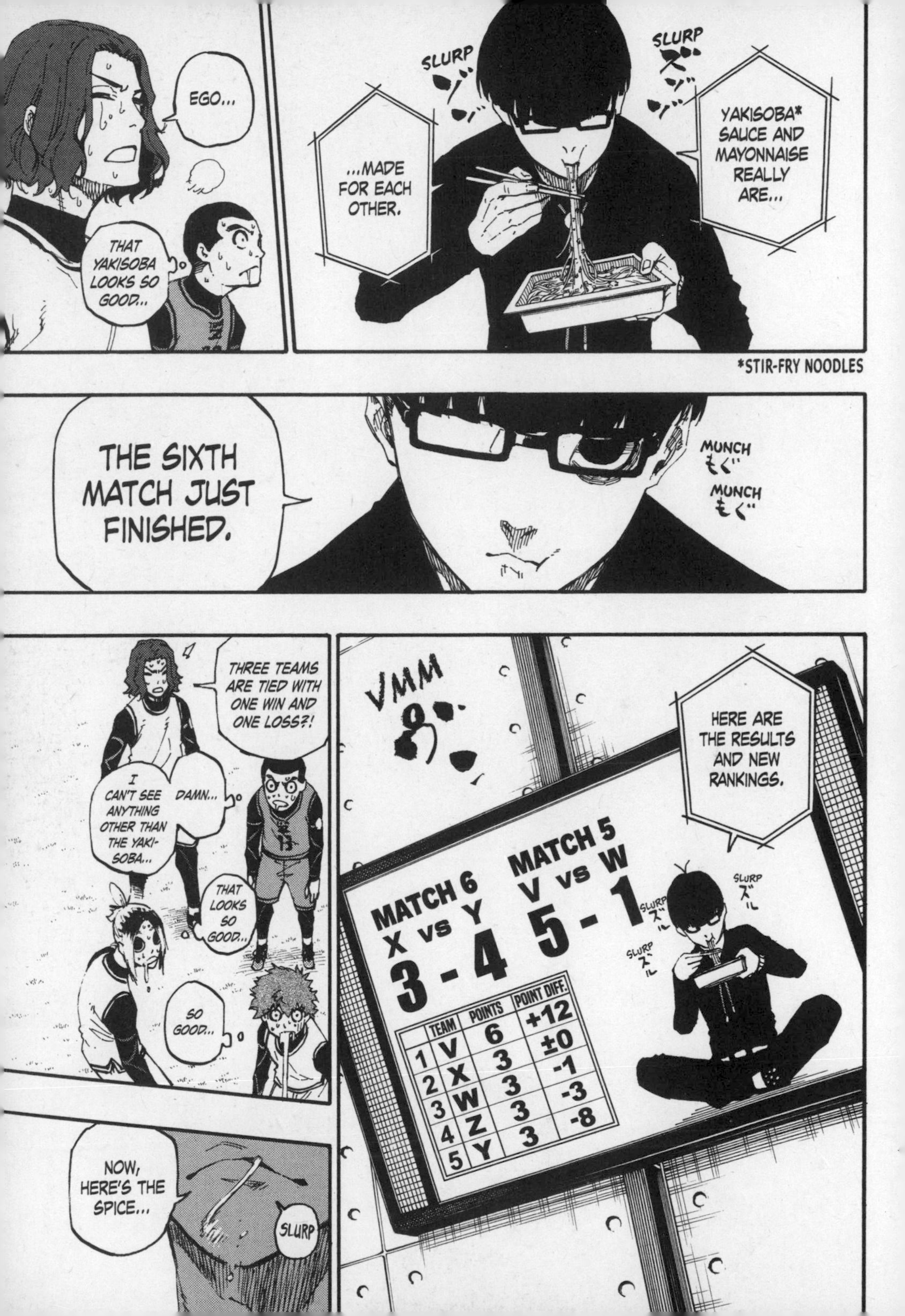
SLURP
SLURP
YAKISOBA* SAUCE AND MAYONNAISE REALLY ARE...
...MADE FOR EACH OTHER.
EGO...
THAT YAKISOBA LOOKS SO GOOD...
MUNCH もぐ
MUNCH もぐ
THE SIXTH MATCH JUST FINISHED.
HERE ARE THE RESULTS AND NEW RANKINGS.
VMM
MATCH 5
V vs W
5 - 1
MATCH 6
X vs Y
3 - 4
TEAM POINTS POINT DIFF.
1 V 6 +12
2 X 3 ±0
3 W 3 -1
4 Z 3 -3
5 Y 3 -8
SLURP
SLURP
SLURP
THREE TEAMS ARE TIED WITH ONE WIN AND ONE LOSS?!
DAMN...
I CAN'T SEE ANYTHING OTHER THAN THE YAKI-SOBA...
THAT LOOKS SO GOOD...
SO GOOD...
NOW, HERE'S THE SPICE...
SLURP

*STIR-FRY NOODLES

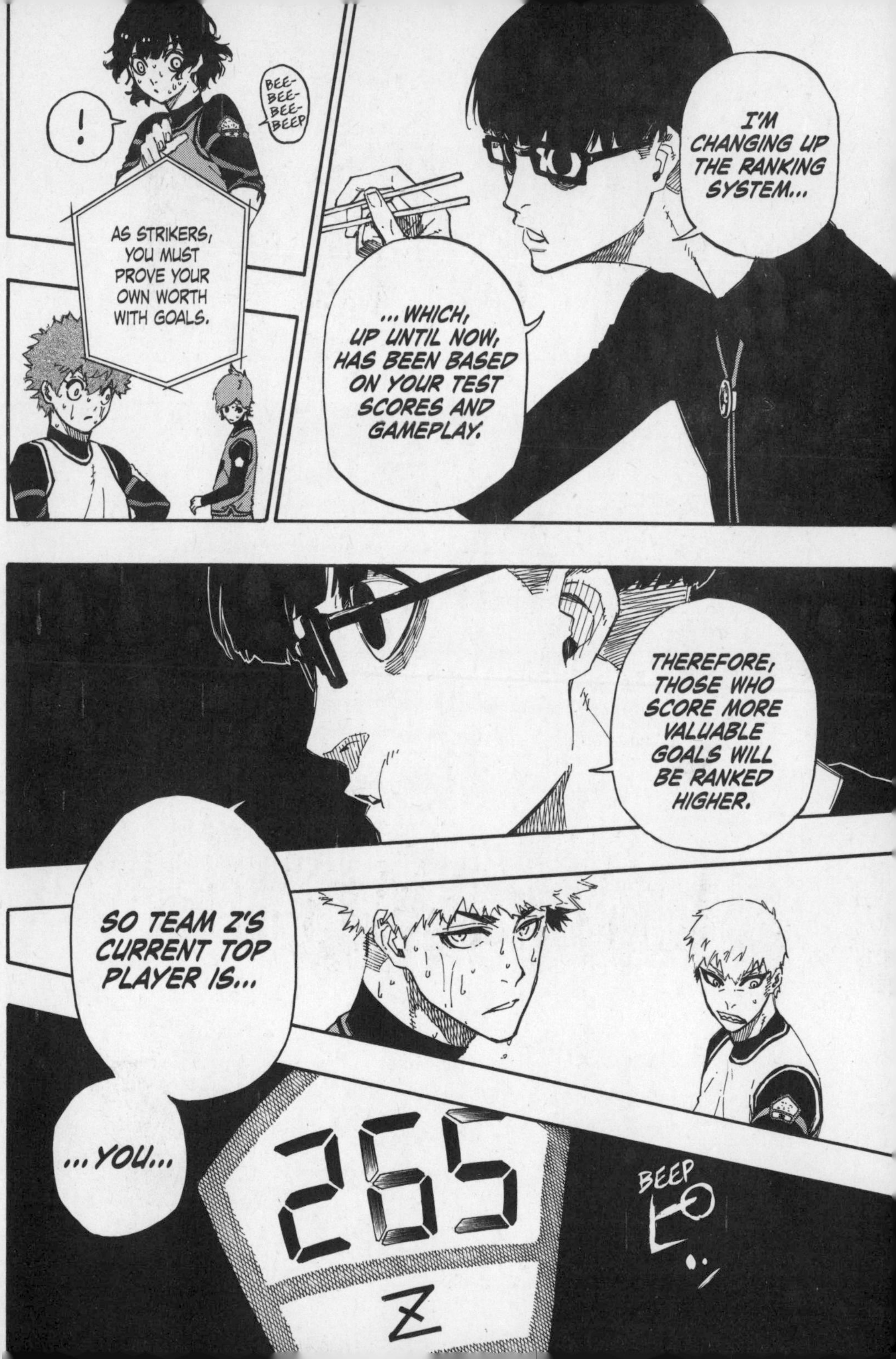
I'M CHANGING UP THE RANKING SYSTEM...
...WHICH, UP UNTIL NOW, HAS BEEN BASED ON YOUR TEST SCORES AND GAMEPLAY.
BEE-BEE-BEE-BEEP
!
AS STRIKERS, YOU MUST PROVE YOUR OWN WORTH WITH GOALS.
THEREFORE, THOSE WHO SCORE MORE VALUABLE GOALS WILL BE RANKED HIGHER.
SO TEAM Z'S CURRENT TOP PLAYER IS...
BEEP
265
Z
...YOU...

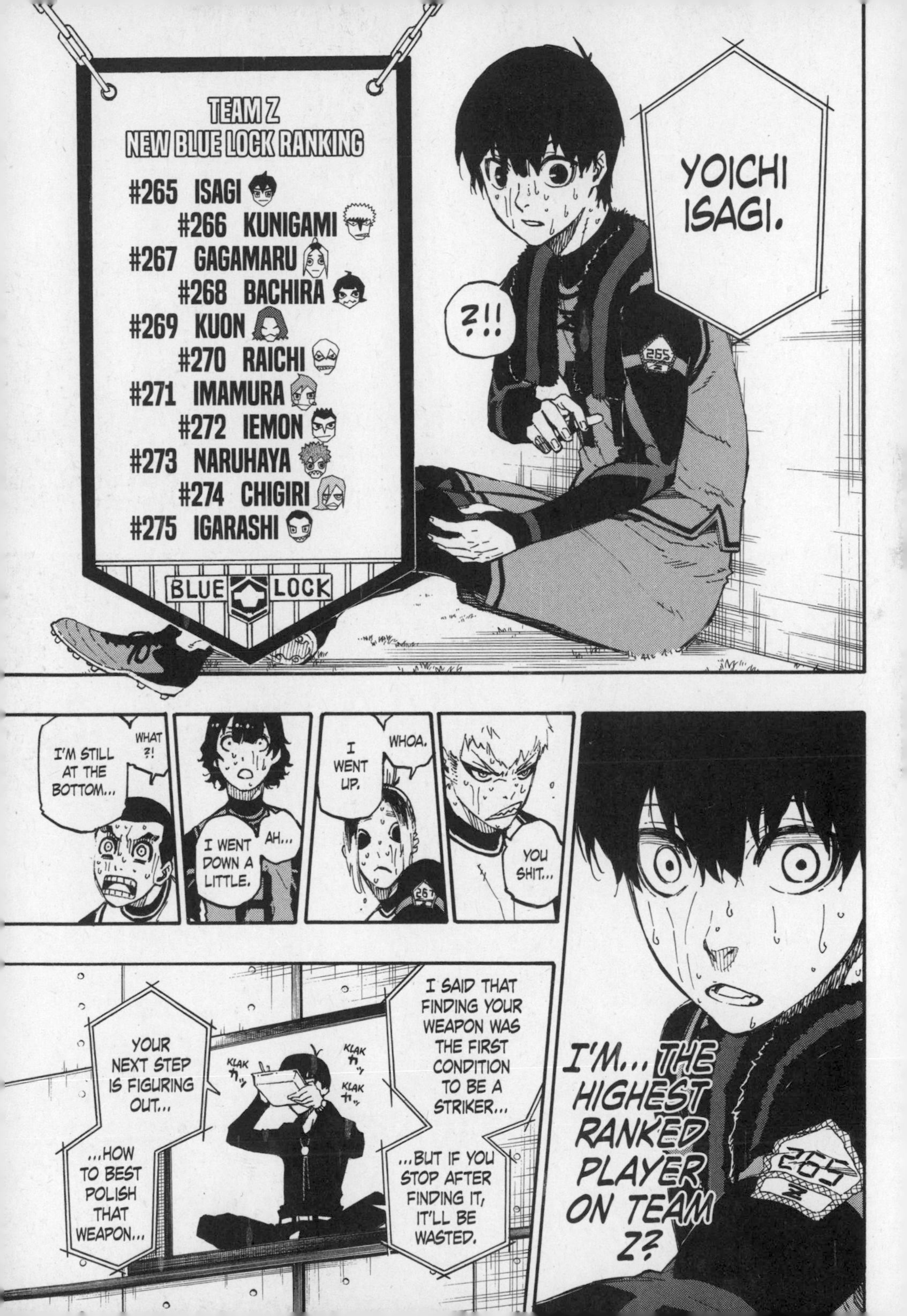
YOICHI ISAGI.
?!!
TEAM Z
NEW BLUE LOCK RANKING
#265 ISAGI
#266 KUNIGAMI
#267 GAGAMARU
#268 BACHIRA
#269 KUON
#270 RAICHI
#271 IMAMURA
#272 IEMON
#273 NARUHAYA
#274 CHIGIRI
#275 IGARASHI
BLUE LOCK
I'M... THE HIGHEST RANKED PLAYER ON TEAM Z?
YOU SHIT...
WHOA.
I WENT UP.
AH...
I WENT DOWN A LITTLE.
WHAT?!
I'M STILL AT THE BOTTOM...
I SAID THAT FINDING YOUR WEAPON WAS THE FIRST CONDITION TO BE A STRIKER...
...BUT IF YOU STOP AFTER FINDING IT, IT'LL BE WASTED.
KLAK
KLAK
KLAK
YOUR NEXT STEP IS FIGURING OUT...
...HOW TO BEST POLISH THAT WEAPON...

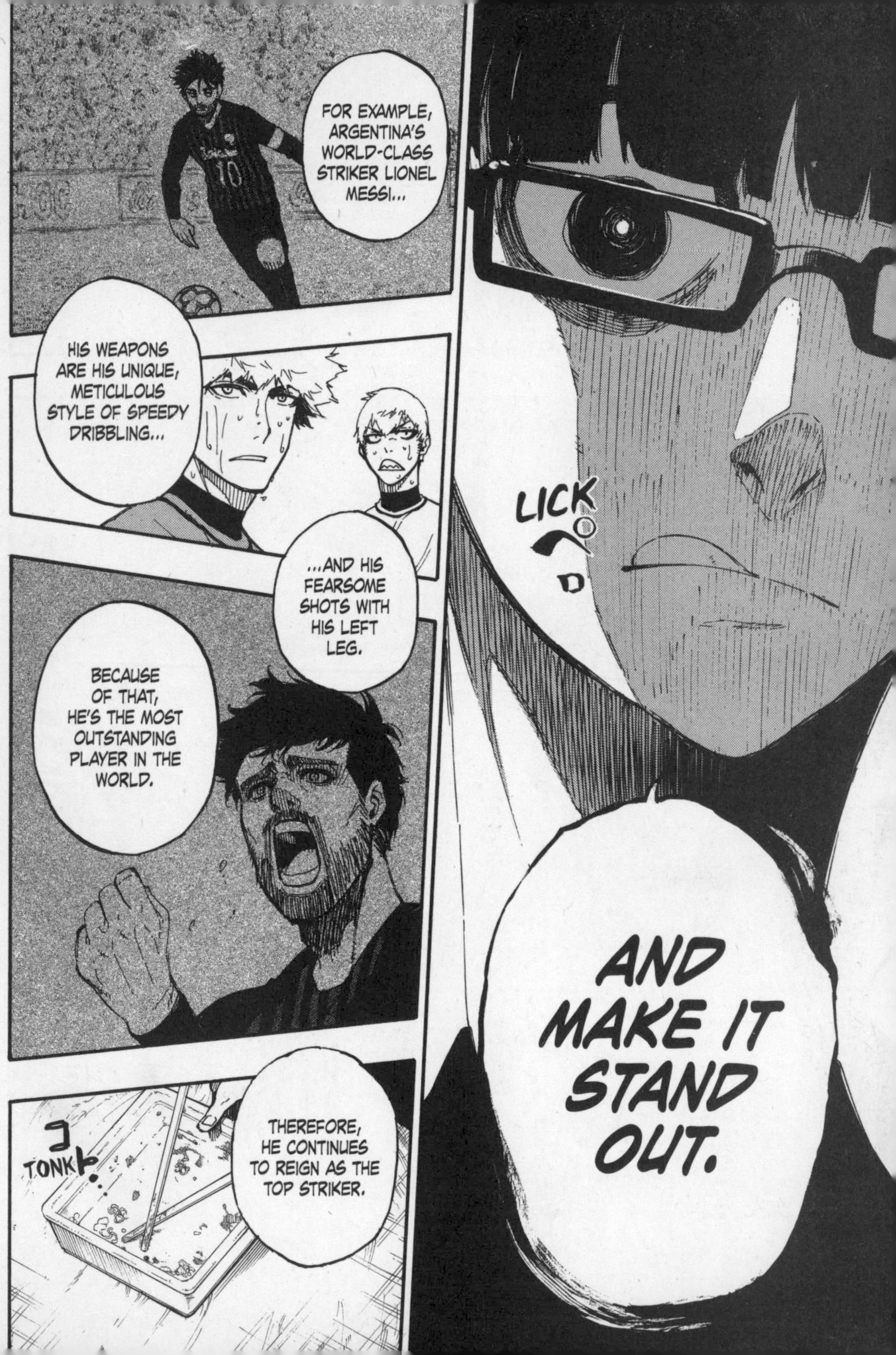
LICK
AND MAKE IT STAND OUT.
FOR EXAMPLE, ARGENTINA'S WORLD-CLASS STRIKER LIONEL MESSI...
HIS WEAPONS ARE HIS UNIQUE, METICULOUS STYLE OF SPEEDY DRIBBLING...
...AND HIS FEARSOME SHOTS WITH HIS LEFT LEG.
BECAUSE OF THAT, HE'S THE MOST OUTSTANDING PLAYER IN THE WORLD.
TONK
THEREFORE, HE CONTINUES TO REIGN AS THE TOP STRIKER.

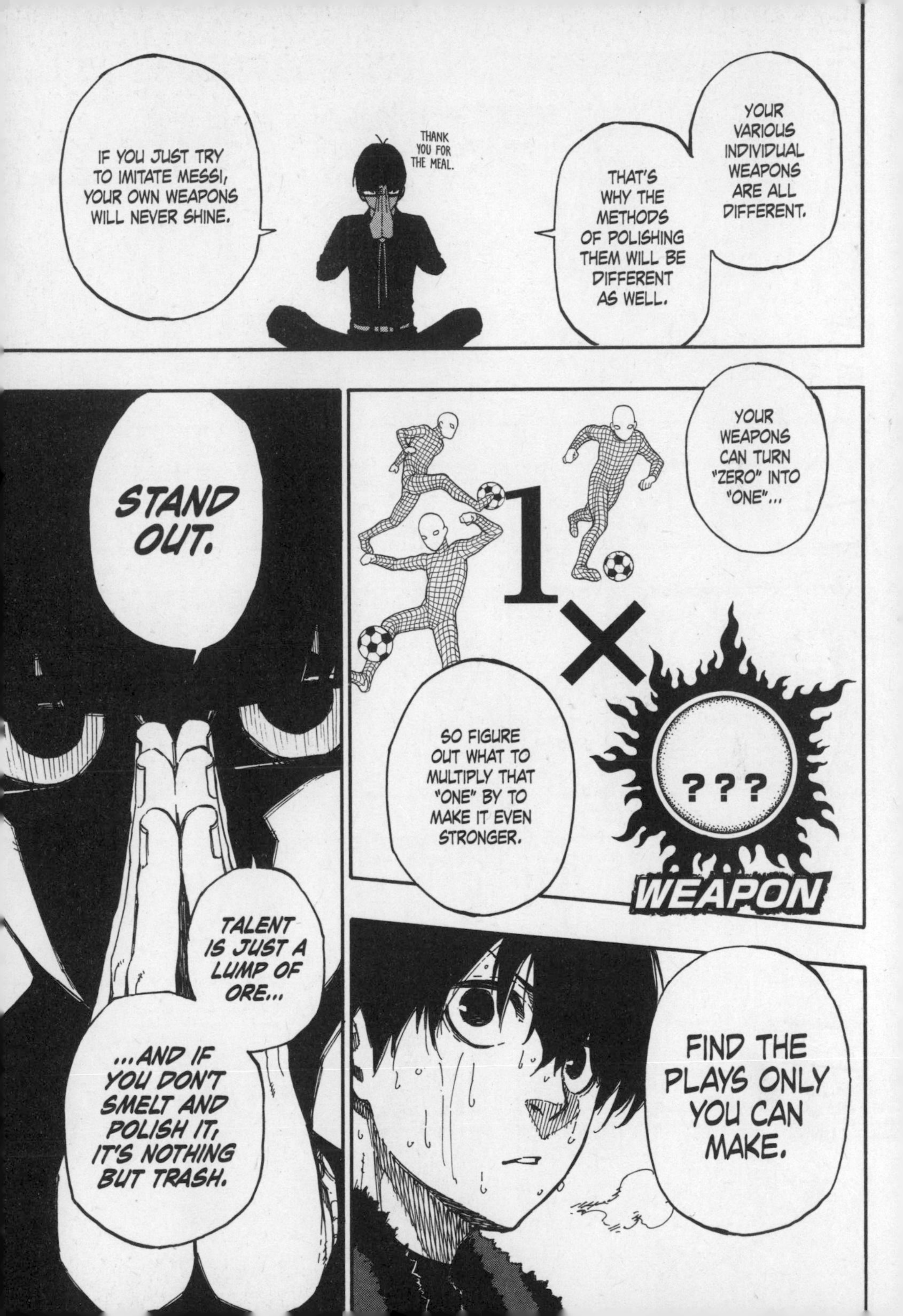
YOUR VARIOUS INDIVIDUAL WEAPONS ARE ALL DIFFERENT.
THAT'S WHY THE METHODS OF POLISHING THEM WILL BE DIFFERENT AS WELL.
THANK YOU FOR THE MEAL.
IF YOU JUST TRY TO IMITATE MESSI, YOUR OWN WEAPONS WILL NEVER SHINE.
YOUR WEAPONS CAN TURN "ZERO" INTO "ONE"...
1
×
SO FIGURE OUT WHAT TO MULTIPLY THAT "ONE" BY TO MAKE IT EVEN STRONGER.
???
WEAPON
FIND THE PLAYS ONLY YOU CAN MAKE.
STAND OUT.
TALENT IS JUST A LUMP OF ORE...
...AND IF YOU DON'T SMELT AND POLISH IT, IT'S NOTHING BUT TRASH.

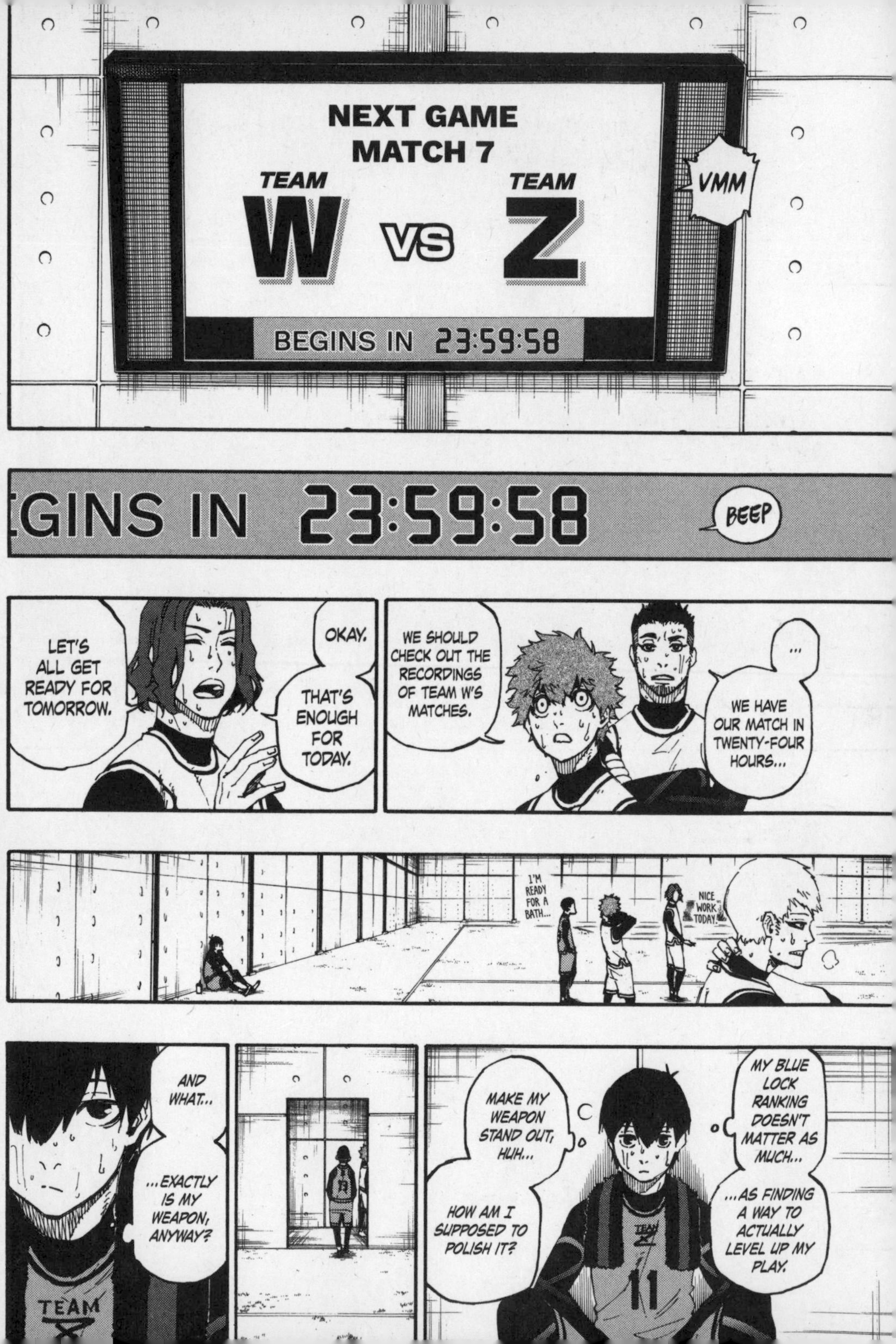
NEXT GAME
MATCH 7
TEAM W VS TEAM Z
BEGINS IN 23:59:58
VMM
GINS IN 23:59:58
BEEP
...
WE HAVE OUR MATCH IN TWENTY-FOUR HOURS...
WE SHOULD CHECK OUT THE RECORDINGS OF TEAM W'S MATCHES.
OKAY.
THAT'S ENOUGH FOR TODAY.
LET'S ALL GET READY FOR TOMORROW.
NICE WORK TODAY.
I'M READY FOR A BATH...
MY BLUE LOCK RANKING DOESN'T MATTER AS MUCH...
...AS FINDING A WAY TO ACTUALLY LEVEL UP MY PLAY.
MAKE MY WEAPON STAND OUT, HUH...
HOW AM I SUPPOSED TO POLISH IT?
AND WHAT...
...EXACTLY IS MY WEAPON, ANYWAY?

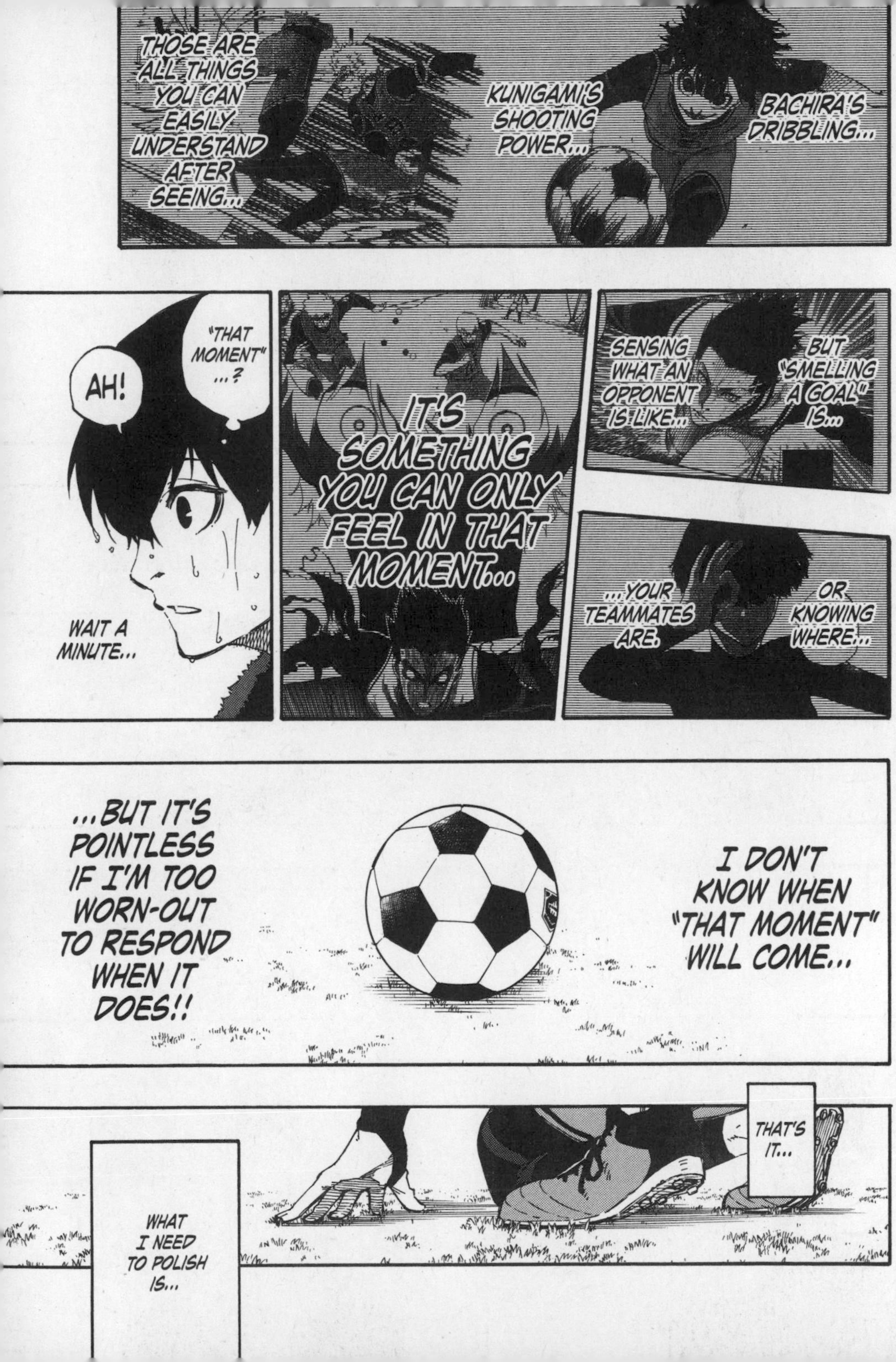
BACHIRA'S DRIBBLING...
KUNIGAMI'S SHOOTING POWER...
THOSE ARE ALL THINGS YOU CAN EASILY UNDERSTAND AFTER SEEING...
BUT "SMELLING A GOAL" IS...
SENSING WHAT AN OPPONENT IS LIKE...
OR KNOWING WHERE...
...YOUR TEAMMATES ARE.
IT'S SOMETHING YOU CAN ONLY FEEL IN THAT MOMENT...
"THAT MOMENT" ...?
AH!
WAIT A MINUTE...
I DON'T KNOW WHEN "THAT MOMENT" WILL COME...
...BUT IT'S POINTLESS IF I'M TOO WORN-OUT TO RESPOND WHEN IT DOES!!
THAT'S IT...
WHAT I NEED TO POLISH IS...

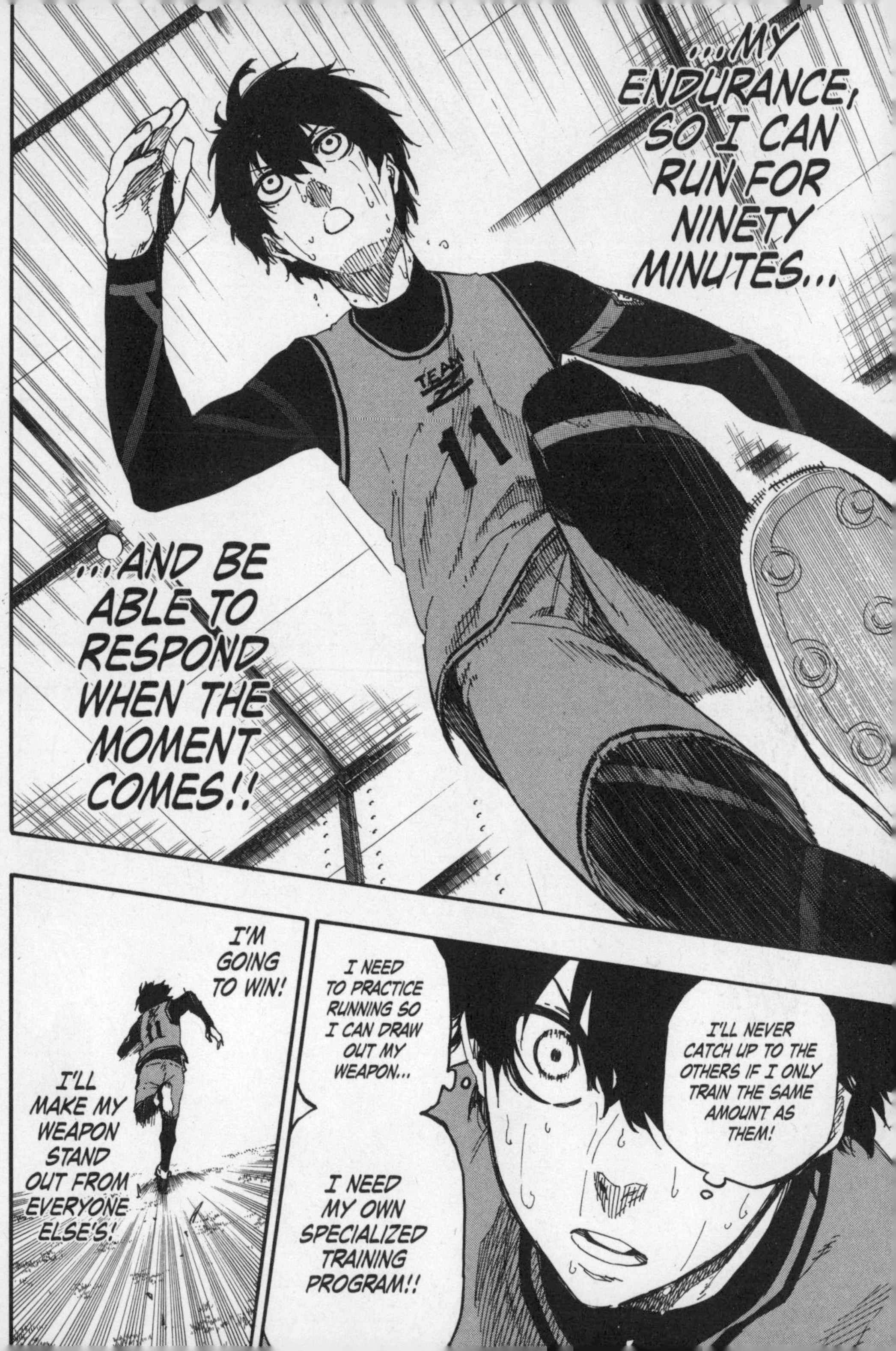
...MY ENDURANCE, SO I CAN RUN FOR NINETY MINUTES...
...AND BE ABLE TO RESPOND WHEN THE MOMENT COMES!!
I'LL NEVER CATCH UP TO THE OTHERS IF I ONLY TRAIN THE SAME AMOUNT AS THEM!
I NEED TO PRACTICE RUNNING SO I CAN DRAW OUT MY WEAPON...
I NEED MY OWN SPECIALIZED TRAINING PROGRAM!!
I'M GOING TO WIN!
I'LL MAKE MY WEAPON STAND OUT FROM EVERYONE ELSE'S!

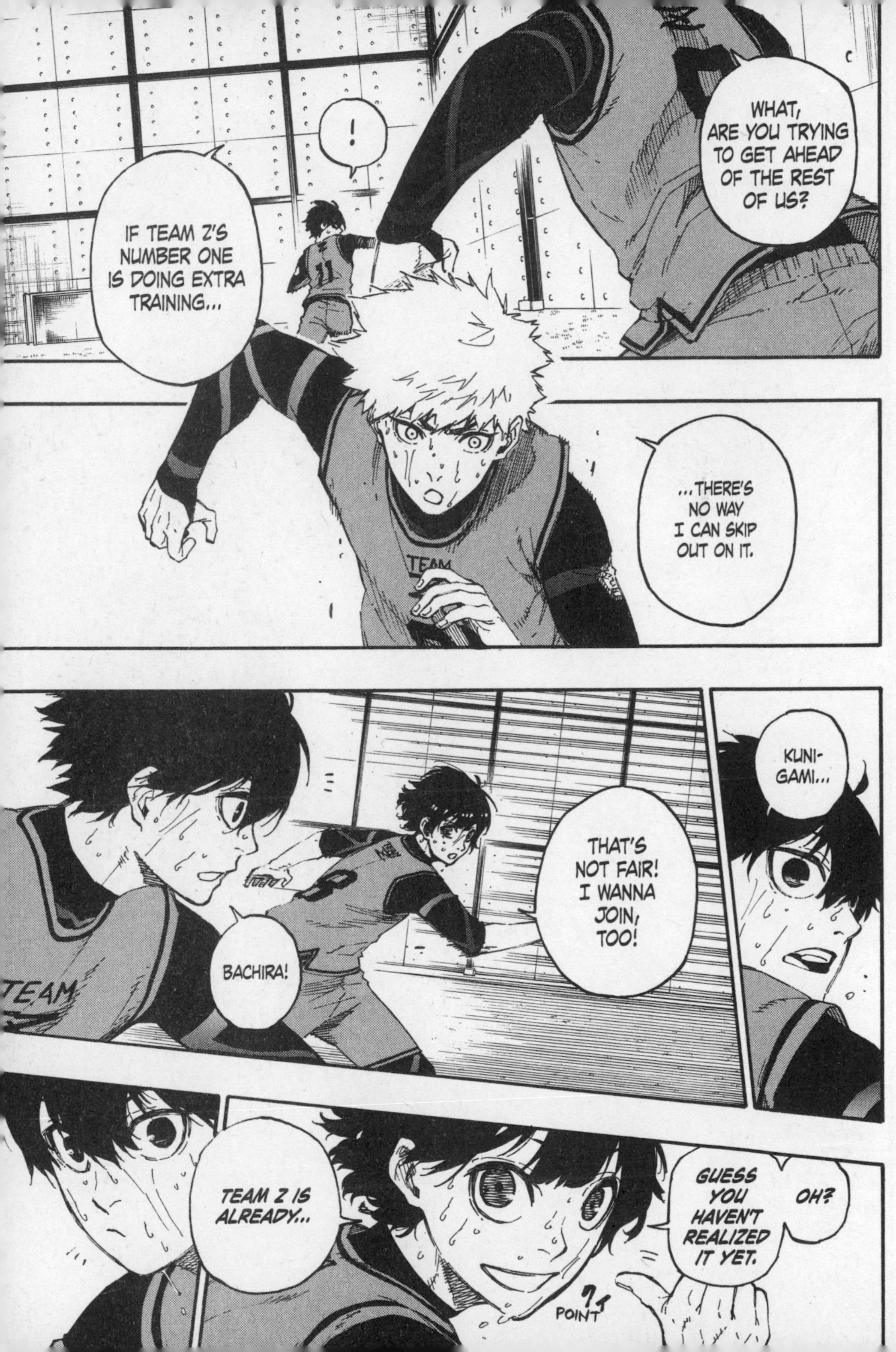
WHAT, ARE YOU TRYING TO GET AHEAD OF THE REST OF US?
!
IF TEAM Z'S NUMBER ONE IS DOING EXTRA TRAINING...
...THERE'S NO WAY I CAN SKIP OUT ON IT.
KUNI-GAMI...
THAT'S NOT FAIR! I WANNA JOIN, TOO!
BACHIRA!
OH?
GUESS YOU HAVEN'T REALIZED IT YET.
POINT
TEAM Z IS ALREADY...

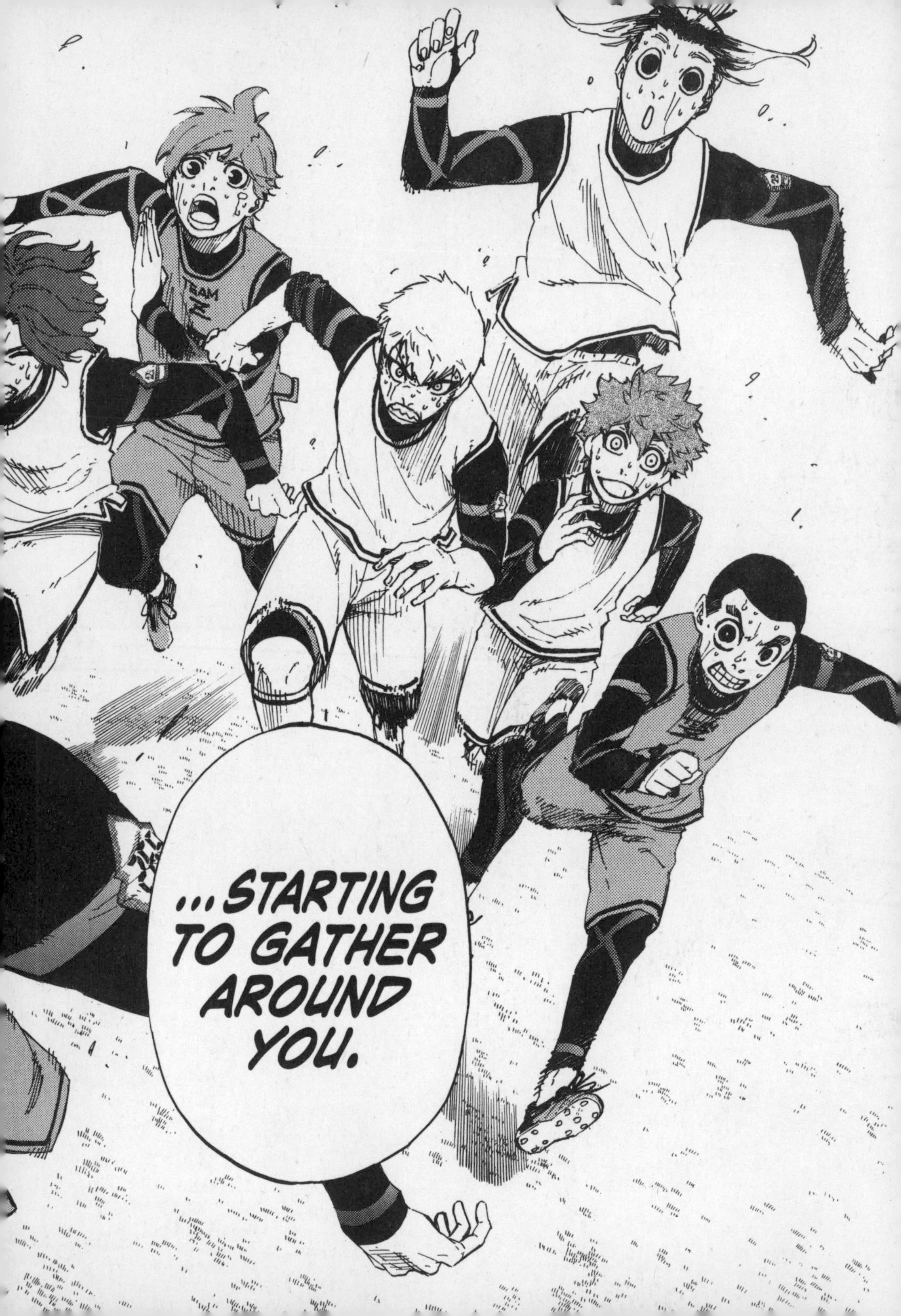
...STARTING TO GATHER AROUND YOU.

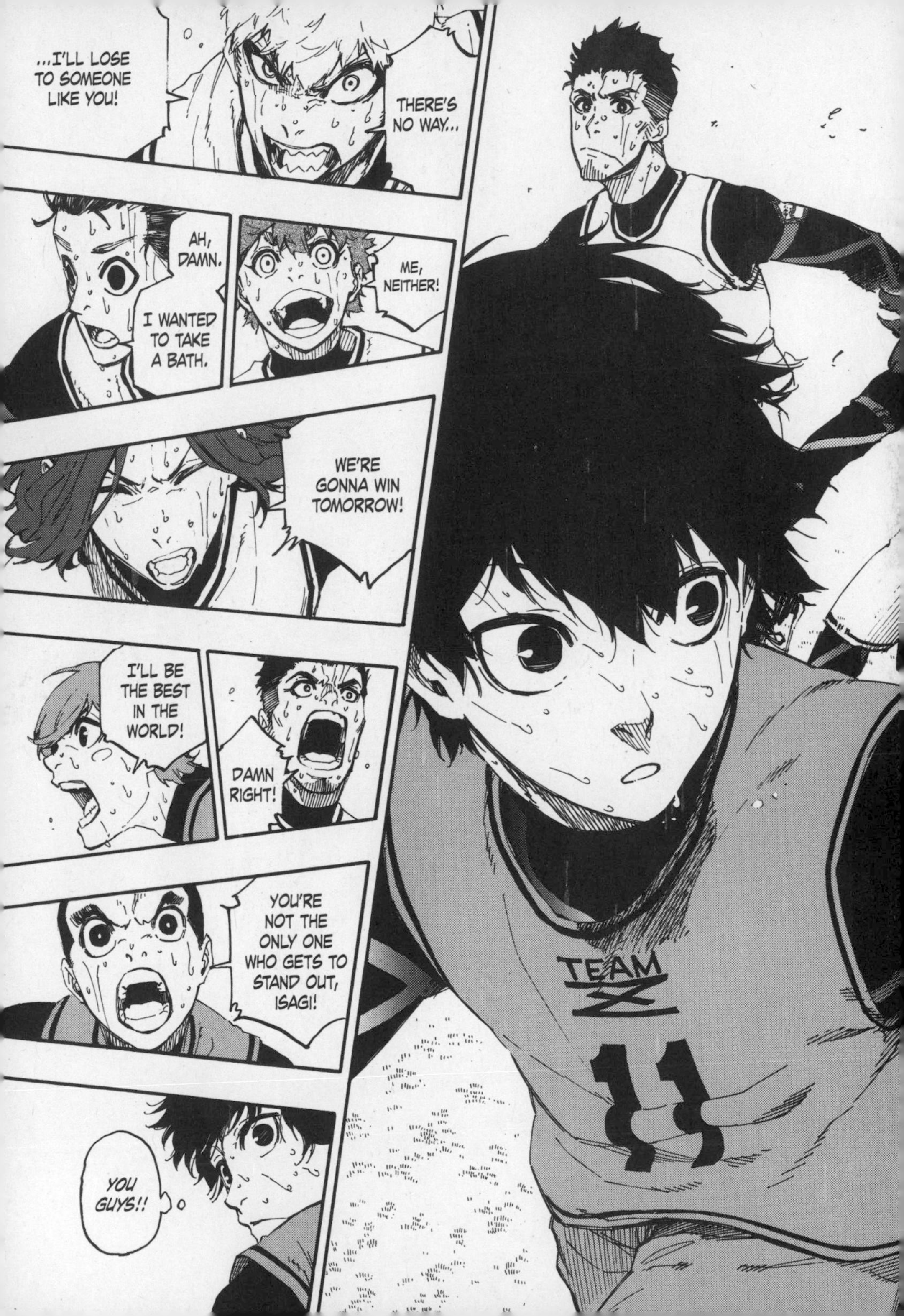
THERE'S NO WAY...
...I'LL LOSE TO SOMEONE LIKE YOU!
ME, NEITHER!
AH, DAMN.
I WANTED TO TAKE A BATH.
WE'RE GONNA WIN TOMORROW!
DAMN RIGHT!
I'LL BE THE BEST IN THE WORLD!
YOU'RE NOT THE ONLY ONE WHO GETS TO STAND OUT, ISAGI!
YOU GUYS!!
TEAM Z
11

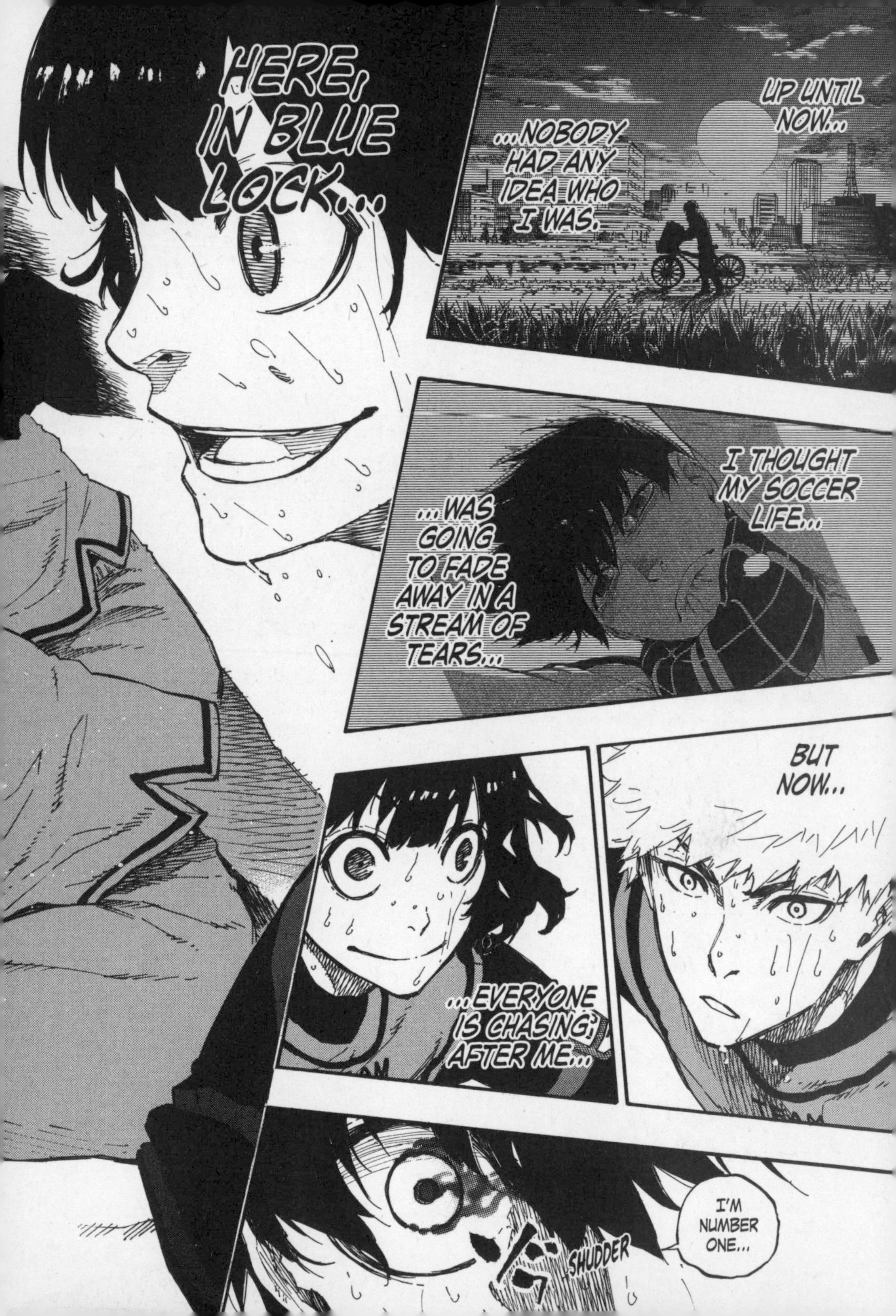
UP UNTIL NOW...
...NOBODY HAD ANY IDEA WHO I WAS.
I THOUGHT MY SOCCER LIFE...
...WAS GOING TO FADE AWAY IN A STREAM OF TEARS...
BUT NOW...
...EVERYONE IS CHASING AFTER ME...
I'M NUMBER ONE...
SHUDDER
HERE, IN BLUE LOCK...

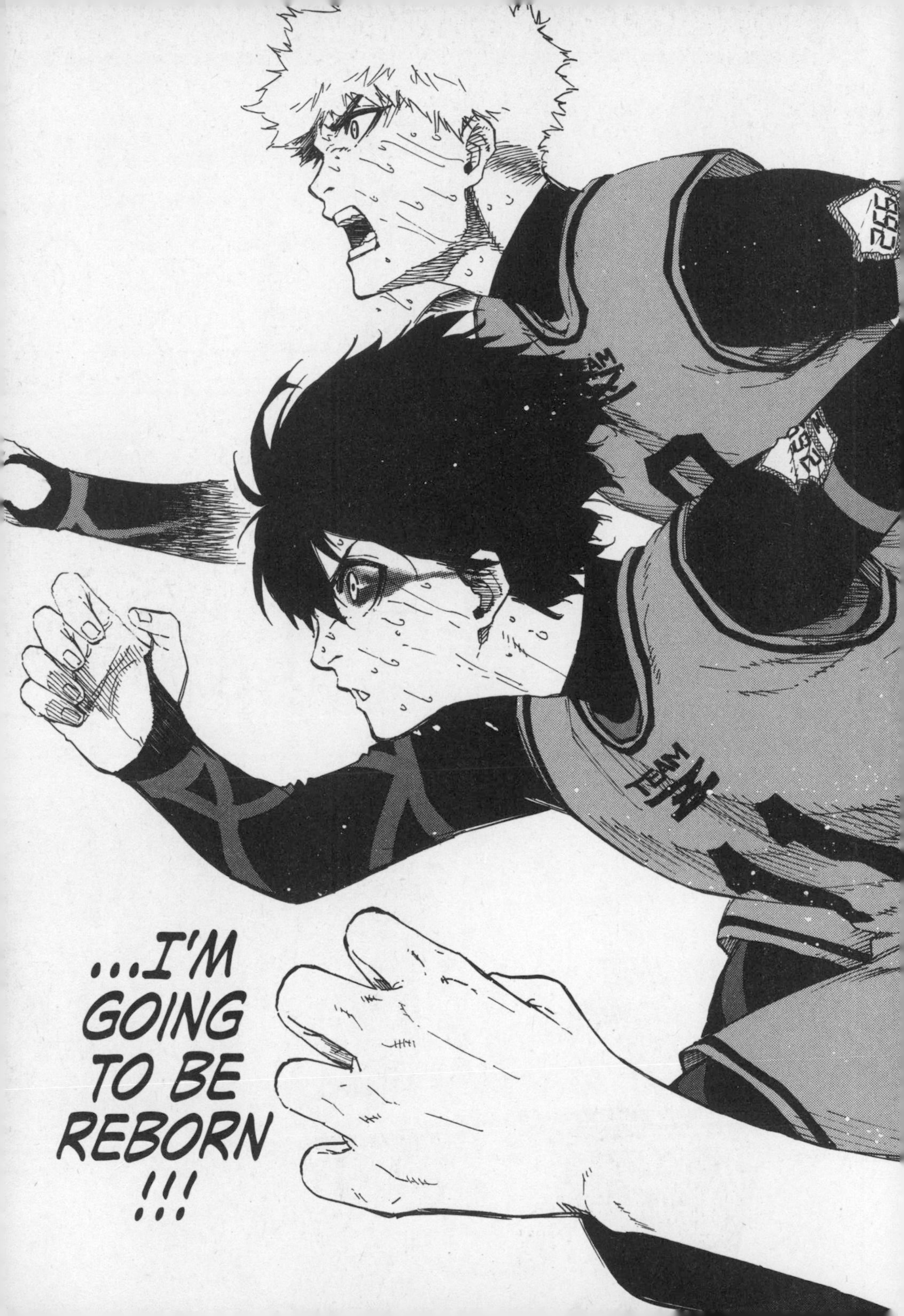
...I'M GOING TO BE REBORN !!!

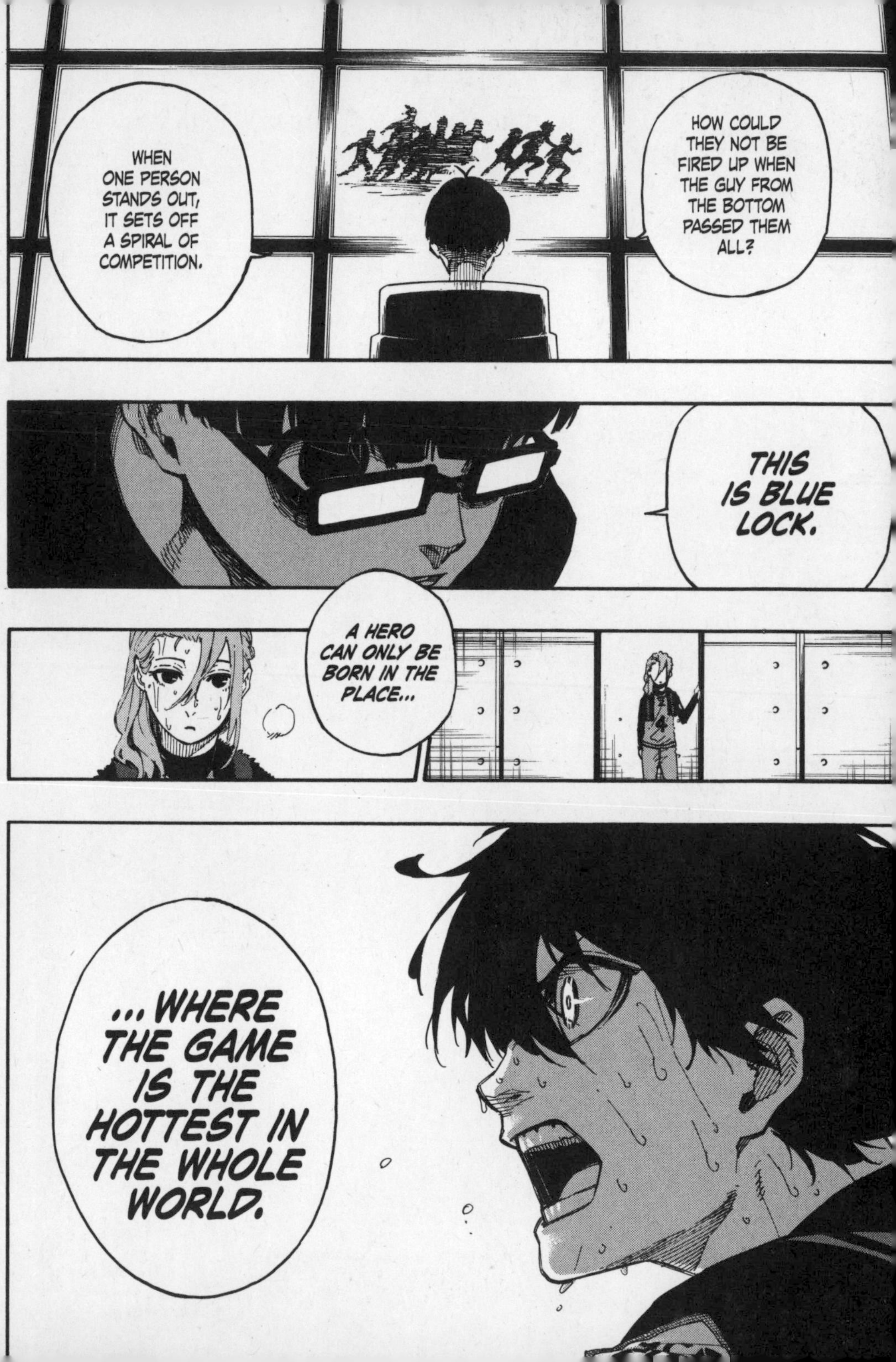
HOW COULD THEY NOT BE FIRED UP WHEN THE GUY FROM THE BOTTOM PASSED THEM ALL?
WHEN ONE PERSON STANDS OUT, IT SETS OFF A SPIRAL OF COMPETITION.
THIS IS BLUE LOCK.
A HERO CAN ONLY BE BORN IN THE PLACE...
...WHERE THE GAME IS THE HOTTEST IN THE WHOLE WORLD.

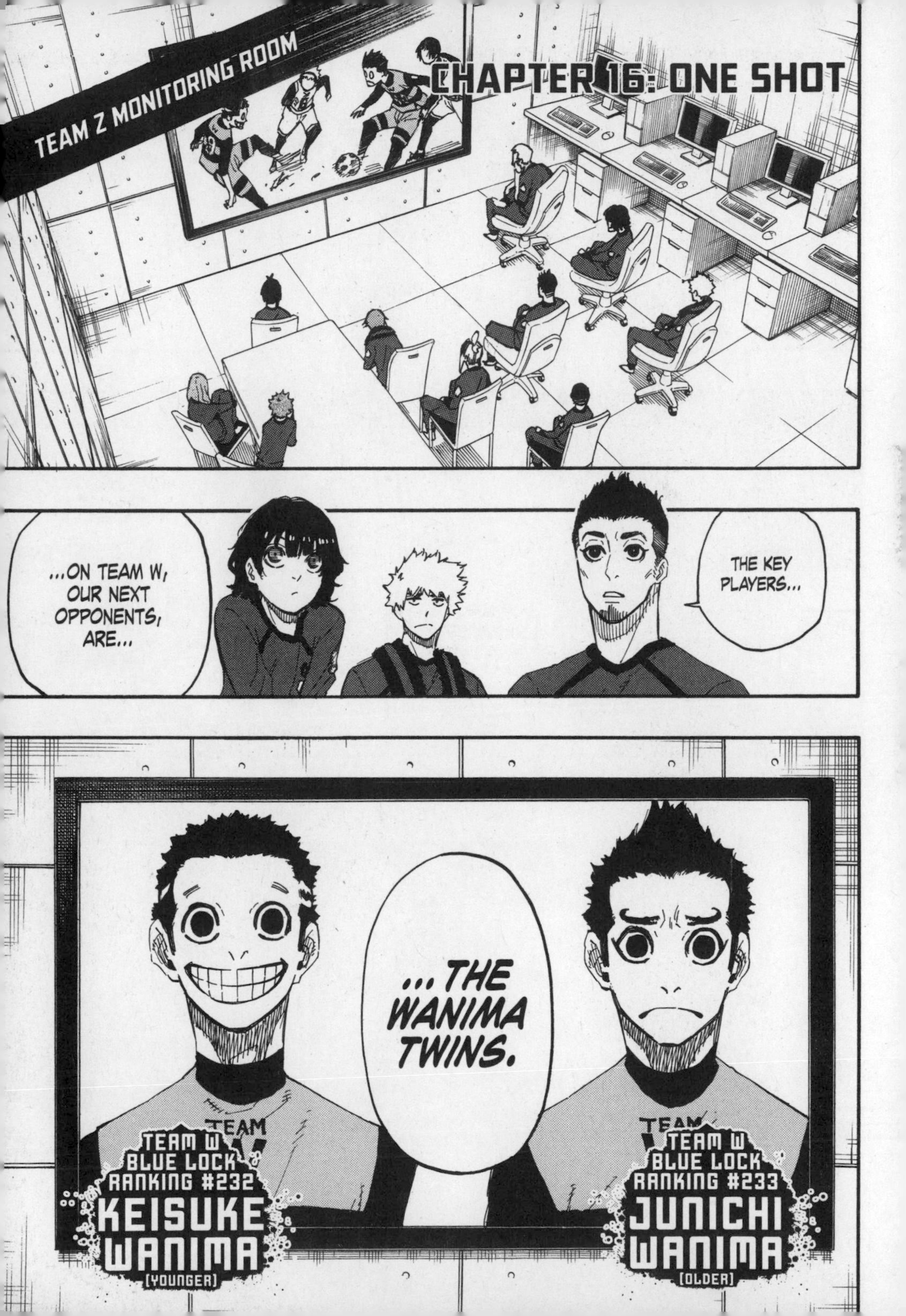
CHAPTER 16: ONE SHOT
TEAM Z MONITORING ROOM
THE KEY PLAYERS...
...ON TEAM W, OUR NEXT OPPONENTS, ARE...
...THE WANIMA TWINS.
TEAM W BLUE LOCK RANKING #233 JUNICHI WANIMA [OLDER]
TEAM W BLUE LOCK RANKING #232 KEISUKE WANIMA [YOUNGER]

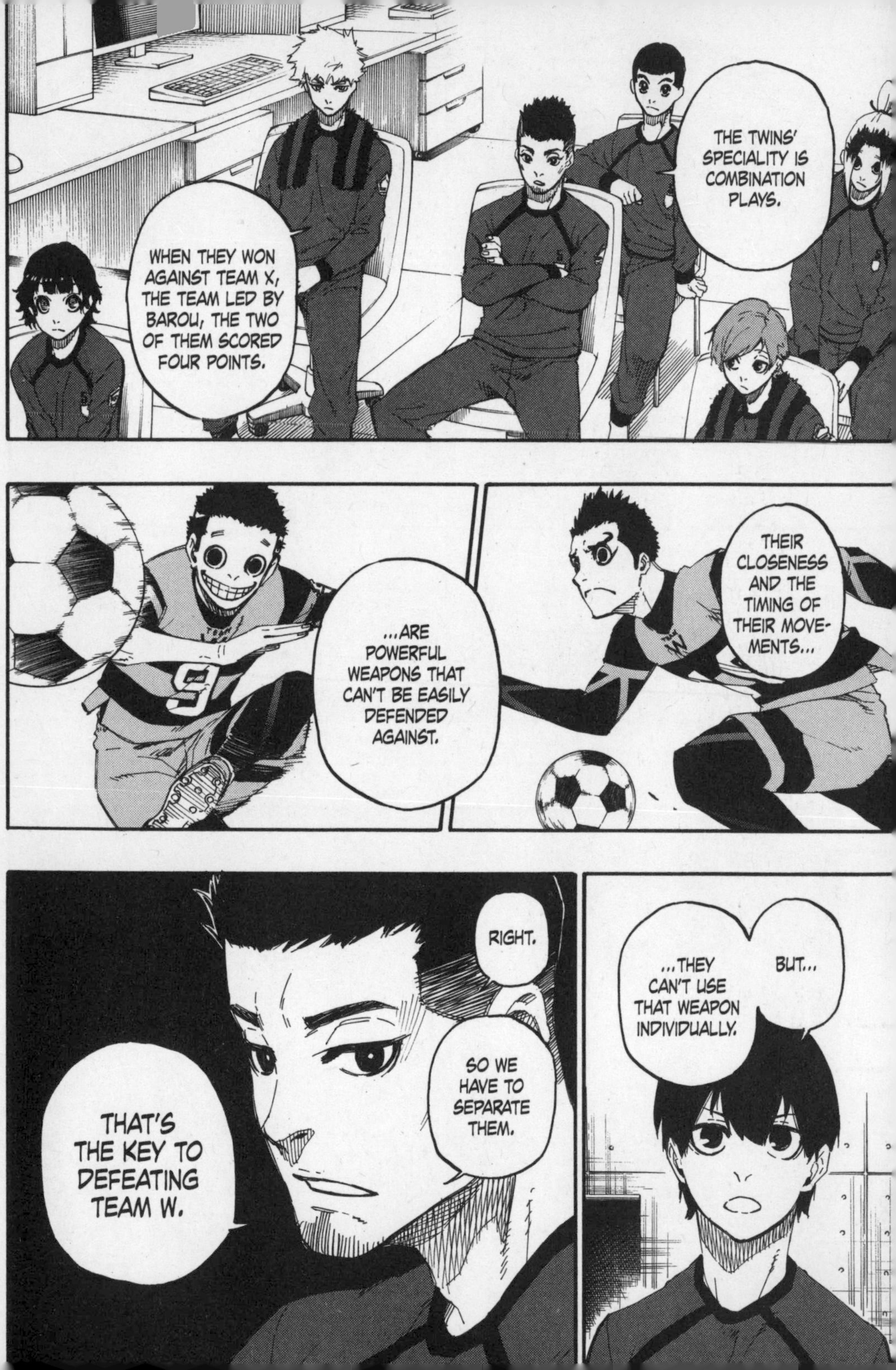
THE TWINS' SPECIALITY IS COMBINATION PLAYS.
WHEN THEY WON AGAINST TEAM X, THE TEAM LED BY BAROU, THE TWO OF THEM SCORED FOUR POINTS.
THEIR CLOSENESS AND THE TIMING OF THEIR MOVEMENTS...
...ARE POWERFUL WEAPONS THAT CAN'T BE EASILY DEFENDED AGAINST.
BUT...
...THEY CAN'T USE THAT WEAPON INDIVIDUALLY.
RIGHT.
SO WE HAVE TO SEPARATE THEM.
THAT'S THE KEY TO DEFEATING TEAM W.

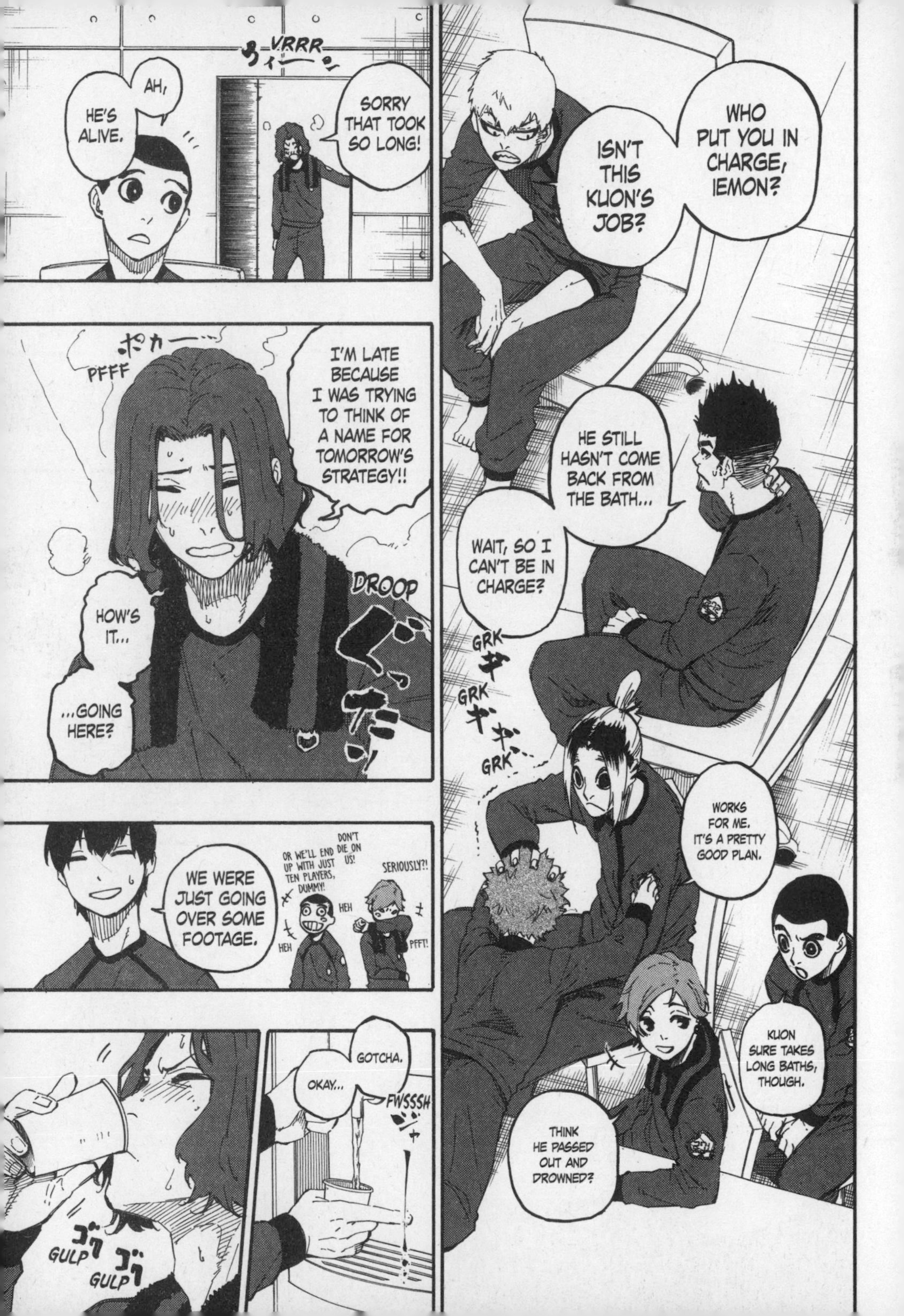
WHO PUT YOU IN CHARGE, IEMON?
ISN'T THIS KUON'S JOB?
HE STILL HASN'T COME BACK FROM THE BATH...
WAIT, SO I CAN'T BE IN CHARGE?
GRK
GRK
GRK
WORKS FOR ME. IT'S A PRETTY GOOD PLAN.
KUON SURE TAKES LONG BATHS, THOUGH.
THINK HE PASSED OUT AND DROWNED?
VRRR
SORRY THAT TOOK SO LONG!
AH,
HE'S ALIVE.
I'M LATE BECAUSE I WAS TRYING TO THINK OF A NAME FOR TOMORROW'S STRATEGY!!
PFFF
DROOP
HOW'S IT...
...GOING HERE?
SERIOUSLY?!
PFFT!
DON'T DIE ON US!
OR WE'LL END UP WITH JUST TEN PLAYERS, DUMMY!
HEH
HEH
WE WERE JUST GOING OVER SOME FOOTAGE.
GOTCHA.
OKAY...
FWSSSH
GULP
GULP

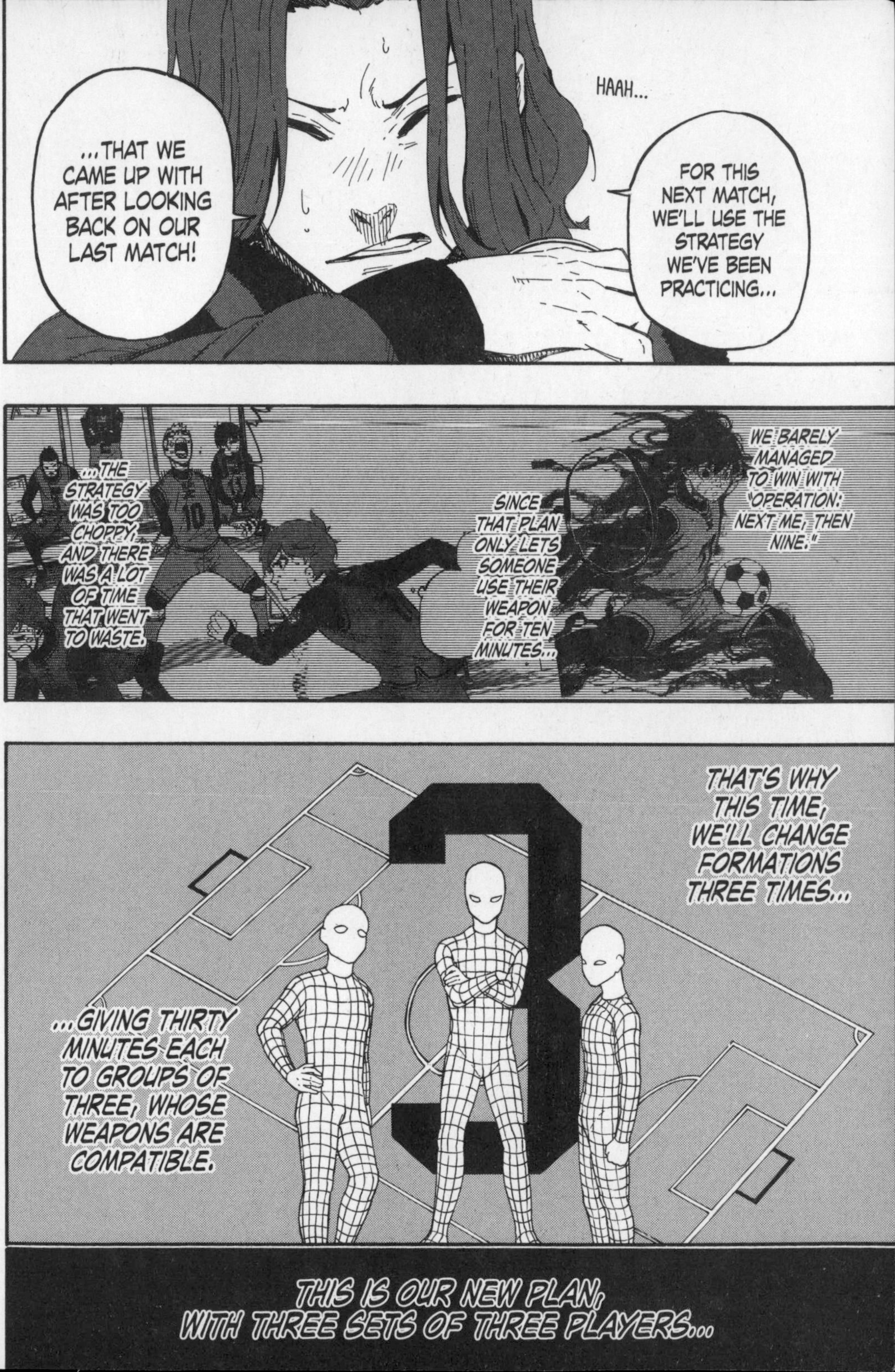
HAAH...
FOR THIS NEXT MATCH, WE'LL USE THE STRATEGY WE'VE BEEN PRACTICING...
...THAT WE CAME UP WITH AFTER LOOKING BACK ON OUR LAST MATCH!
WE BARELY MANAGED TO WIN WITH "OPERATION: NEXT ME, THEN NINE."
SINCE THAT PLAN ONLY LETS SOMEONE USE THEIR WEAPON FOR TEN MINUTES...
...THE STRATEGY WAS TOO CHOPPY, AND THERE WAS A LOT OF TIME THAT WENT TO WASTE.
THAT'S WHY THIS TIME, WE'LL CHANGE FORMATIONS THREE TIMES...
...GIVING THIRTY MINUTES EACH TO GROUPS OF THREE, WHOSE WEAPONS ARE COMPATIBLE.
THIS IS OUR NEW PLAN, WITH THREE SETS OF THREE PLAYERS...

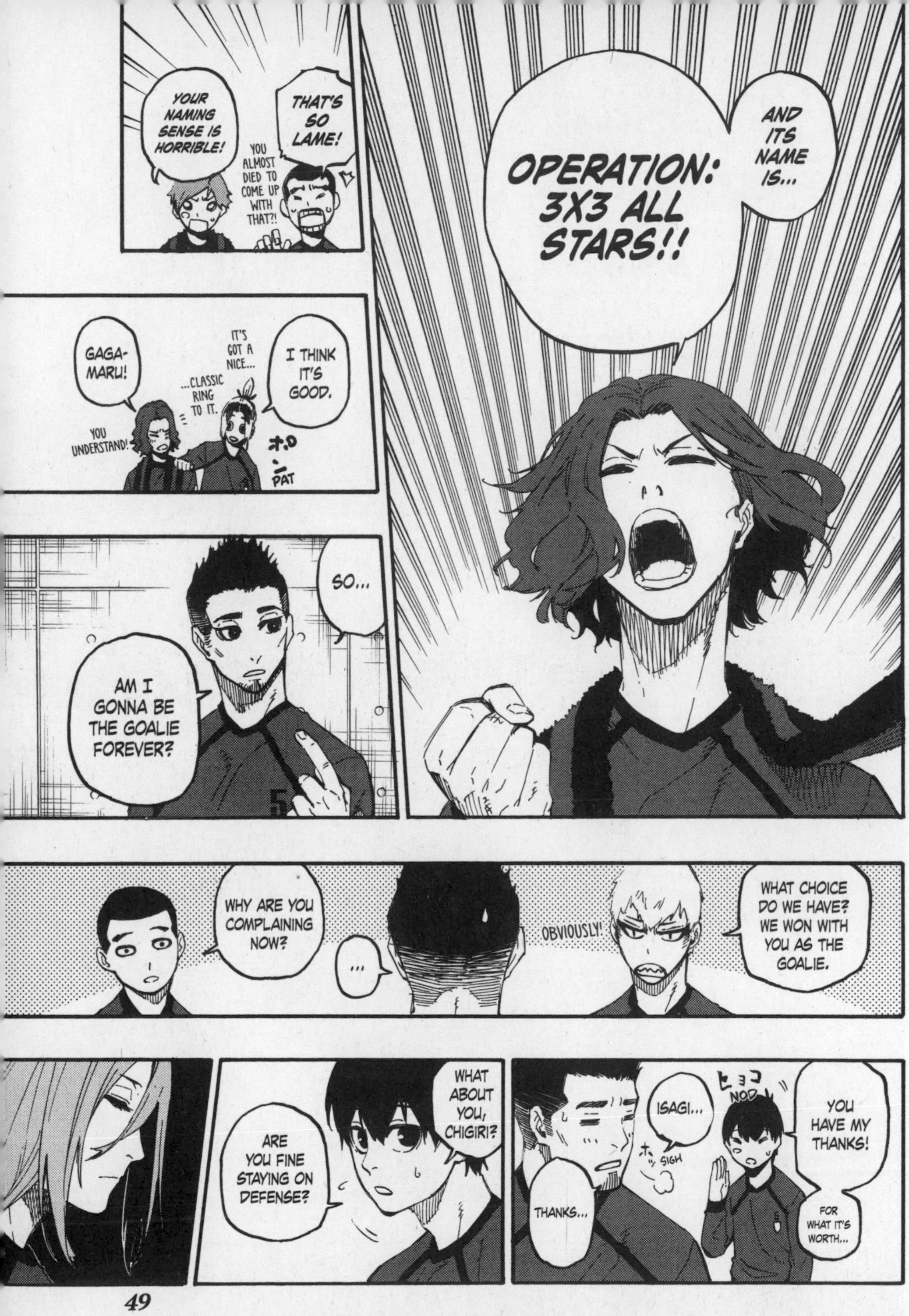
AND ITS NAME IS...
OPERATION: 3X3 ALL STARS!!
THAT'S SO LAME!
YOU ALMOST DIED TO COME UP WITH THAT?!
YOUR NAMING SENSE IS HORRIBLE!
I THINK IT'S GOOD.
IT'S GOT A NICE...
...CLASSIC RING TO IT.
GAGA-MARU!
YOU UNDERSTAND!
PAT
SO...
AM I GONNA BE THE GOALIE FOREVER?
WHAT CHOICE DO WE HAVE? WE WON WITH YOU AS THE GOALIE.
OBVIOUSLY!
...
WHY ARE YOU COMPLAINING NOW?
YOU HAVE MY THANKS!
NOD
FOR WHAT IT'S WORTH...
ISAGI...
SIGH
THANKS...
WHAT ABOUT YOU, CHIGIRI?
ARE YOU FINE STAYING ON DEFENSE?

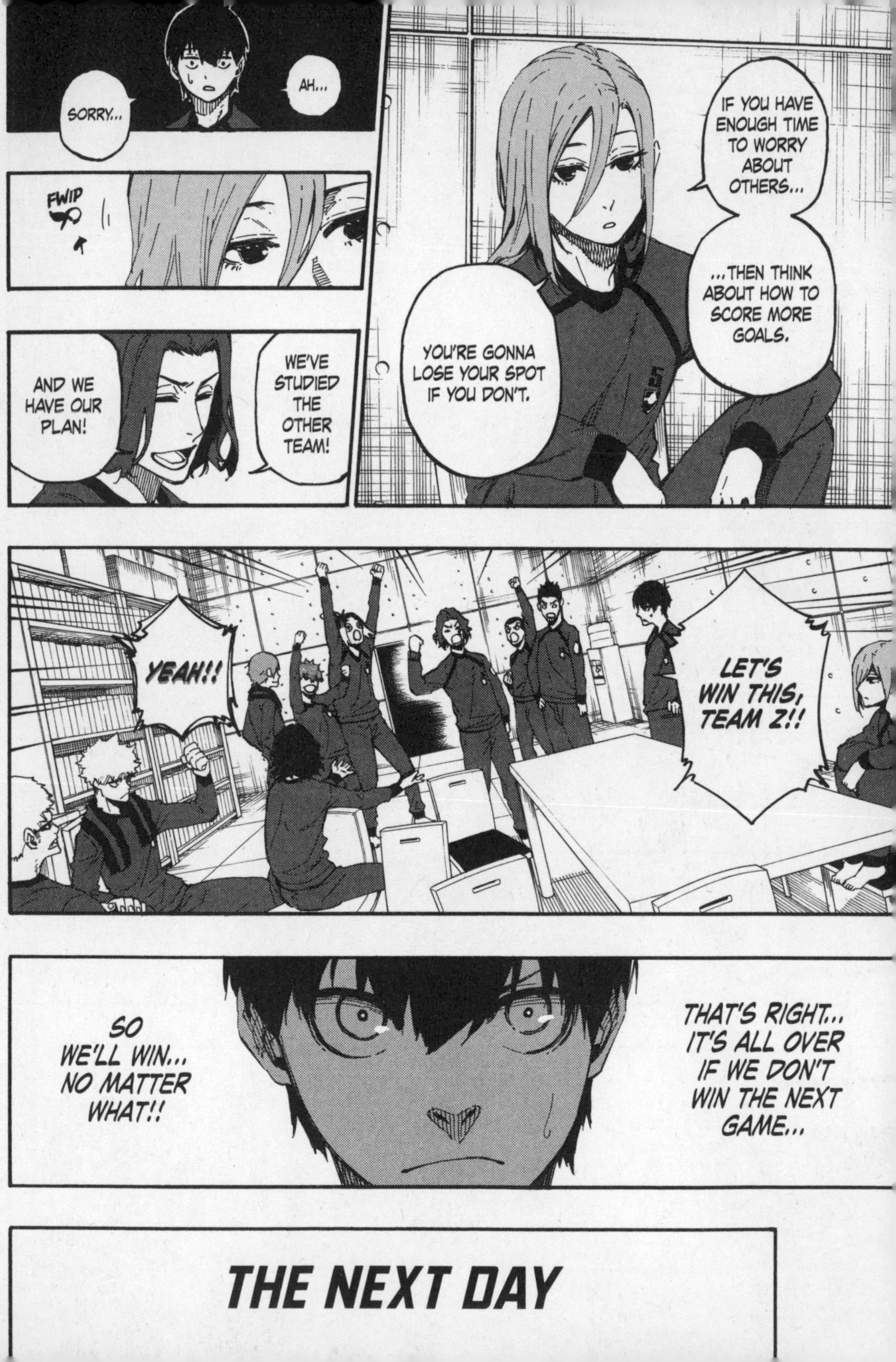
IF YOU HAVE ENOUGH TIME TO WORRY ABOUT OTHERS...
...THEN THINK ABOUT HOW TO SCORE MORE GOALS.
YOU'RE GONNA LOSE YOUR SPOT IF YOU DON'T.
AH...
SORRY...
FWIP
WE'VE STUDIED THE OTHER TEAM!
AND WE HAVE OUR PLAN!
LET'S WIN THIS, TEAM Z!!
YEAH!!
THAT'S RIGHT... IT'S ALL OVER IF WE DON'T WIN THE NEXT GAME...
SO WE'LL WIN... NO MATTER WHAT!!
THE NEXT DAY

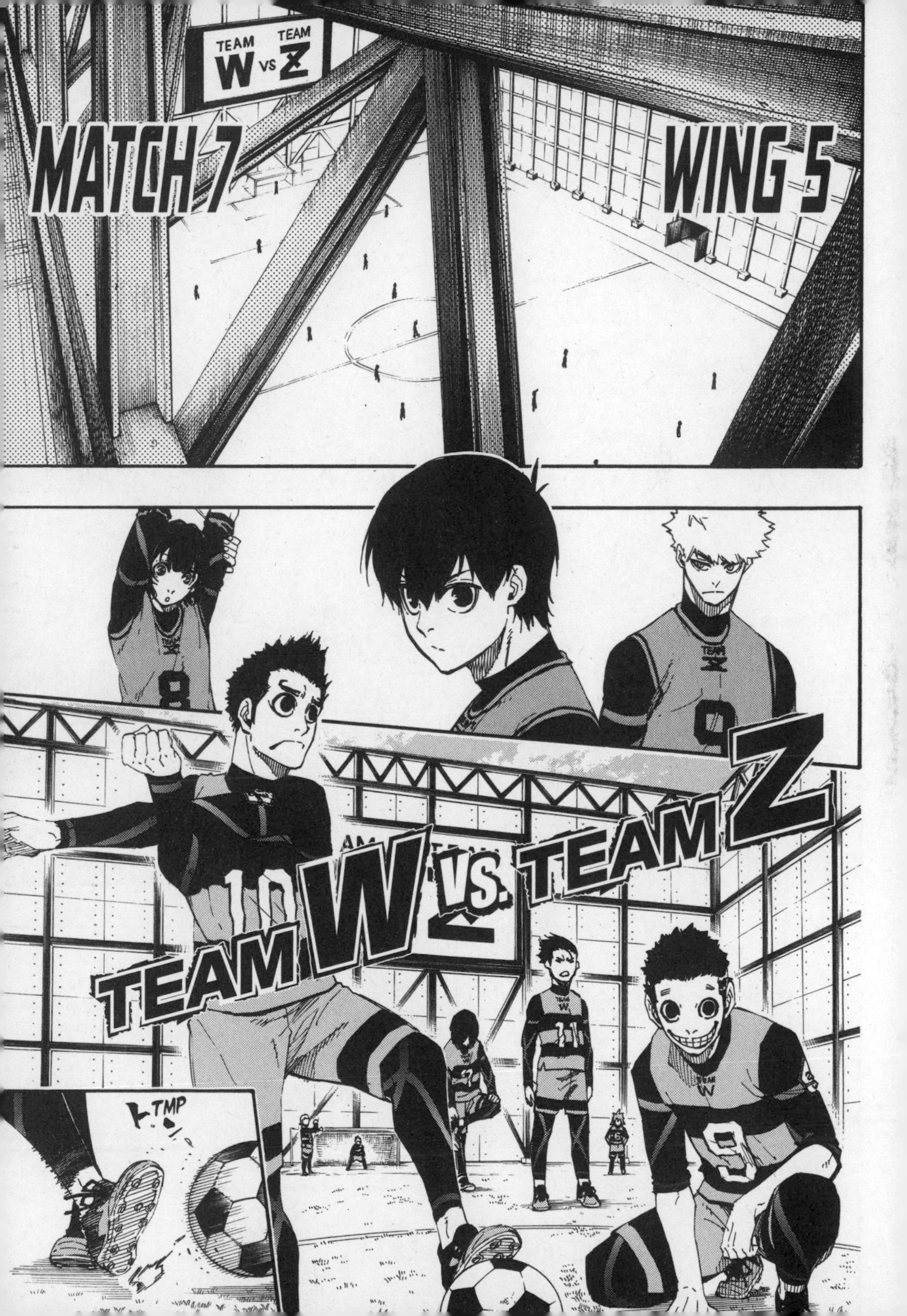

TEAM W VS TEAM Z
WING 5
MATCH 7
TEAM W VS. TEAM Z
TMP

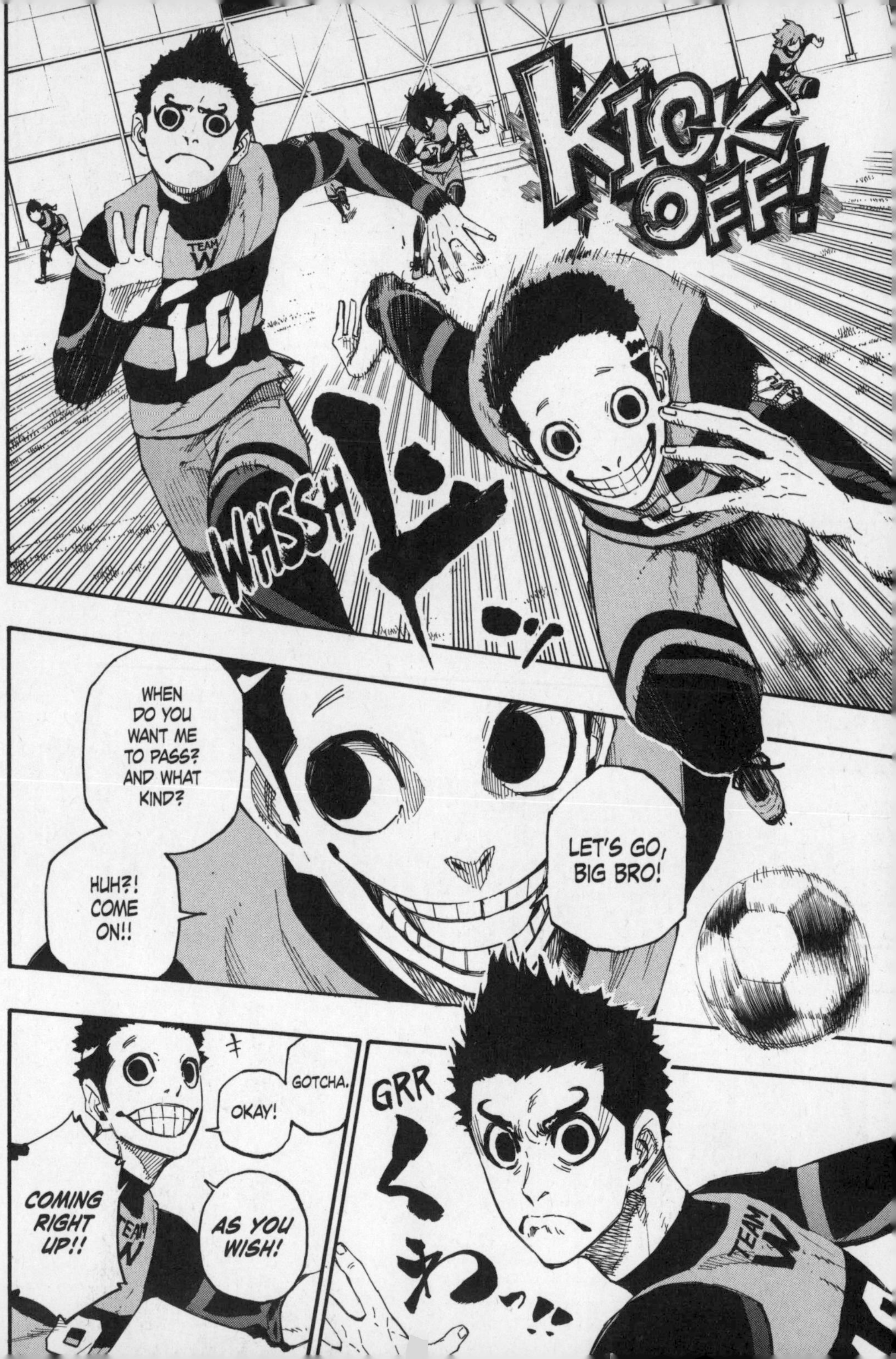
KICK OFF!
WHSSH
LET'S GO, BIG BRO!
WHEN DO YOU WANT ME TO PASS? AND WHAT KIND?
HUH?! COME ON!!
GRR
GOTCHA.
OKAY!
AS YOU WISH!
COMING RIGHT UP!!

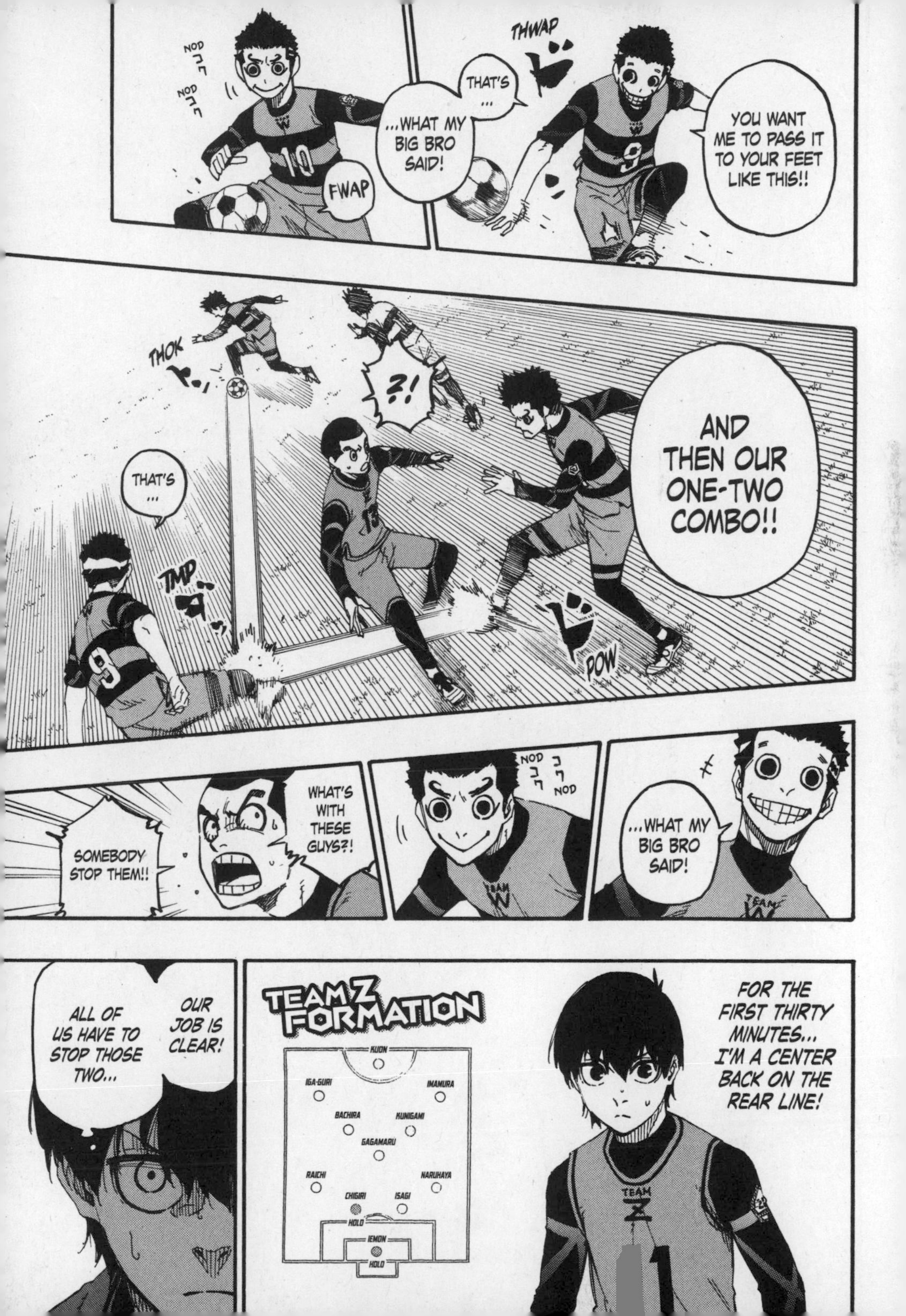
THWAP
YOU WANT ME TO PASS IT TO YOUR FEET LIKE THIS!!
THAT'S ...
...WHAT MY BIG BRO SAID!
NOD
NOD
FWAP
AND THEN OUR ONE-TWO COMBO!!
POW
?!
THOK
THAT'S ...
TMP
...WHAT MY BIG BRO SAID!
NOD
NOD
WHAT'S WITH THESE GUYS?!
SOMEBODY STOP THEM!!
FOR THE FIRST THIRTY MINUTES... I'M A CENTER BACK ON THE REAR LINE!
TEAM Z FORMATION
KUON
IGA-GURI
IMAMURA
BACHIRA
KUNIGAMI
GAGAMARU
RAICHI
NARUHAYA
CHIGIRI
ISAGI
HOLD
IEMON
HOLD
OUR JOB IS CLEAR!
ALL OF US HAVE TO STOP THOSE TWO...

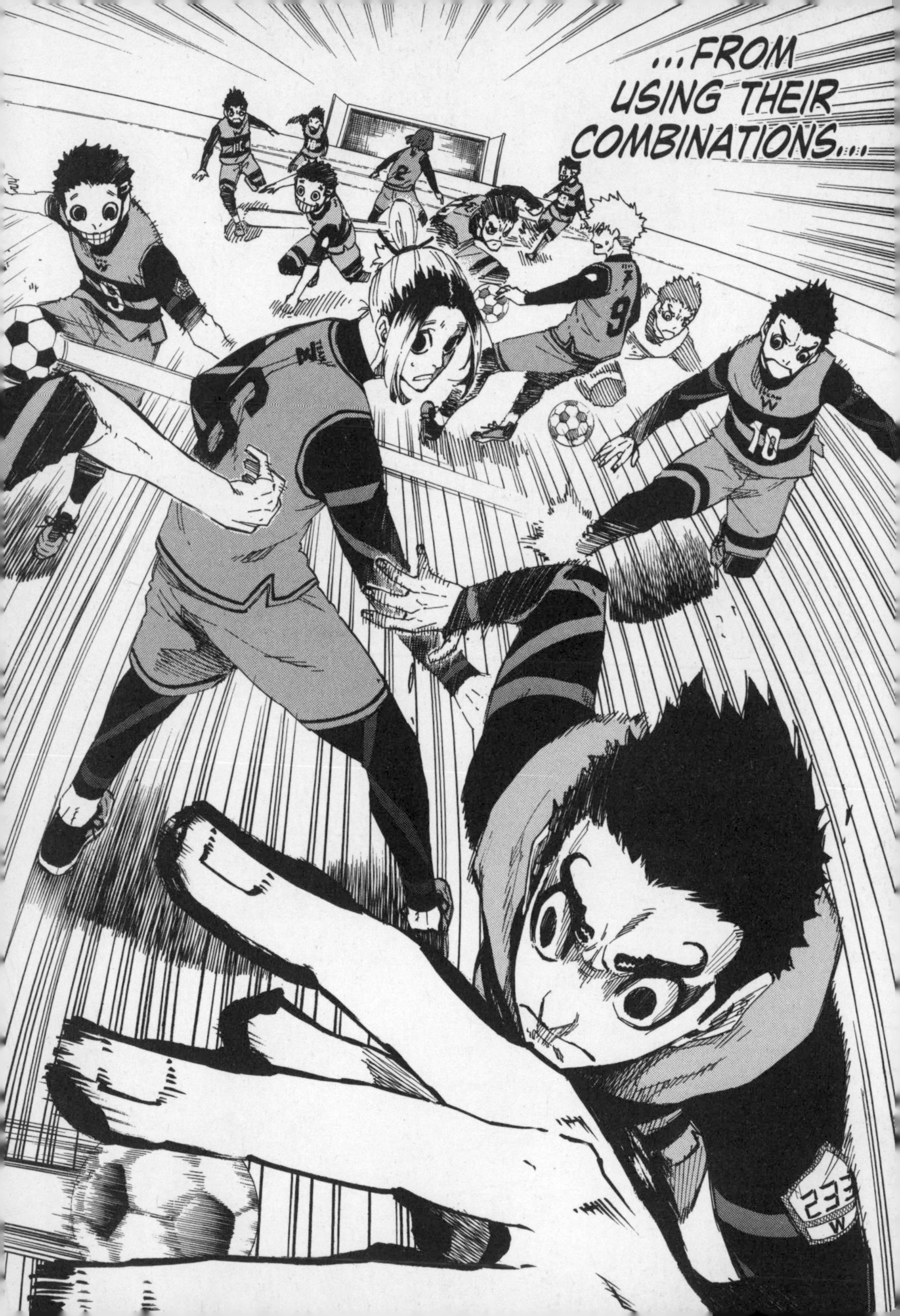
...FROM USING THEIR COMBINATIONS...

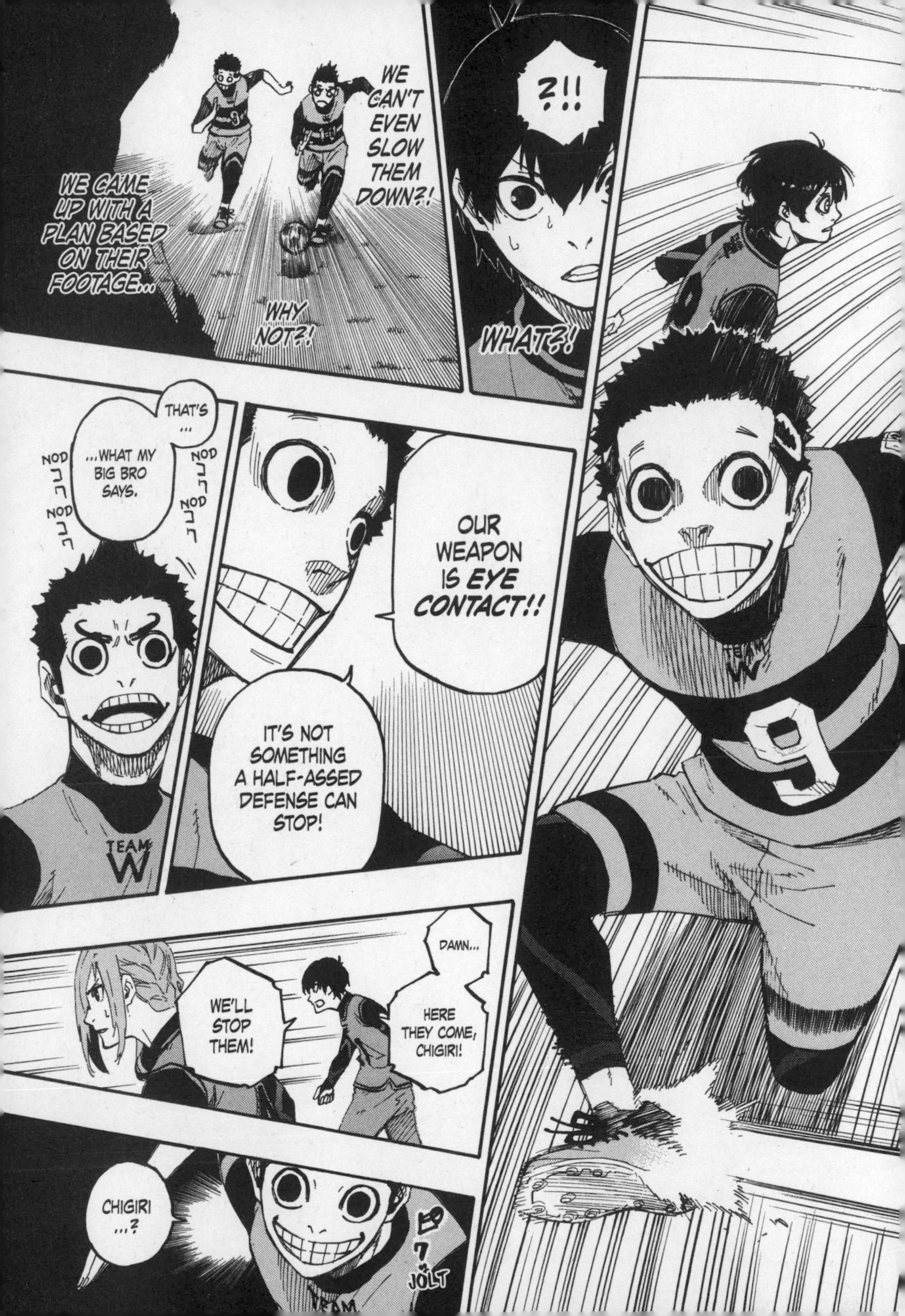
?!!
WHAT?!
WE CAN'T EVEN SLOW THEM DOWN?!
WHY NOT?!
WE CAME UP WITH A PLAN BASED ON THEIR FOOTAGE...
OUR WEAPON IS EYE CONTACT!!
IT'S NOT SOMETHING A HALF-ASSED DEFENSE CAN STOP!
THAT'S ...
...WHAT MY BIG BRO SAYS.
NOD
NOD
NOD
NOD
DAMN...
HERE THEY COME, CHIGIRI!
WE'LL STOP THEM!
JOLT
CHIGIRI ...?

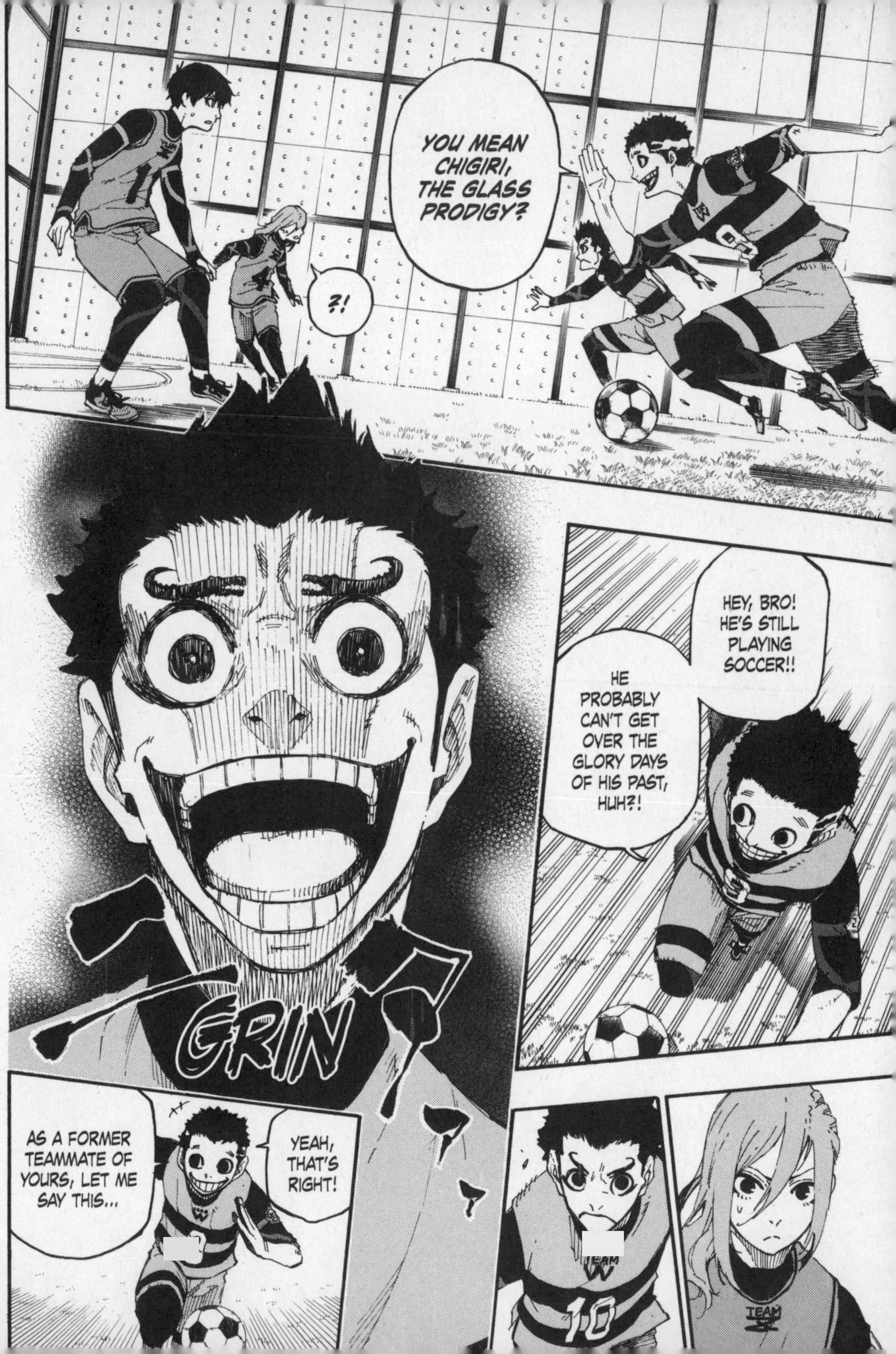
YOU MEAN CHIGIRI, THE GLASS PRODIGY?
?!
HEY, BRO! HE'S STILL PLAYING SOCCER!!
HE PROBABLY CAN'T GET OVER THE GLORY DAYS OF HIS PAST, HUH?!
GRIN
YEAH, THAT'S RIGHT!
AS A FORMER TEAMMATE OF YOURS, LET ME SAY THIS...

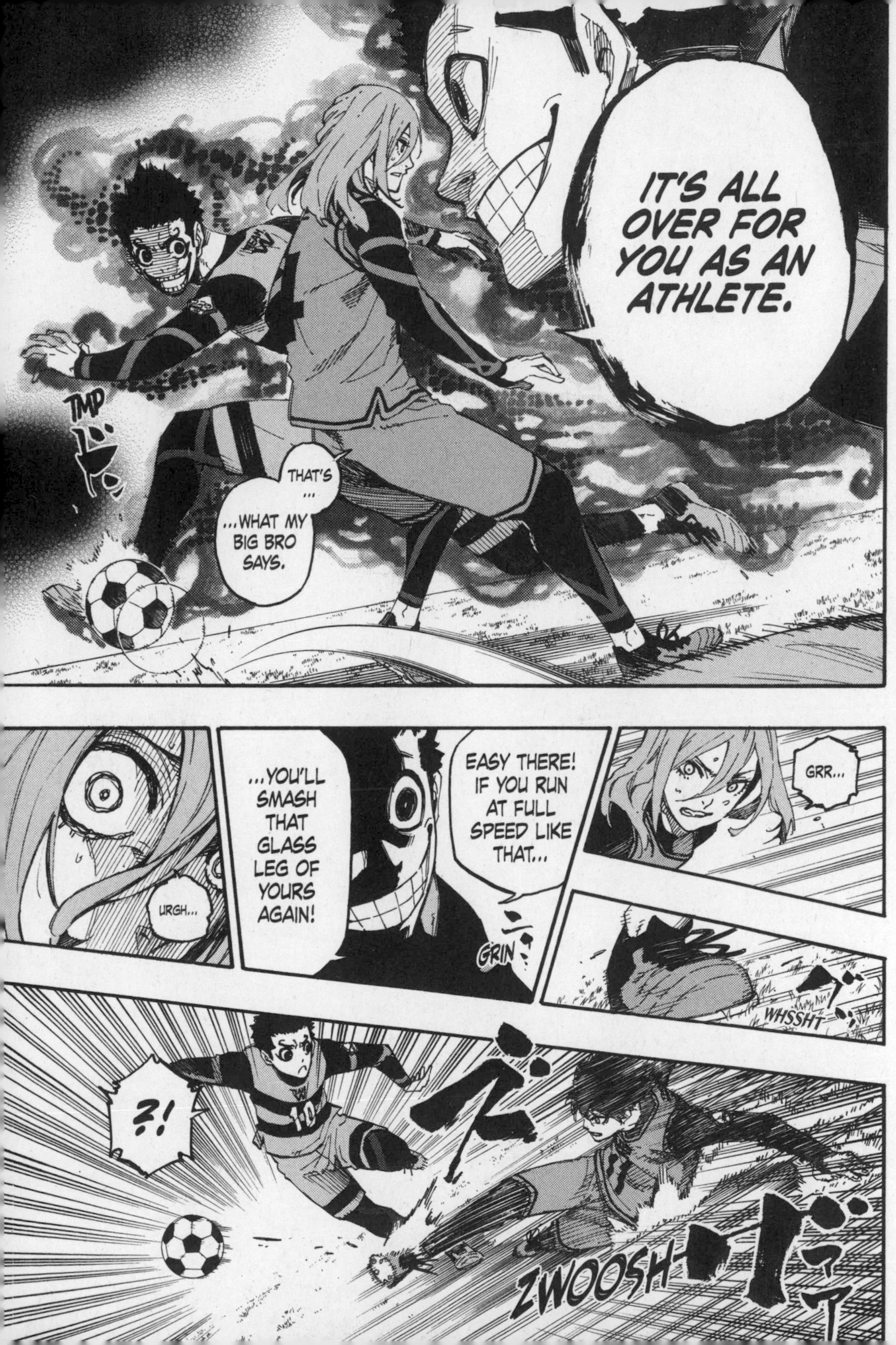
IT'S ALL OVER FOR YOU AS AN ATHLETE.
THAT'S ...
...WHAT MY BIG BRO SAYS.
TMP
GRR...
WHSSHT
EASY THERE! IF YOU RUN AT FULL SPEED LIKE THAT...
...YOU'LL SMASH THAT GLASS LEG OF YOURS AGAIN!
GRIN
URGH...
ZWOOSH
?!

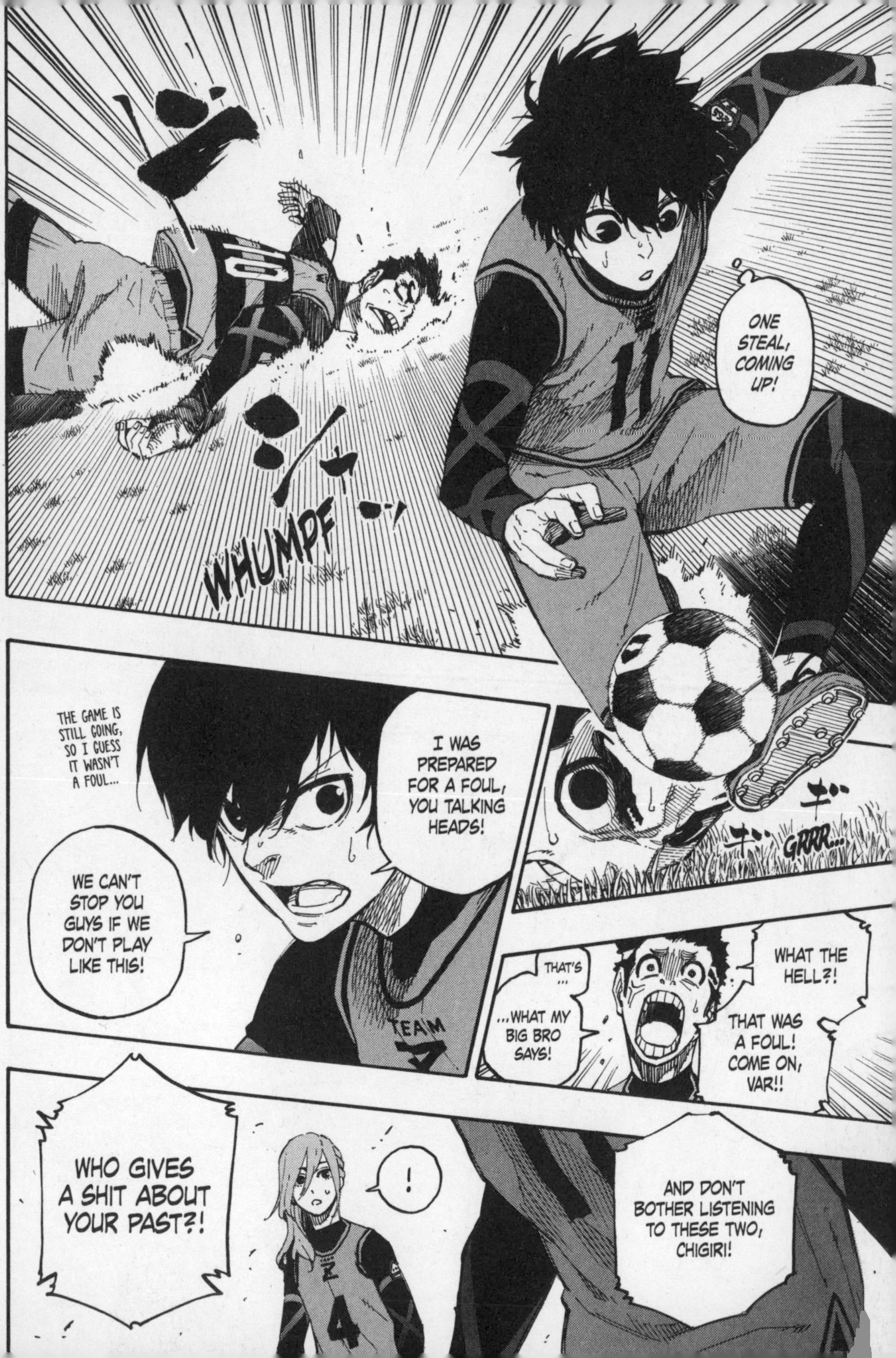
ONE STEAL, COMING UP!
WHUMPF
GRRR...
WHAT THE HELL?!
THAT WAS A FOUL! COME ON, VAR!!
THAT'S ...
...WHAT MY BIG BRO SAYS!
I WAS PREPARED FOR A FOUL, YOU TALKING HEADS!
THE GAME IS STILL GOING, SO I GUESS IT WASN'T A FOUL...
WE CAN'T STOP YOU GUYS IF WE DON'T PLAY LIKE THIS!
TEAM Z
AND DON'T BOTHER LISTENING TO THESE TWO, CHIGIRI!
!
WHO GIVES A SHIT ABOUT YOUR PAST?!

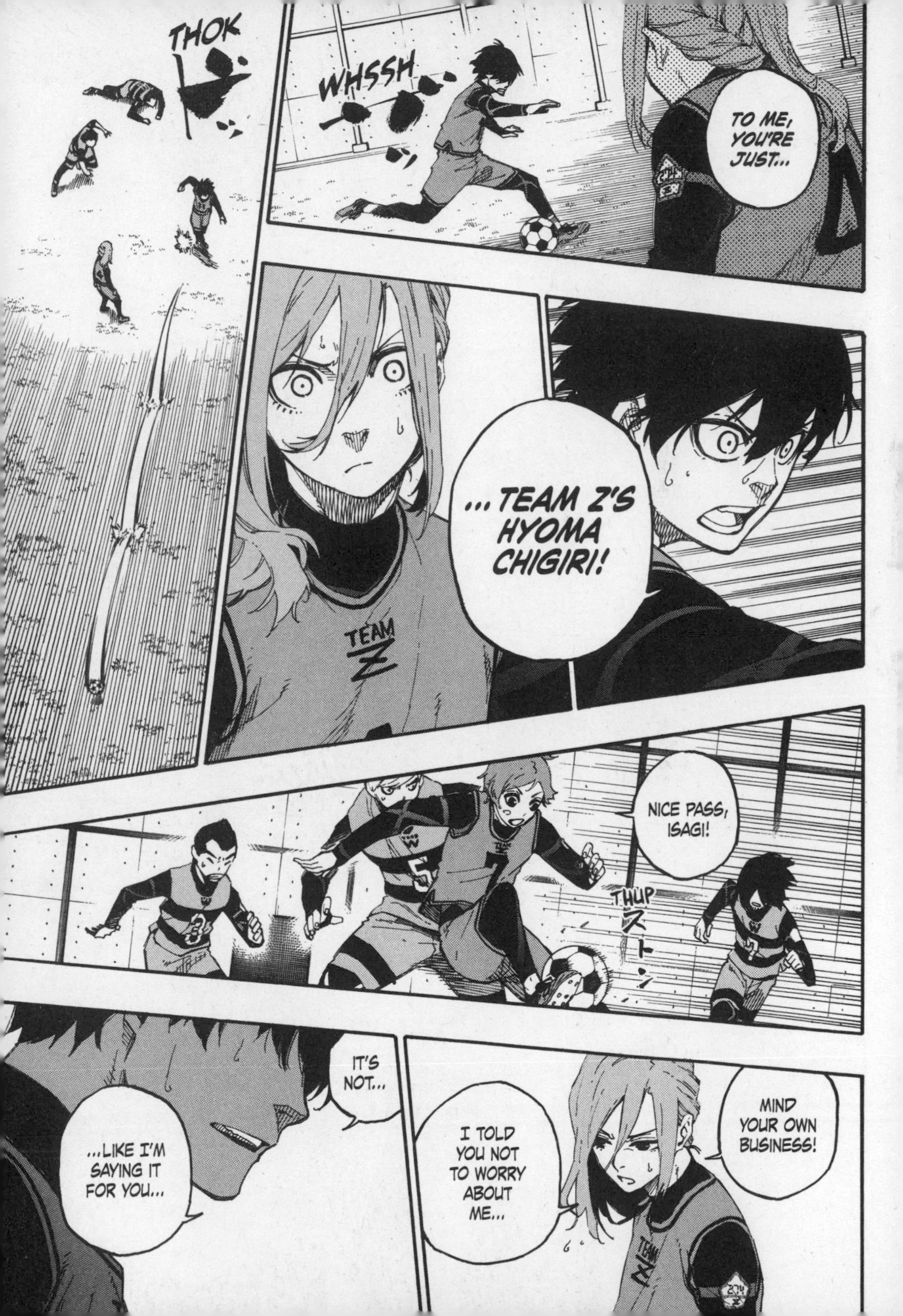
TO ME, YOU'RE JUST...
WHSSH
...TEAM Z'S HYOMA CHIGIRI!
THOK
NICE PASS, ISAGI!
THUP
MIND YOUR OWN BUSINESS!
I TOLD YOU NOT TO WORRY ABOUT ME...
IT'S NOT...
...LIKE I'M SAYING IT FOR YOU...

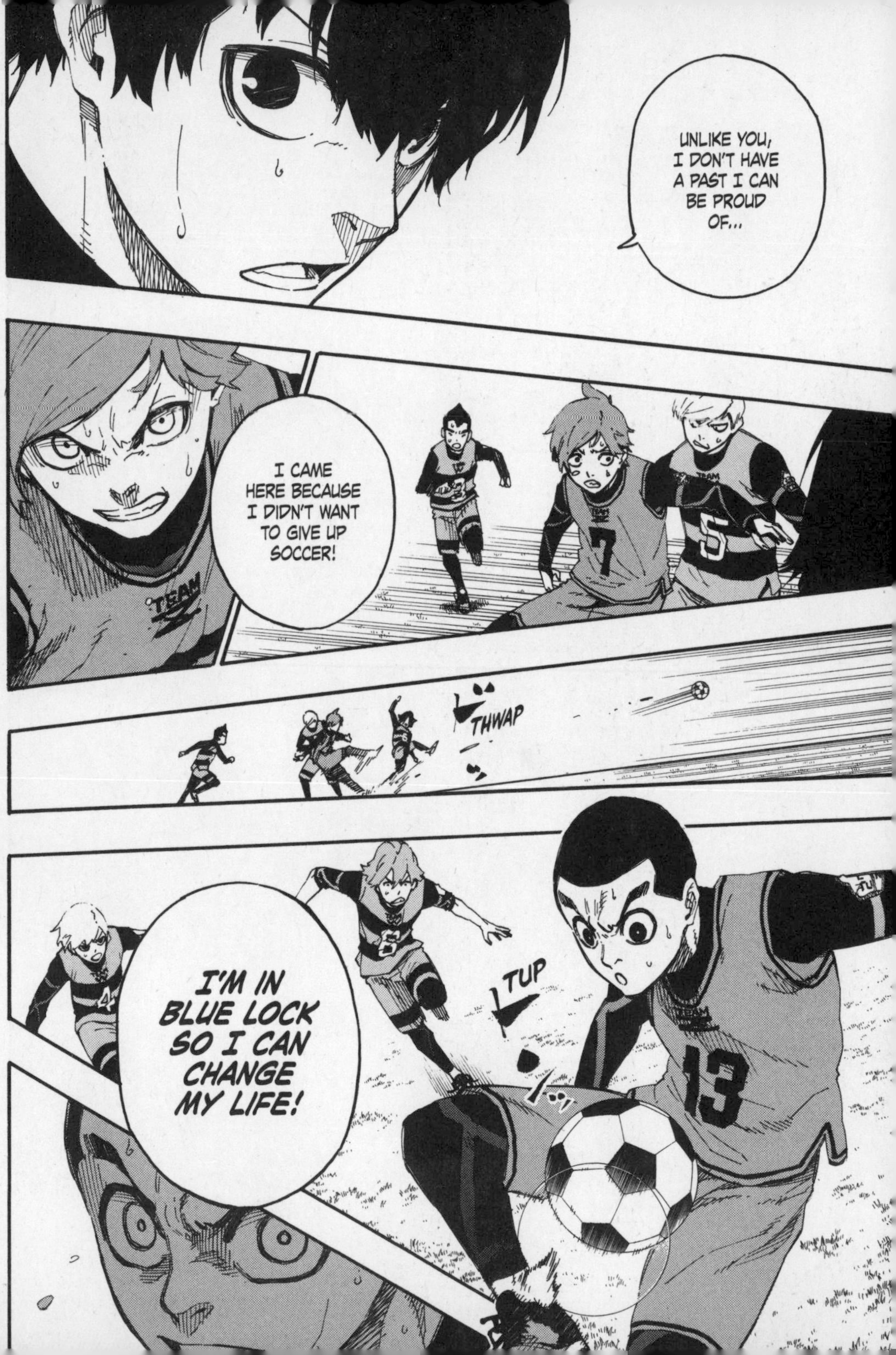
UNLIKE YOU, I DON'T HAVE A PAST I CAN BE PROUD OF...
I CAME HERE BECAUSE I DIDN'T WANT TO GIVE UP SOCCER!
THWAP
TUP
I'M IN BLUE LOCK SO I CAN CHANGE MY LIFE!

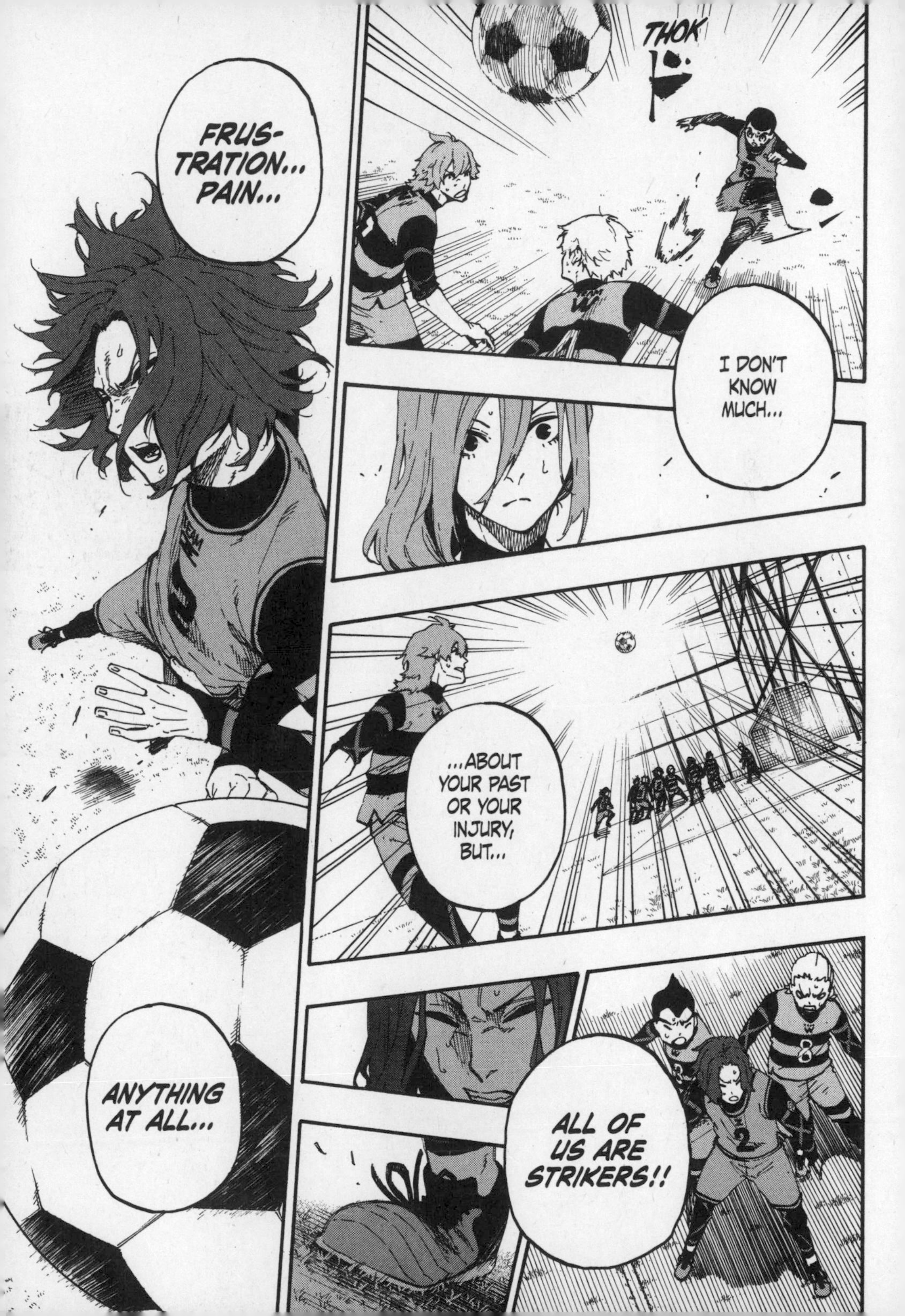
THOK
I DON'T KNOW MUCH...
...ABOUT YOUR PAST OR YOUR INJURY, BUT...
ALL OF US ARE STRIKERS!!
FRUS-TRATION... PAIN...
ANYTHING AT ALL...

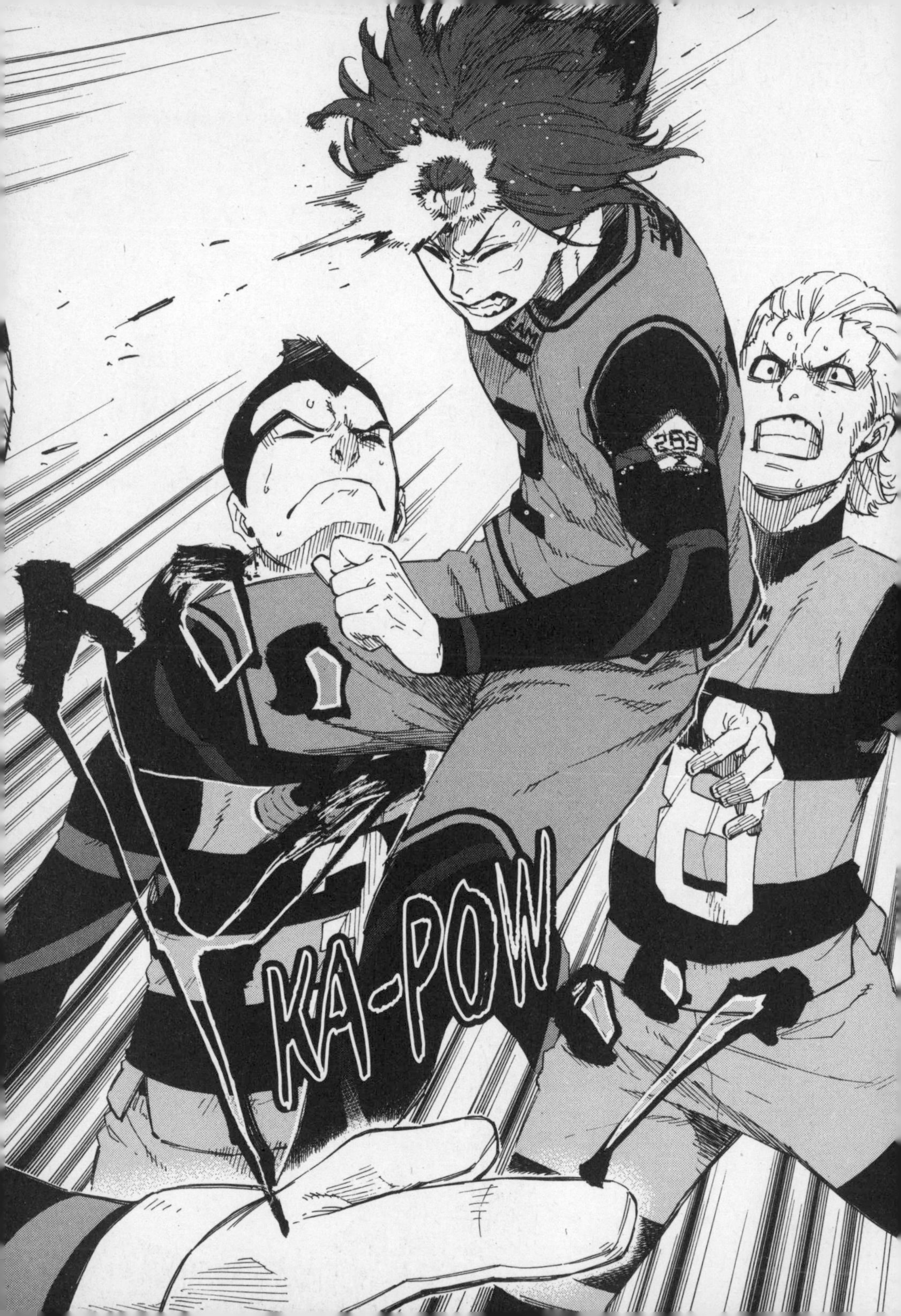
KA-POW
269

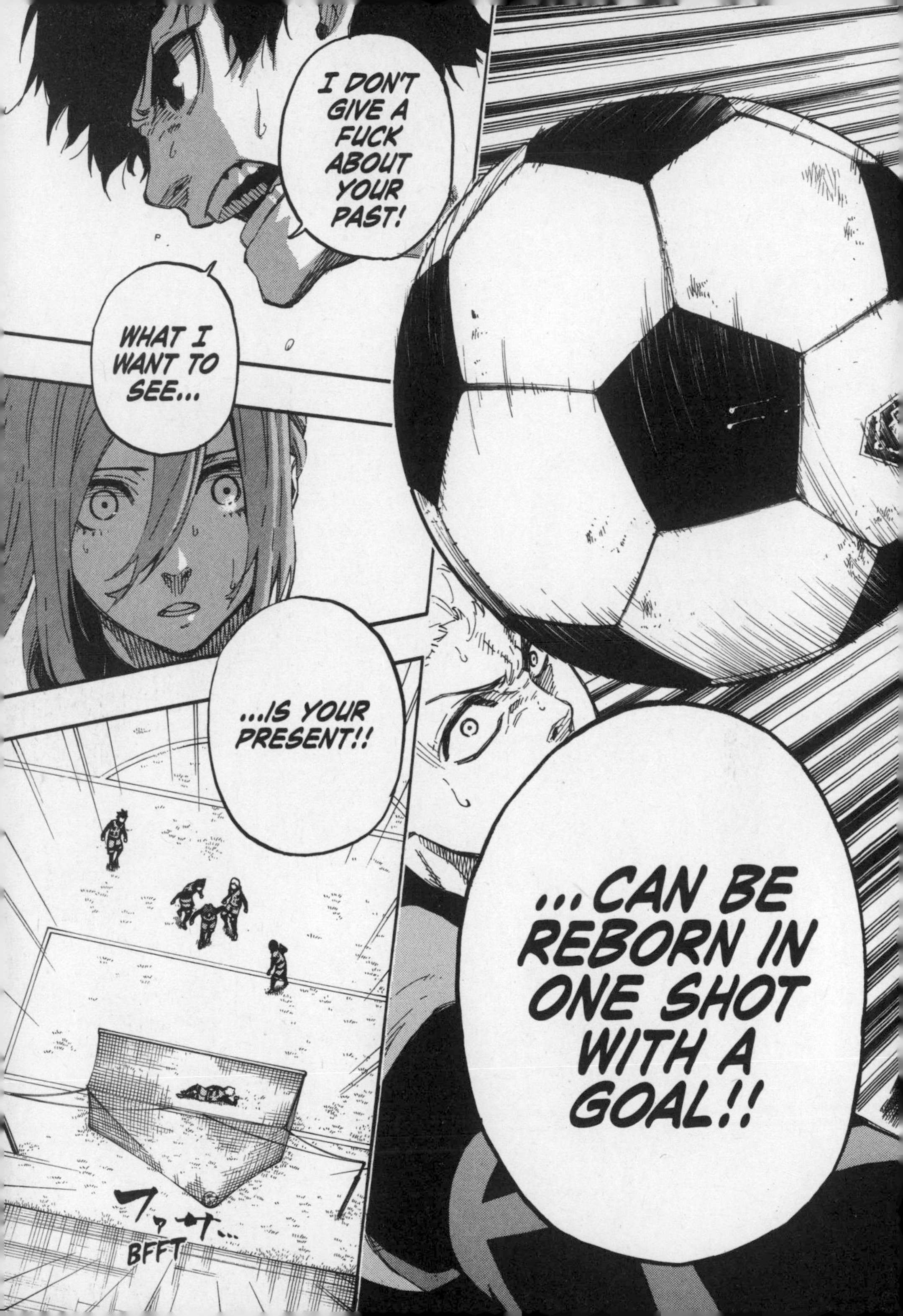
I DON'T GIVE A FUCK ABOUT YOUR PAST!
WHAT I WANT TO SEE...
...IS YOUR PRESENT!!
ファサ...
BFFT
...CAN BE REBORN IN ONE SHOT WITH A GOAL!!

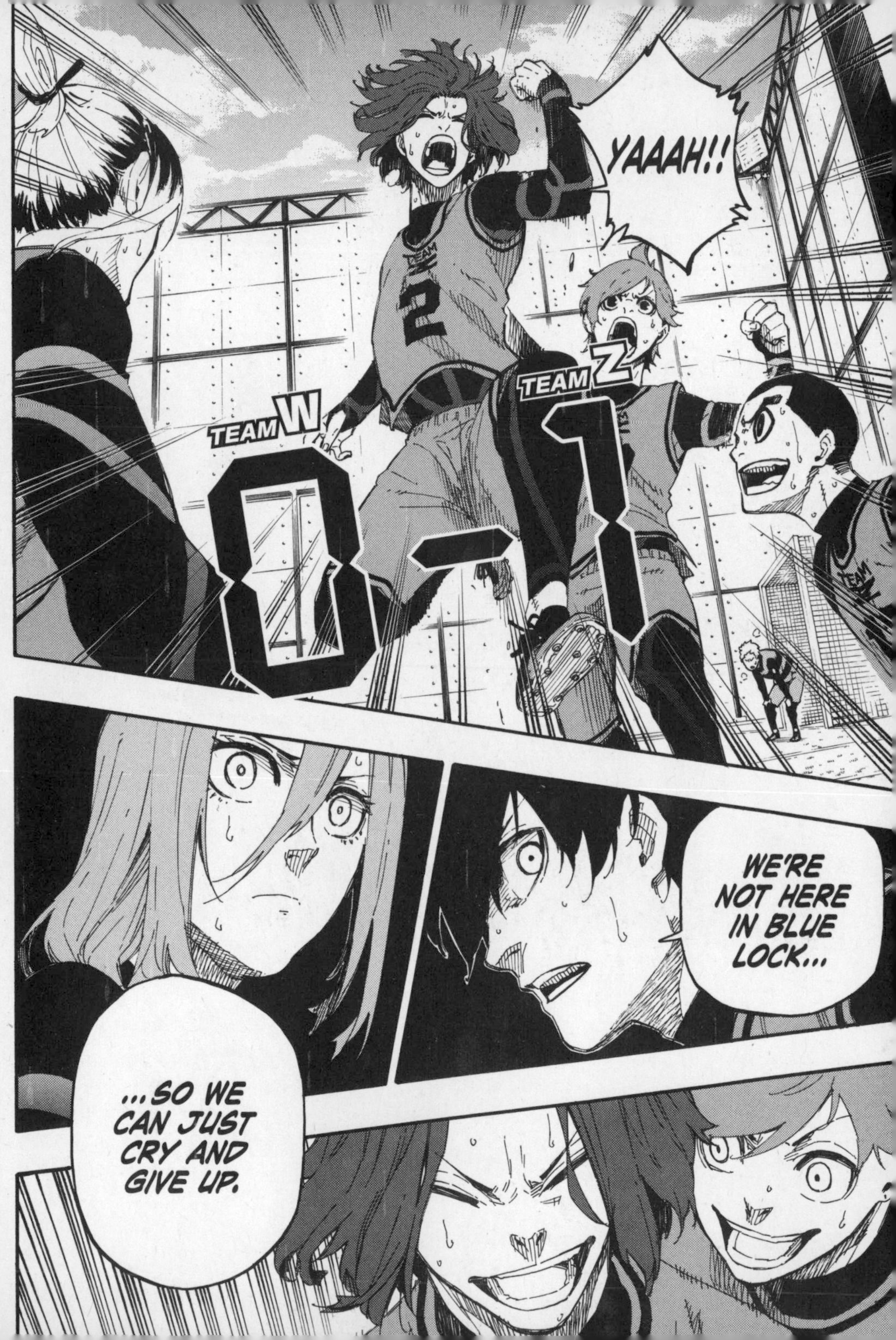
YAAAH!!
TEAM W
8-1
TEAM Z
2
WE'RE NOT HERE IN BLUE LOCK...
...SO WE CAN JUST CRY AND GIVE UP.

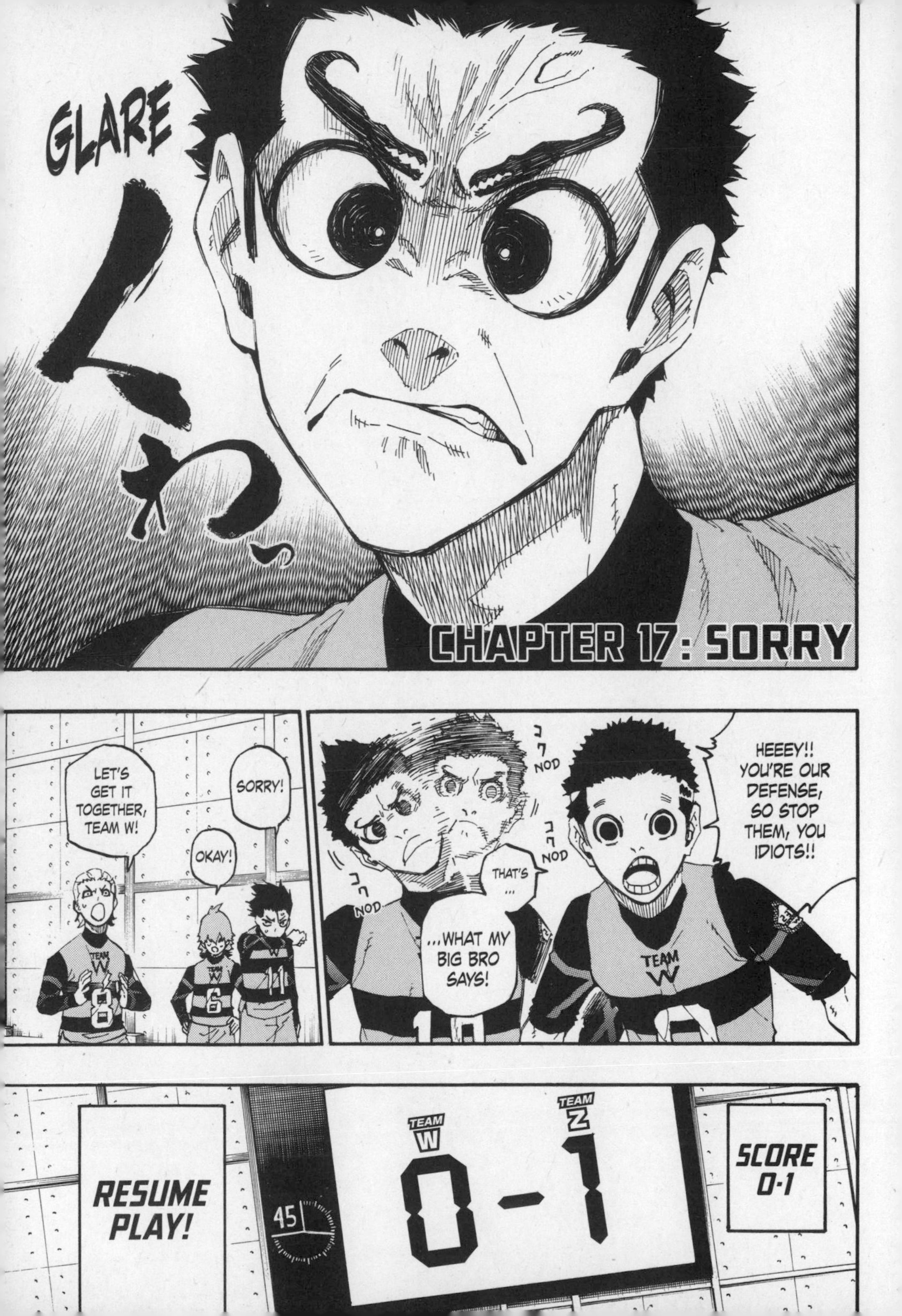
GLARE
CHAPTER 17: SORRY
HEEEY!! YOU'RE OUR DEFENSE, SO STOP THEM, YOU IDIOTS!!
NOD
NOD
NOD
THAT'S ...
...WHAT MY BIG BRO SAYS!
TEAM W
SORRY!
LET'S GET IT TOGETHER, TEAM W!
OKAY!
TEAM W
TEAM W
SCORE 0-1
TEAM Z
TEAM W
0 - 1
45
RESUME PLAY!

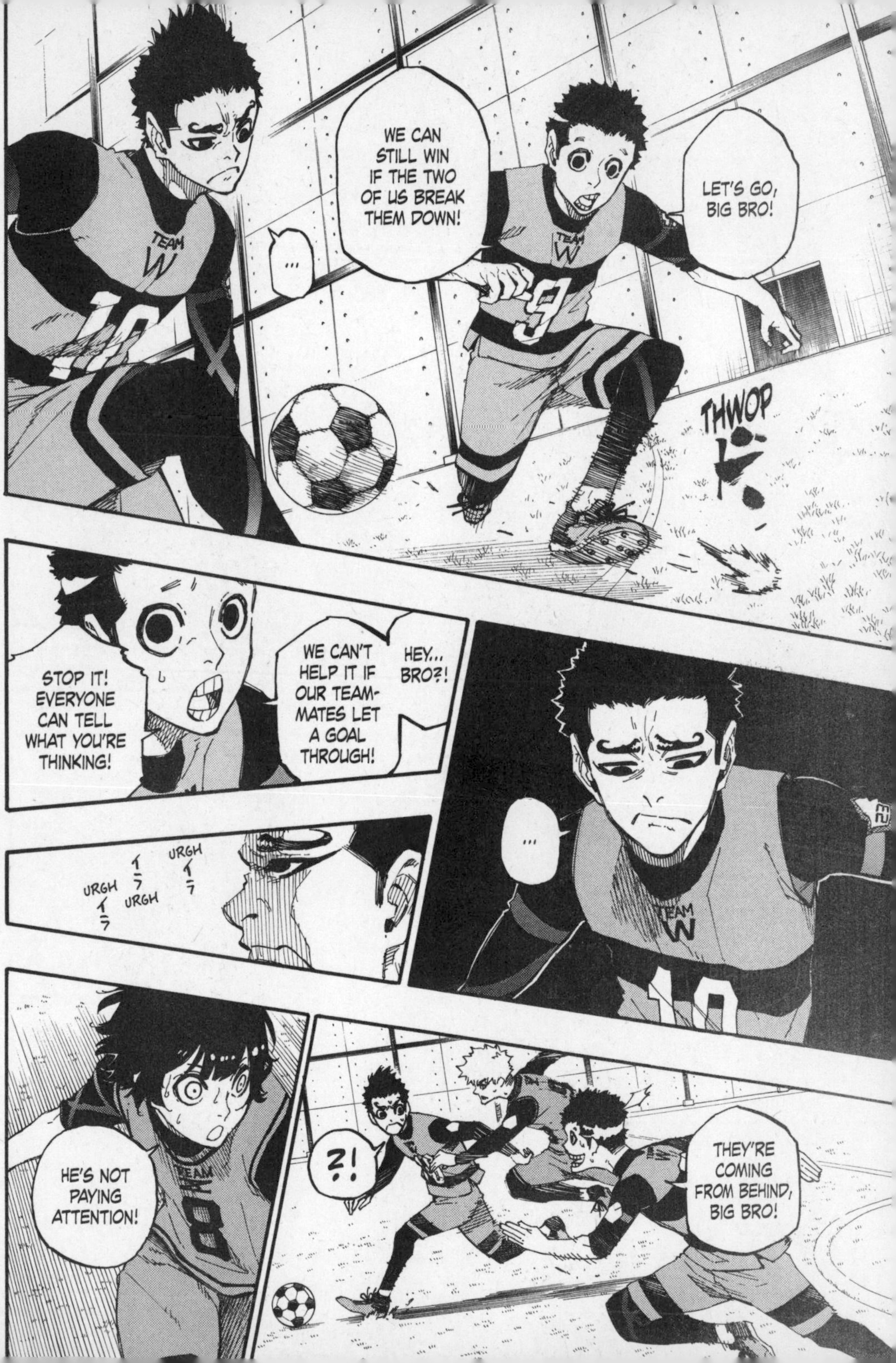
LET'S GO, BIG BRO!
WE CAN STILL WIN IF THE TWO OF US BREAK THEM DOWN!
...
THWOP
...
HEY... BRO?!
WE CAN'T HELP IT IF OUR TEAM-MATES LET A GOAL THROUGH!
STOP IT! EVERYONE CAN TELL WHAT YOU'RE THINKING!
URGH
URGH
URGH
THEY'RE COMING FROM BEHIND, BIG BRO!
?!
HE'S NOT PAYING ATTENTION!

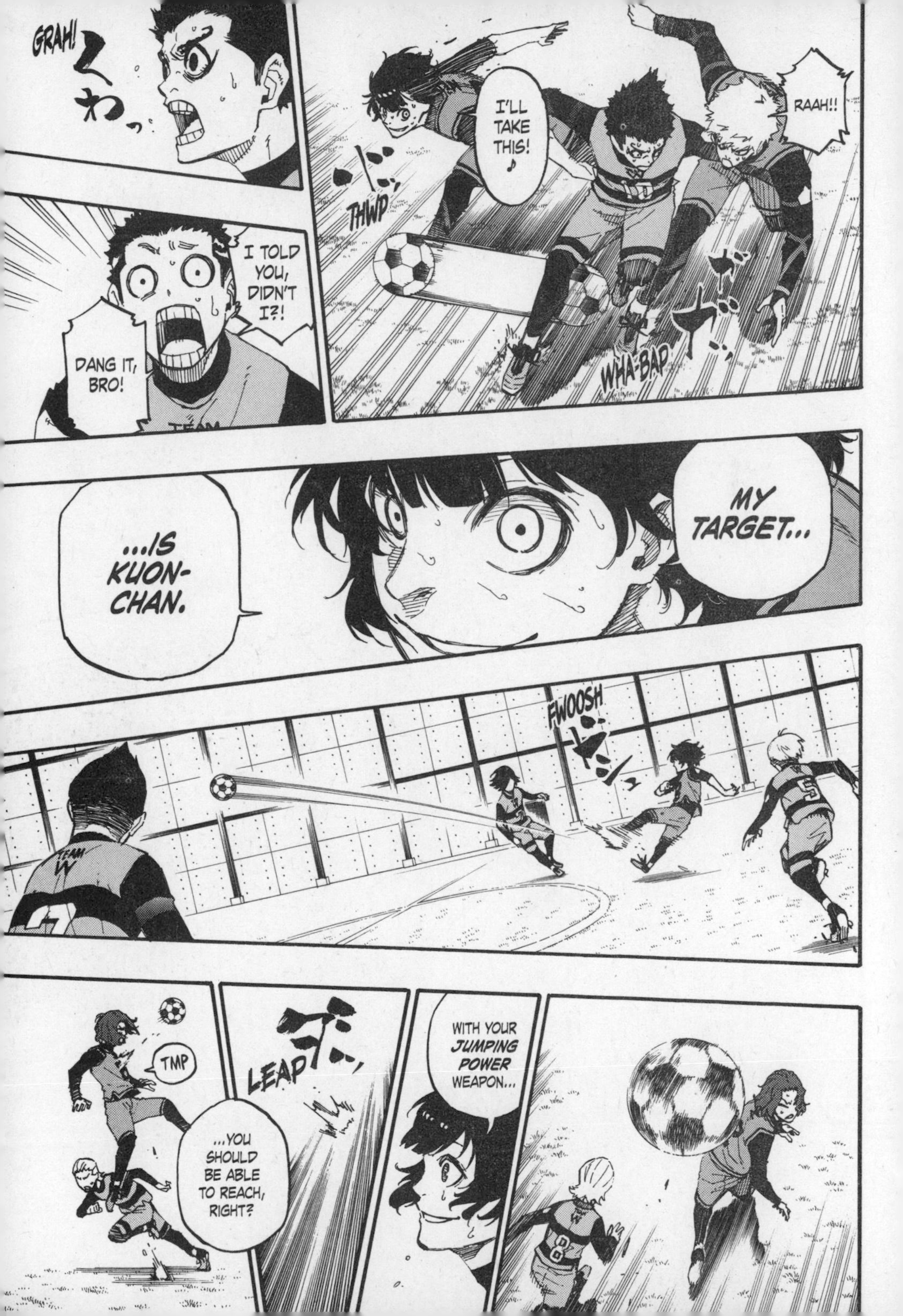
RAAH!!
I'LL TAKE THIS! ♪
THWP
WHA-BAP
GRAH!
くわっ
I TOLD YOU, DIDN'T I?!
DANG IT, BRO!
MY TARGET...
...IS KUON-CHAN.
FWOOSH
WITH YOUR JUMPING POWER WEAPON...
LEAP
...YOU SHOULD BE ABLE TO REACH, RIGHT?
TMP

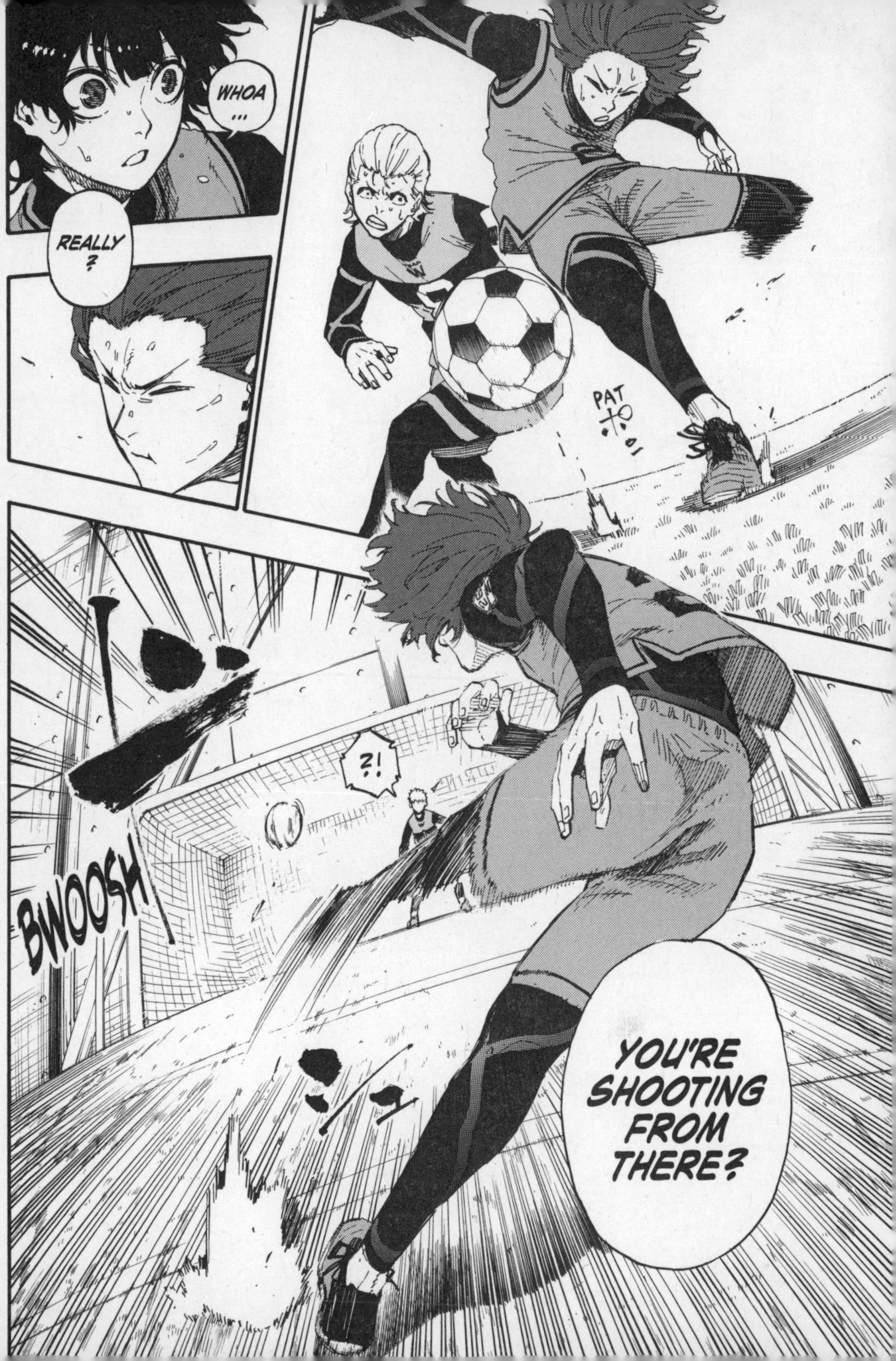
PAT
WHOA ...
REALLY ?
?!
BWOOSH
YOU'RE SHOOTING FROM THERE?

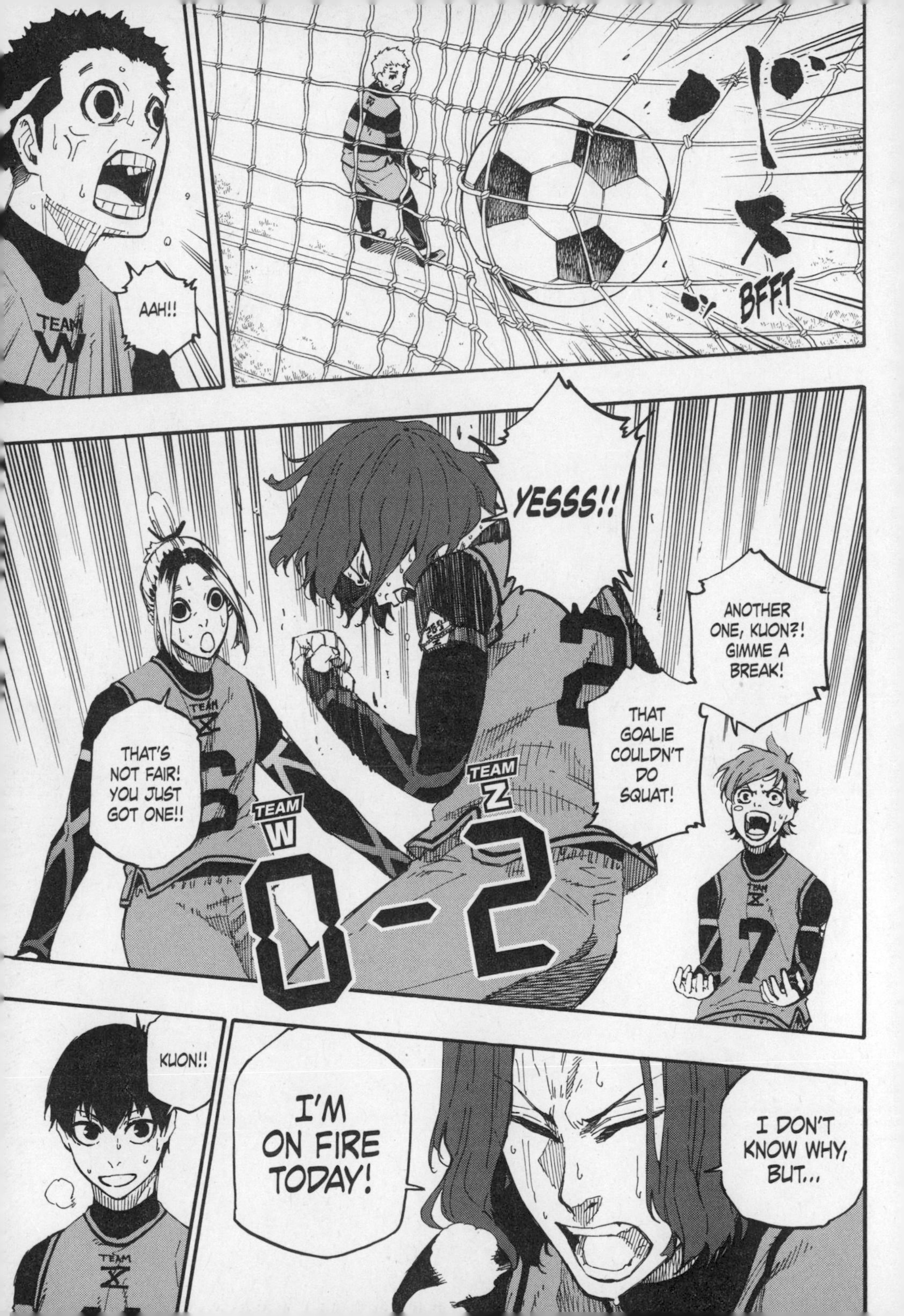
BFFT
AAH!!
YESSS!!
ANOTHER ONE, KUON?! GIMME A BREAK!
THAT GOALIE COULDN'T DO SQUAT!
THAT'S NOT FAIR! YOU JUST GOT ONE!!
TEAM Z
TEAM W
0-2
I DON'T KNOW WHY, BUT...
I'M ON FIRE TODAY!
KUON!!

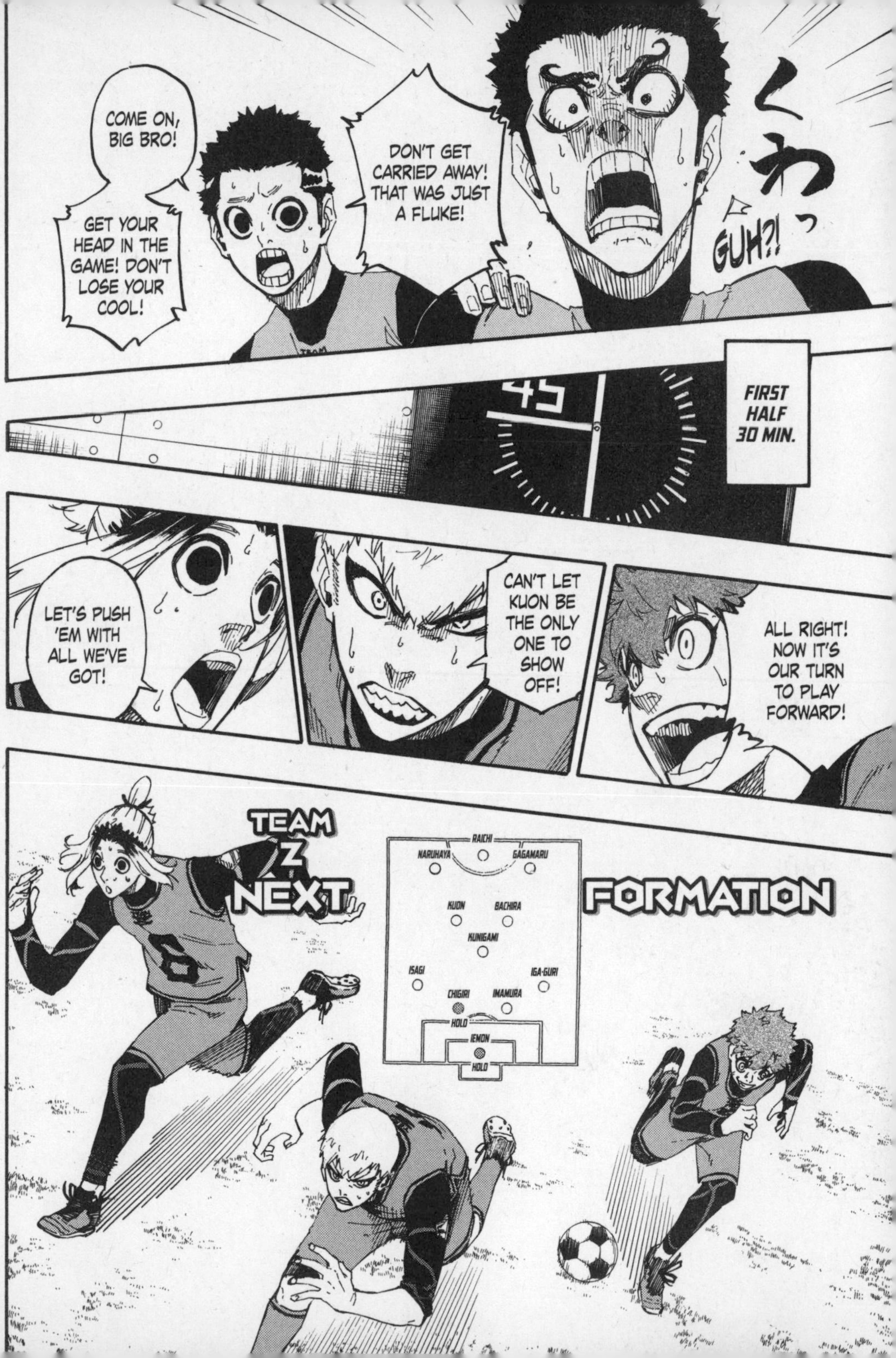
くわっ
GUH?!
DON'T GET CARRIED AWAY! THAT WAS JUST A FLUKE!
COME ON, BIG BRO!
GET YOUR HEAD IN THE GAME! DON'T LOSE YOUR COOL!
FIRST HALF 30 MIN.
45
ALL RIGHT! NOW IT'S OUR TURN TO PLAY FORWARD!
CAN'T LET KUON BE THE ONLY ONE TO SHOW OFF!
LET'S PUSH 'EM WITH ALL WE'VE GOT!
TEAM Z NEXT FORMATION
RAICHI
NARUHAYA
GAGAMARU
KUON
BACHIRA
KUNIGAMI
ISAGI
IGA-GURI
CHIGIRI
IMAMURA
HOLD
IEMON
HOLD

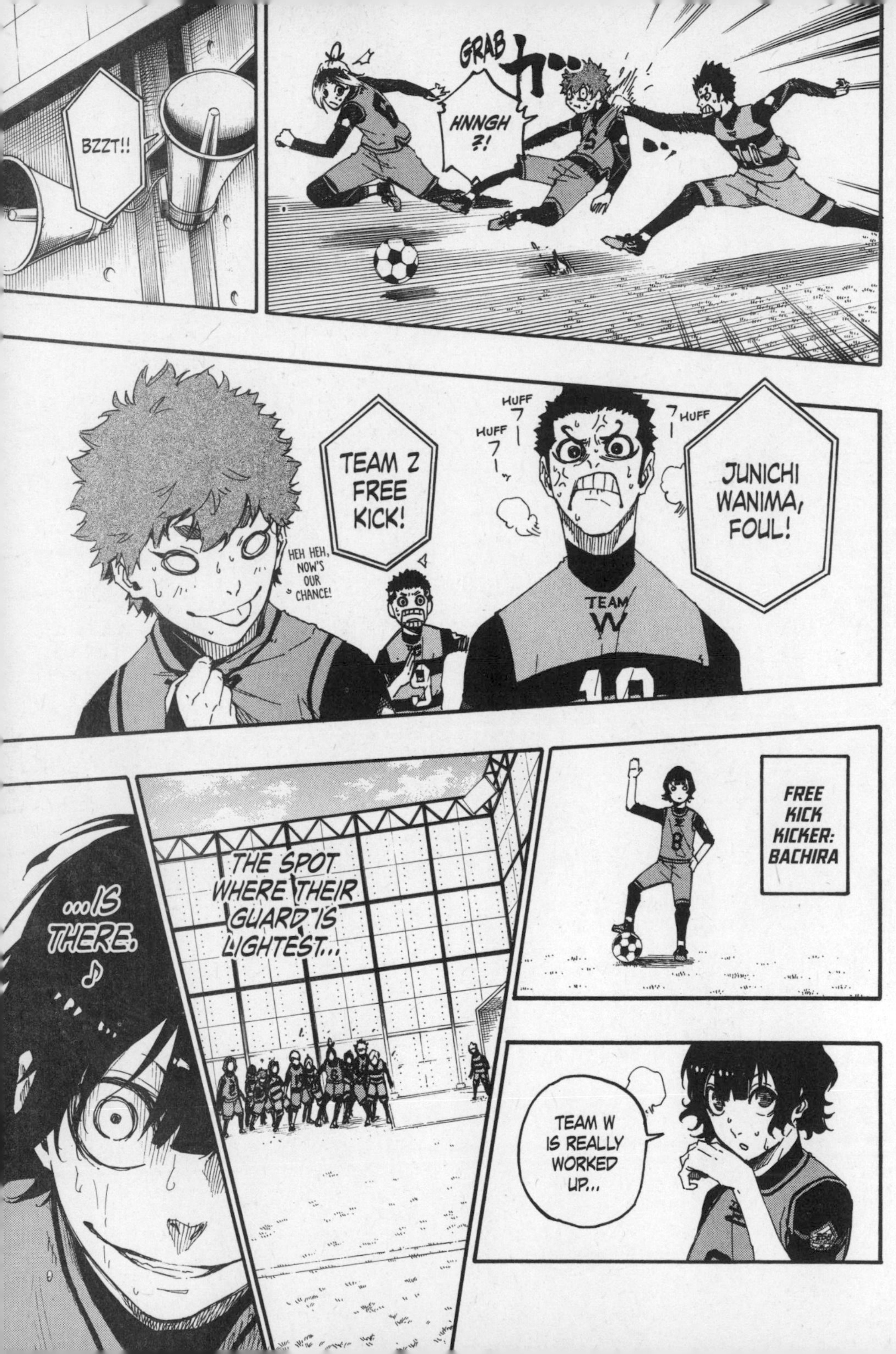
GRAB
HNNGH ?!
BZZT!!
JUNICHI WANIMA, FOUL!
HUFF
HUFF
HUFF
TEAM Z FREE KICK!
HEH HEH, NOW'S OUR CHANCE!
FREE KICK KICKER: BACHIRA
TEAM W IS REALLY WORKED UP...
THE SPOT WHERE THEIR GUARD IS LIGHTEST...
...IS THERE. ♪

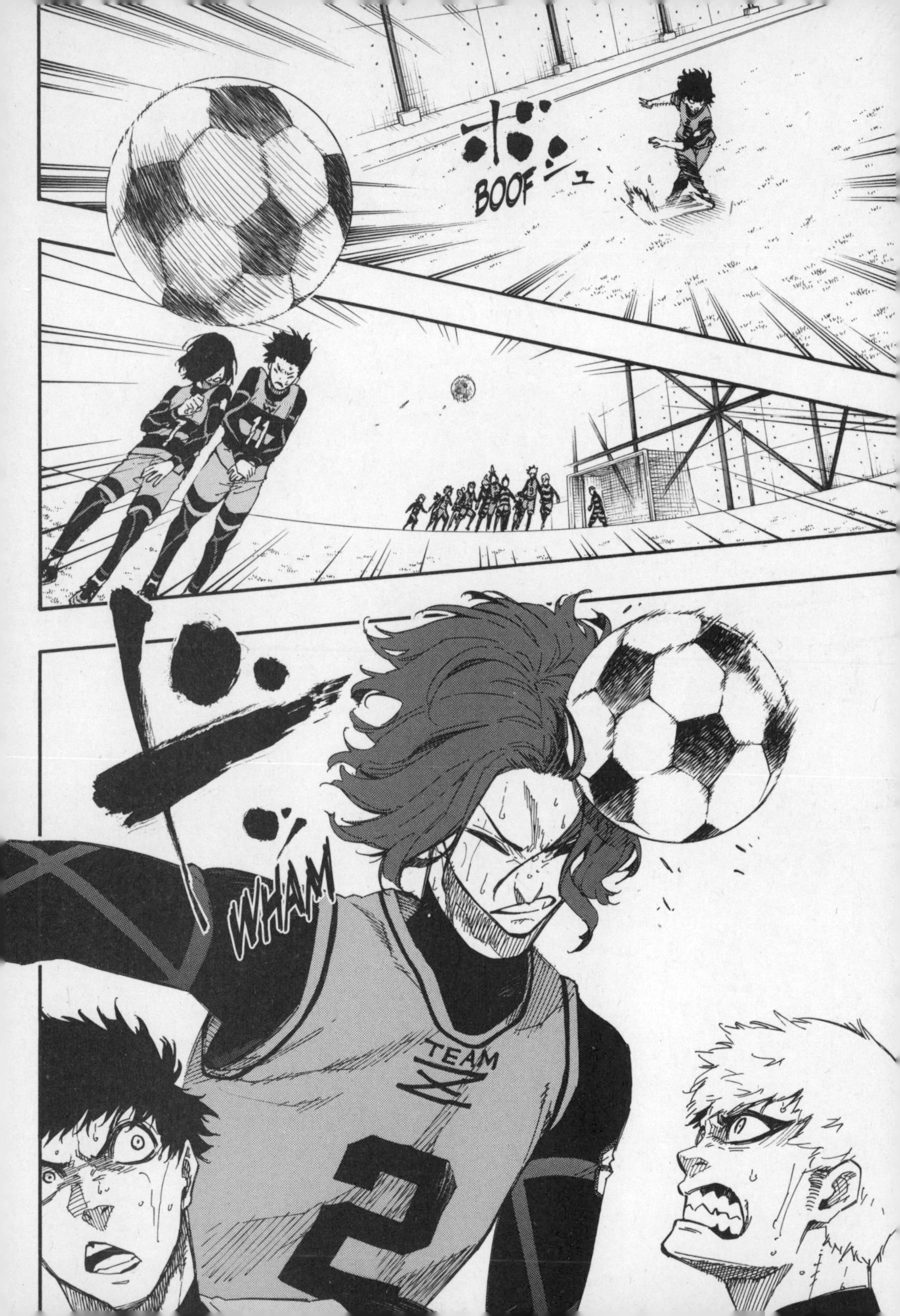
BOOF
WHAM
TEAM

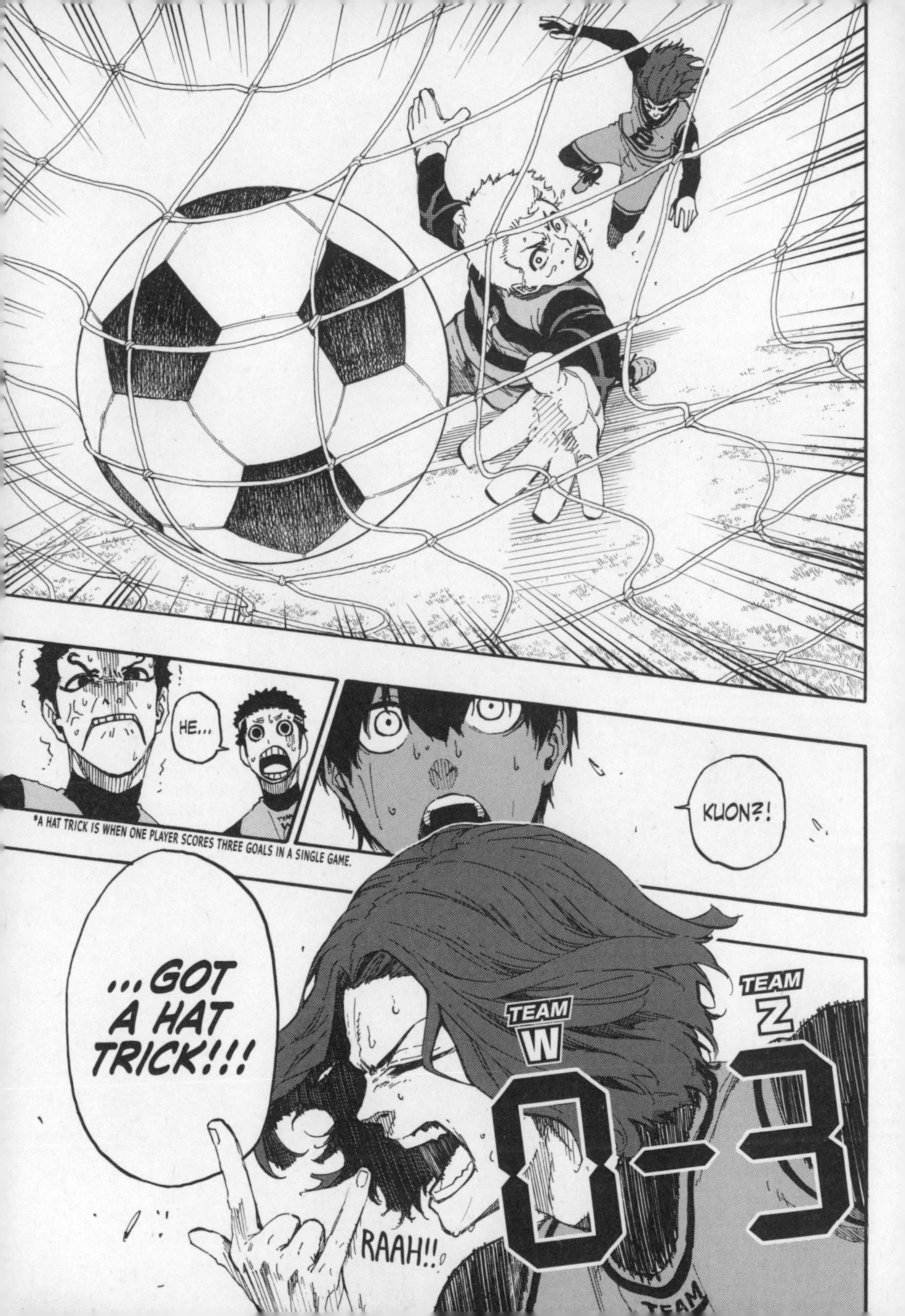
KUON?!
HE...
...GOT A HAT TRICK!!!
TEAM W
TEAM Z
0-3
RAAH!!

*A HAT TRICK IS WHEN ONE PLAYER SCORES THREE GOALS IN A SINGLE GAME.

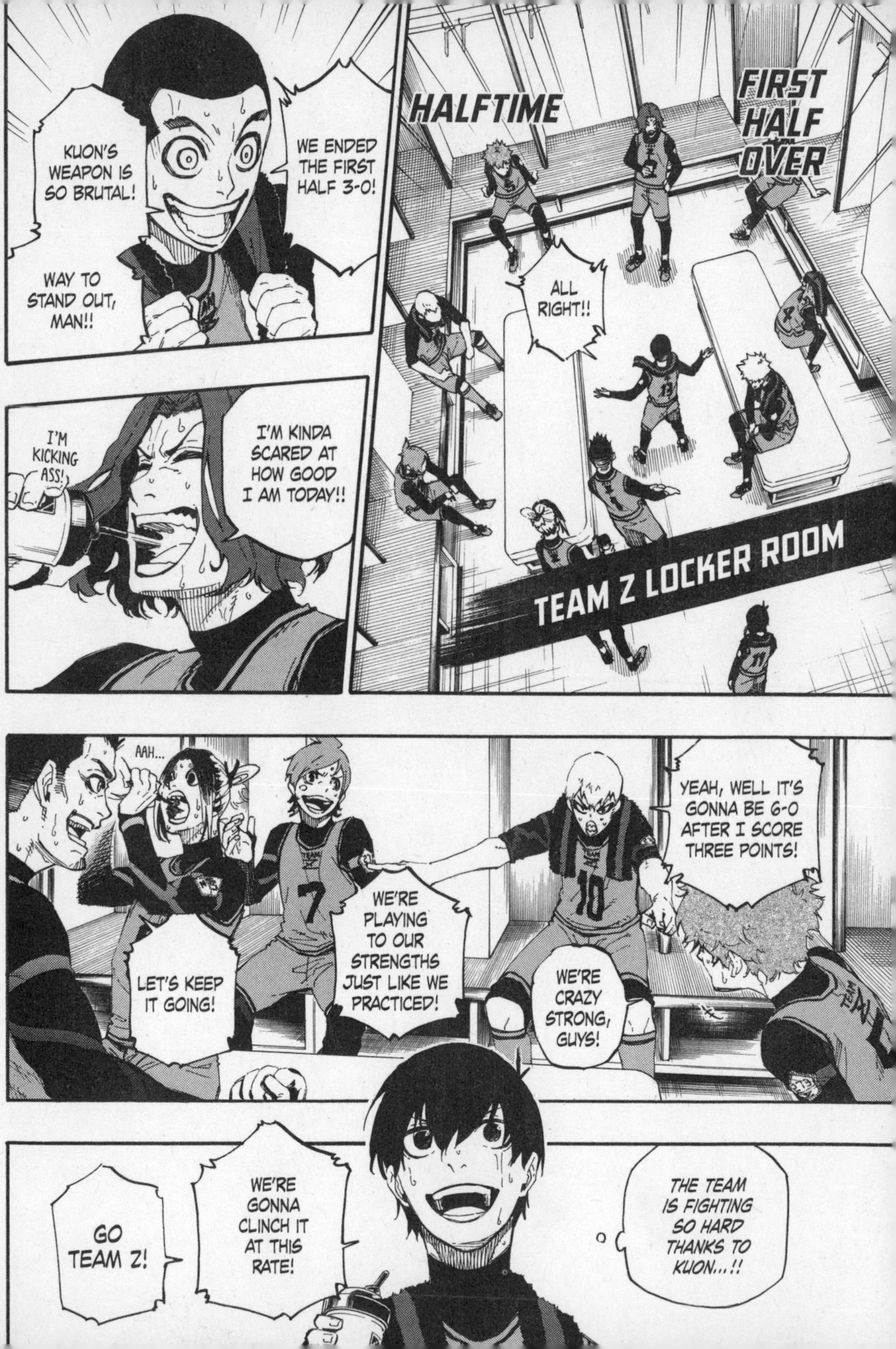
FIRST HALF OVER
HALFTIME
ALL RIGHT!!
TEAM Z LOCKER ROOM
WE ENDED THE FIRST HALF 3-0!
KUON'S WEAPON IS SO BRUTAL!
WAY TO STAND OUT, MAN!!
I'M KINDA SCARED AT HOW GOOD I AM TODAY!!
I'M KICKING ASS!
YEAH, WELL IT'S GONNA BE 6-0 AFTER I SCORE THREE POINTS!
WE'RE CRAZY STRONG, GUYS!
WE'RE PLAYING TO OUR STRENGTHS JUST LIKE WE PRACTICED!
AAH...
LET'S KEEP IT GOING!
THE TEAM IS FIGHTING SO HARD THANKS TO KUON...!!
WE'RE GONNA CLINCH IT AT THIS RATE!
GO TEAM Z!

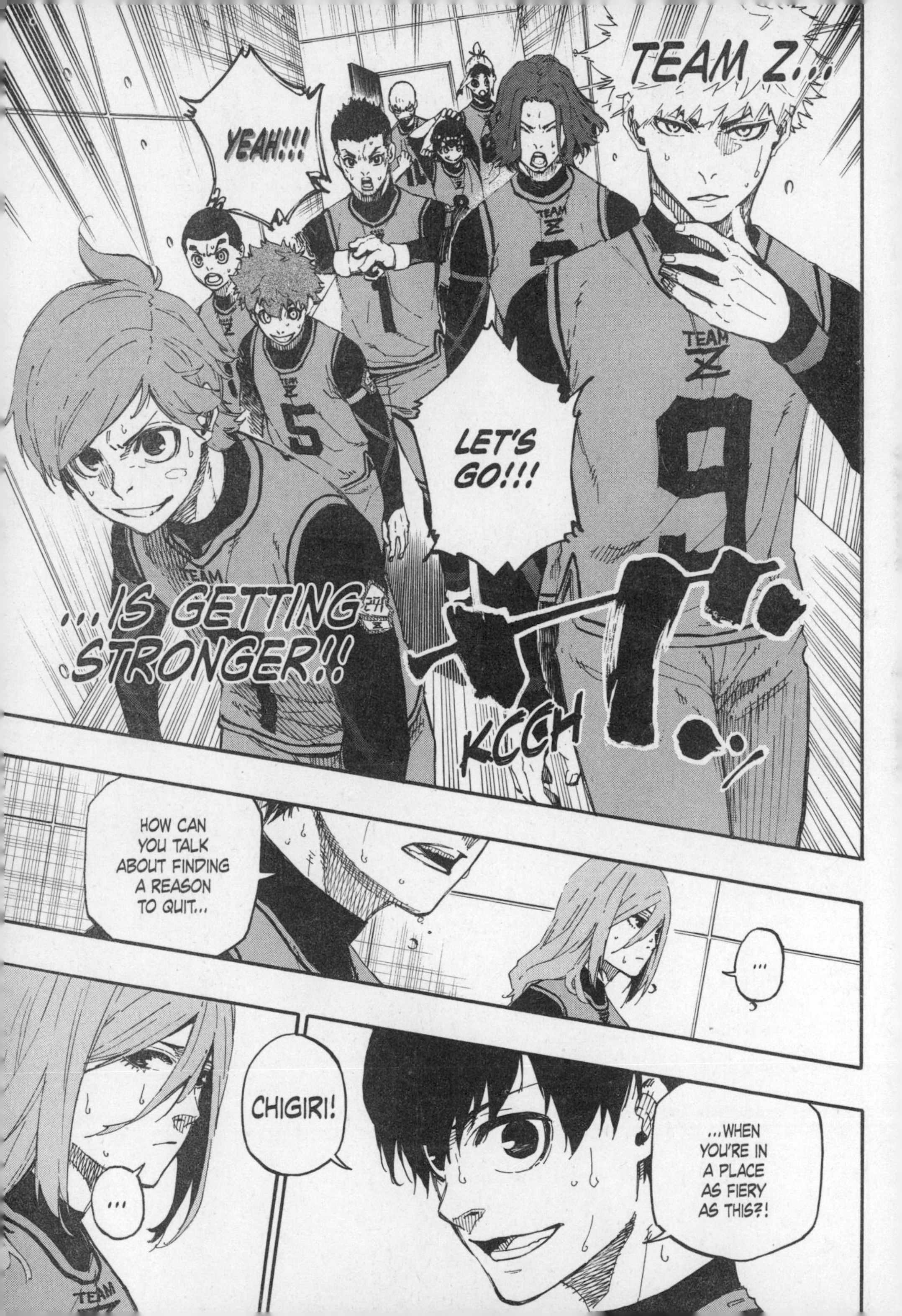
TEAM Z...
YEAH!!!
LET'S GO!!!
...IS GETTING STRONGER!!
KCCH
HOW CAN YOU TALK ABOUT FINDING A REASON TO QUIT...
...
...WHEN YOU'RE IN A PLACE AS FIERY AS THIS?!
CHIGIRI!
...

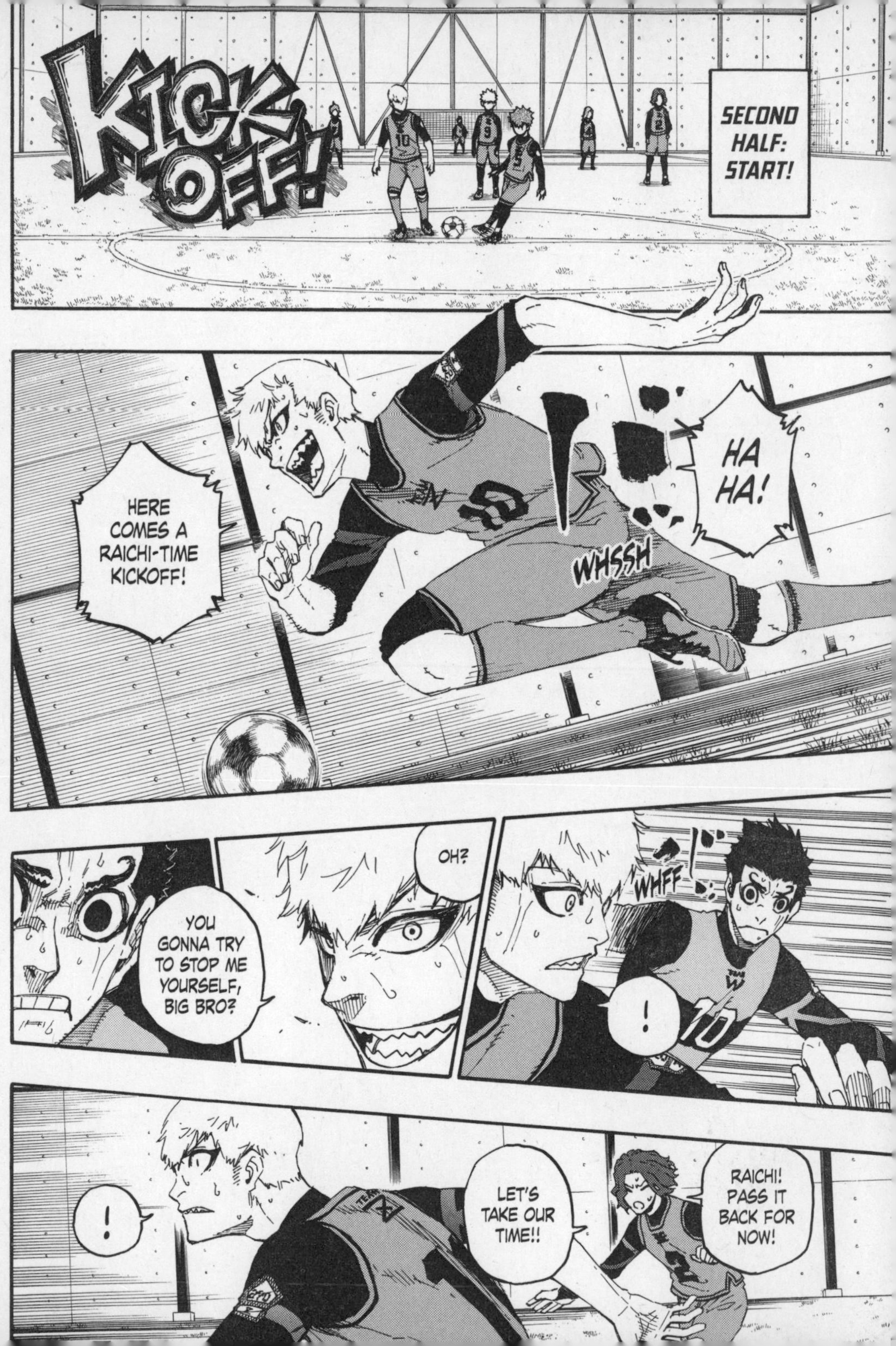
SECOND HALF: START!
KICK OFF!
HA HA!
WHSSH
HERE COMES A RAICHI-TIME KICKOFF!
WHFF
!
OH?
YOU GONNA TRY TO STOP ME YOURSELF, BIG BRO?
RAICHI! PASS IT BACK FOR NOW!
LET'S TAKE OUR TIME!!
!

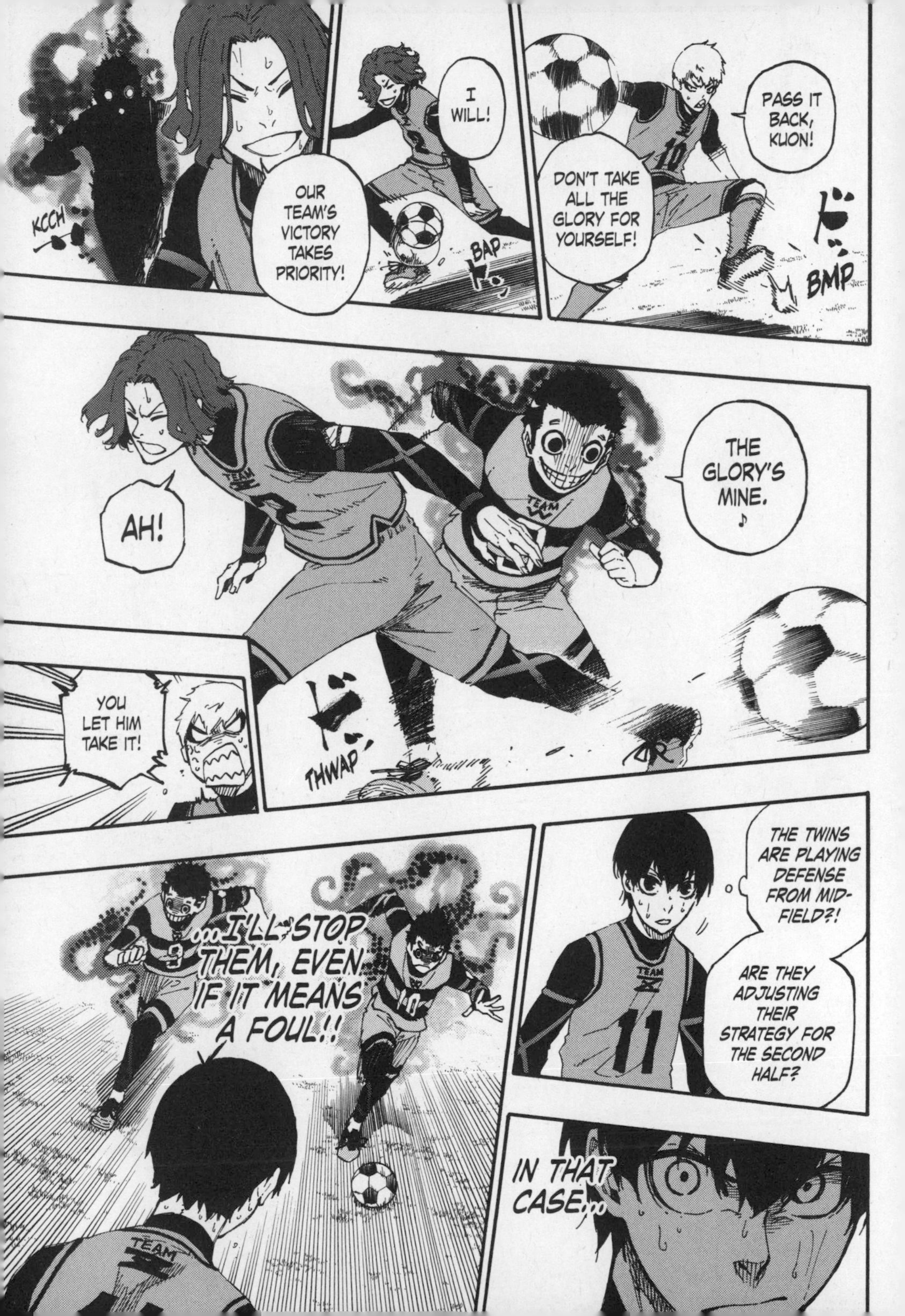
PASS IT BACK, KUON!
DON'T TAKE ALL THE GLORY FOR YOURSELF!
BMP
I WILL!
OUR TEAM'S VICTORY TAKES PRIORITY!
BAP
KCCH
THE GLORY'S MINE. ♪
AH!
THWAP
YOU LET HIM TAKE IT!
THE TWINS ARE PLAYING DEFENSE FROM MID-FIELD?!
ARE THEY ADJUSTING THEIR STRATEGY FOR THE SECOND HALF?
IN THAT CASE...
...I'LL STOP THEM, EVEN IF IT MEANS A FOUL!!

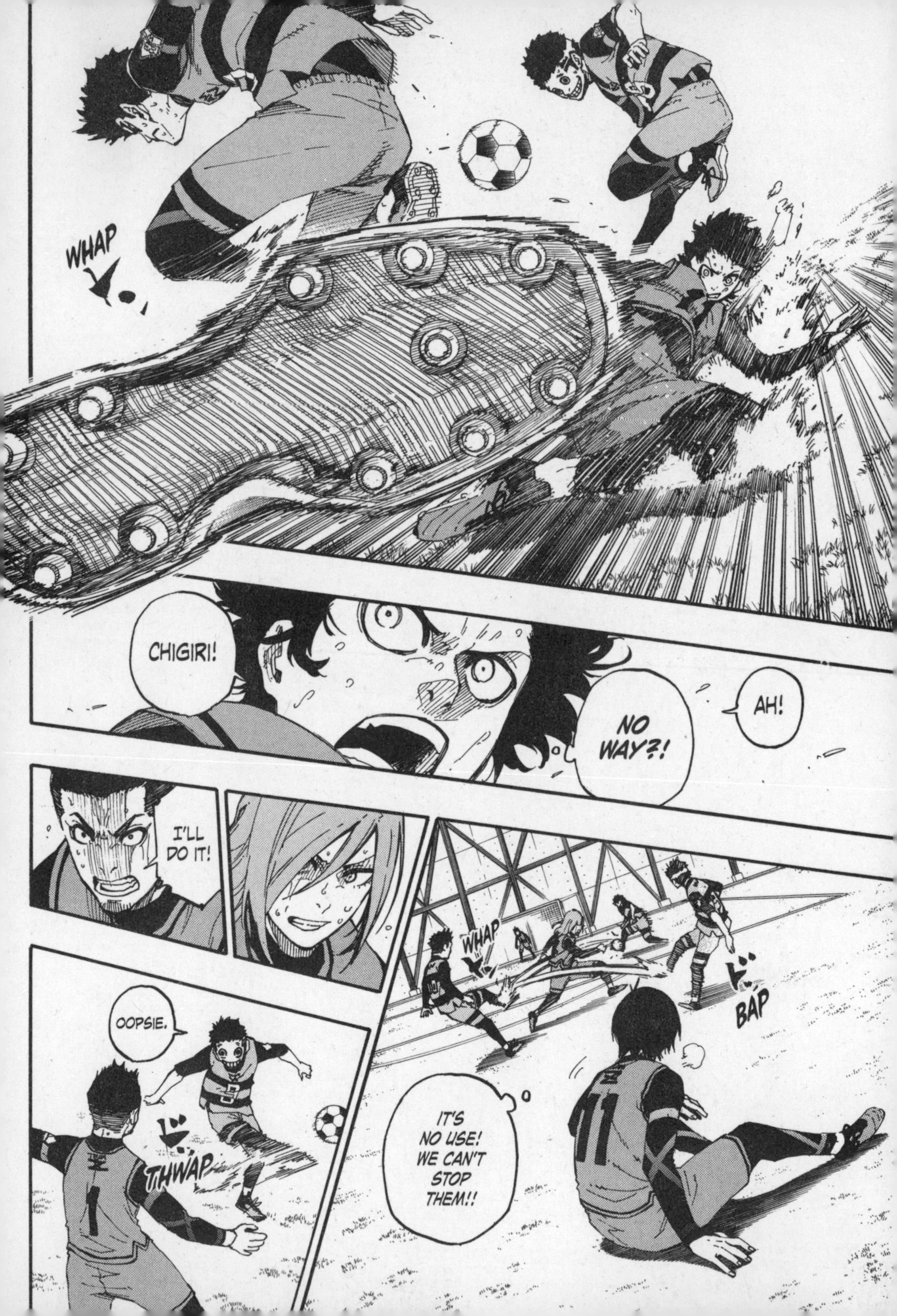
WHAP
AH!
NO WAY?!
CHIGIRI!
WHAP
BAP
IT'S NO USE! WE CAN'T STOP THEM!!
I'LL DO IT!
OOPSIE.
THWAP

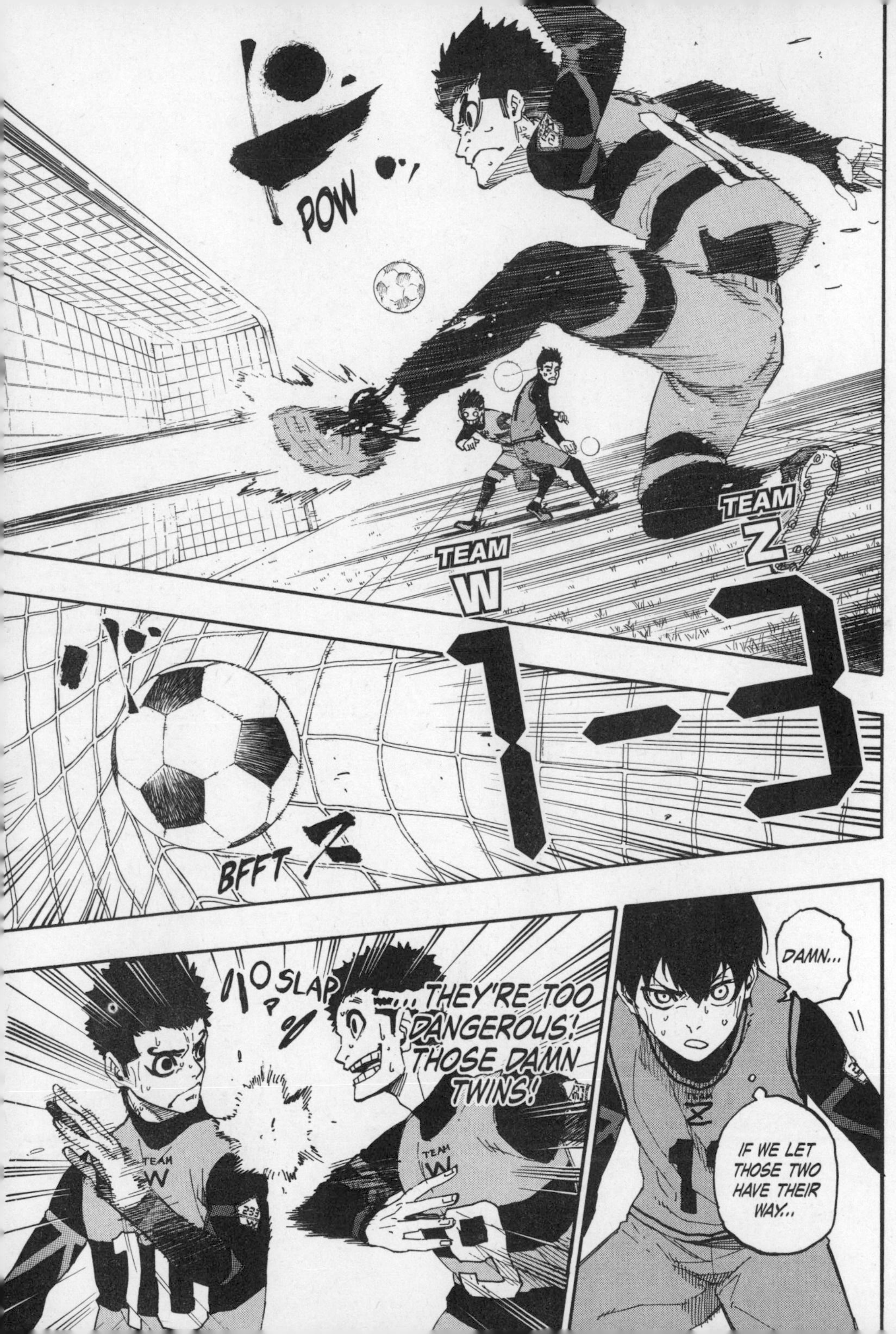
POW
TEAM W
1-3
TEAM Z
BFFT
DAMN...
IF WE LET THOSE TWO HAVE THEIR WAY...
SLAP
...THEY'RE TOO DANGEROUS! THOSE DAMN TWINS!

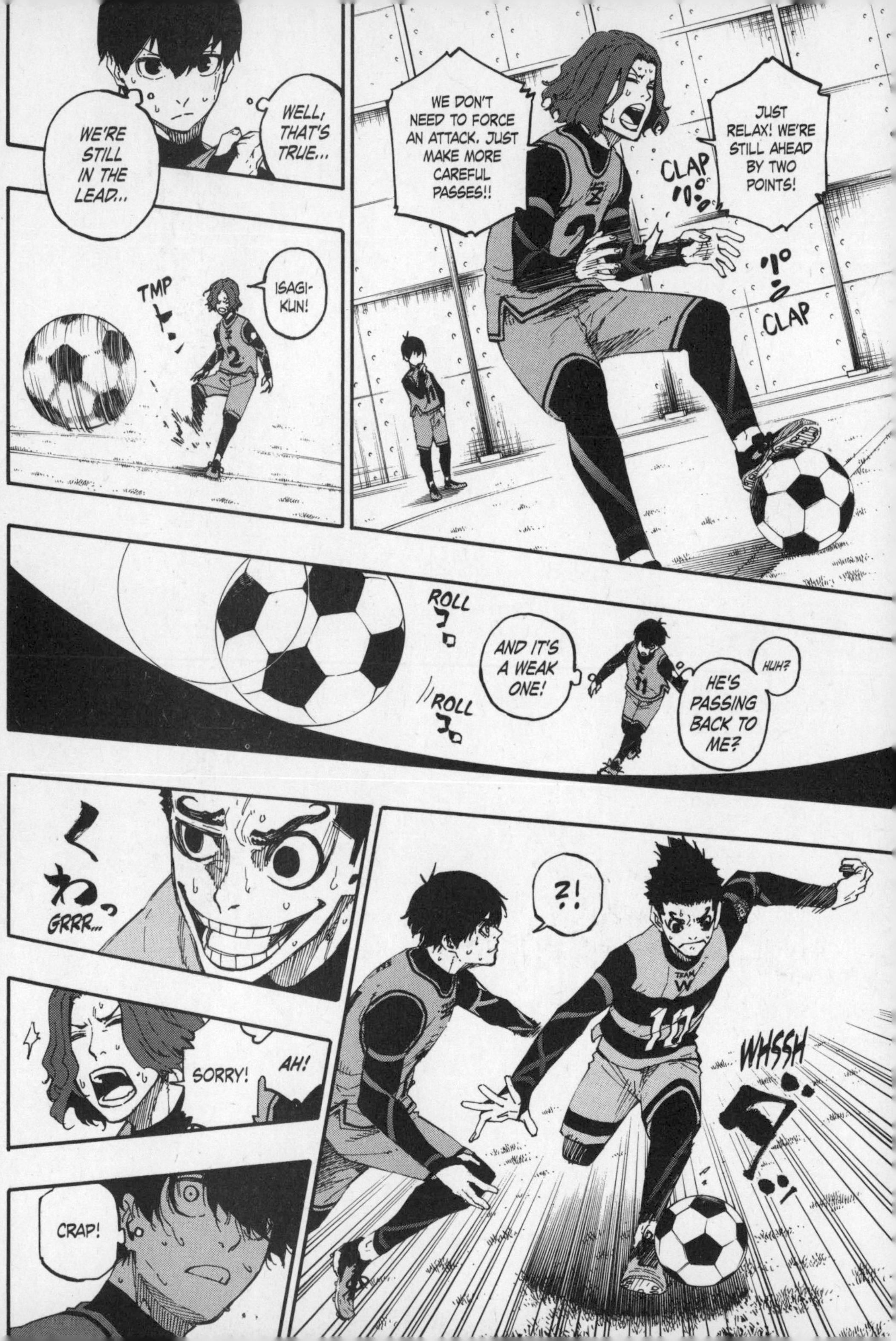
JUST RELAX! WE'RE STILL AHEAD BY TWO POINTS!
CLAP
WE DON'T NEED TO FORCE AN ATTACK. JUST MAKE MORE CAREFUL PASSES!!
CLAP
WELL, THAT'S TRUE...
WE'RE STILL IN THE LEAD...
ISAGI-KUN!
TMP
HUH?
HE'S PASSING BACK TO ME?
AND IT'S A WEAK ONE!
ROLL
ROLL
?!
WHSSH
くわっ
GRRR...
AH!
SORRY!
CRAP!

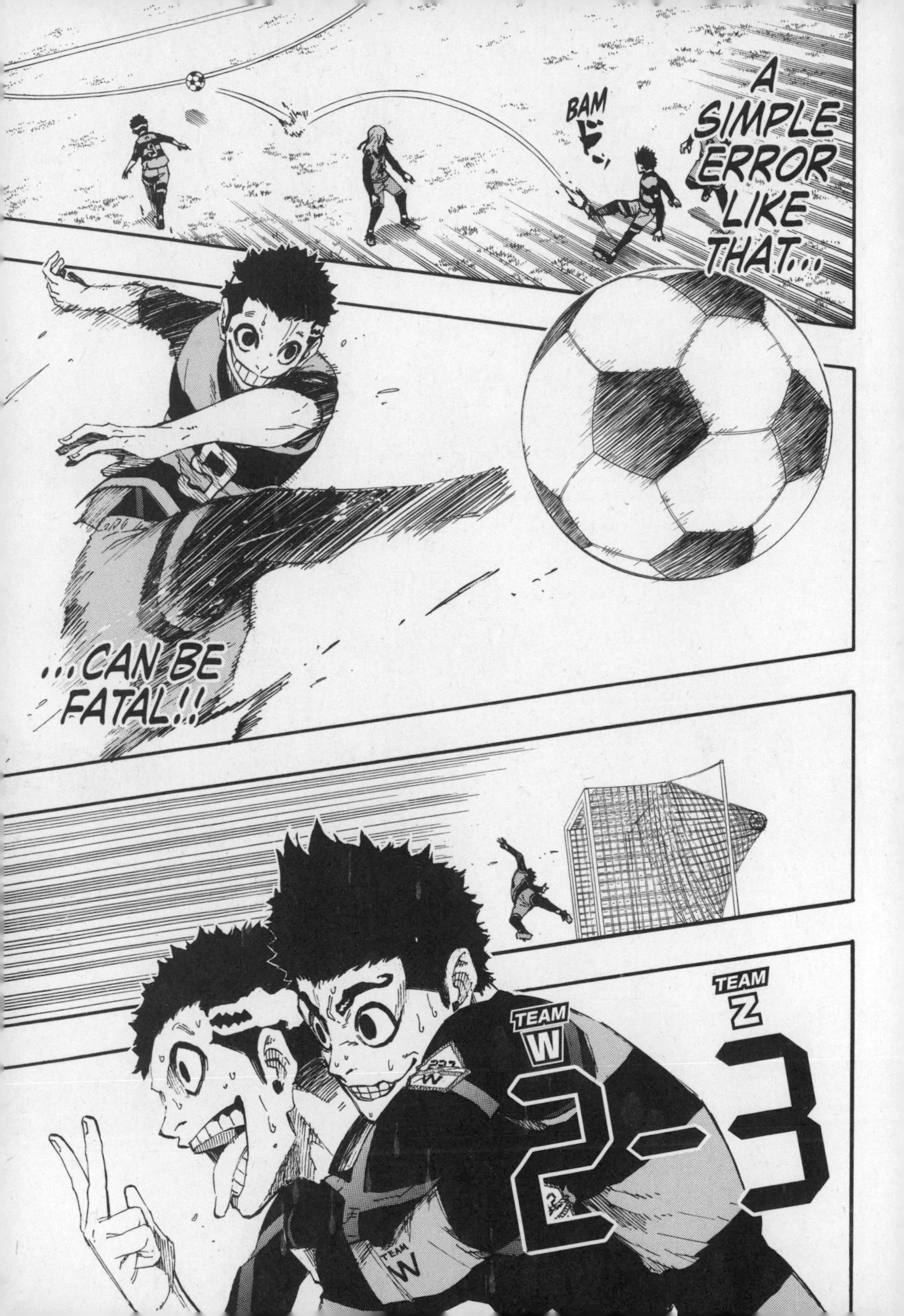
A SIMPLE ERROR LIKE THAT...
BAM
...CAN BE FATAL!!
TEAM Z
TEAM W
2-3

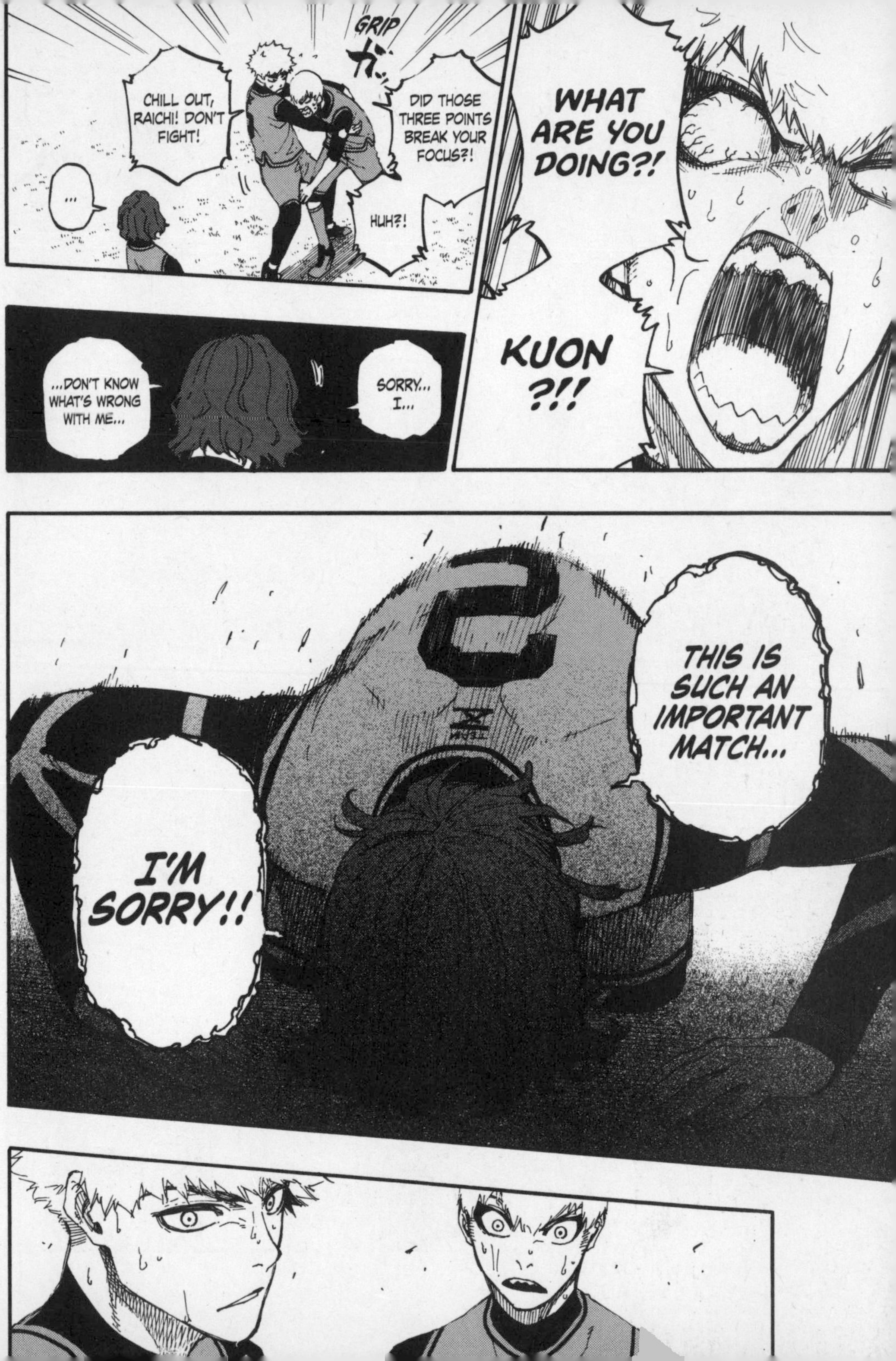
WHAT ARE YOU DOING?!
KUON ?!!
GRIP
DID THOSE THREE POINTS BREAK YOUR FOCUS?!
HUH?!
CHILL OUT, RAICHI! DON'T FIGHT!
...
SORRY... I...
...DON'T KNOW WHAT'S WRONG WITH ME...
THIS IS SUCH AN IMPORTANT MATCH...
I'M SORRY!!

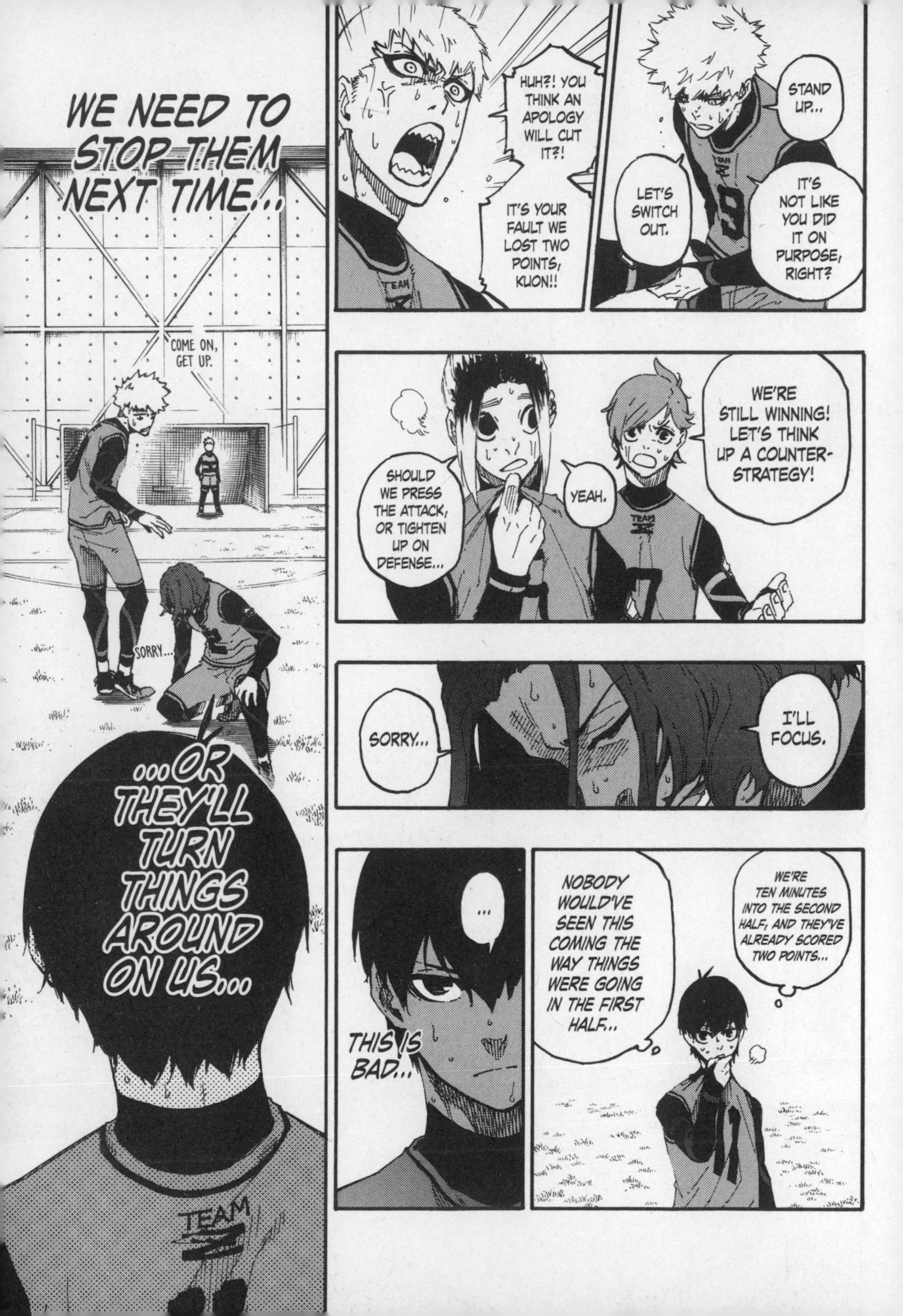
STAND UP...
IT'S NOT LIKE YOU DID IT ON PURPOSE, RIGHT?
LET'S SWITCH OUT.
HUH?! YOU THINK AN APOLOGY WILL CUT IT?!
IT'S YOUR FAULT WE LOST TWO POINTS, KUON!!
WE'RE STILL WINNING! LET'S THINK UP A COUNTER-STRATEGY!
YEAH.
SHOULD WE PRESS THE ATTACK, OR TIGHTEN UP ON DEFENSE...
I'LL FOCUS.
SORRY...
WE'RE TEN MINUTES INTO THE SECOND HALF, AND THEY'VE ALREADY SCORED TWO POINTS...
NOBODY WOULD'VE SEEN THIS COMING THE WAY THINGS WERE GOING IN THE FIRST HALF...
...
THIS IS BAD...
WE NEED TO STOP THEM NEXT TIME...
COME ON, GET UP.
SORRY...
...OR THEY'LL TURN THINGS AROUND ON US...

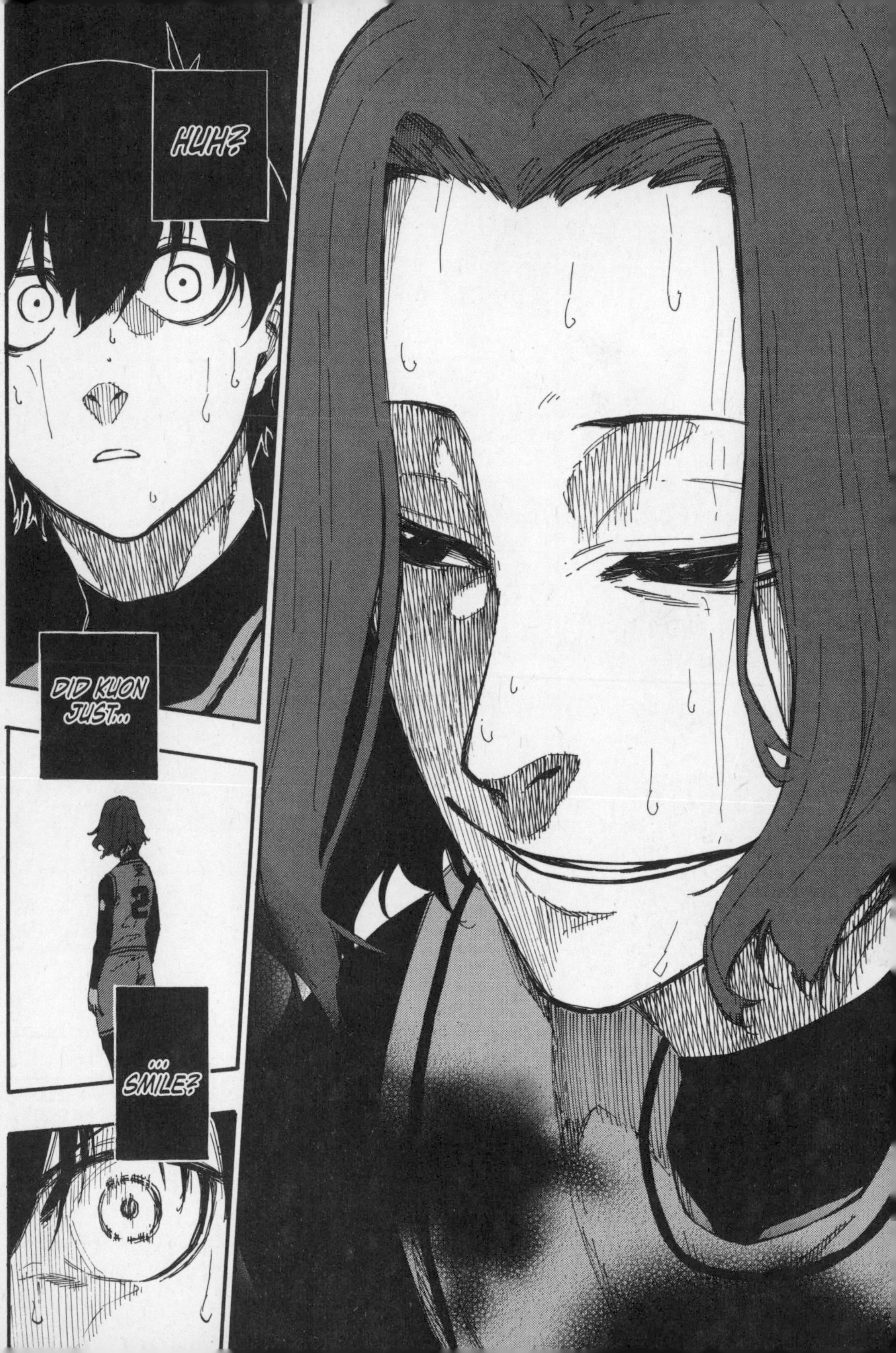
HUH?
DID KUON JUST...
...SMILE?

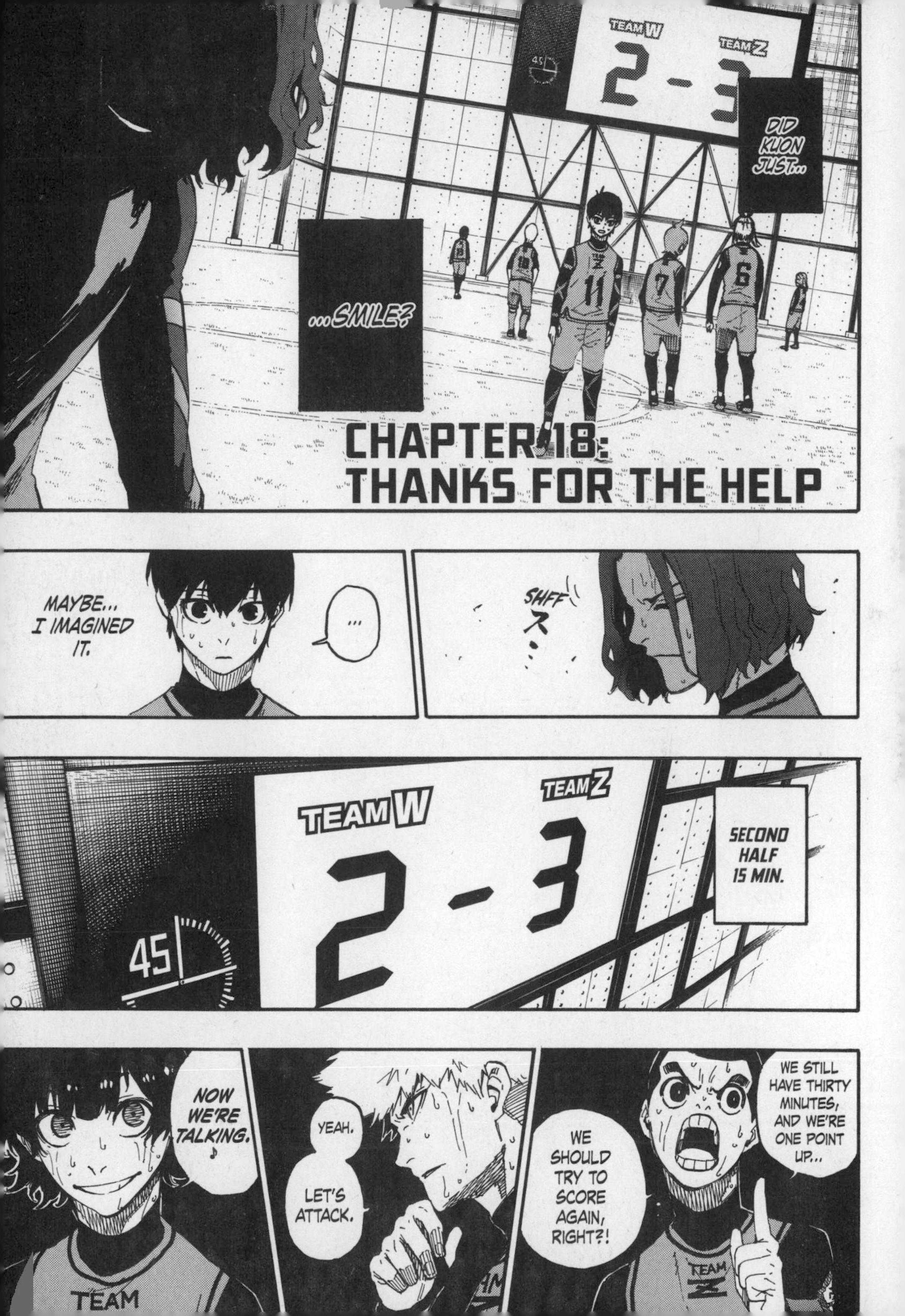
TEAM W
TEAM Z
2 - 3
DID KUON JUST...
...SMILE?
CHAPTER 18: THANKS FOR THE HELP
SHFF
ス
...
MAYBE... I IMAGINED IT.
SECOND HALF 15 MIN.
TEAM Z
TEAM W
2 - 3
45
WE STILL HAVE THIRTY MINUTES, AND WE'RE ONE POINT UP...
WE SHOULD TRY TO SCORE AGAIN, RIGHT?!
YEAH.
LET'S ATTACK.
NOW WE'RE TALKING.♪

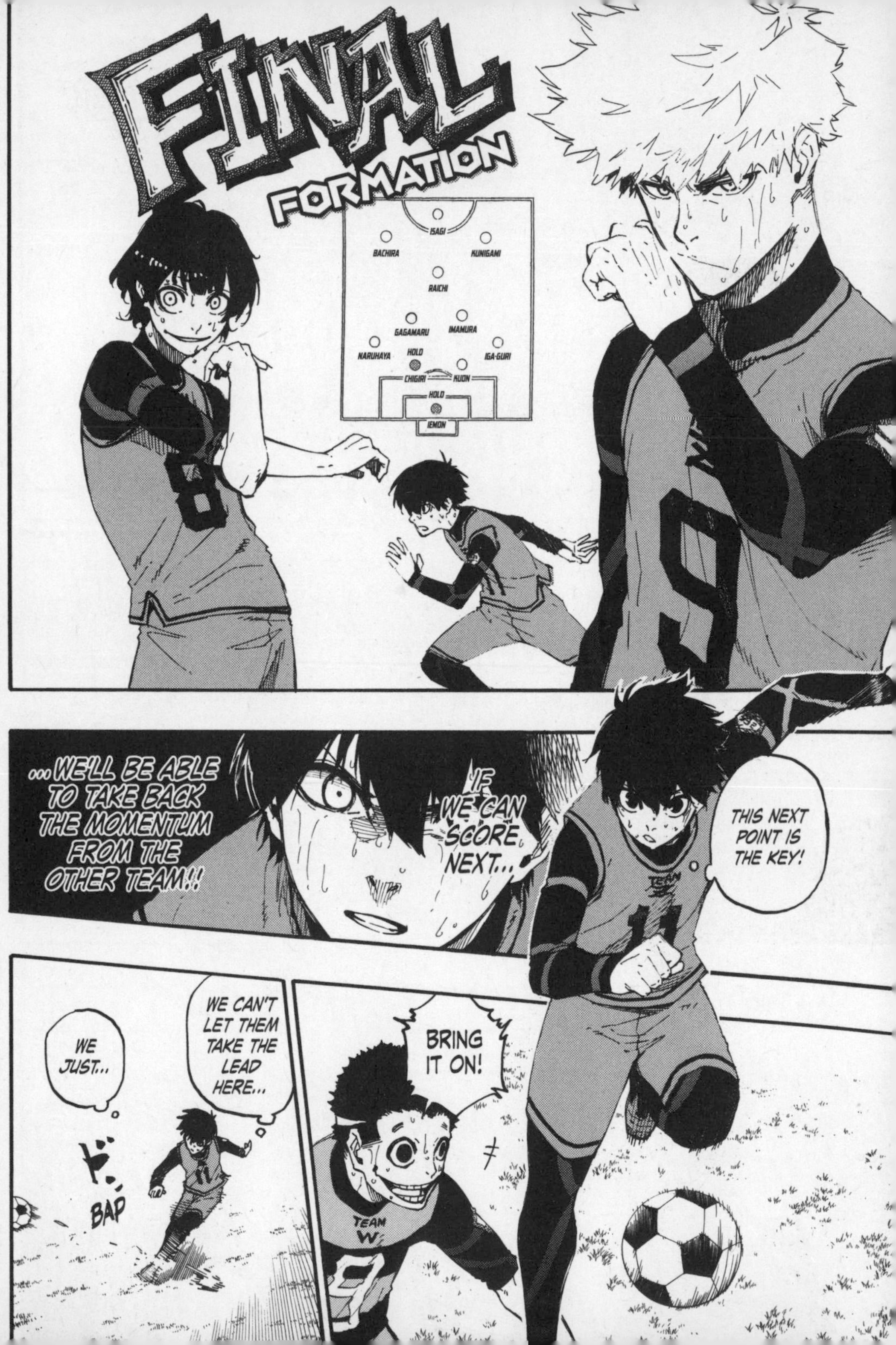
FINAL FORMATION
ISAGI
BACHIRA
KUNIGAMI
RAICHI
GAGAMARU
IMAMURA
NARUHAYA
HOLD
IGA-GURI
CHIGIRI
KUON
HOLD
IEMON
THIS NEXT POINT IS THE KEY!
IF WE CAN SCORE NEXT...
...WE'LL BE ABLE TO TAKE BACK THE MOMENTUM FROM THE OTHER TEAM!!
BRING IT ON!
TEAM W
WE CAN'T LET THEM TAKE THE LEAD HERE...
WE JUST...
BAP

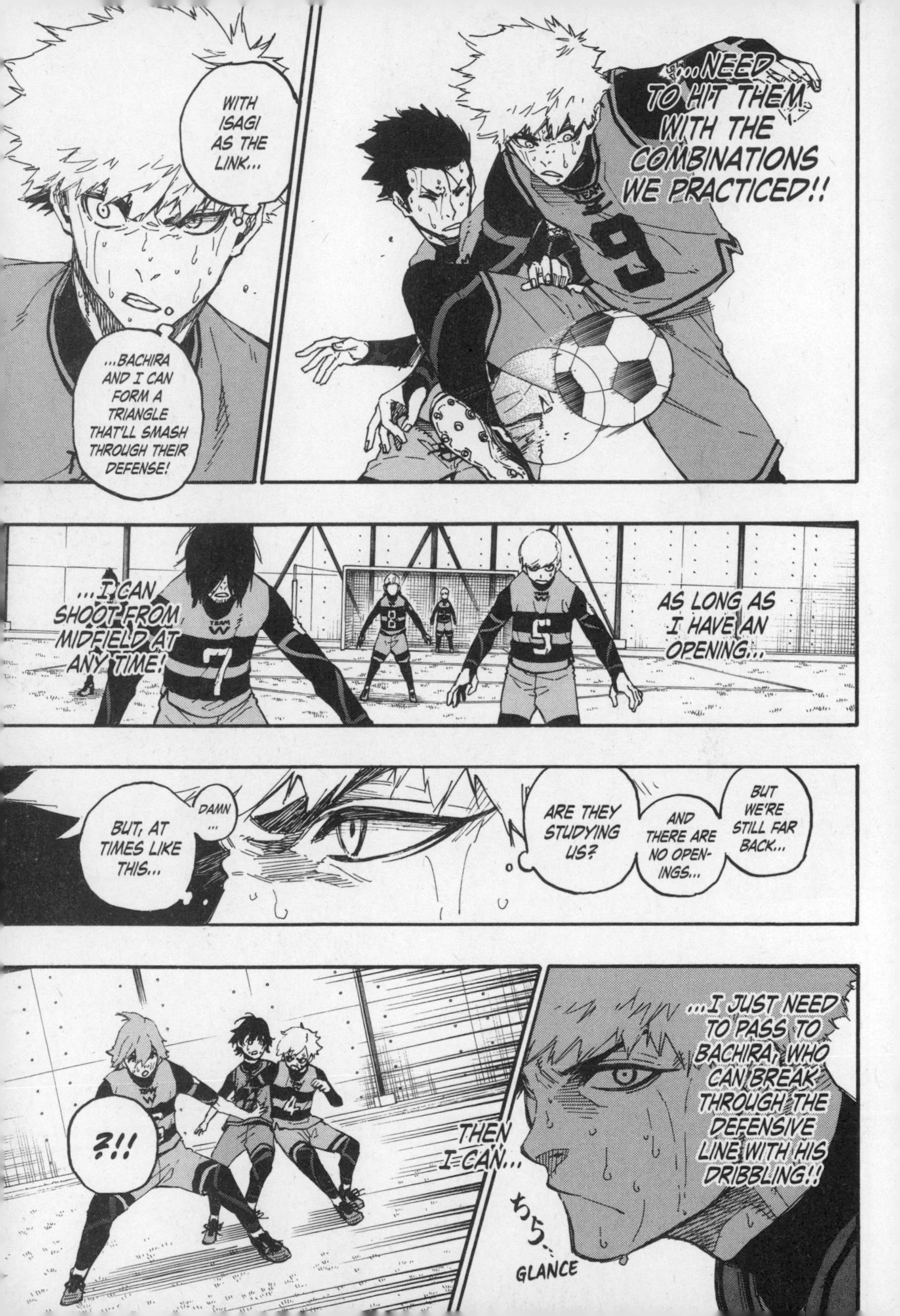
...NEED TO HIT THEM WITH THE COMBINATIONS WE PRACTICED!!
WITH ISAGI AS THE LINK...
...BACHIRA AND I CAN FORM A TRIANGLE THAT'LL SMASH THROUGH THEIR DEFENSE!
AS LONG AS I HAVE AN OPENING...
...I CAN SHOOT FROM MIDFIELD AT ANY TIME!
BUT WE'RE STILL FAR BACK...
AND THERE ARE NO OPEN-INGS...
ARE THEY STUDYING US?
DAMN...
BUT, AT TIMES LIKE THIS...
...I JUST NEED TO PASS TO BACHIRA, WHO CAN BREAK THROUGH THE DEFENSIVE LINE WITH HIS DRIBBLING!!
THEN I CAN...
ちら…
GLANCE
?!!

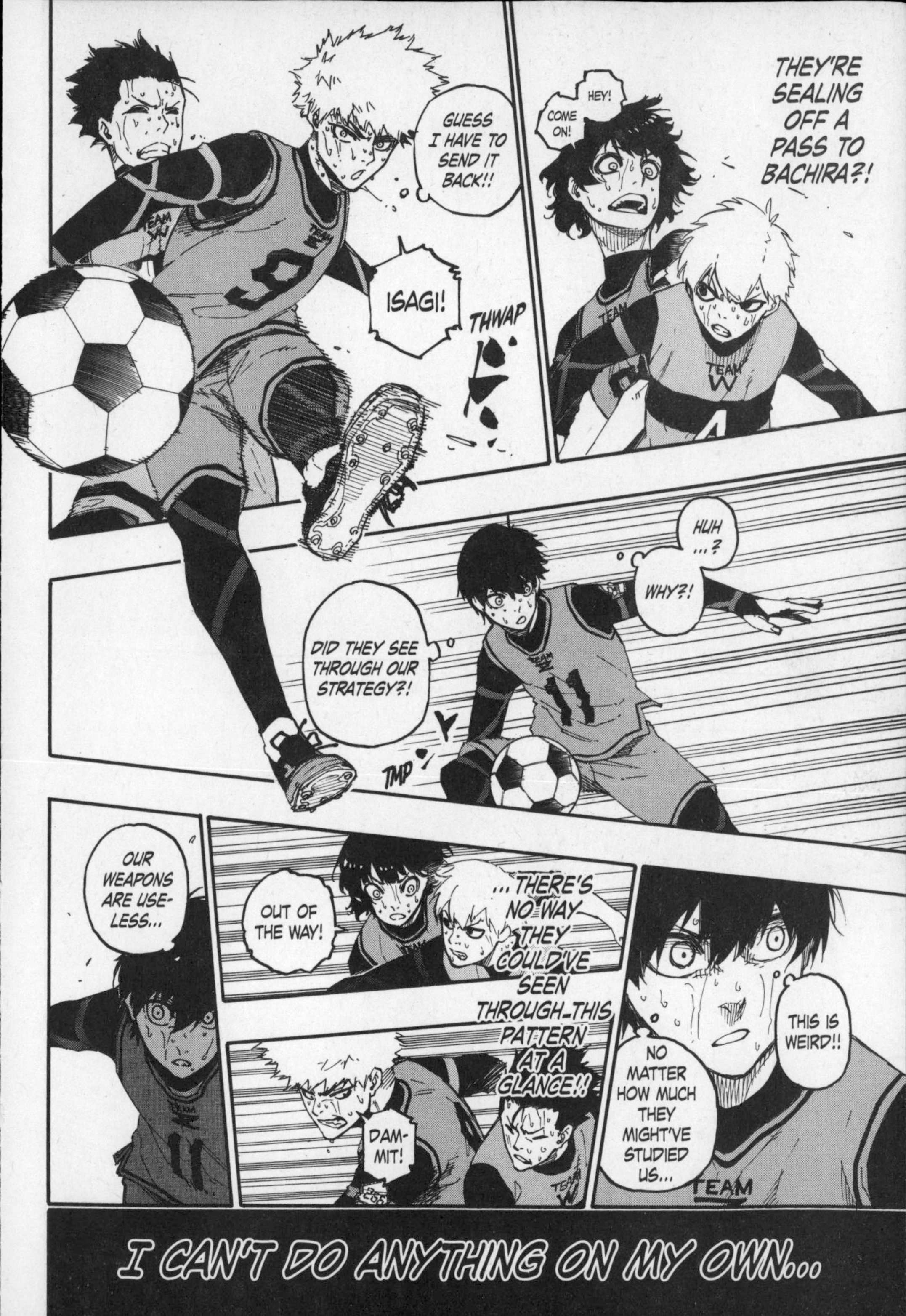
THEY'RE SEALING OFF A PASS TO BACHIRA?!
HEY!
COME ON!
GUESS I HAVE TO SEND IT BACK!!
ISAGI!
THWAP
HUH ...?
WHY?!
DID THEY SEE THROUGH OUR STRATEGY?!
TMP
THIS IS WEIRD!!
NO MATTER HOW MUCH THEY MIGHT'VE STUDIED US...
...THERE'S NO WAY THEY COULD'VE SEEN THROUGH THIS PATTERN AT A GLANCE!!
OUT OF THE WAY!
DAM-MIT!
OUR WEAPONS ARE USE-LESS...
I CAN'T DO ANYTHING ON MY OWN...

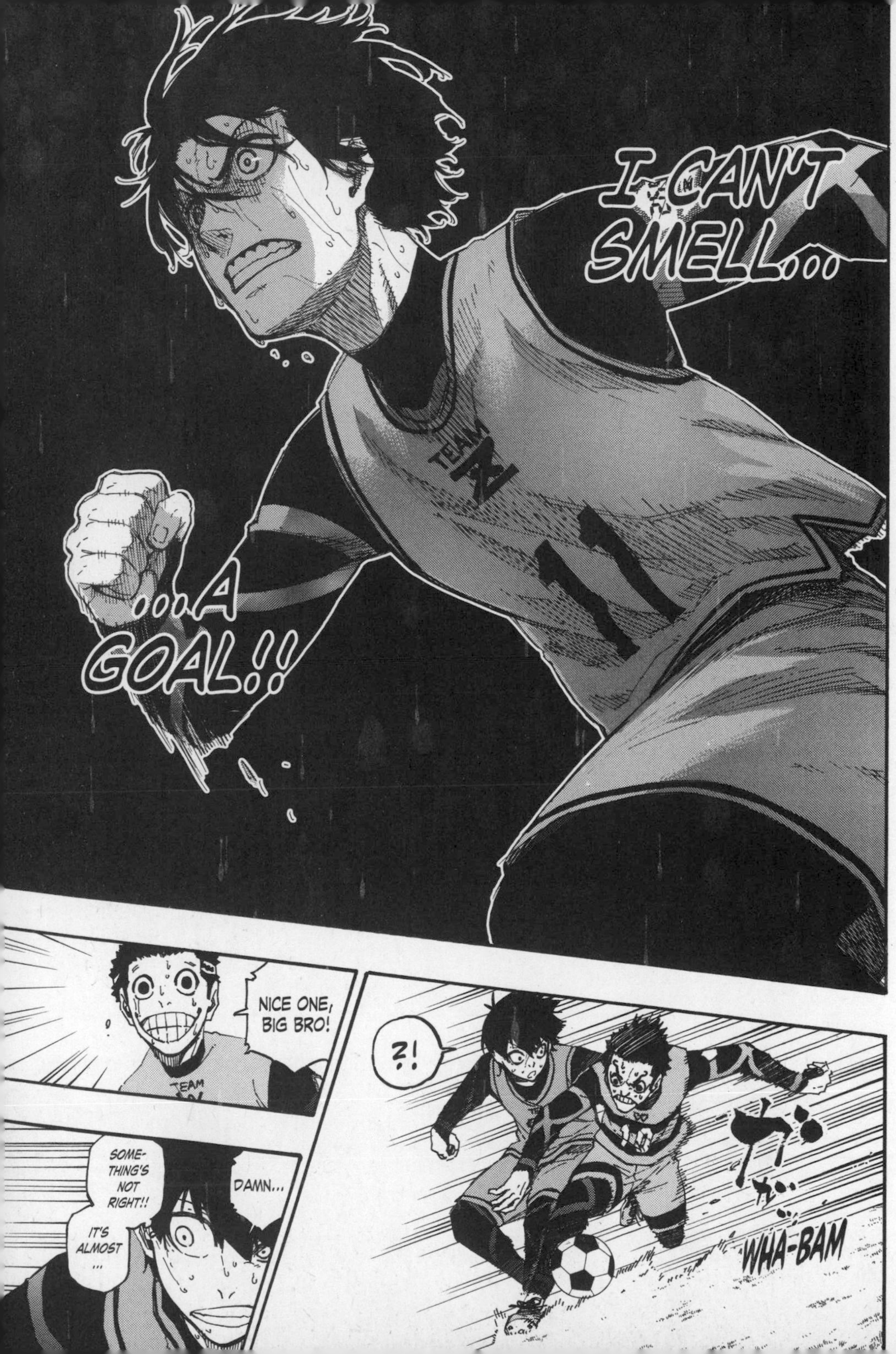
I CAN'T SMELL...
...A GOAL!!
?!
WHA-BAM
NICE ONE, BIG BRO!
DAMN...
SOME-THING'S NOT RIGHT!!
IT'S ALMOST...

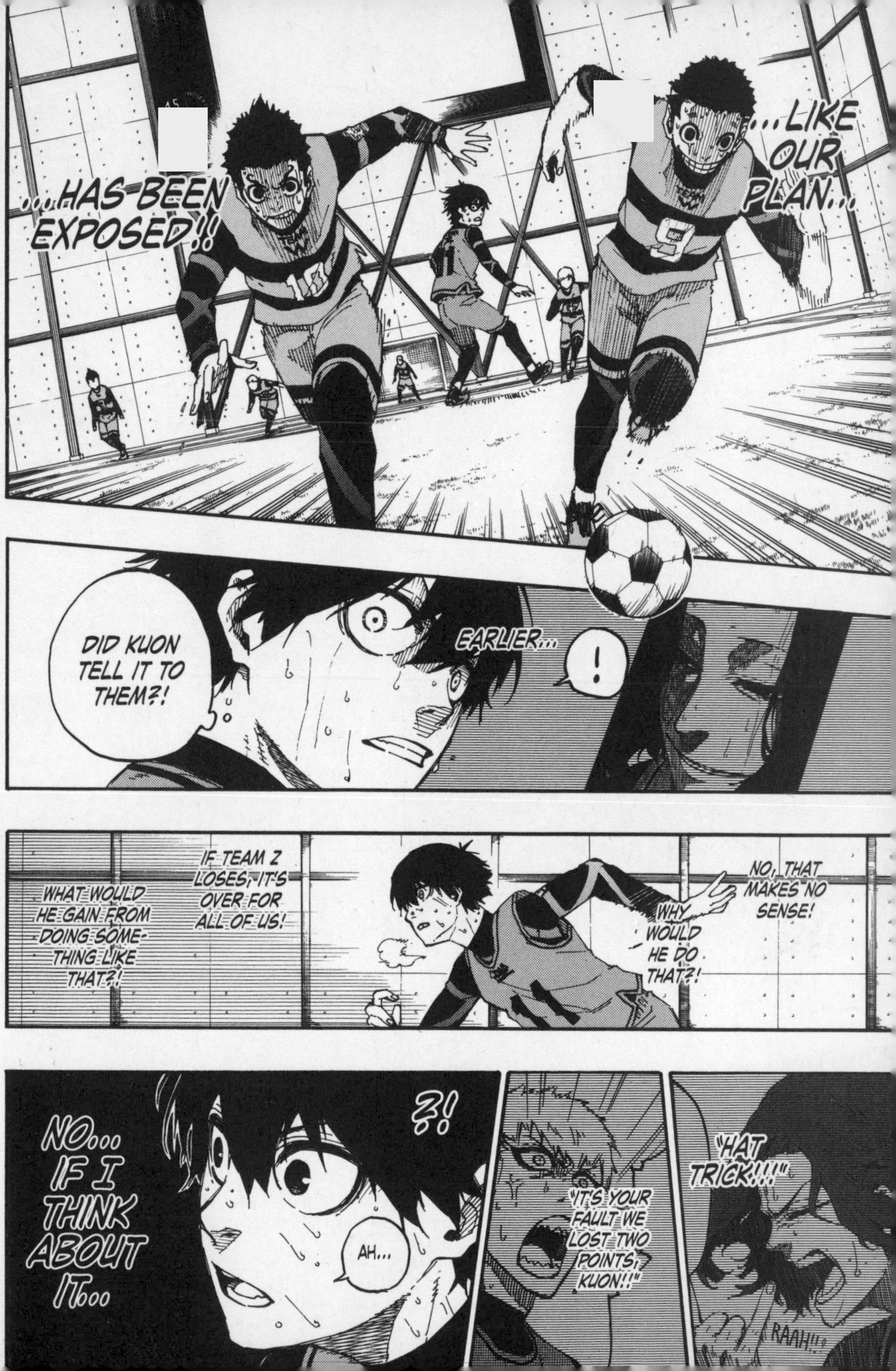
...LIKE OUR PLAN...
...HAS BEEN EXPOSED!!
!
EARLIER...
DID KUON TELL IT TO THEM?!
NO, THAT MAKES NO SENSE!
WHY WOULD HE DO THAT?!
IF TEAM Z LOSES, IT'S OVER FOR ALL OF US!
WHAT WOULD HE GAIN FROM DOING SOME-THING LIKE THAT?!
"HAT TRICK!!!"
RAAH!!
"IT'S YOUR FAULT WE LOST TWO POINTS, KUON!!"
?!
NO... IF I THINK ABOUT IT...
AH...

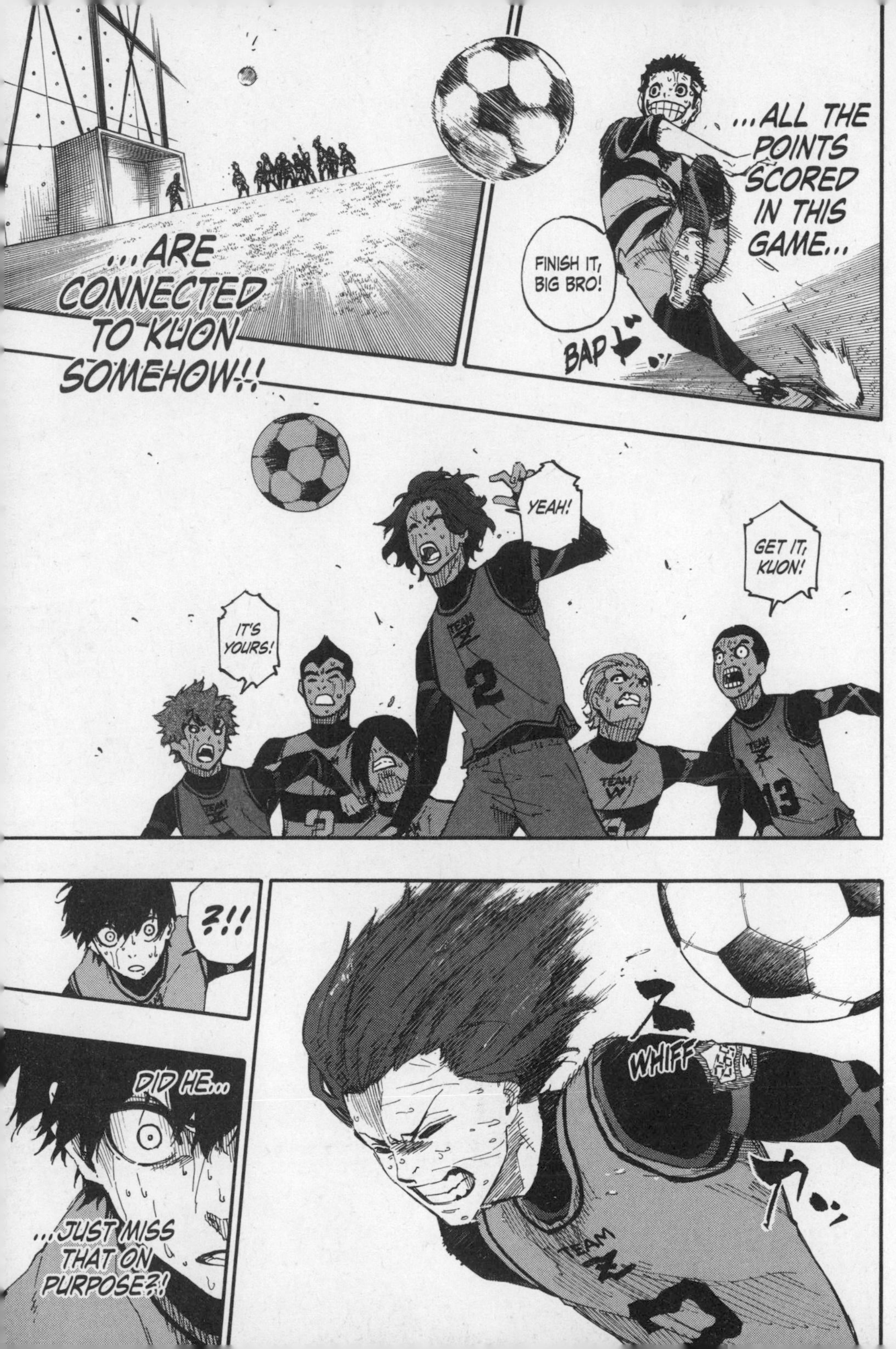

...ALL THE POINTS SCORED IN THIS GAME...
FINISH IT, BIG BRO!
BAP
...ARE CONNECTED TO KUON SOMEHOW!!
GET IT, KUON!
YEAH!
IT'S YOURS!
WHIFF
?!!
DID HE...
...JUST MISS THAT ON PURPOSE?!

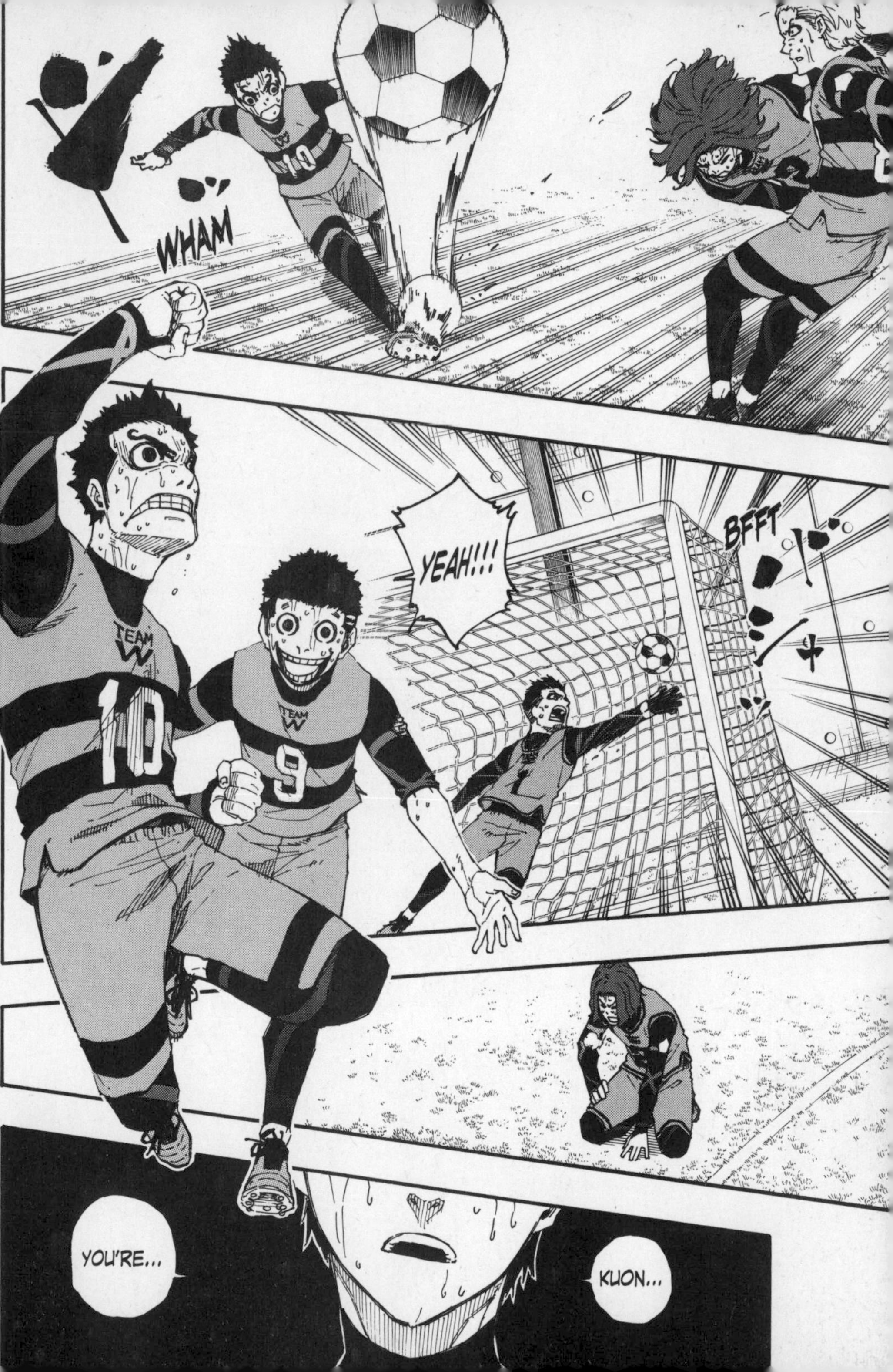
WHAM
BFFT
YEAH!!!
KUON...
YOU'RE...

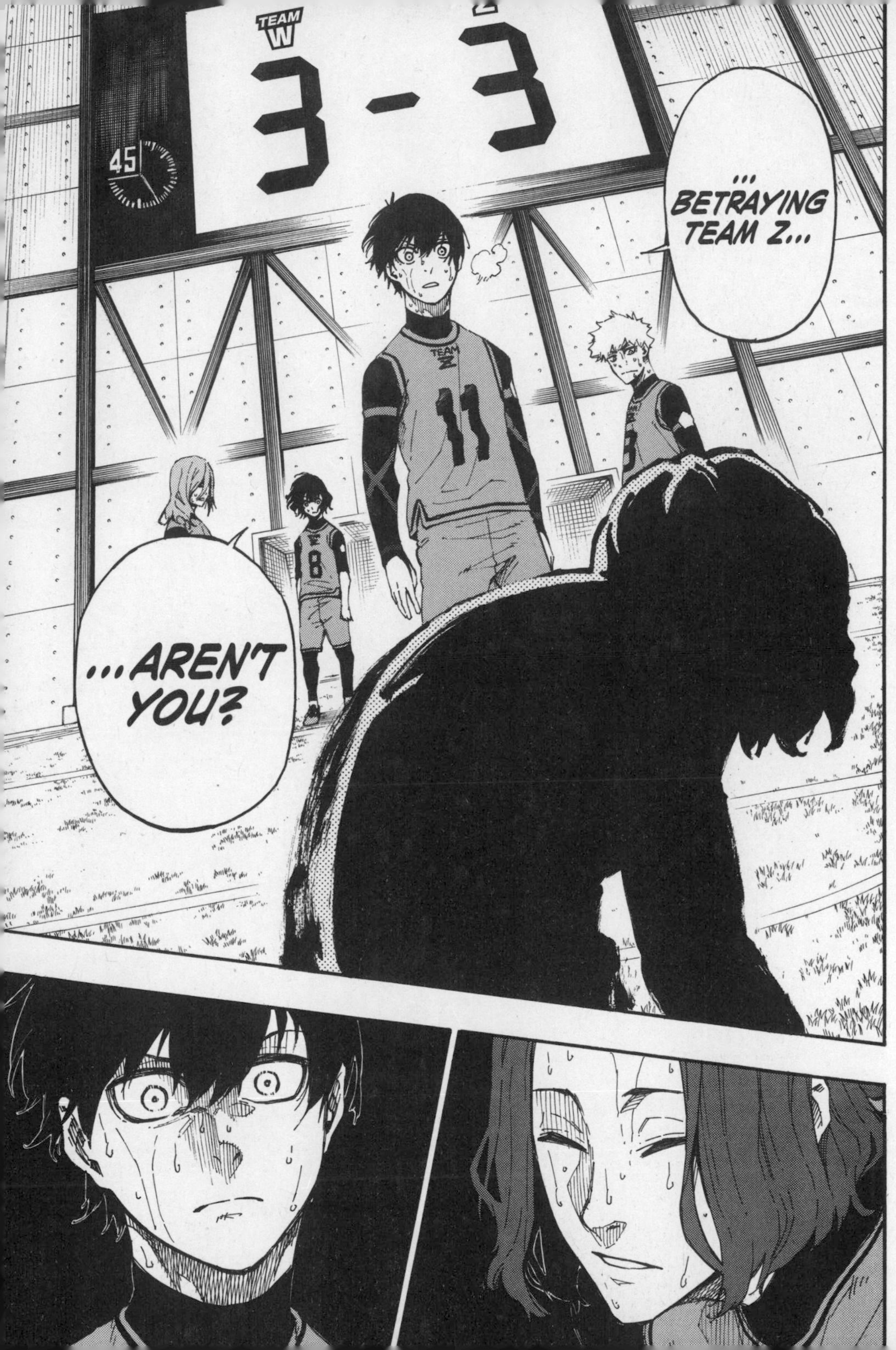
TEAM W
3 - 3
45
... BETRAYING TEAM Z...
TEAM Z
... AREN'T YOU?

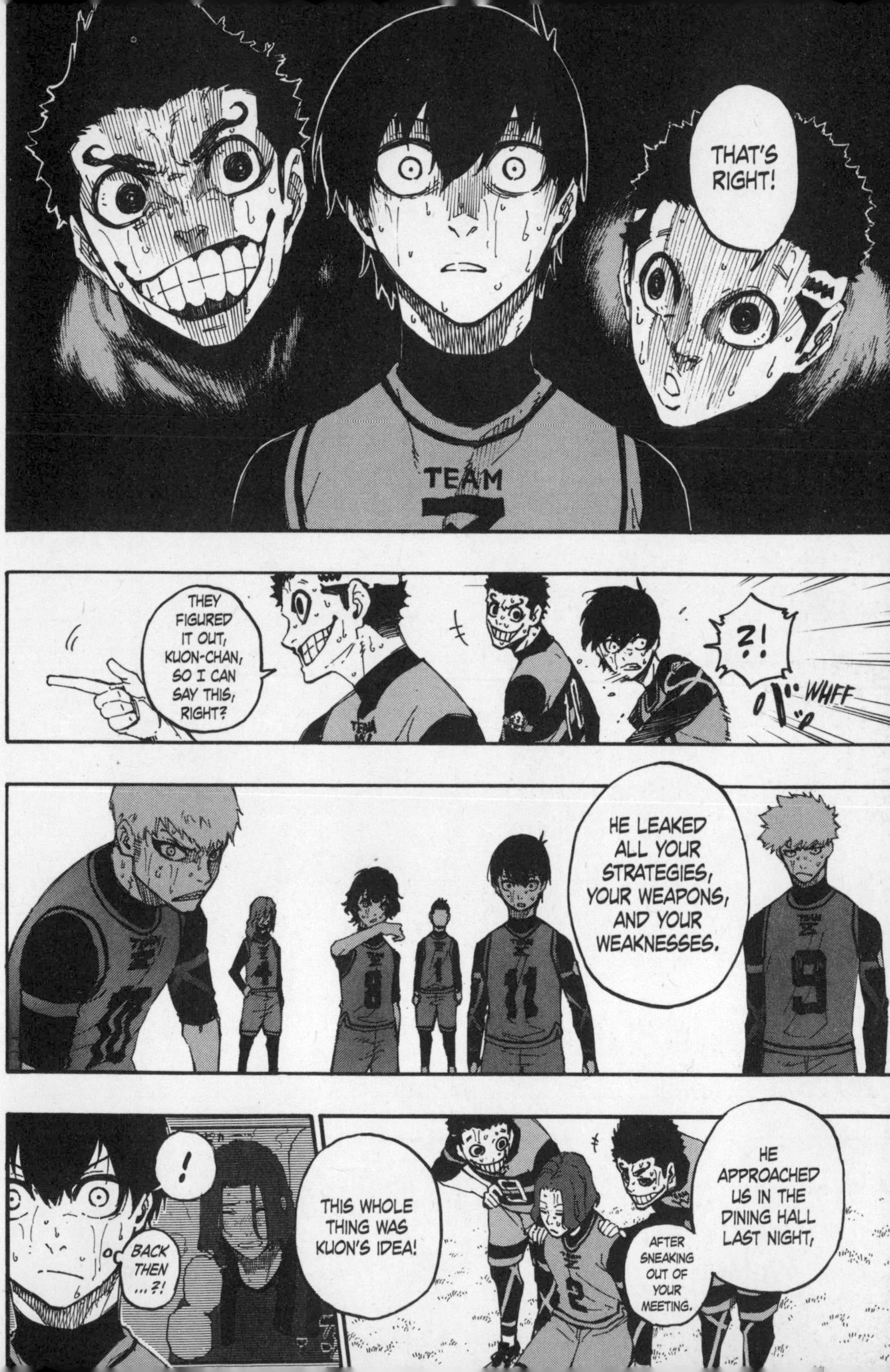
THAT'S RIGHT!
?!
WHFF
THEY FIGURED IT OUT, KUON-CHAN, SO I CAN SAY THIS, RIGHT?
HE LEAKED ALL YOUR STRATEGIES, YOUR WEAPONS, AND YOUR WEAKNESSES.
HE APPROACHED US IN THE DINING HALL LAST NIGHT,
AFTER SNEAKING OUT OF YOUR MEETING.
THIS WHOLE THING WAS KUON'S IDEA!
!
BACK THEN ...?!

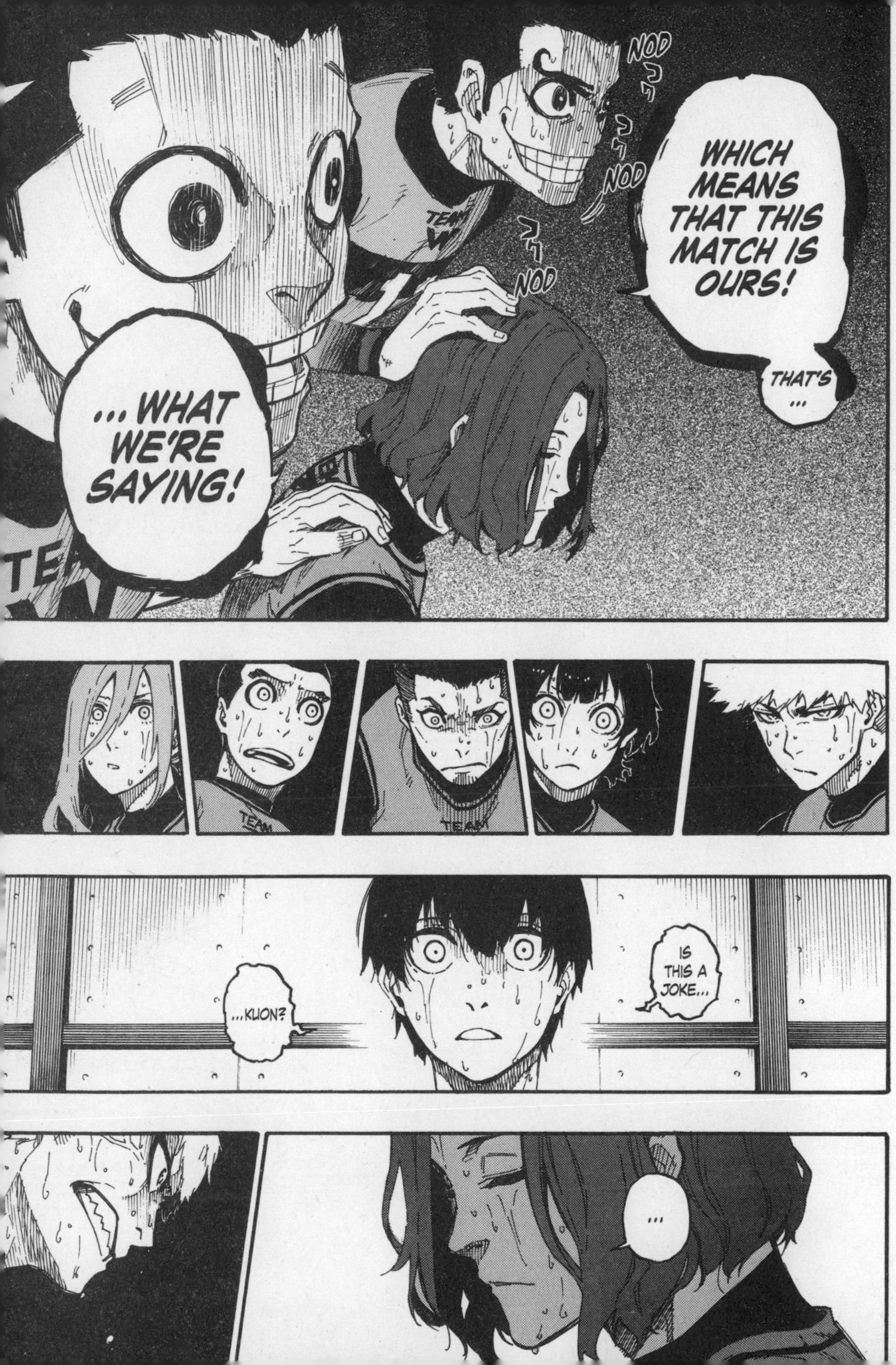
NOD
WHICH MEANS THAT THIS MATCH IS OURS!
THAT'S ...
NOD
NOD
...WHAT WE'RE SAYING!
IS THIS A JOKE...
...KUON?
...

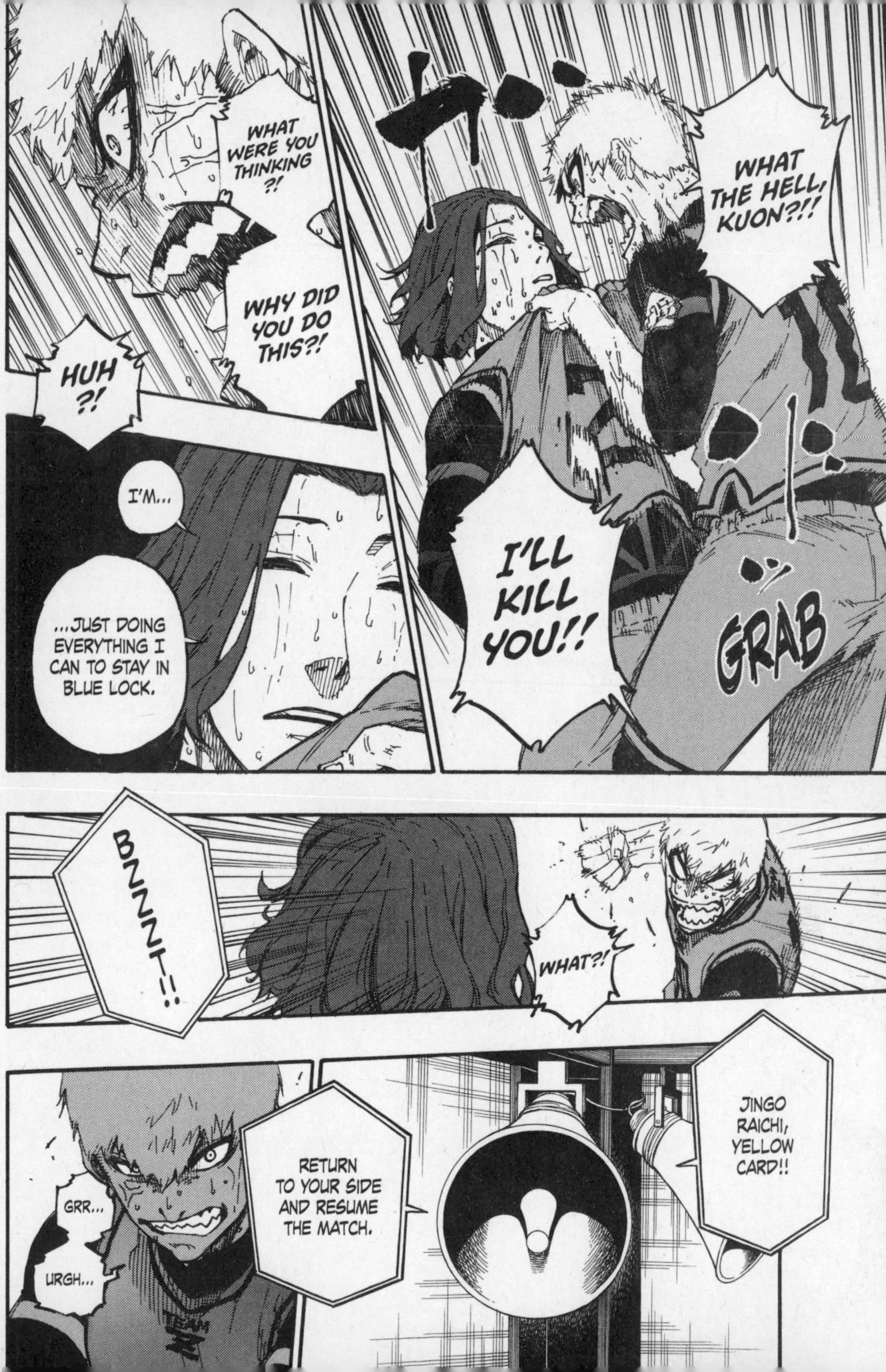
WHAT THE HELL, KUON?!!
GRAB
I'LL KILL YOU!!
WHAT WERE YOU THINKING?!
WHY DID YOU DO THIS?!
HUH?!
I'M...
...JUST DOING EVERYTHING I CAN TO STAY IN BLUE LOCK.
BZZZZT!!
WHAT?!
JINGO RAICHI, YELLOW CARD!!
RETURN TO YOUR SIDE AND RESUME THE MATCH.
GRR...
URGH...

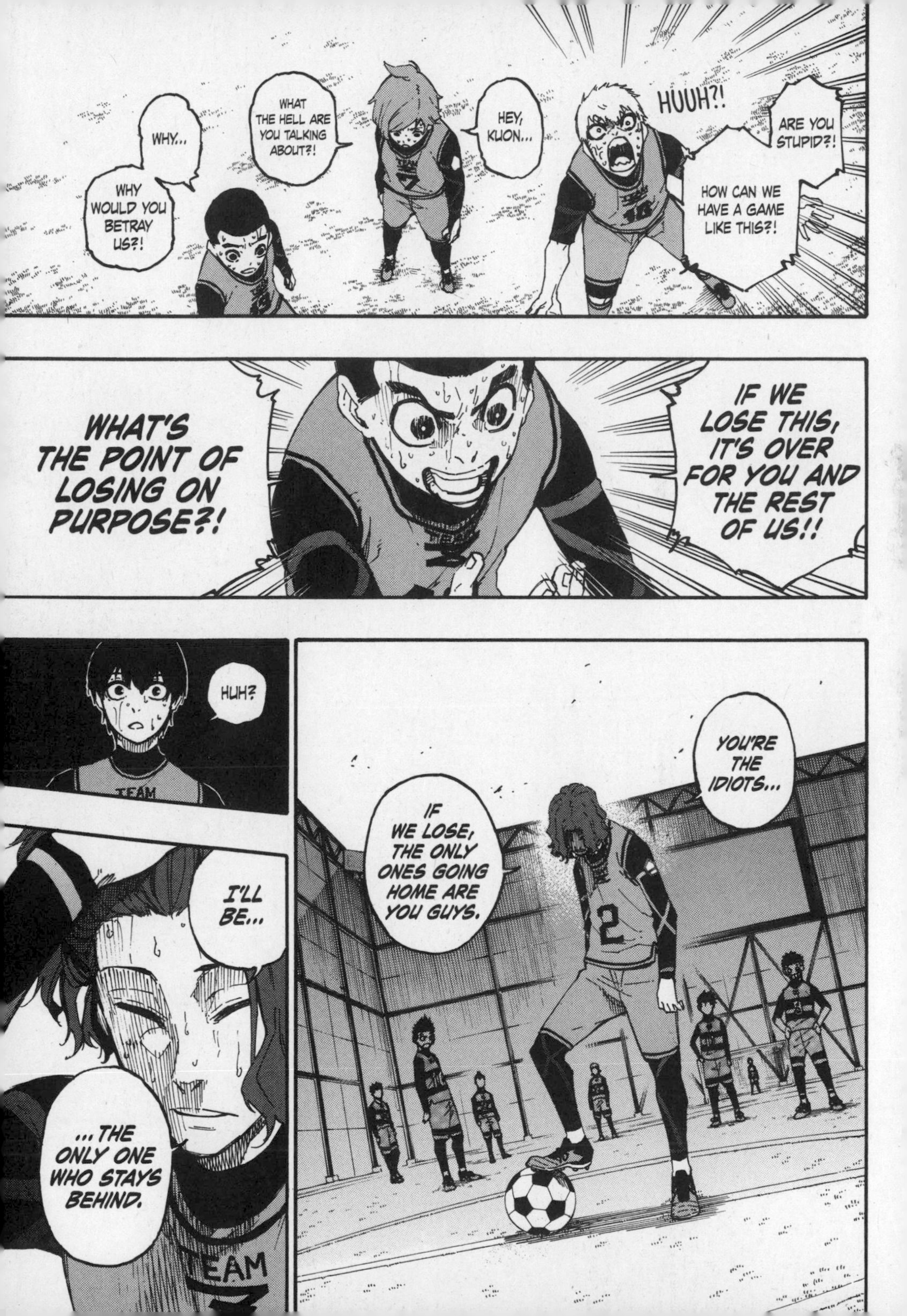
HUUH?!
ARE YOU STUPID?!
HOW CAN WE HAVE A GAME LIKE THIS?!
HEY, KUON...
WHAT THE HELL ARE YOU TALKING ABOUT?!
WHY...
WHY WOULD YOU BETRAY US?!
IF WE LOSE THIS, IT'S OVER FOR YOU AND THE REST OF US!!
WHAT'S THE POINT OF LOSING ON PURPOSE?!
YOU'RE THE IDIOTS...
IF WE LOSE, THE ONLY ONES GOING HOME ARE YOU GUYS.
HUH?
I'LL BE...
...THE ONLY ONE WHO STAYS BEHIND.

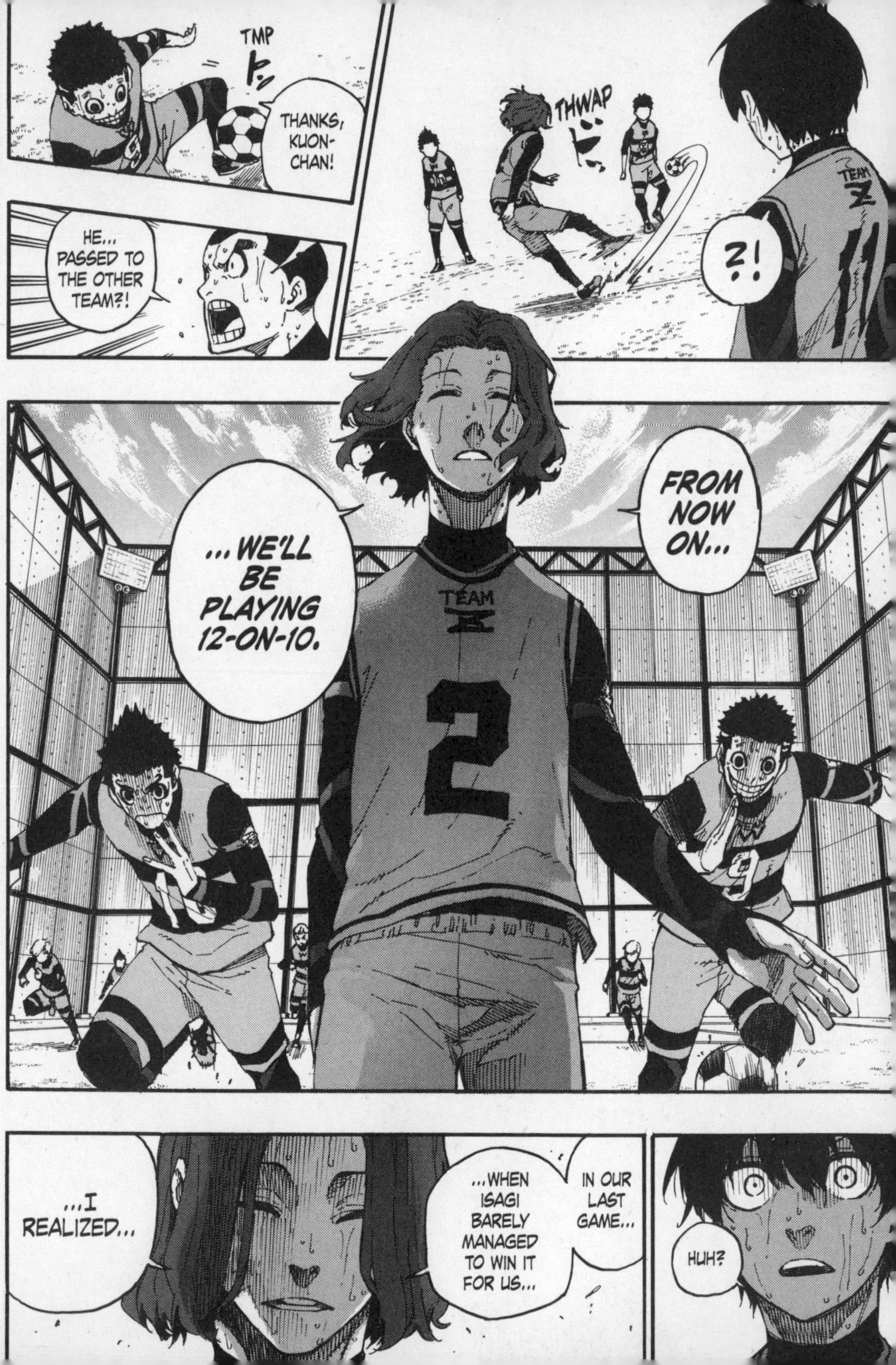
THWAP
?!
TMP
THANKS, KUON-CHAN!
HE... PASSED TO THE OTHER TEAM?!
FROM NOW ON...
...WE'LL BE PLAYING 12-ON-10.
TEAM Z
2
HUH?
IN OUR LAST GAME...
...WHEN ISAGI BARELY MANAGED TO WIN IT FOR US...
...I REALIZED...

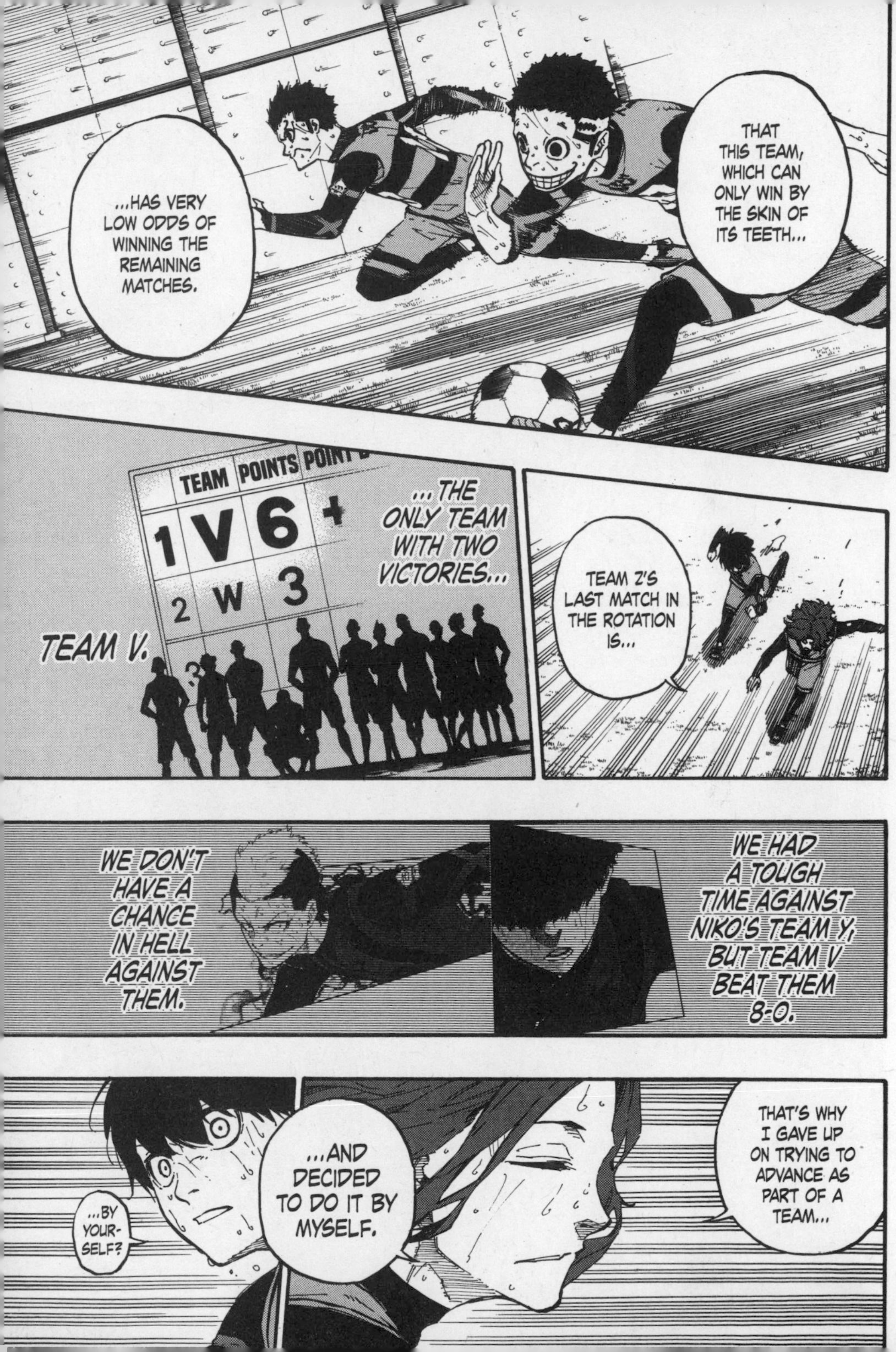
THAT THIS TEAM, WHICH CAN ONLY WIN BY THE SKIN OF ITS TEETH...
...HAS VERY LOW ODDS OF WINNING THE REMAINING MATCHES.
TEAM Z'S LAST MATCH IN THE ROTATION IS...
TEAM POINTS
1 V 6
2 W 3
...THE ONLY TEAM WITH TWO VICTORIES...
TEAM V.
WE HAD A TOUGH TIME AGAINST NIKO'S TEAM Y, BUT TEAM V BEAT THEM 8-0.
WE DON'T HAVE A CHANCE IN HELL AGAINST THEM.
THAT'S WHY I GAVE UP ON TRYING TO ADVANCE AS PART OF A TEAM...
...AND DECIDED TO DO IT BY MYSELF.
...BY YOURSELF?

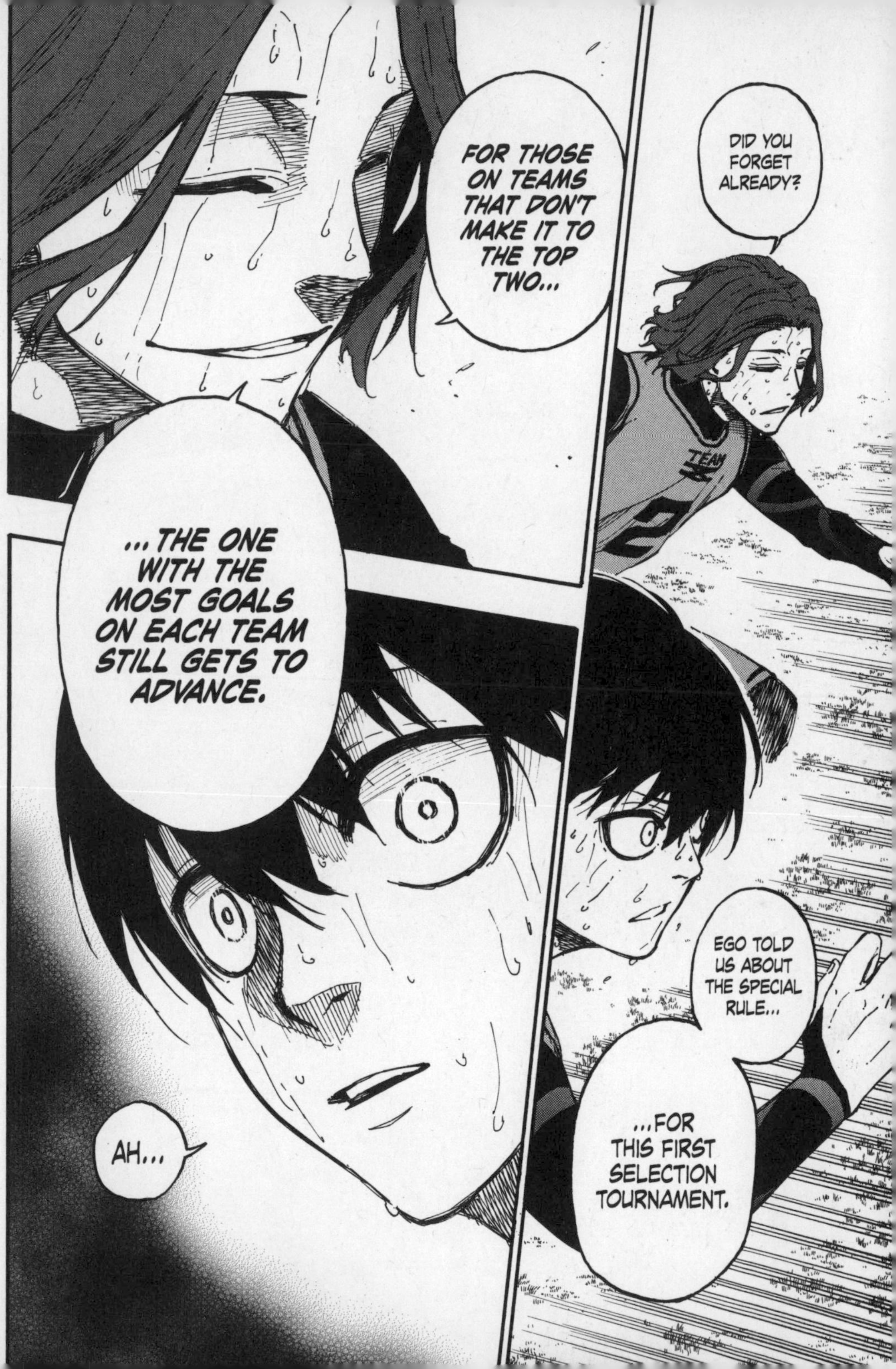
DID YOU FORGET ALREADY?
EGO TOLD US ABOUT THE SPECIAL RULE...
...FOR THIS FIRST SELECTION TOURNAMENT.
FOR THOSE ON TEAMS THAT DON'T MAKE IT TO THE TOP TWO...
...THE ONE WITH THE MOST GOALS ON EACH TEAM STILL GETS TO ADVANCE.
AH...

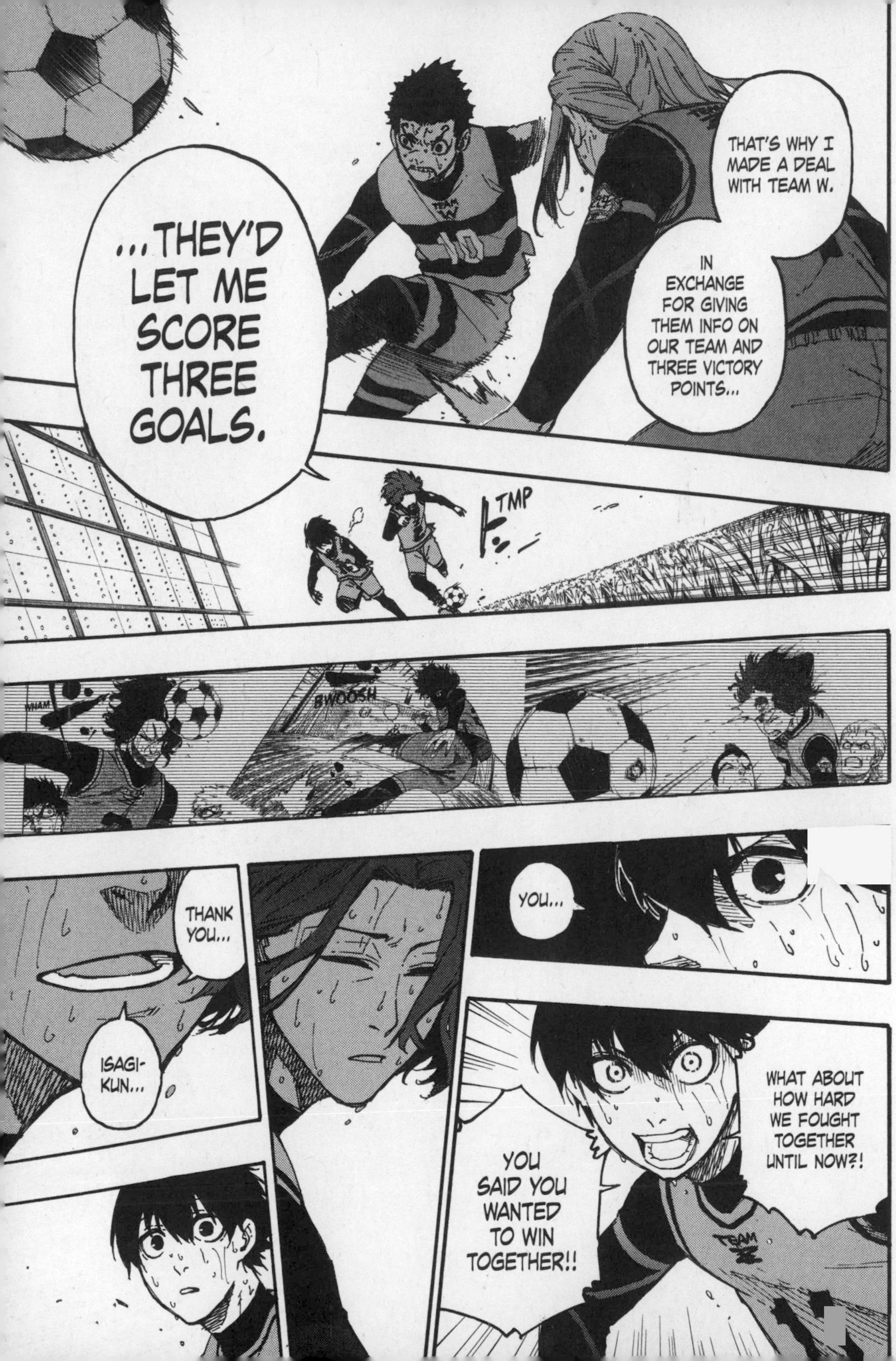
THAT'S WHY I MADE A DEAL WITH TEAM W.
IN EXCHANGE FOR GIVING THEM INFO ON OUR TEAM AND THREE VICTORY POINTS...
...THEY'D LET ME SCORE THREE GOALS.
TMP
BWOOSH
WHAM
YOU...
THANK YOU...
ISAGI-KUN...
WHAT ABOUT HOW HARD WE FOUGHT TOGETHER UNTIL NOW?!
YOU SAID YOU WANTED TO WIN TOGETHER!!

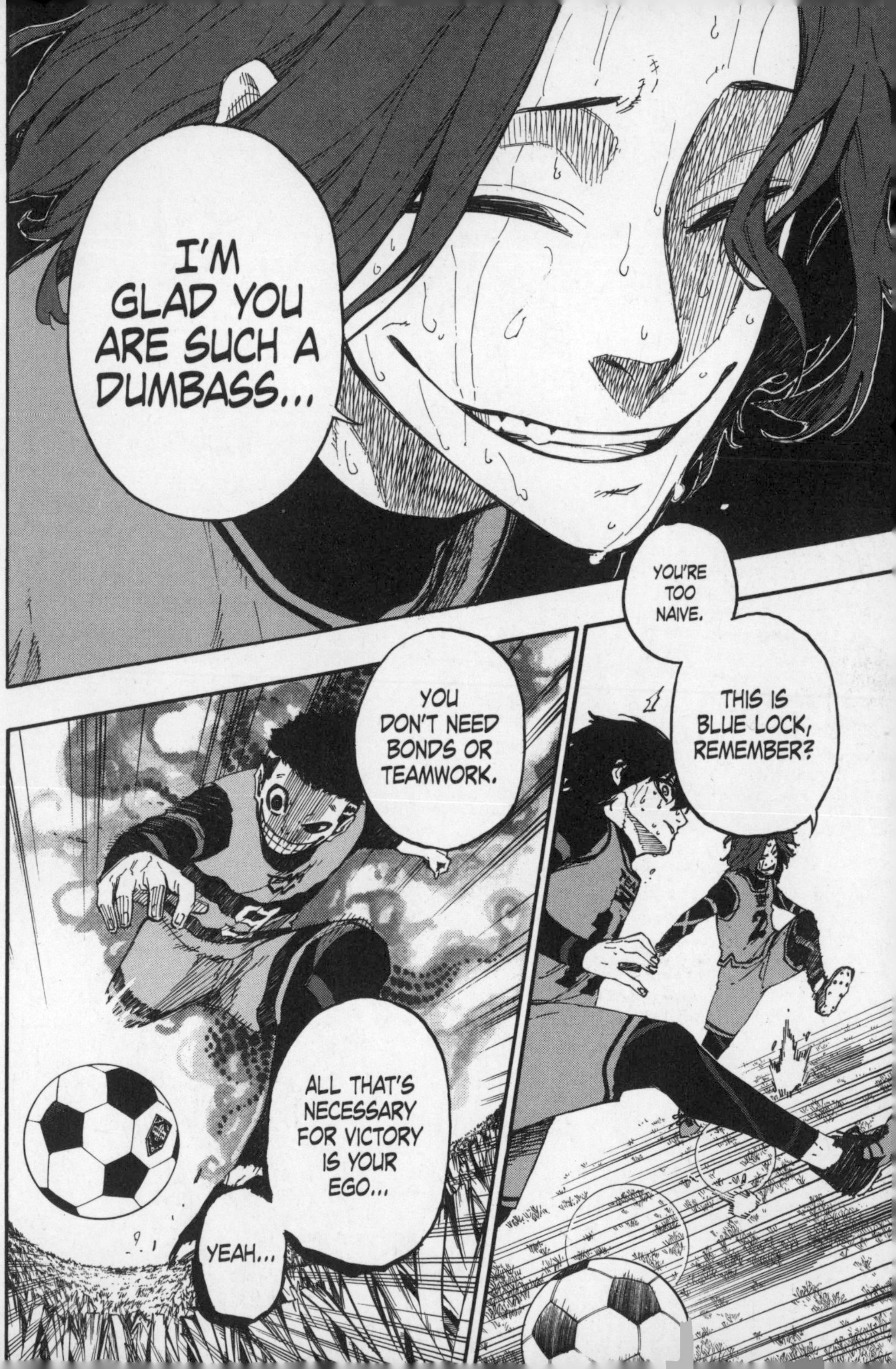
I'M GLAD YOU ARE SUCH A DUMBASS...
YOU'RE TOO NAIVE.
THIS IS BLUE LOCK, REMEMBER?
YOU DON'T NEED BONDS OR TEAMWORK.
ALL THAT'S NECESSARY FOR VICTORY IS YOUR EGO...
YEAH...

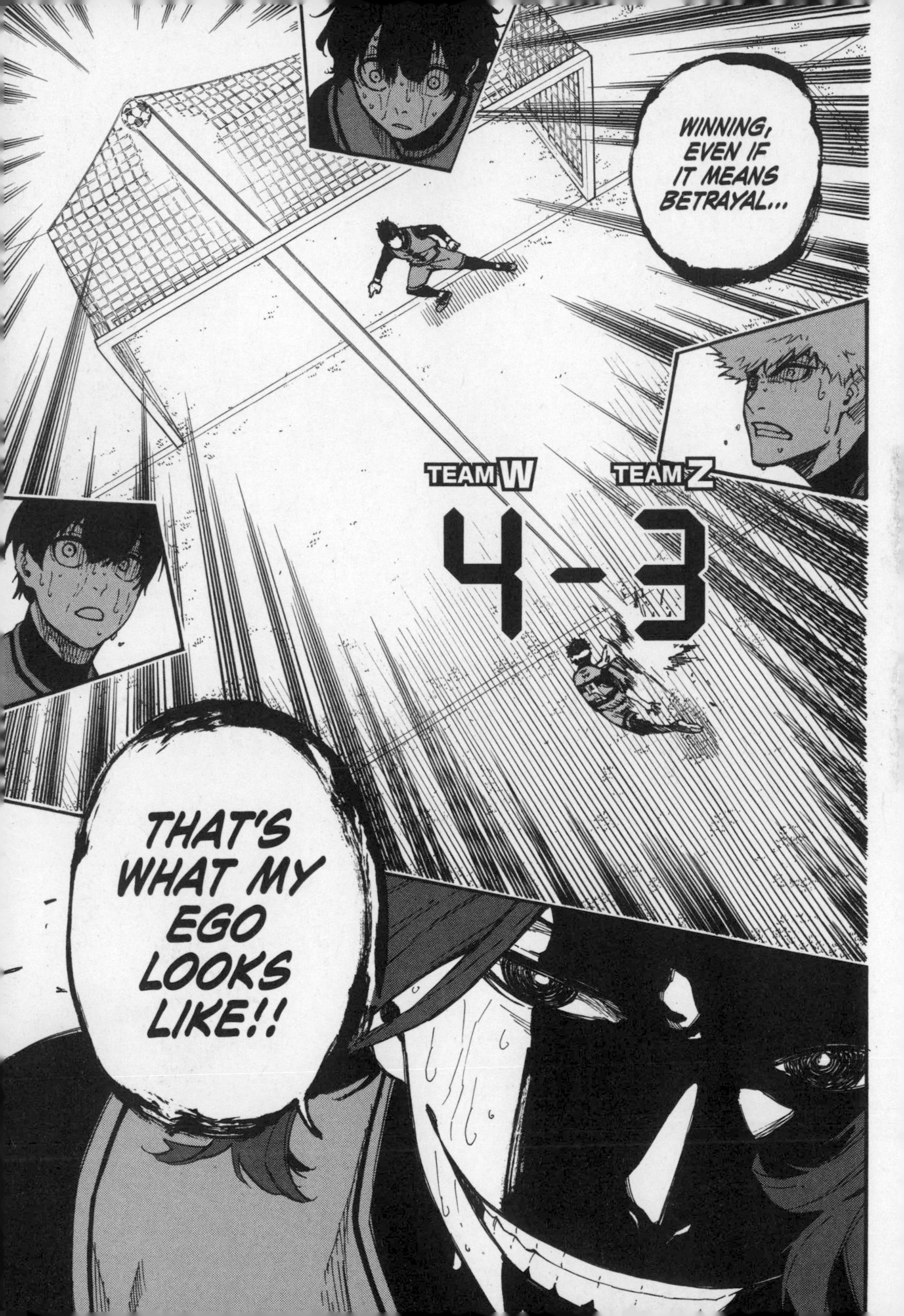
WINNING, EVEN IF IT MEANS BETRAYAL...
TEAM W TEAM Z
4-3
THAT'S WHAT MY EGO LOOKS LIKE!!

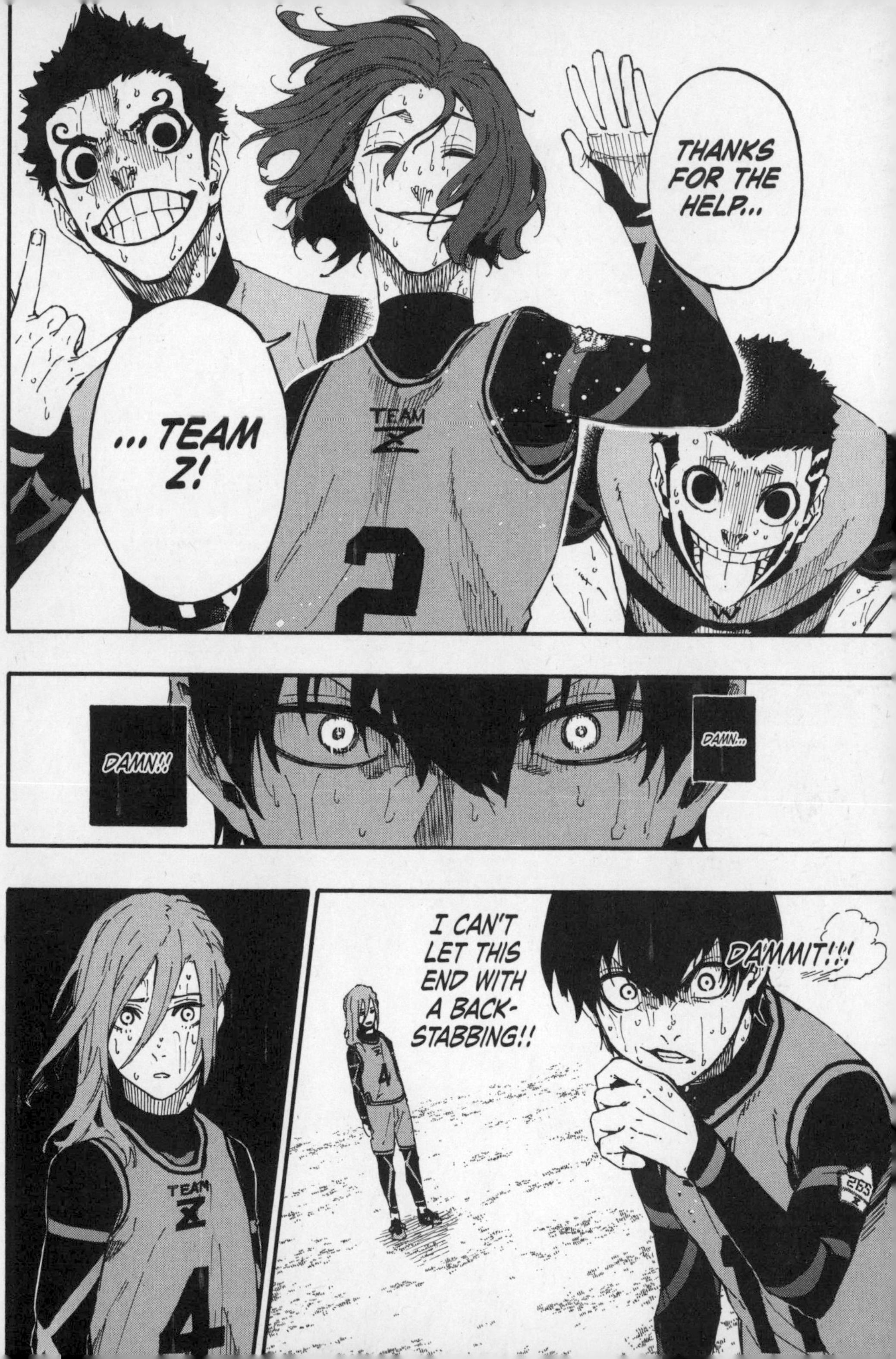
THANKS FOR THE HELP...
...TEAM Z!
DAMN...
DAMN!!
DAMMIT!!!
I CAN'T LET THIS END WITH A BACK-STABBING!!

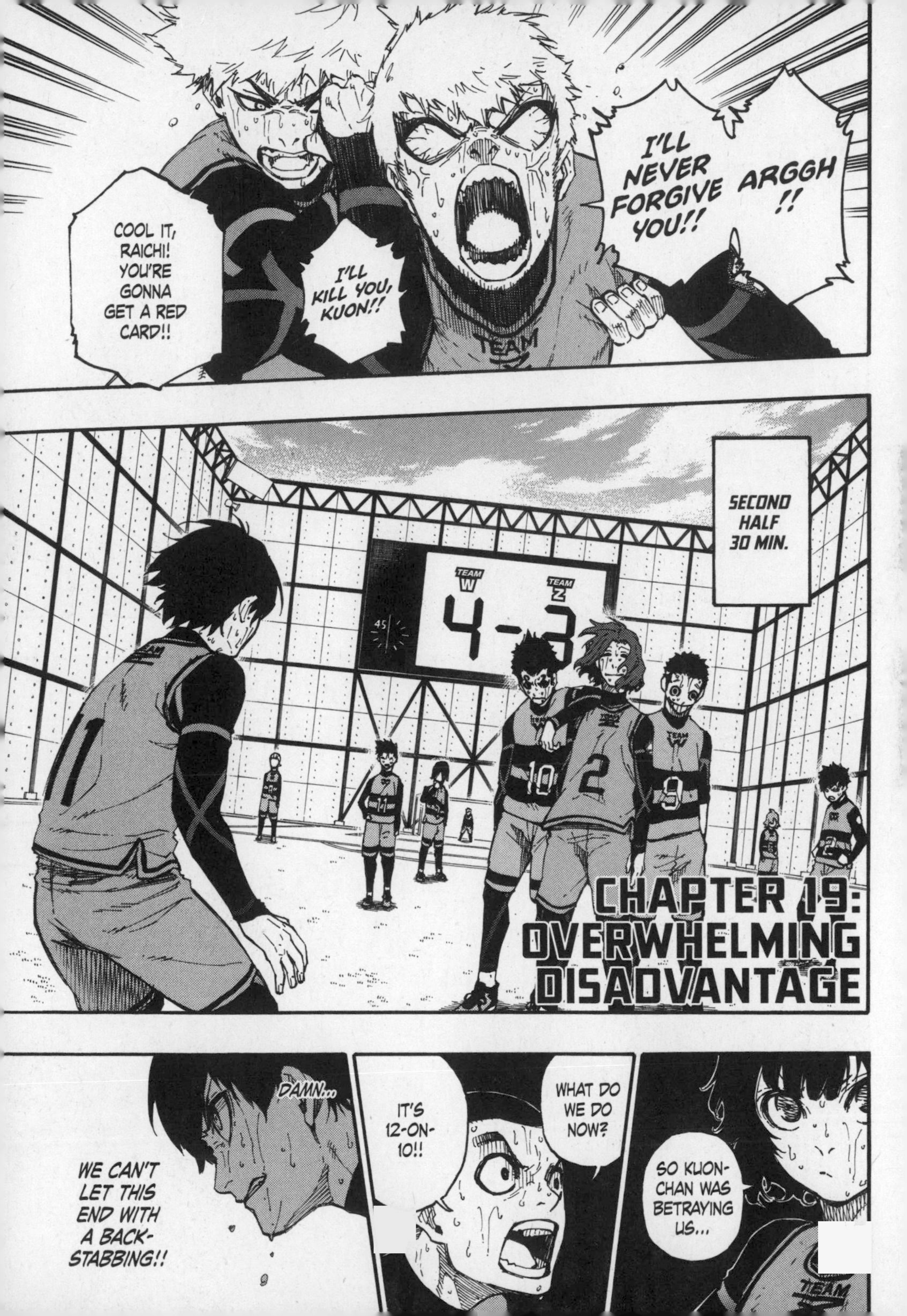
ARGGH!!
I'LL NEVER FORGIVE YOU!!
I'LL KILL YOU, KUON!!
COOL IT, RAICHI! YOU'RE GONNA GET A RED CARD!!
SECOND HALF 30 MIN.
TEAM W
TEAM Z
4-3
CHAPTER 19: OVERWHELMING DISADVANTAGE
SO KUON-CHAN WAS BETRAYING US...
WHAT DO WE DO NOW?
IT'S 12-ON-10!!
DAMN...
WE CAN'T LET THIS END WITH A BACK-STABBING!!

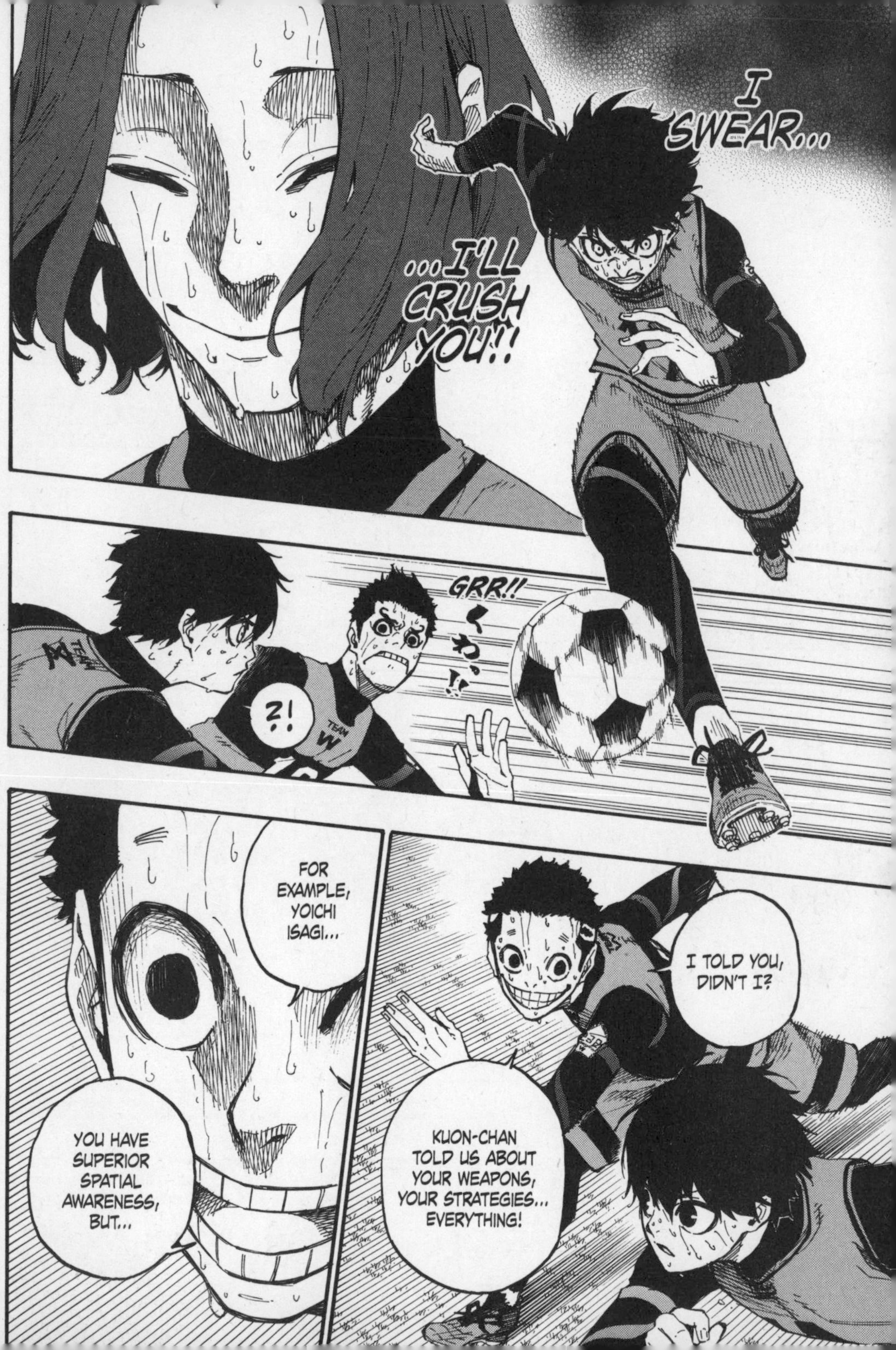
I SWEAR...
...I'LL CRUSH YOU!!
GRR!!
くわっ!!
?!
I TOLD YOU, DIDN'T I?
KUON-CHAN TOLD US ABOUT YOUR WEAPONS, YOUR STRATEGIES... EVERYTHING!
FOR EXAMPLE, YOICHI ISAGI...
YOU HAVE SUPERIOR SPATIAL AWARENESS, BUT...

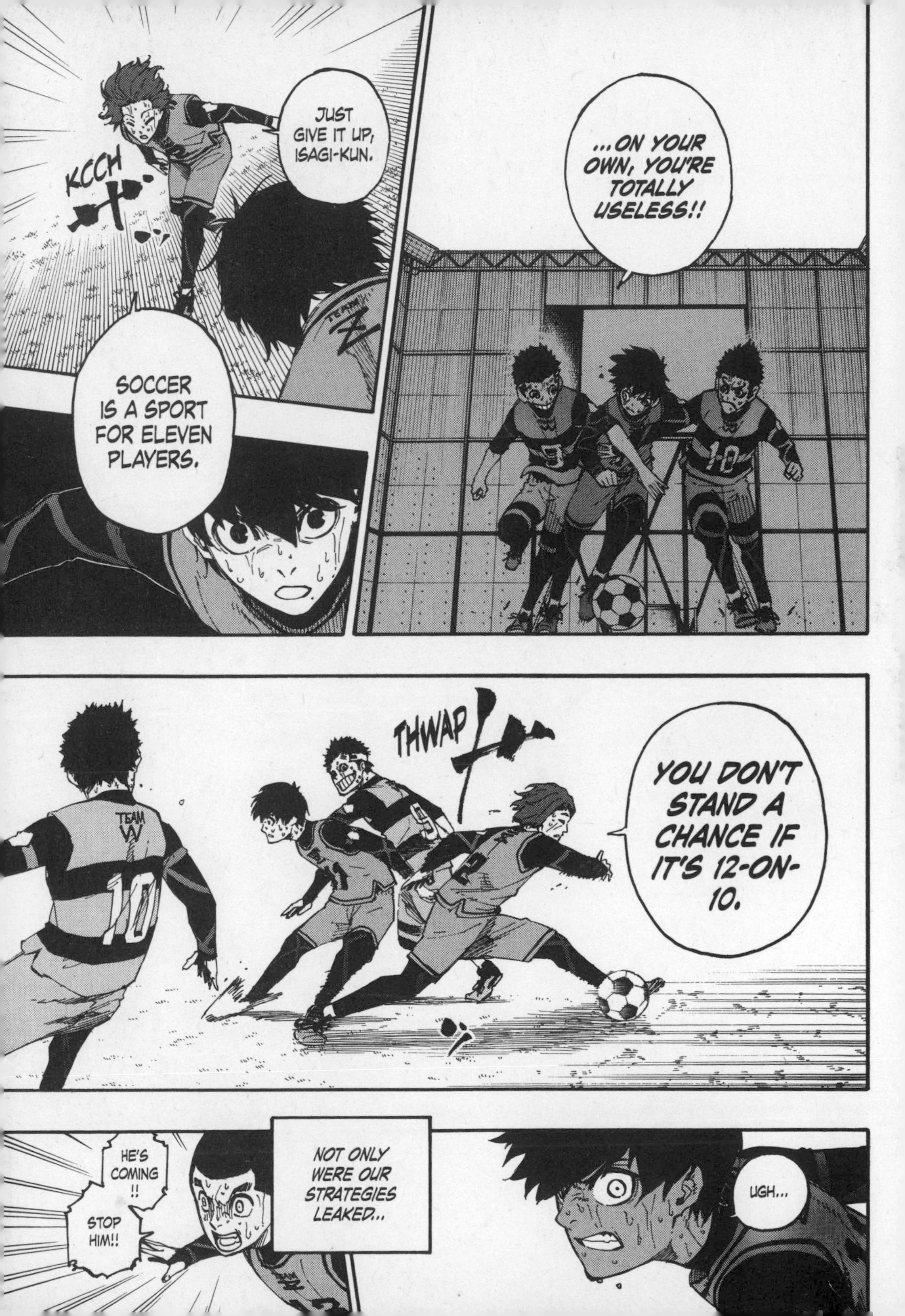
...ON YOUR OWN, YOU'RE TOTALLY USELESS!!
JUST GIVE IT UP, ISAGI-KUN.
KCCH
SOCCER IS A SPORT FOR ELEVEN PLAYERS.
YOU DON'T STAND A CHANCE IF IT'S 12-ON-10.
THWAP
UGH...
NOT ONLY WERE OUR STRATEGIES LEAKED...
HE'S COMING!!
STOP HIM!!

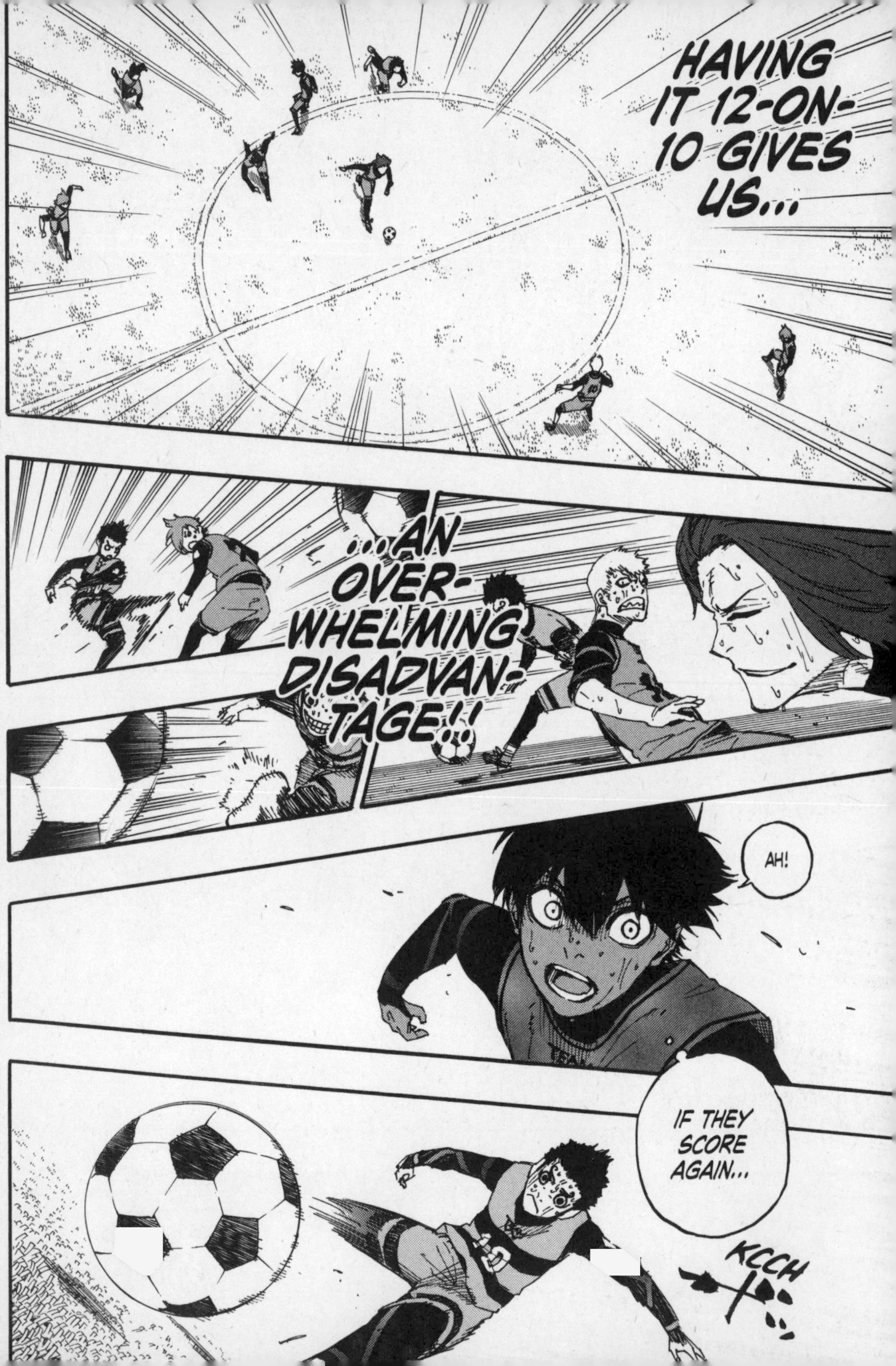
HAVING IT 12-ON-10 GIVES US...
...AN OVER-WHELMING DISADVAN-TAGE!!
AH!
IF THEY SCORE AGAIN...
KCCH

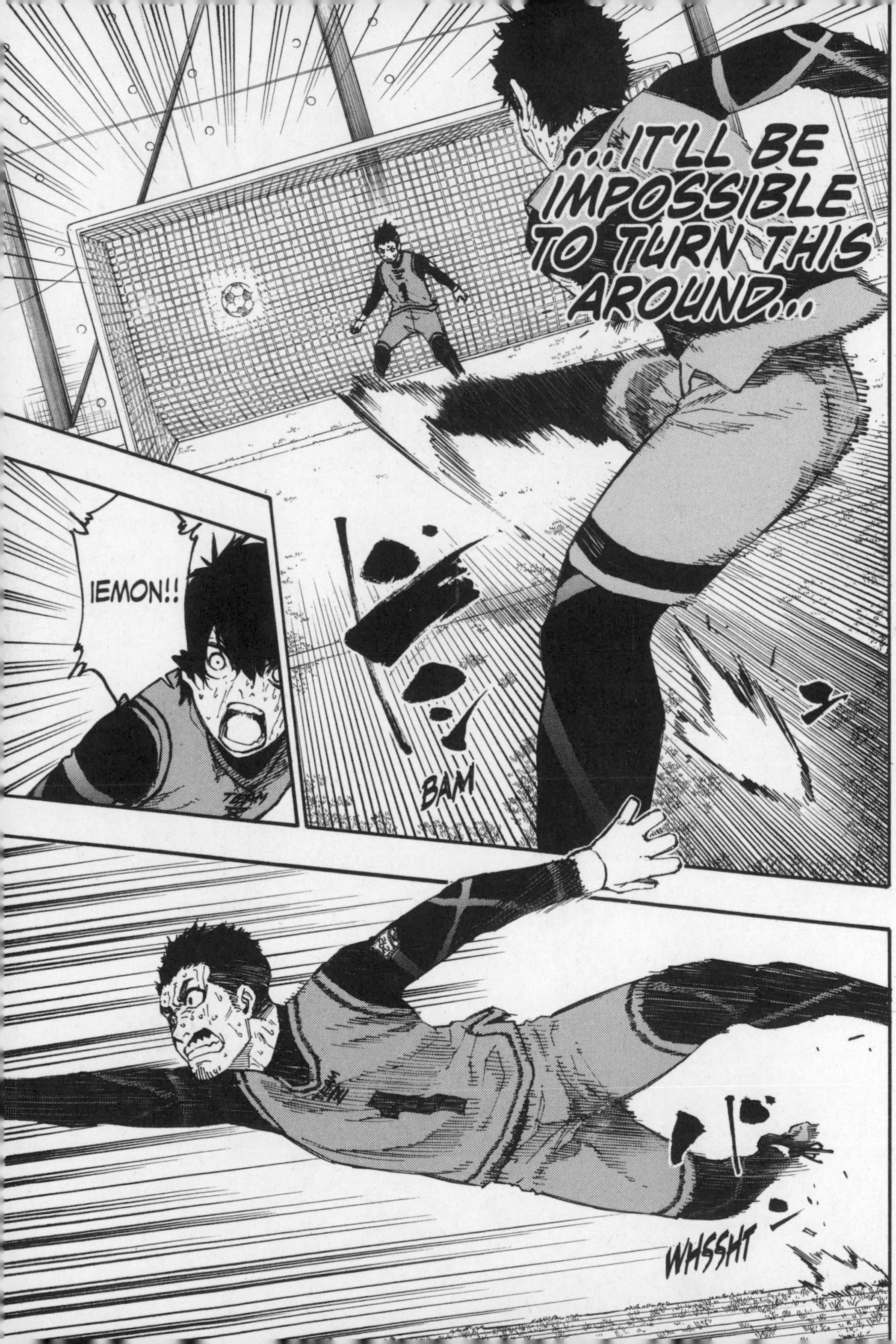
...IT'LL BE IMPOSSIBLE TO TURN THIS AROUND...
BAM
IEMON!!
WHSSHT

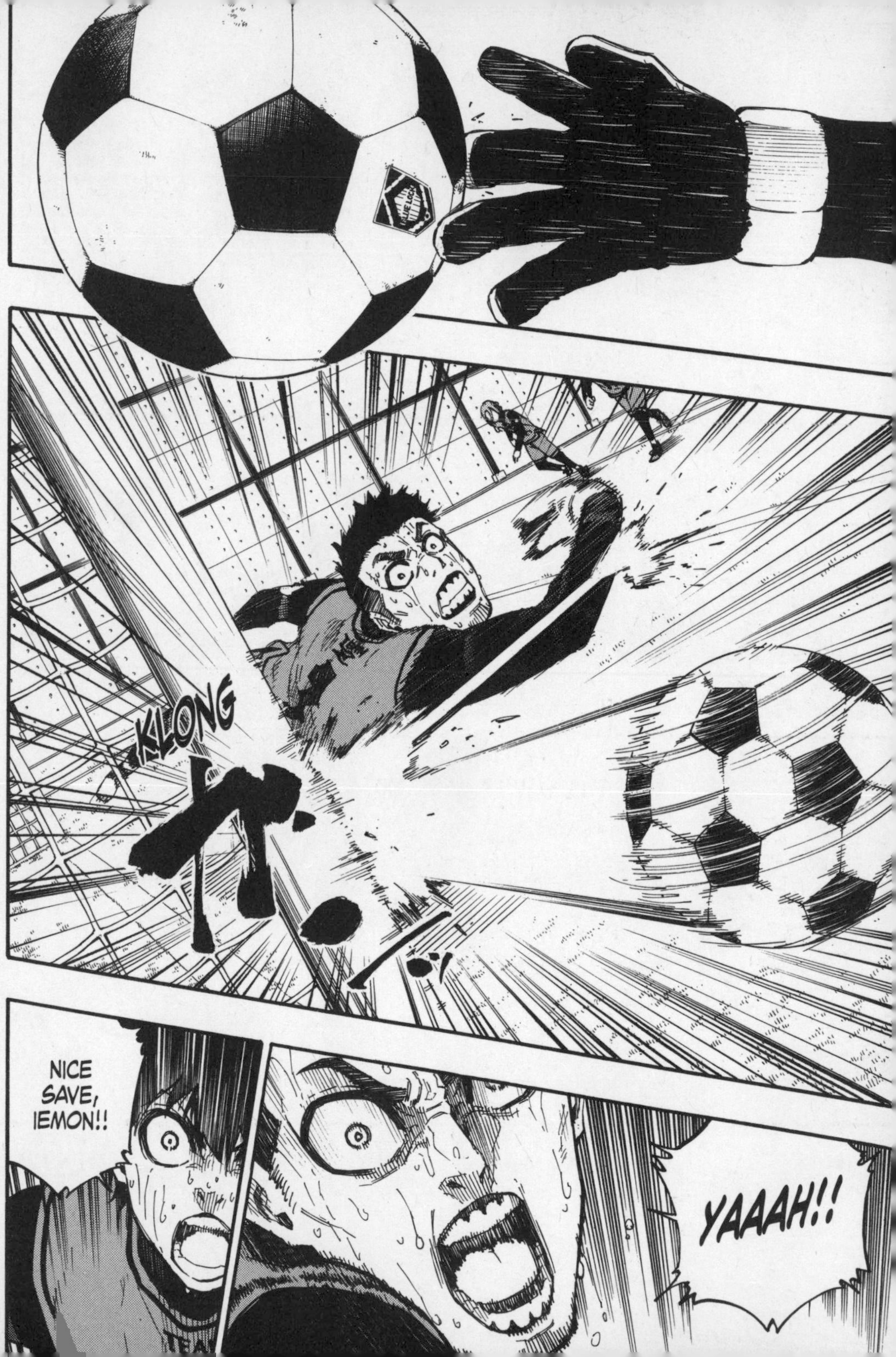
KLONG
YAAAH!!
NICE SAVE, IEMON!!

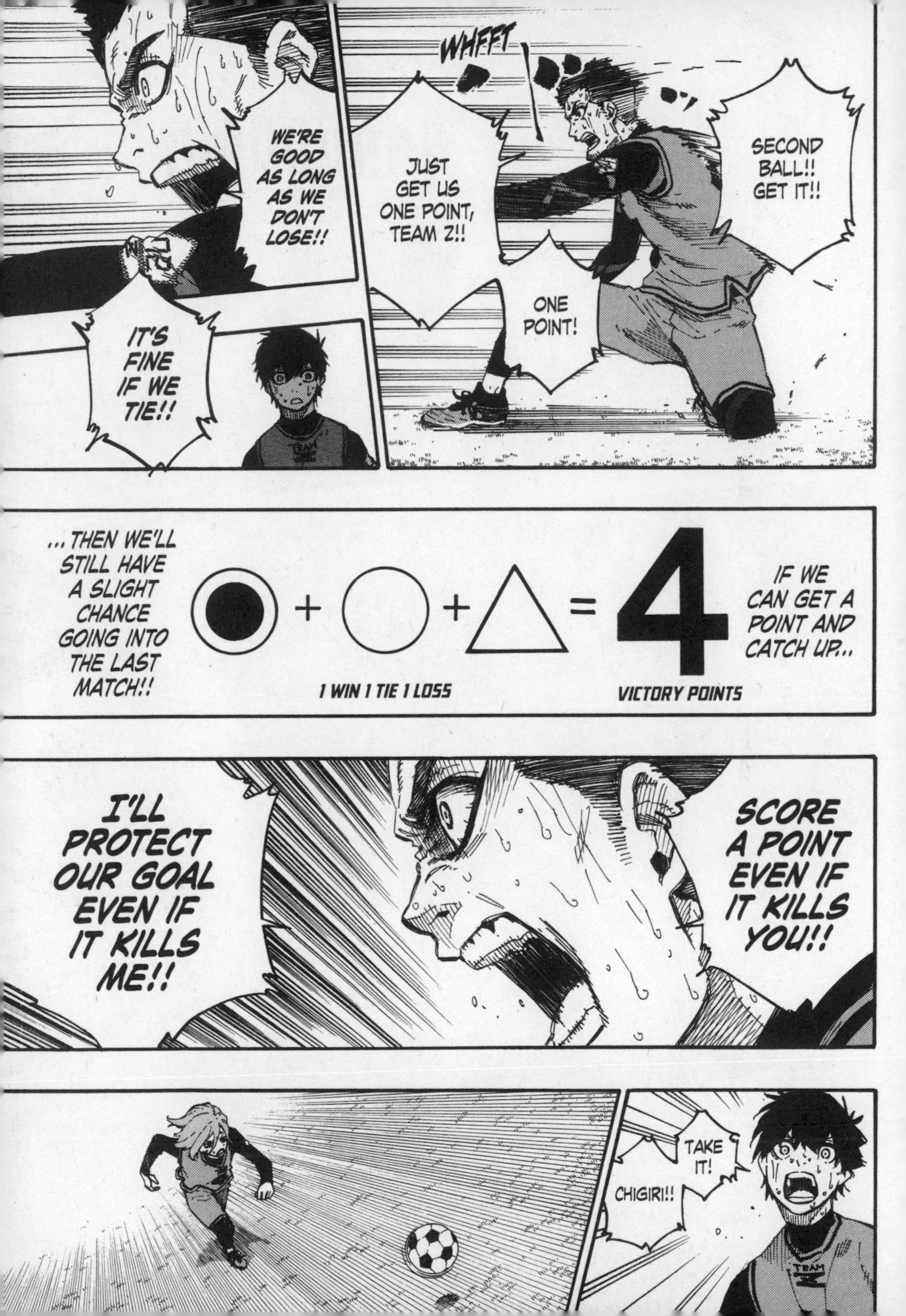
WHFFT
SECOND BALL!! GET IT!!
JUST GET US ONE POINT, TEAM Z!!
ONE POINT!
WE'RE GOOD AS LONG AS WE DON'T LOSE!!
IT'S FINE IF WE TIE!!
IF WE CAN GET A POINT AND CATCH UP...
4
VICTORY POINTS
1 WIN 1 TIE 1 LOSS
...THEN WE'LL STILL HAVE A SLIGHT CHANCE GOING INTO THE LAST MATCH!!
SCORE A POINT EVEN IF IT KILLS YOU!!
I'LL PROTECT OUR GOAL EVEN IF IT KILLS ME!!
TAKE IT!
CHIGIRI!!

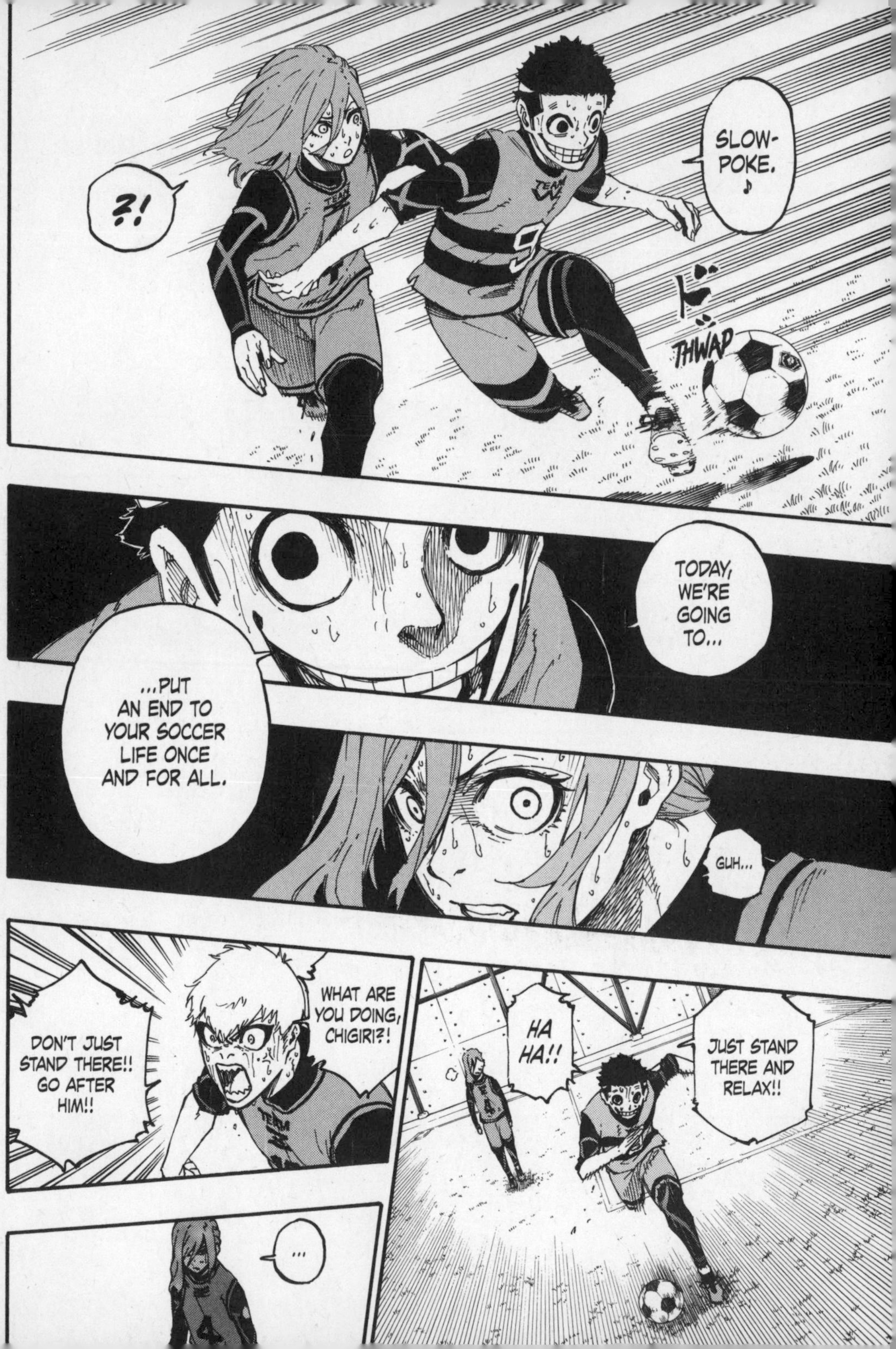
SLOW-POKE. ♪
THWAP
?!
TODAY, WE'RE GOING TO...
...PUT AN END TO YOUR SOCCER LIFE ONCE AND FOR ALL.
GUH...
JUST STAND THERE AND RELAX!!
HA HA!!
WHAT ARE YOU DOING, CHIGIRI?!
DON'T JUST STAND THERE!! GO AFTER HIM!!
...

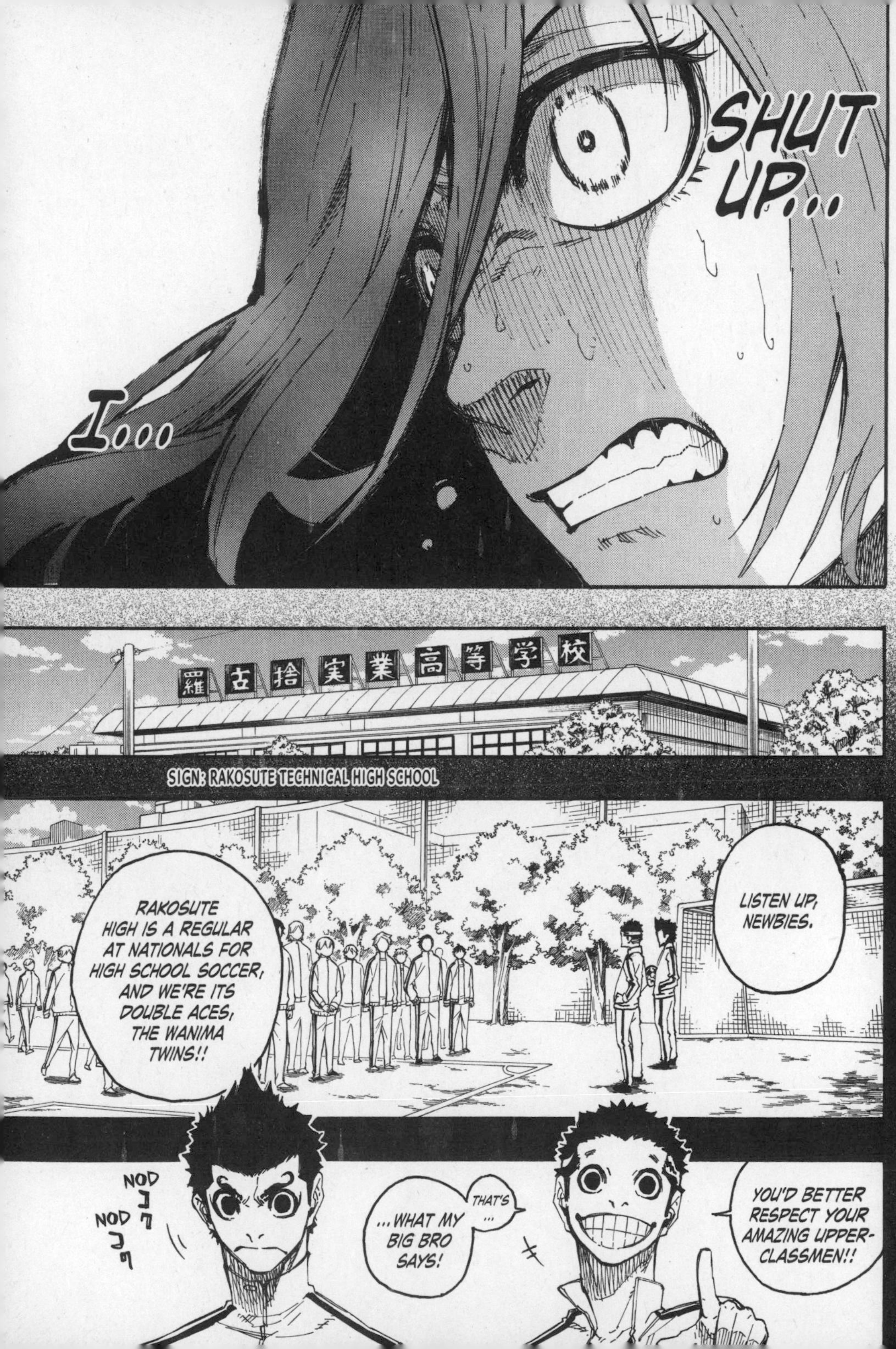
SHUT UP...
I...
羅古捨実業高等学校
SIGN: RAKOSUTE TECHNICAL HIGH SCHOOL
LISTEN UP, NEWBIES.
RAKOSUTE HIGH IS A REGULAR AT NATIONALS FOR HIGH SCHOOL SOCCER, AND WE'RE ITS DOUBLE ACES, THE WANIMA TWINS!!
YOU'D BETTER RESPECT YOUR AMAZING UPPER-CLASSMEN!!
THAT'S...
...WHAT MY BIG BRO SAYS!
NOD NOD

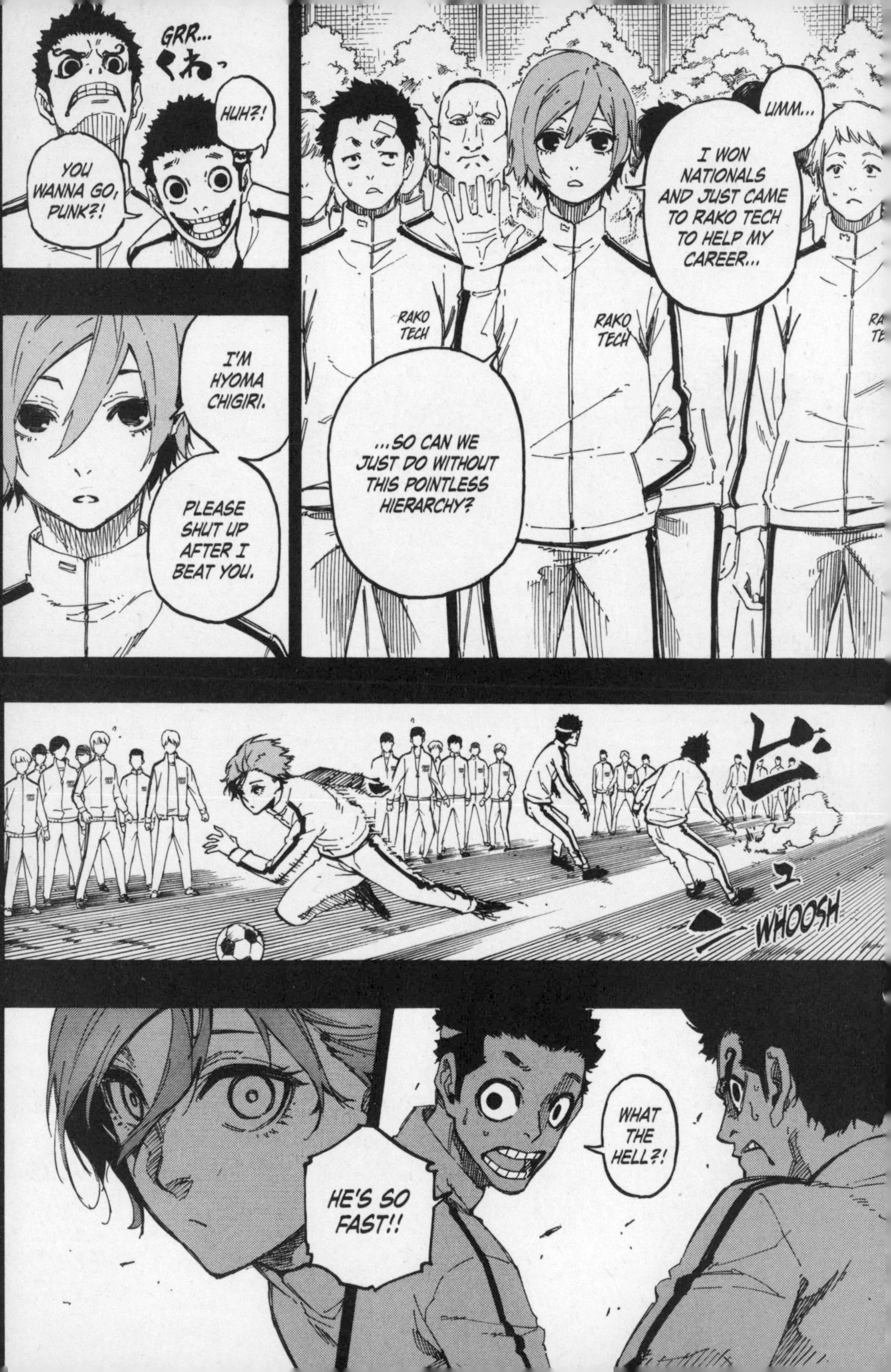
UMM...
I WON NATIONALS AND JUST CAME TO RAKO TECH TO HELP MY CAREER...
RAKO TECH
RAKO TECH
...SO CAN WE JUST DO WITHOUT THIS POINTLESS HIERARCHY?
GRR...
HUH?!
YOU WANNA GO, PUNK?!
I'M HYOMA CHIGIRI.
PLEASE SHUT UP AFTER I BEAT YOU.
WHOOSH
WHAT THE HELL?!
HE'S SO FAST!!

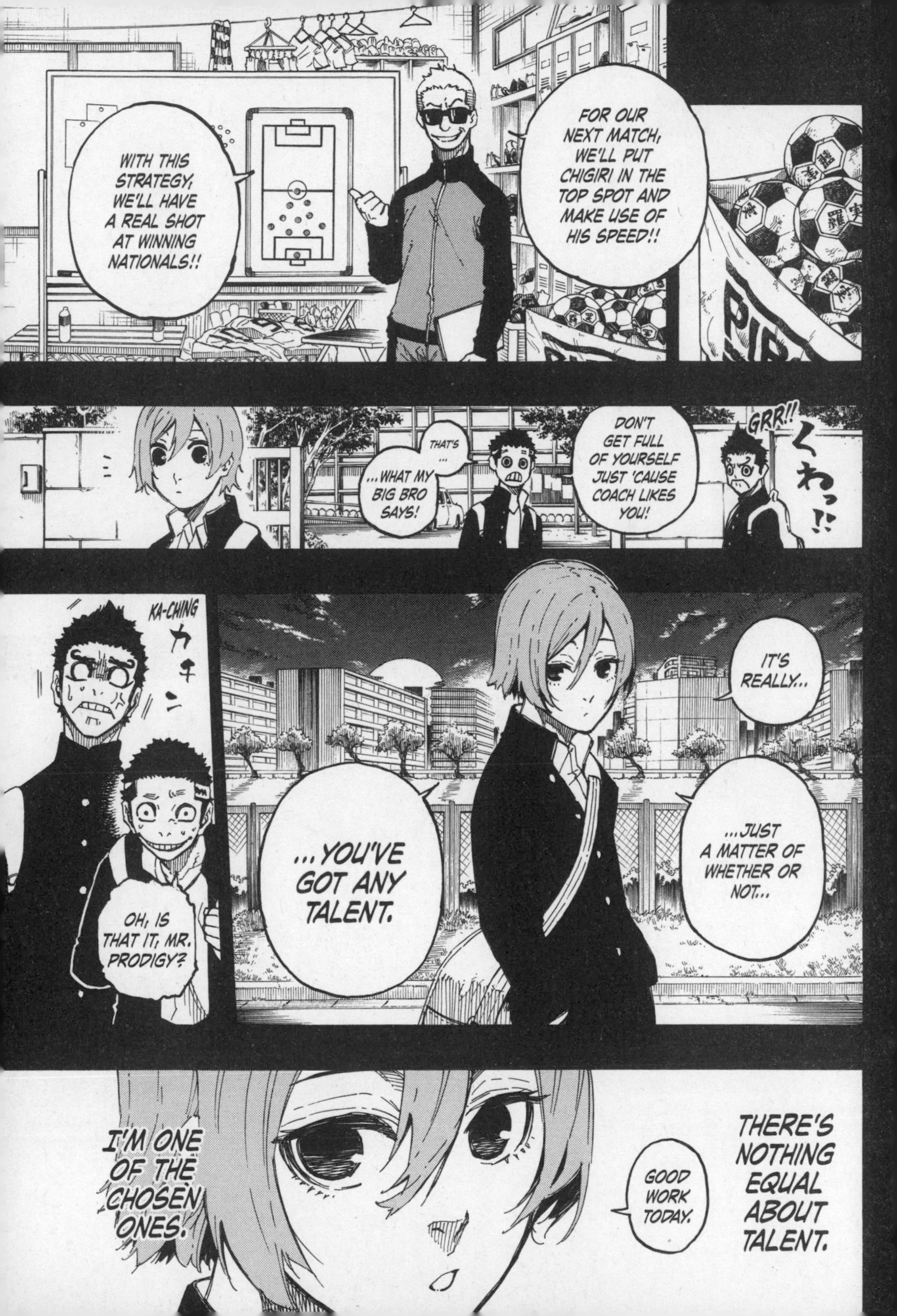
FOR OUR NEXT MATCH, WE'LL PUT CHIGIRI IN THE TOP SPOT AND MAKE USE OF HIS SPEED!!
WITH THIS STRATEGY, WE'LL HAVE A REAL SHOT AT WINNING NATIONALS!!
GRR!!
くわっ!!
DON'T GET FULL OF YOURSELF JUST 'CAUSE COACH LIKES YOU!
THAT'S...
...WHAT MY BIG BRO SAYS!
IT'S REALLY...
...JUST A MATTER OF WHETHER OR NOT...
...YOU'VE GOT ANY TALENT.
KA-CHING
カチン
OH, IS THAT IT, MR. PRODIGY?
THERE'S NOTHING EQUAL ABOUT TALENT.
GOOD WORK TODAY.
I'M ONE OF THE CHOSEN ONES.

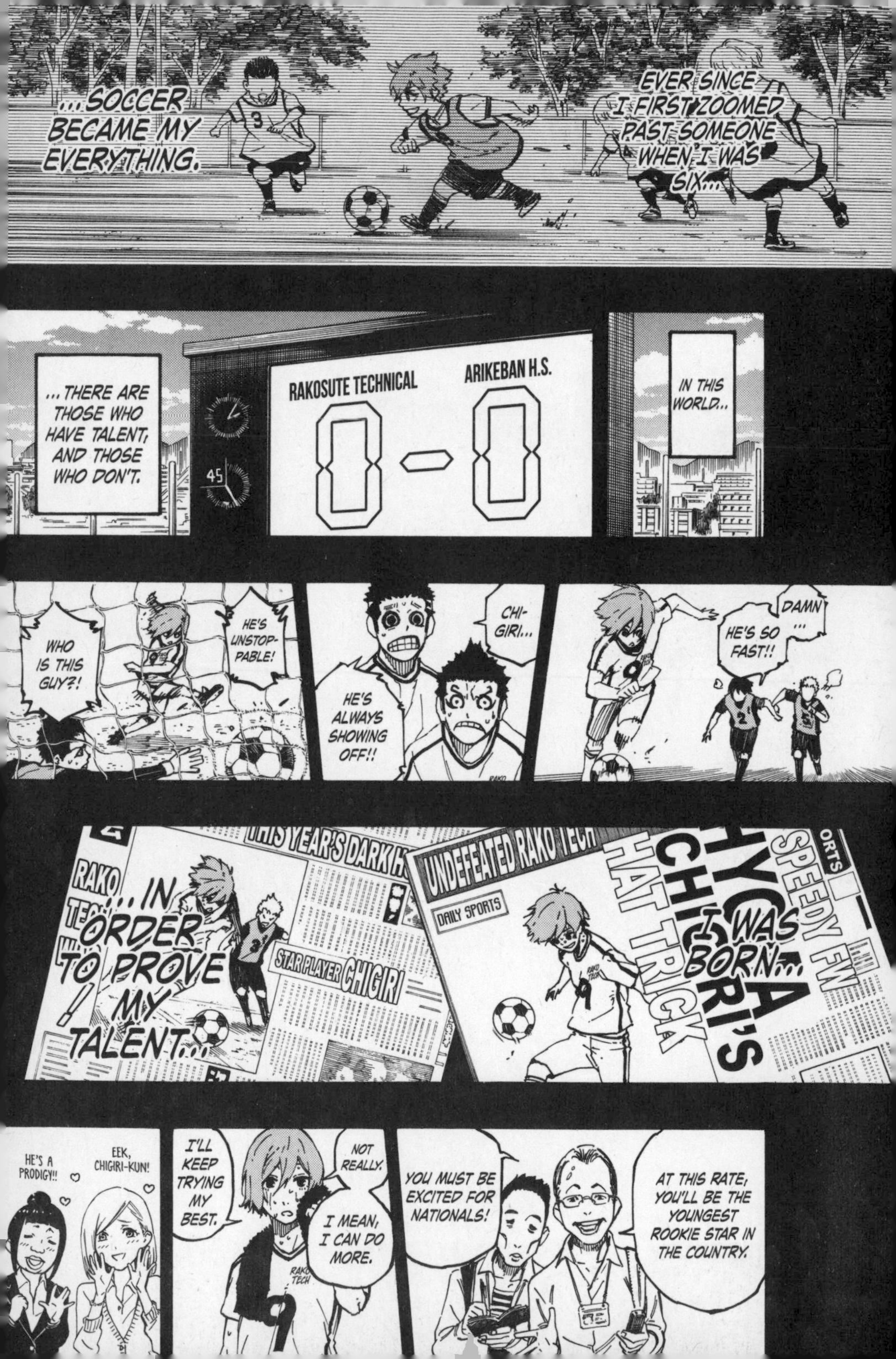
EVER SINCE I FIRST ZOOMED PAST SOMEONE WHEN I WAS SIX...
...SOCCER BECAME MY EVERYTHING.
IN THIS WORLD...
RAKOSUTE TECHNICAL
ARIKEBAN H.S.
0-0
45
...THERE ARE THOSE WHO HAVE TALENT, AND THOSE WHO DON'T.
DAMN...
HE'S SO FAST!!
CHI-GIRI...
HE'S ALWAYS SHOWING OFF!!
HE'S UNSTOPPABLE!
WHO IS THIS GUY?!
SPEEDY FW
HAT TRICK
UNDEFEATED RAKO TECH
DAILY SPORTS
I WAS BORN...
STAR PLAYER CHIGIRI
...IN ORDER TO PROVE MY TALENT...
AT THIS RATE, YOU'LL BE THE YOUNGEST ROOKIE STAR IN THE COUNTRY.
YOU MUST BE EXCITED FOR NATIONALS!
NOT REALLY.
I MEAN, I CAN DO MORE.
I'LL KEEP TRYING MY BEST.
EEK, CHIGIRI-KUN!
HE'S A PRODIGY!!

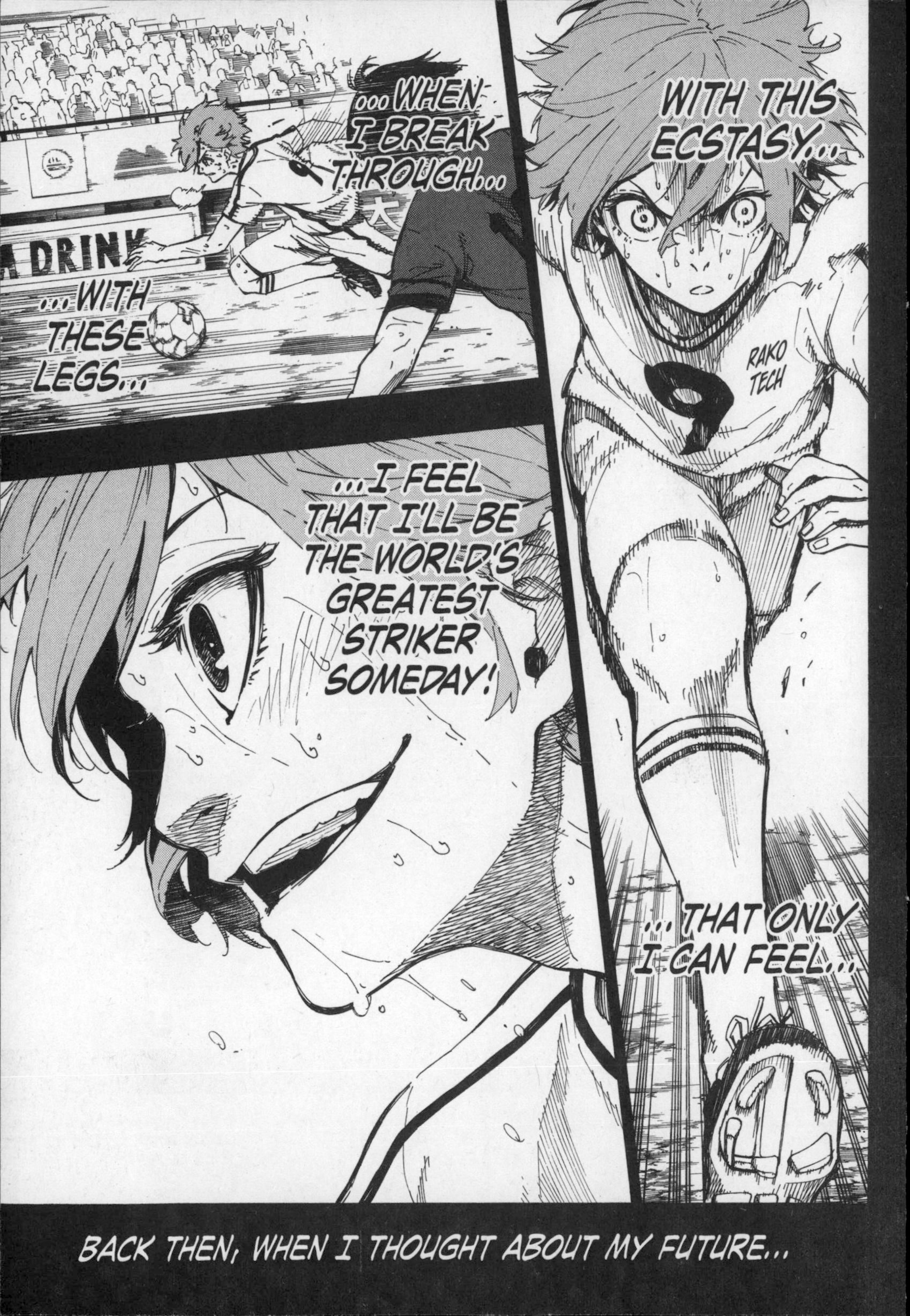
WITH THIS ECSTASY...
RAKO TECH
...THAT ONLY I CAN FEEL...
...WHEN I BREAK THROUGH...
A DRINK
...WITH THESE LEGS...
...I FEEL THAT I'LL BE THE WORLD'S GREATEST STRIKER SOMEDAY!
BACK THEN, WHEN I THOUGHT ABOUT MY FUTURE...

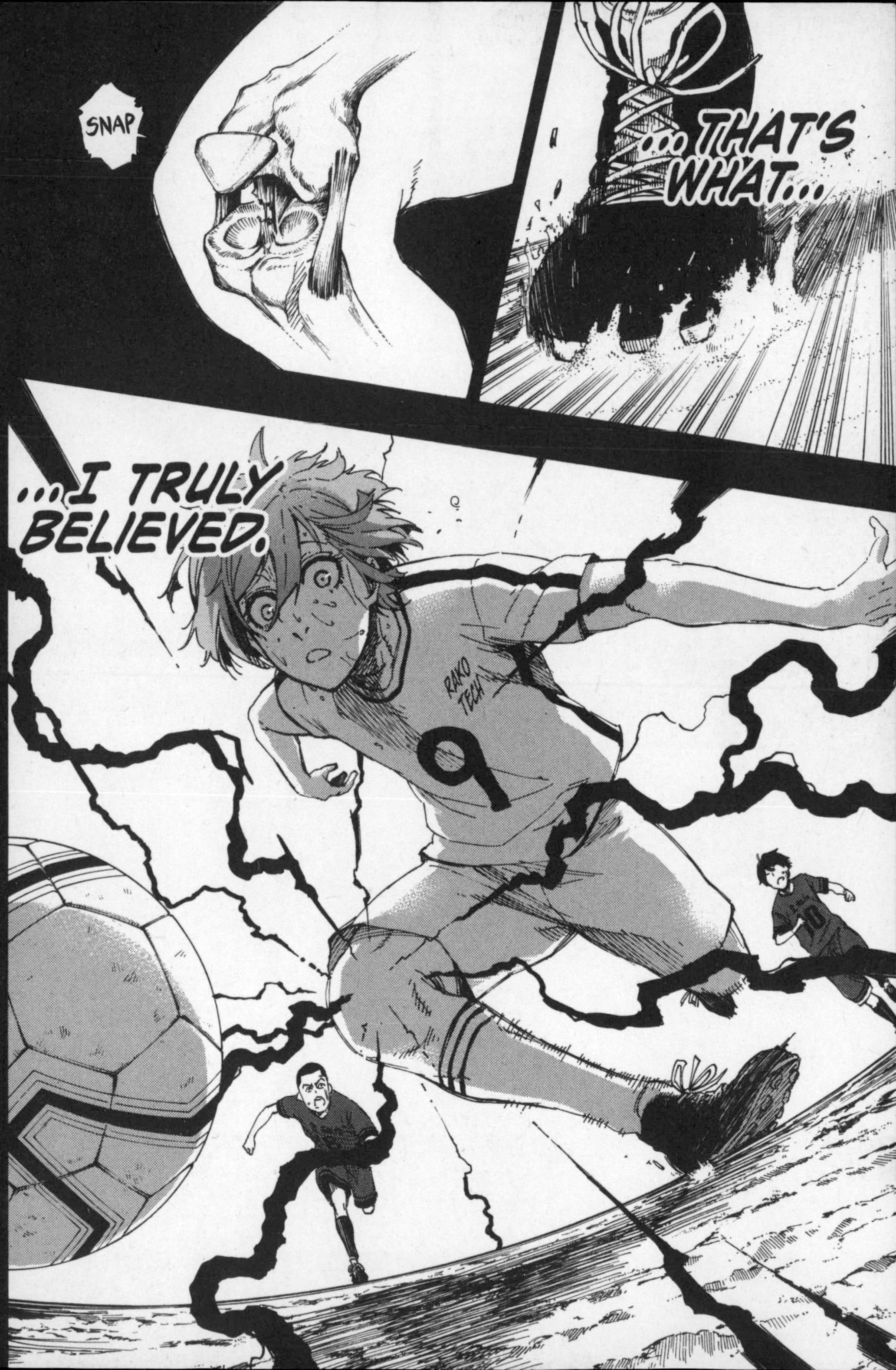
...THAT'S WHAT...
SNAP
...I TRULY BELIEVED.
RAKO TECH
9

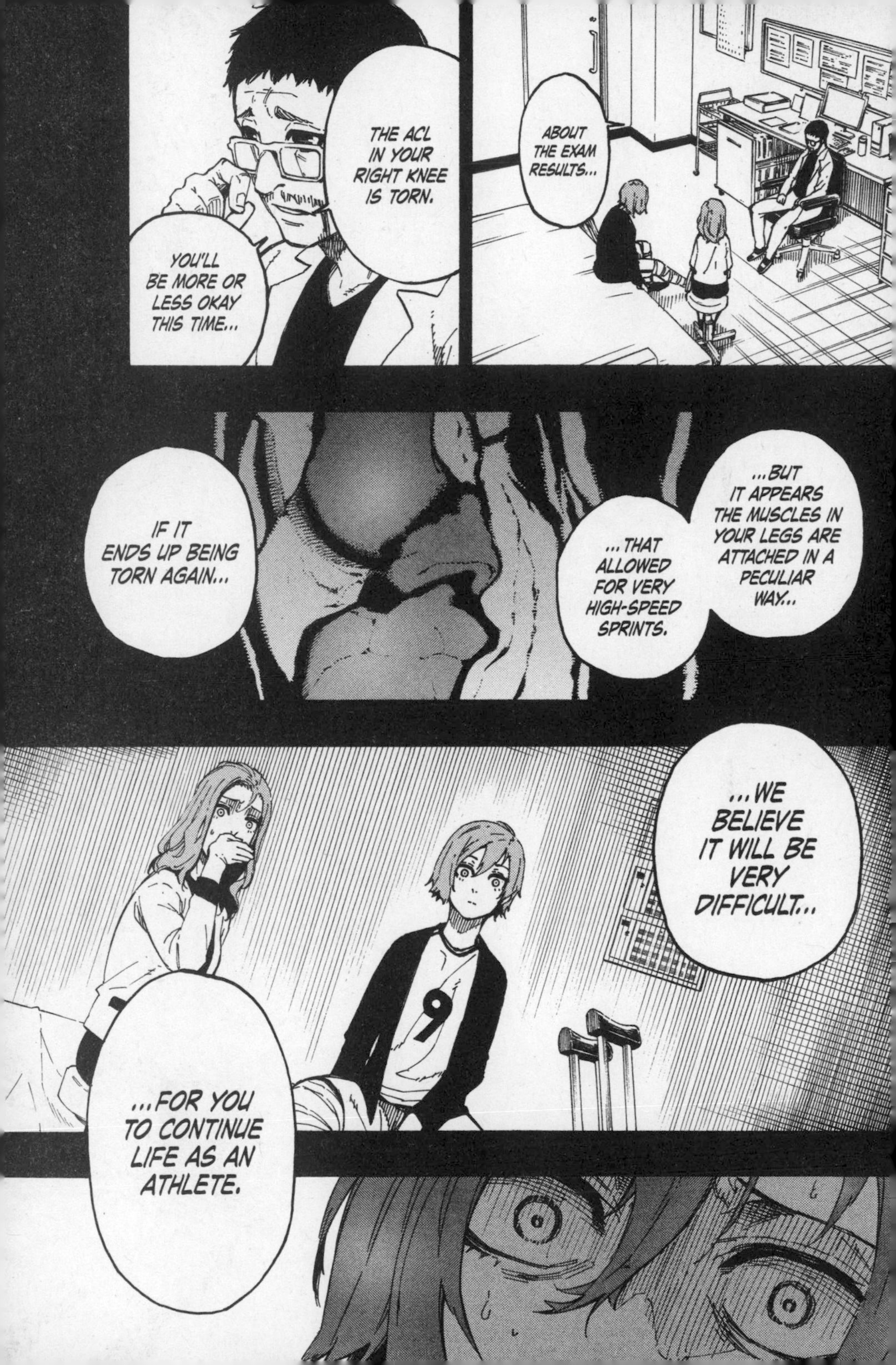
ABOUT THE EXAM RESULTS...
THE ACL IN YOUR RIGHT KNEE IS TORN.
YOU'LL BE MORE OR LESS OKAY THIS TIME...
...BUT IT APPEARS THE MUSCLES IN YOUR LEGS ARE ATTACHED IN A PECULIAR WAY...
...THAT ALLOWED FOR VERY HIGH-SPEED SPRINTS.
IF IT ENDS UP BEING TORN AGAIN...
...WE BELIEVE IT WILL BE VERY DIFFICULT...
...FOR YOU TO CONTINUE LIFE AS AN ATHLETE.

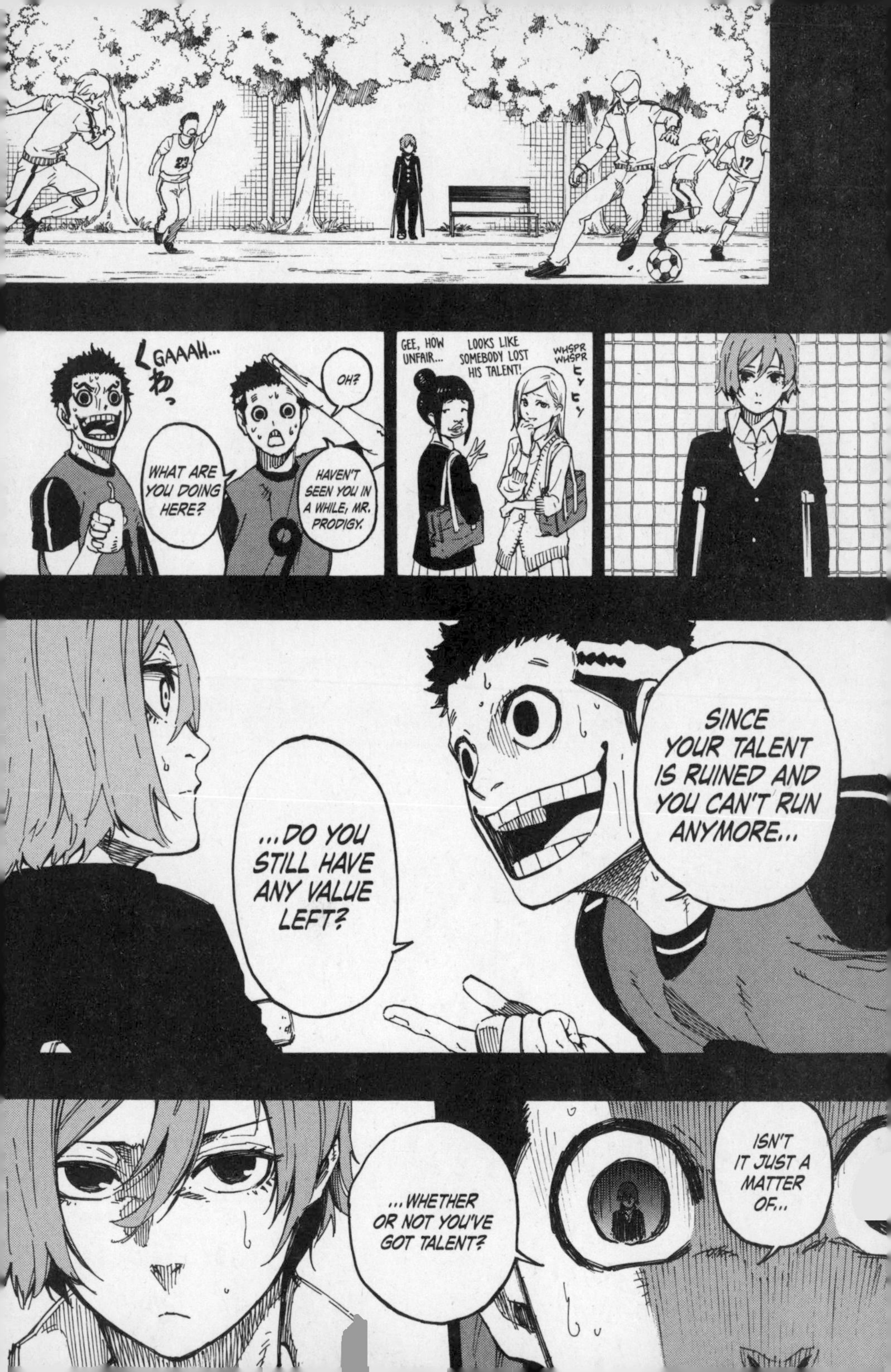
WHSPR WHSPR ヒソヒソ
LOOKS LIKE SOMEBODY LOST HIS TALENT!
GEE, HOW UNFAIR...
OH?
HAVEN'T SEEN YOU IN A WHILE, MR. PRODIGY.
GAAAH... わっ
WHAT ARE YOU DOING HERE?
SINCE YOUR TALENT IS RUINED AND YOU CAN'T RUN ANYMORE...
...DO YOU STILL HAVE ANY VALUE LEFT?
ISN'T IT JUST A MATTER OF...
...WHETHER OR NOT YOU'VE GOT TALENT?

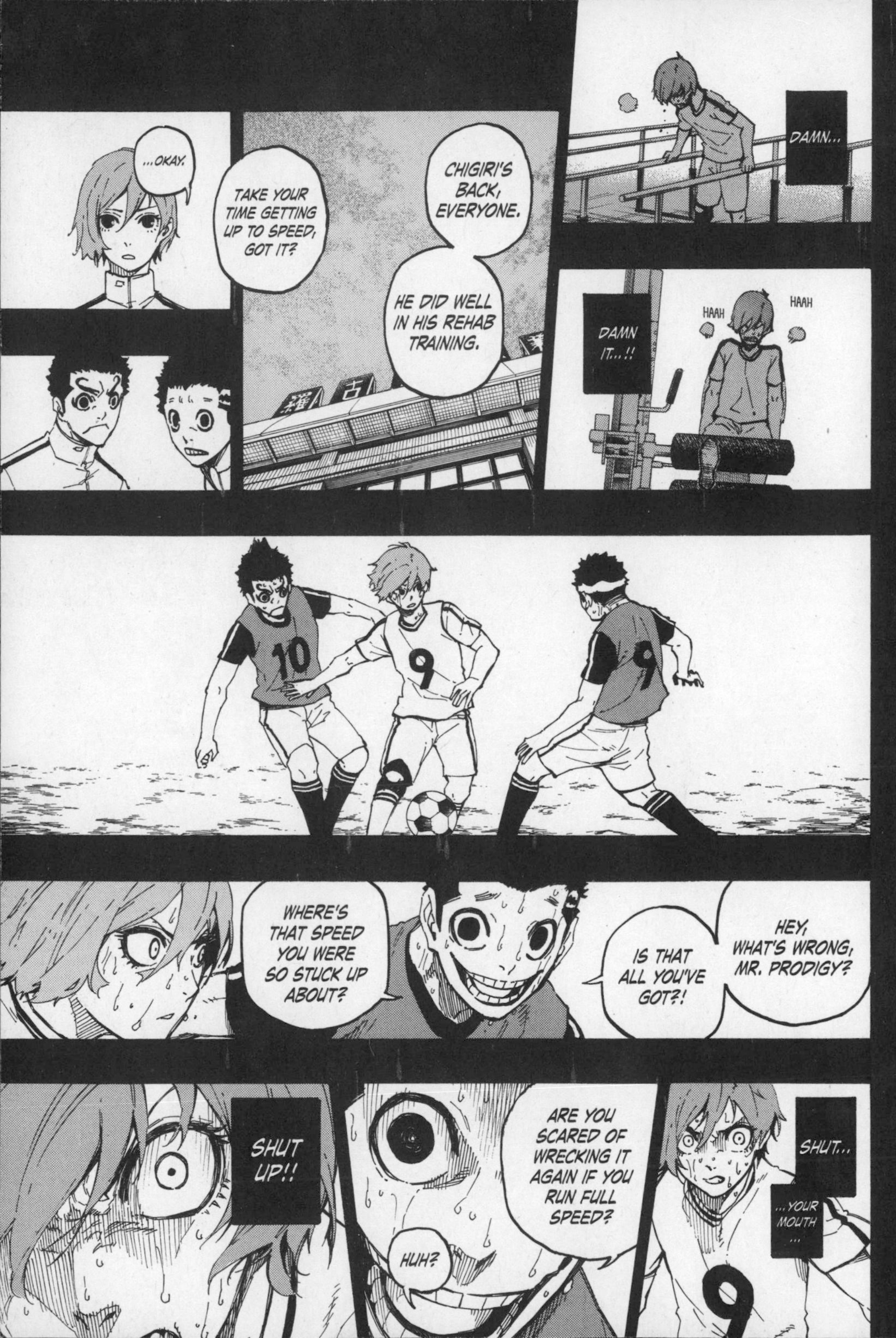
DAMN...
HAAH
HAAH
DAMN IT...!!
CHIGIRI'S BACK, EVERYONE.
HE DID WELL IN HIS REHAB TRAINING.
TAKE YOUR TIME GETTING UP TO SPEED, GOT IT?
...OKAY.
HEY, WHAT'S WRONG, MR. PRODIGY?
IS THAT ALL YOU'VE GOT?!
WHERE'S THAT SPEED YOU WERE SO STUCK UP ABOUT?
SHUT...
...YOUR MOUTH...
ARE YOU SCARED OF WRECKING IT AGAIN IF YOU RUN FULL SPEED?
HUH?
SHUT UP!!

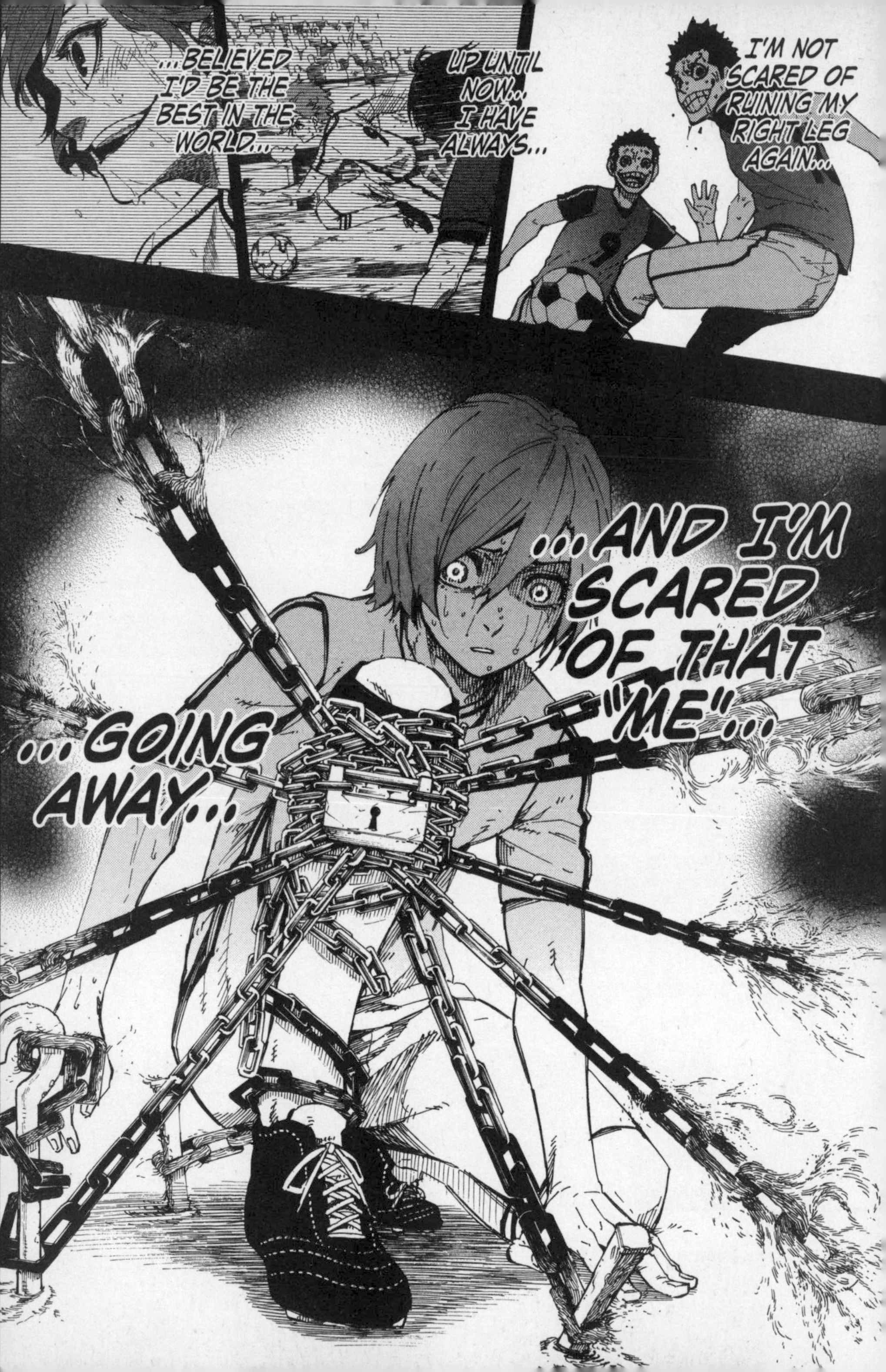
I'M NOT SCARED OF RUINING MY RIGHT LEG AGAIN..
UP UNTIL NOW.. I HAVE ALWAYS...
...BELIEVED I'D BE THE BEST IN THE WORLD...
...AND I'M SCARED OF THAT "ME"...
...GOING AWAY...

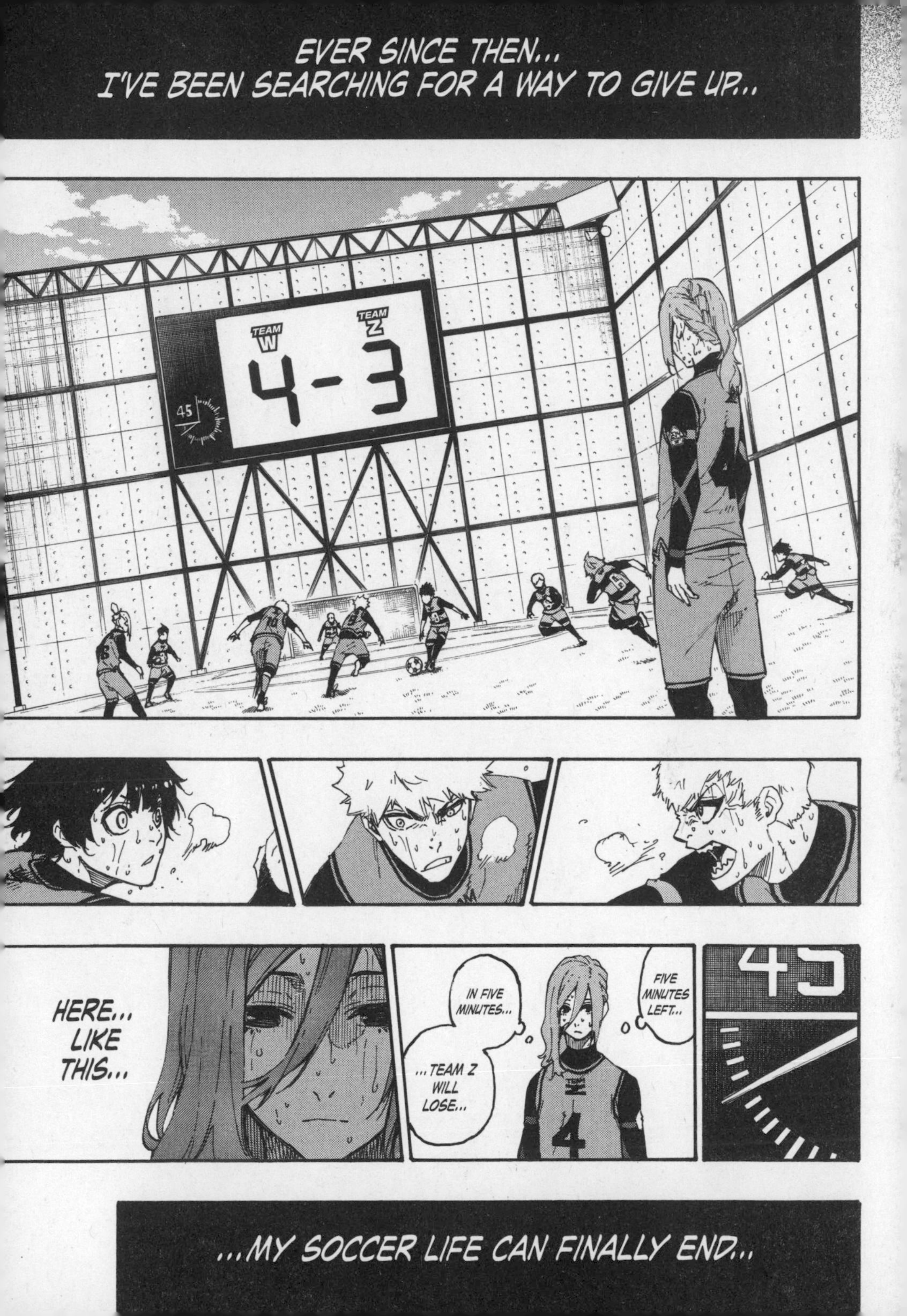
EVER SINCE THEN... I'VE BEEN SEARCHING FOR A WAY TO GIVE UP...
TEAM W
TEAM Z
4-3
45
45
FIVE MINUTES LEFT...
IN FIVE MINUTES...
...TEAM Z WILL LOSE...
HERE... LIKE THIS...
...MY SOCCER LIFE CAN FINALLY END...

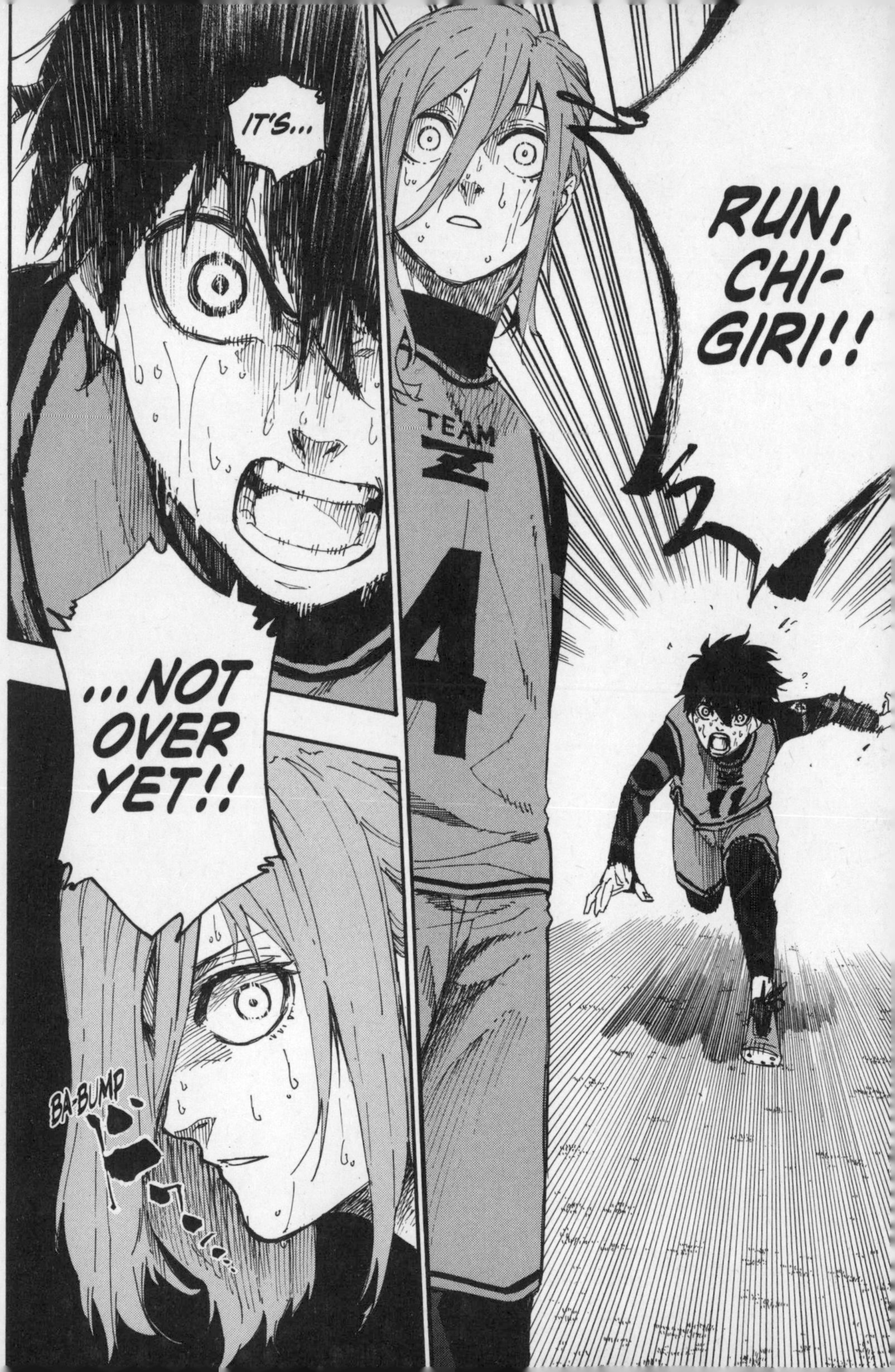
RUN, CHI-GIRI!!
IT'S...
...NOT OVER YET!!
BA-BUMP

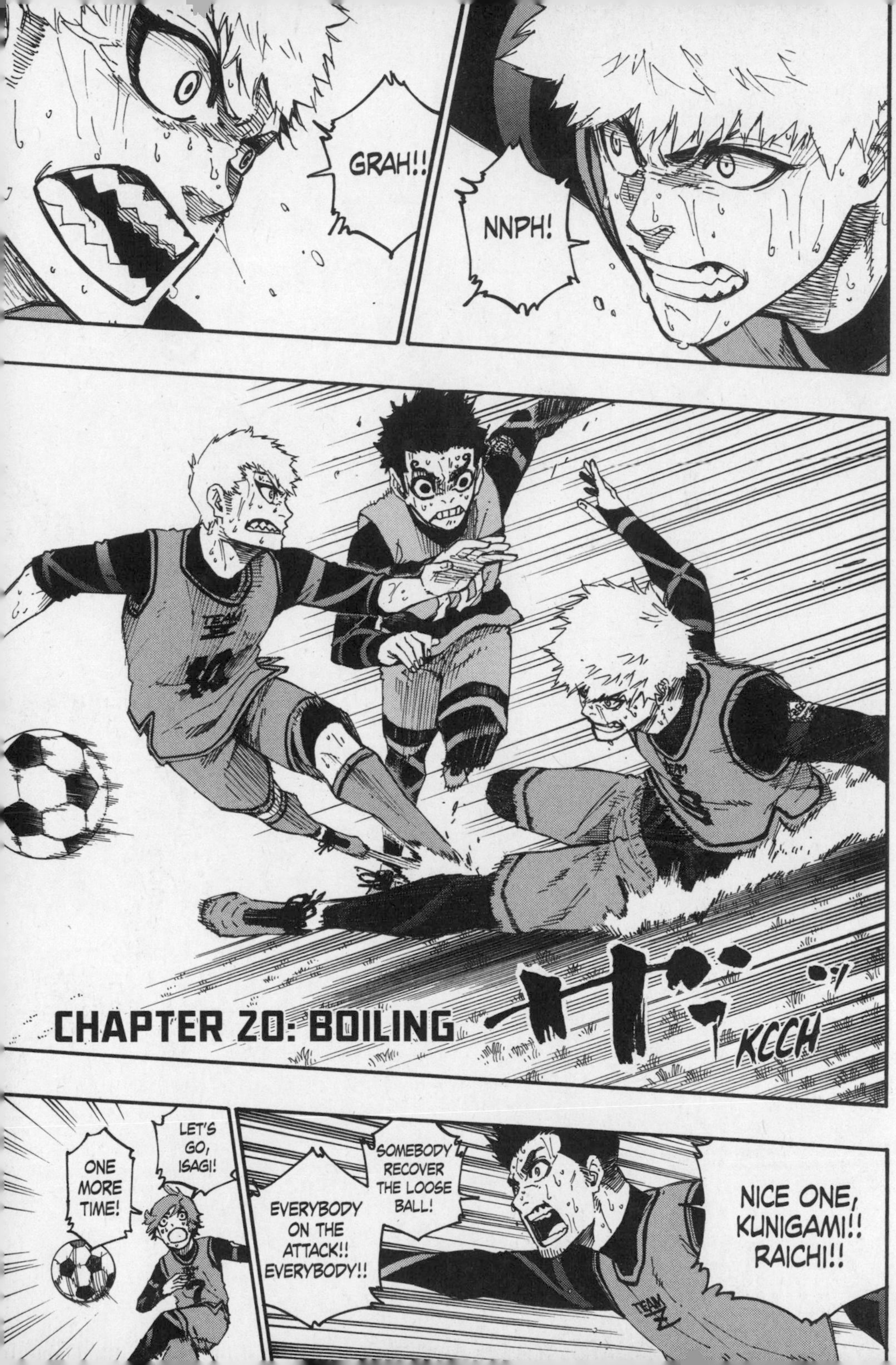
NNPH!
GRAH!!
CHAPTER 20: BOILING
KCCH
NICE ONE, KUNIGAMI!! RAICHI!!
SOMEBODY RECOVER THE LOOSE BALL!
EVERYBODY ON THE ATTACK!! EVERYBODY!!
LET'S GO, ISAGI!
ONE MORE TIME!

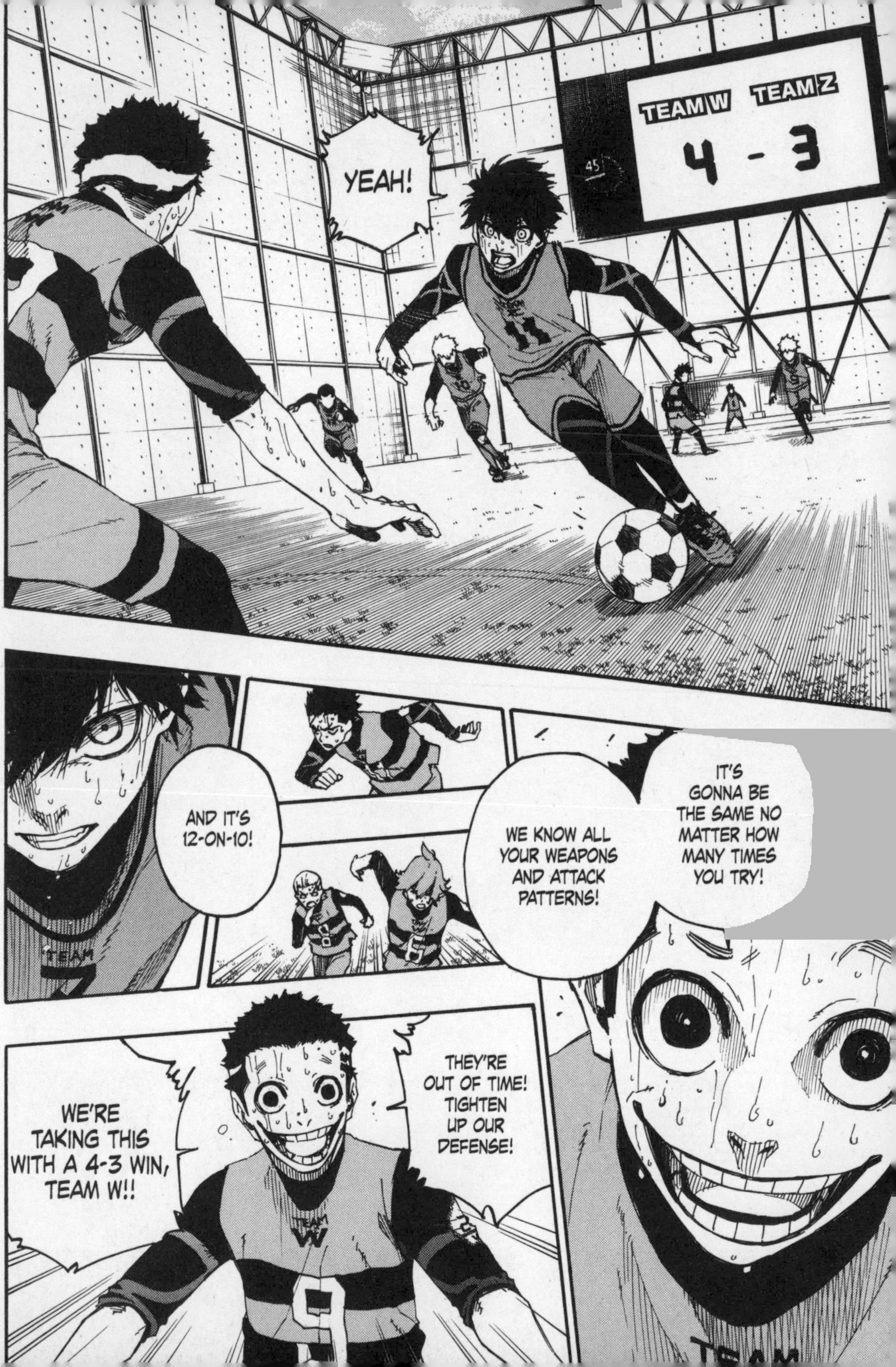
TEAM W TEAM Z
4 - 3
YEAH!
IT'S GONNA BE THE SAME NO MATTER HOW MANY TIMES YOU TRY!
WE KNOW ALL YOUR WEAPONS AND ATTACK PATTERNS!
AND IT'S 12-ON-10!
THEY'RE OUT OF TIME! TIGHTEN UP OUR DEFENSE!
WE'RE TAKING THIS WITH A 4-3 WIN, TEAM W!!

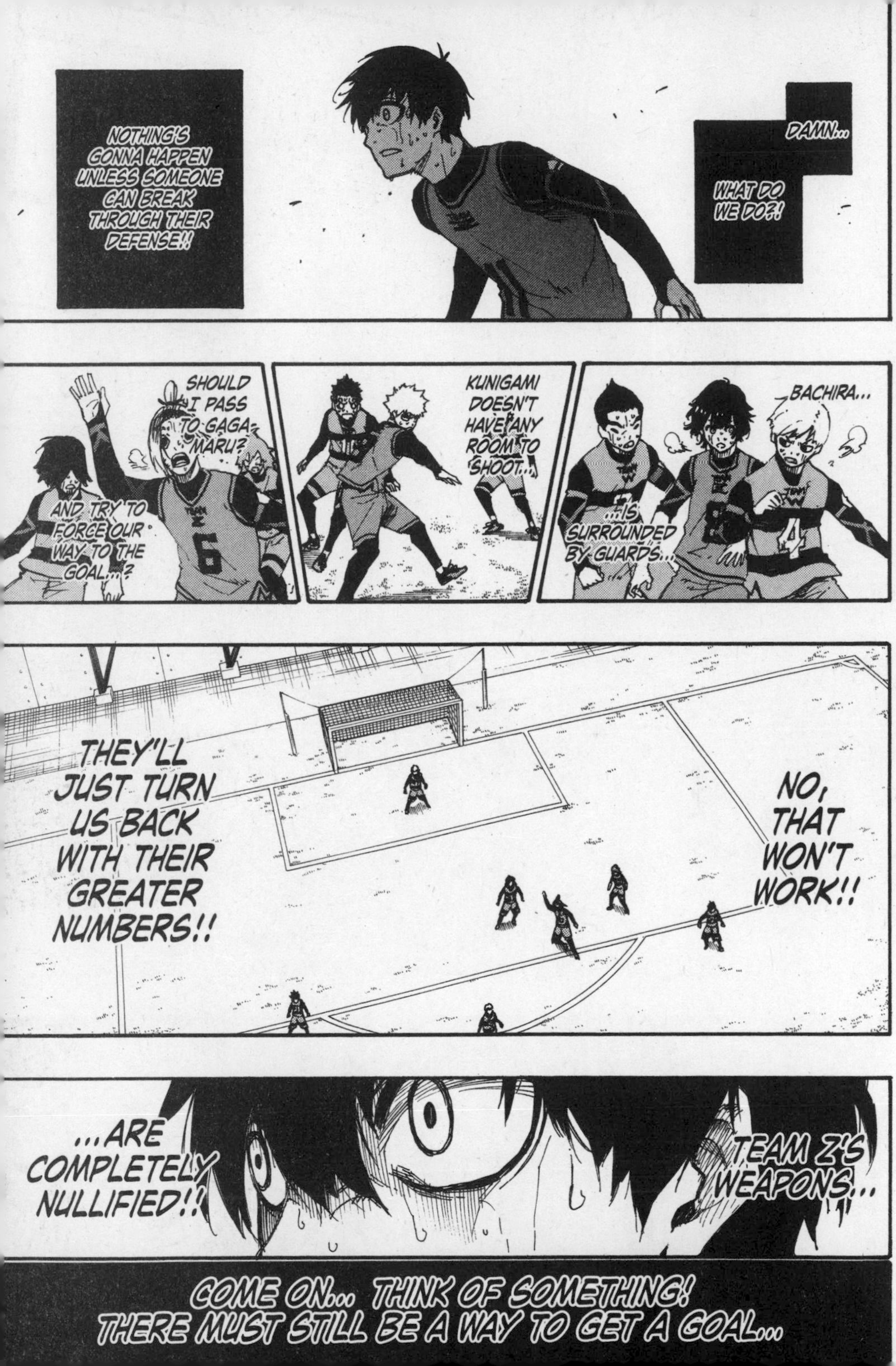
DAMN...
WHAT DO WE DO?!
NOTHING'S GONNA HAPPEN UNLESS SOMEONE CAN BREAK THROUGH THEIR DEFENSE!!
BACHIRA...
...IS SURROUNDED BY GUARDS...
KUNIGAMI DOESN'T HAVE ANY ROOM TO SHOOT...
SHOULD I PASS TO GAGAMARU?
AND TRY TO FORCE OUR WAY TO THE GOAL...?
NO, THAT WON'T WORK!!
THEY'LL JUST TURN US BACK WITH THEIR GREATER NUMBERS!!
TEAM Z'S WEAPONS...
...ARE COMPLETELY NULLIFIED!!
COME ON... THINK OF SOMETHING!
THERE MUST STILL BE A WAY TO GET A GOAL...

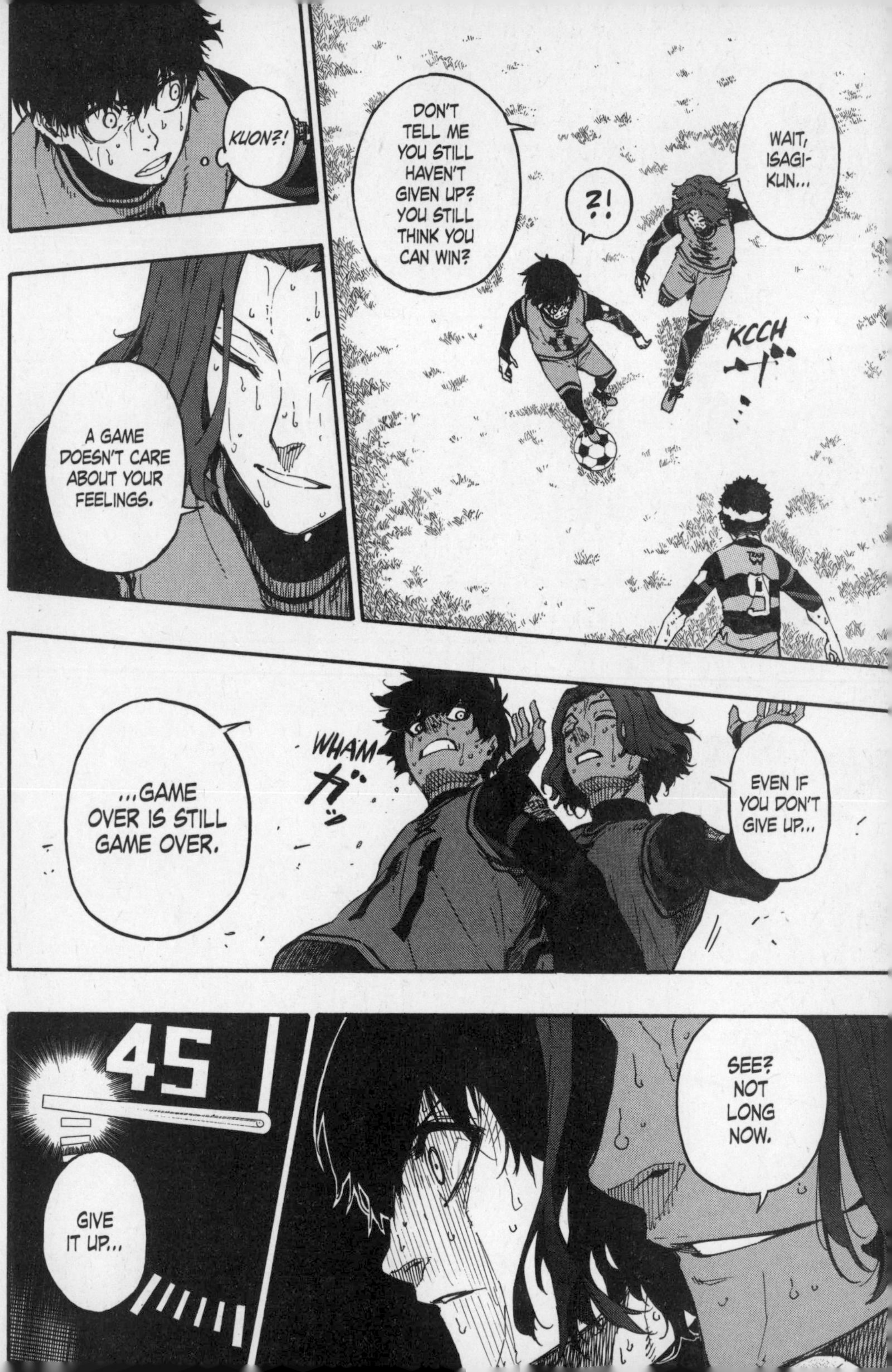
WAIT, ISAGI-KUN...
?!
DON'T TELL ME YOU STILL HAVEN'T GIVEN UP? YOU STILL THINK YOU CAN WIN?
KCCH
KUON?!
A GAME DOESN'T CARE ABOUT YOUR FEELINGS.
EVEN IF YOU DON'T GIVE UP...
WHAM
ガッ
...GAME OVER IS STILL GAME OVER.
SEE? NOT LONG NOW.
45
GIVE IT UP...

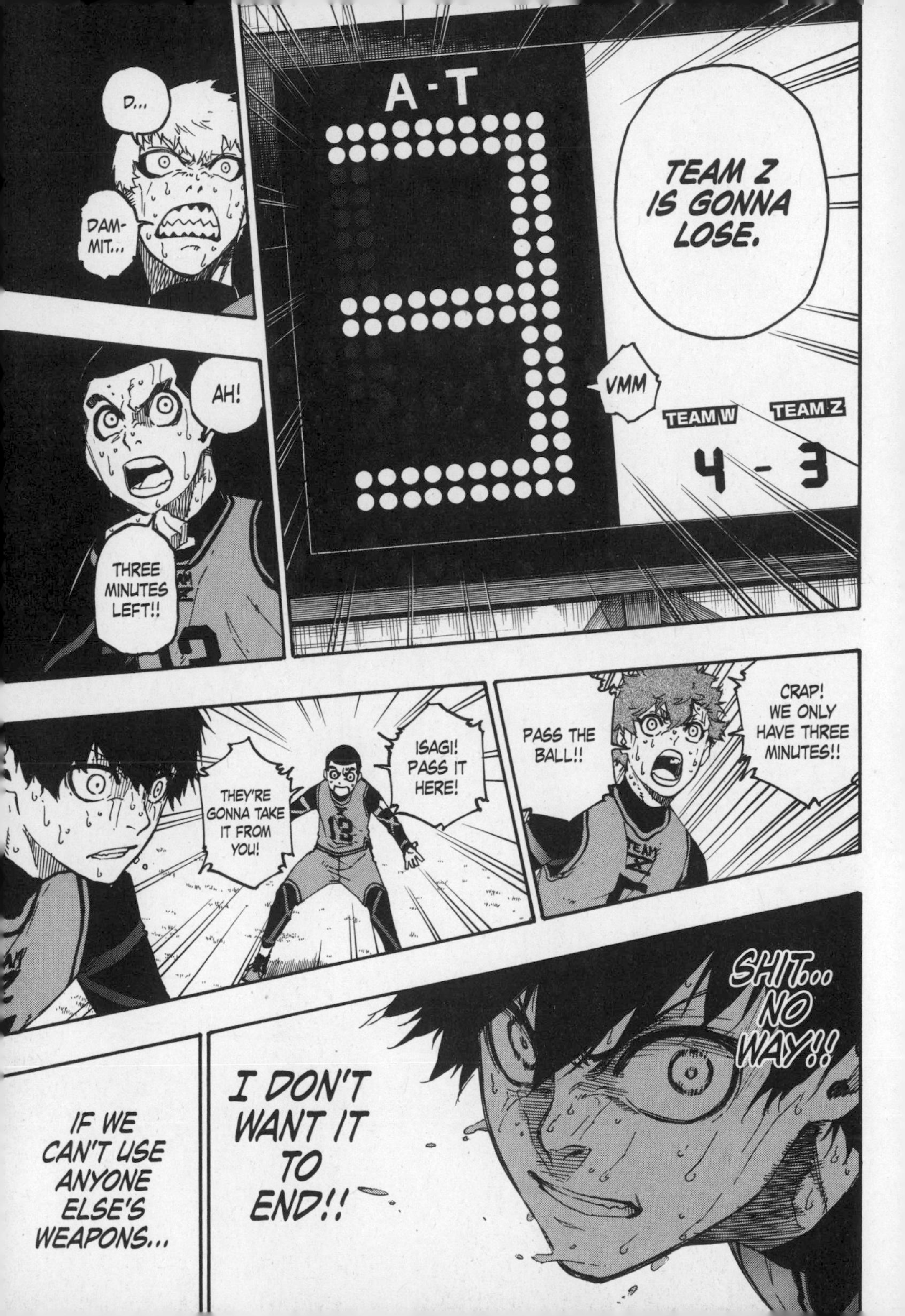
TEAM Z IS GONNA LOSE.
A-T
VMM
TEAM W
TEAM Z
4 - 3
D...
DAM-MIT...
AH!
THREE MINUTES LEFT!!
CRAP! WE ONLY HAVE THREE MINUTES!!
PASS THE BALL!!
ISAGI! PASS IT HERE!
THEY'RE GONNA TAKE IT FROM YOU!
SHIT... NO WAY!!
I DON'T WANT IT TO END!!
IF WE CAN'T USE ANYONE ELSE'S WEAPONS...

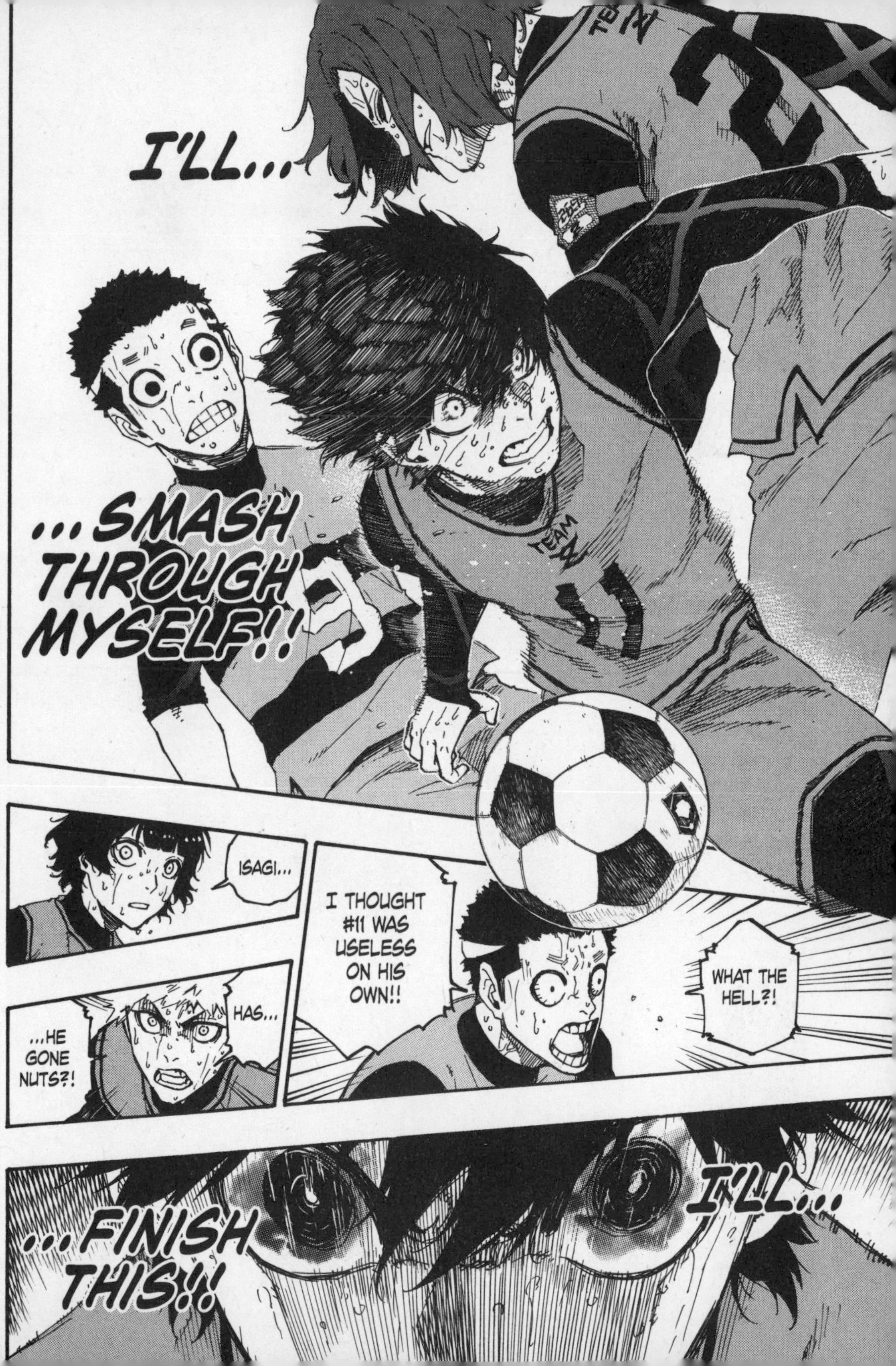
I'LL...
...SMASH THROUGH MYSELF!!
WHAT THE HELL?!
I THOUGHT #11 WAS USELESS ON HIS OWN!!
ISAGI...
HAS...
...HE GONE NUTS?!
I'LL...
...FINISH THIS!!

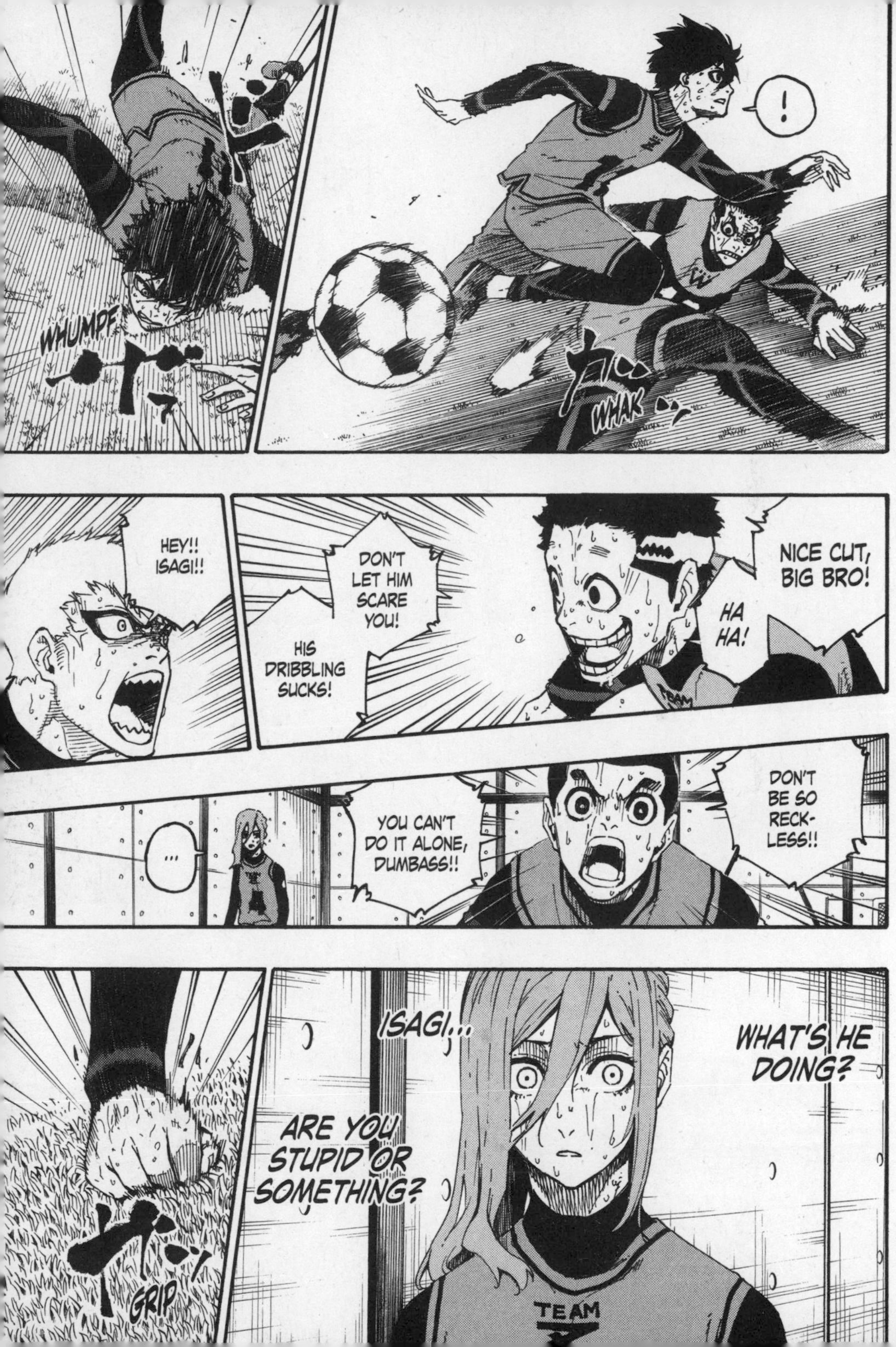
!
WHAK
WHUMPF
NICE CUT, BIG BRO!
HA HA!
DON'T LET HIM SCARE YOU!
HIS DRIBBLING SUCKS!
HEY!! ISAGI!!
DON'T BE SO RECK-LESS!!
YOU CAN'T DO IT ALONE, DUMBASS!!
...
WHAT'S HE DOING?
ISAGI...
ARE YOU STUPID OR SOMETHING?
GRIP

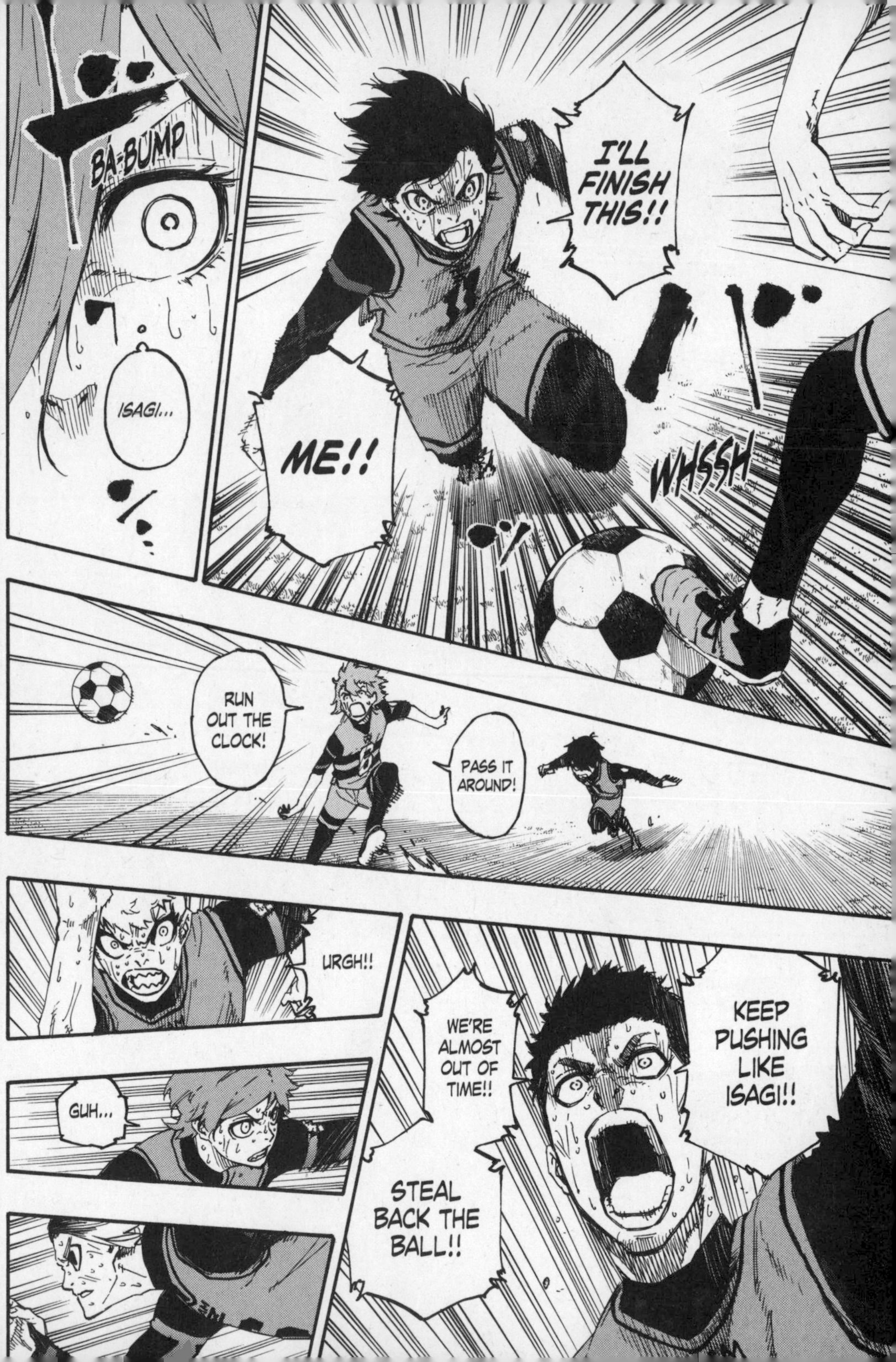
I'LL FINISH THIS!!
ME!!
WHSSH
BA-BUMP
ISAGI...
PASS IT AROUND!
RUN OUT THE CLOCK!
KEEP PUSHING LIKE ISAGI!!
WE'RE ALMOST OUT OF TIME!!
STEAL BACK THE BALL!!
URGH!!
GUH...

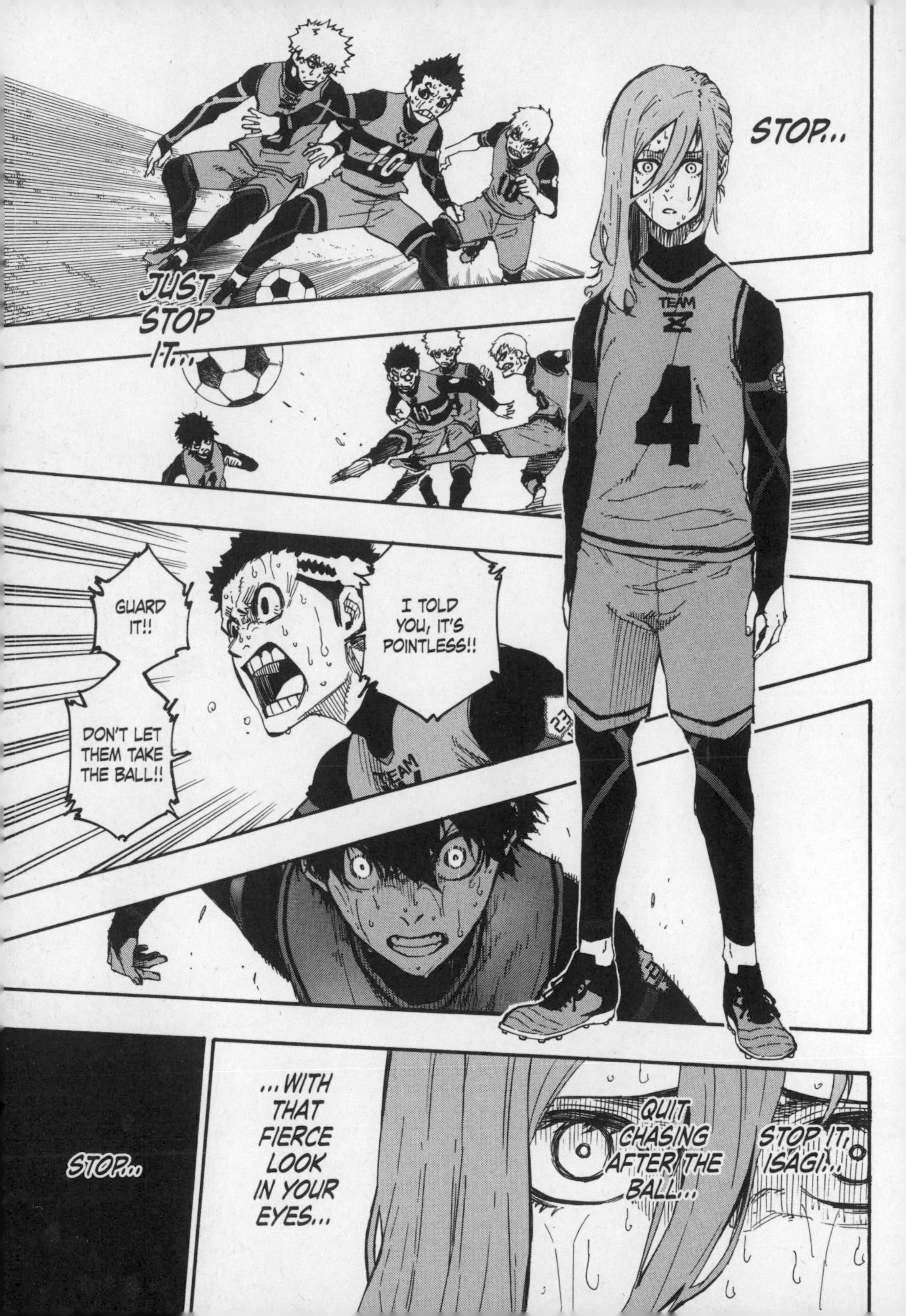
STOP...
JUST STOP IT...
I TOLD YOU, IT'S POINTLESS!!
GUARD IT!!
DON'T LET THEM TAKE THE BALL!!
STOP IT, ISAGI...
QUIT CHASING AFTER THE BALL...
...WITH THAT FIERCE LOOK IN YOUR EYES...
STOP...

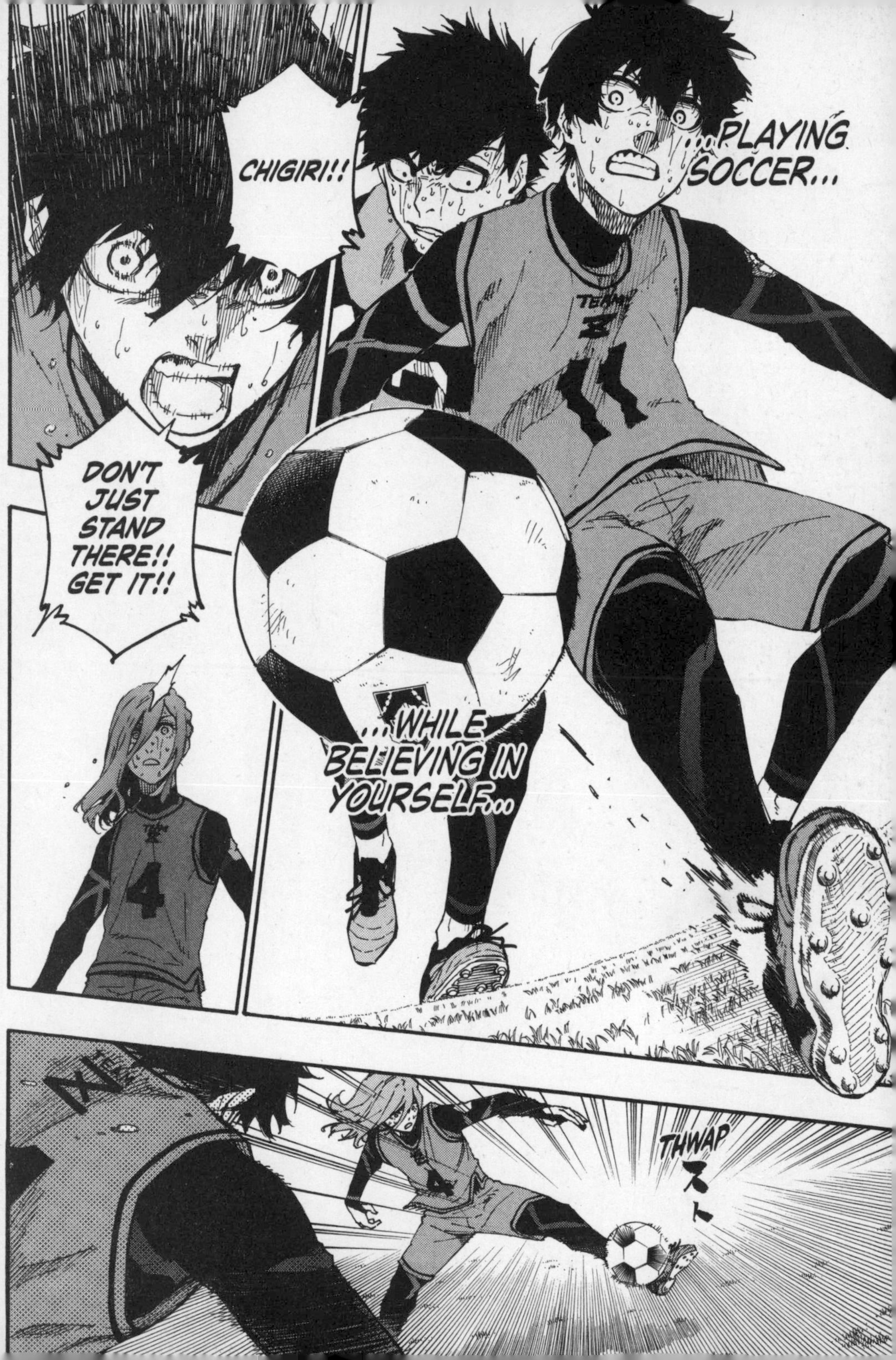
...PLAYING SOCCER...
...WHILE BELIEVING IN YOURSELF...
CHIGIRI!!
DON'T JUST STAND THERE!! GET IT!!
THWAP

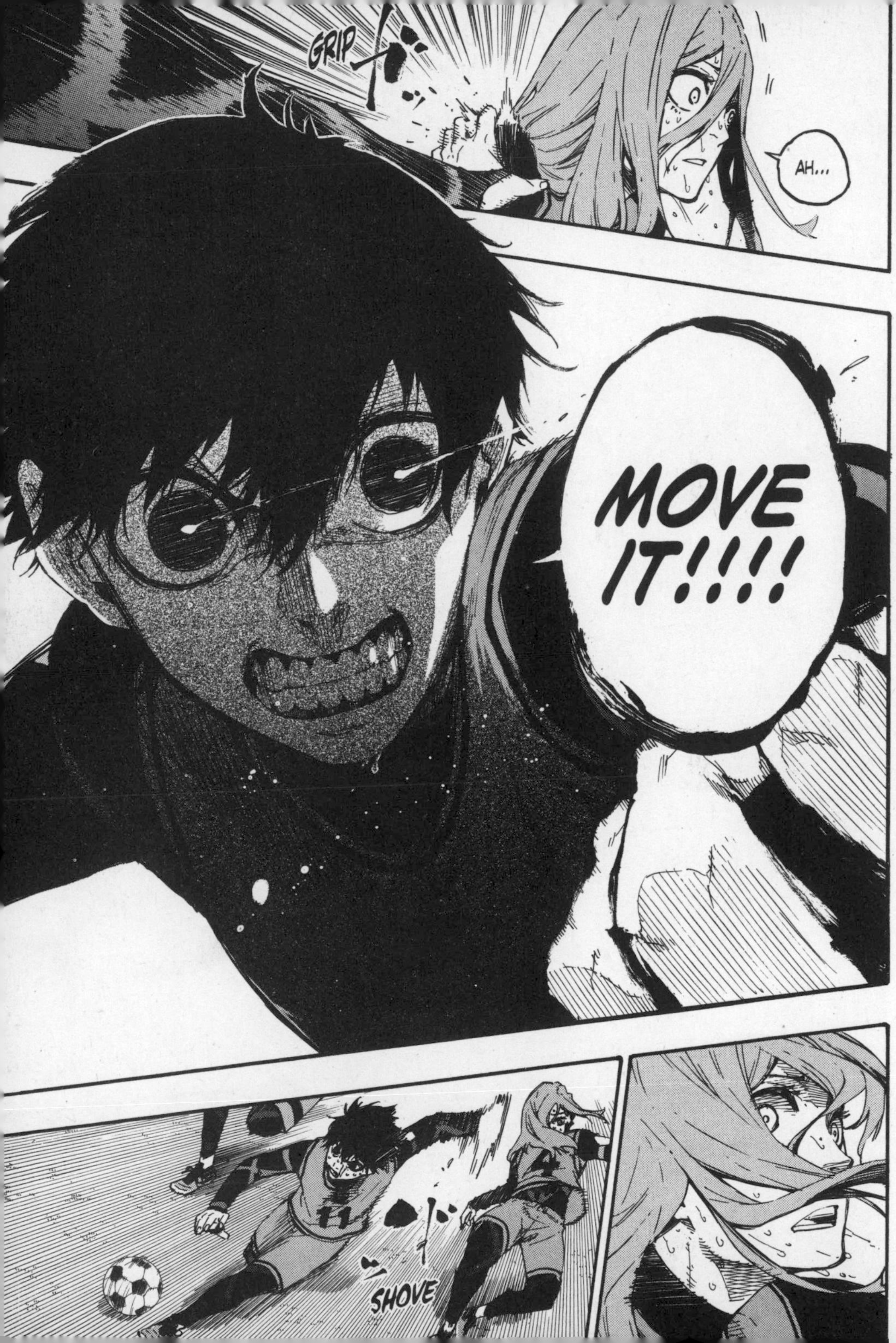
AH...
GRIP
MOVE IT!!!!
SHOVE

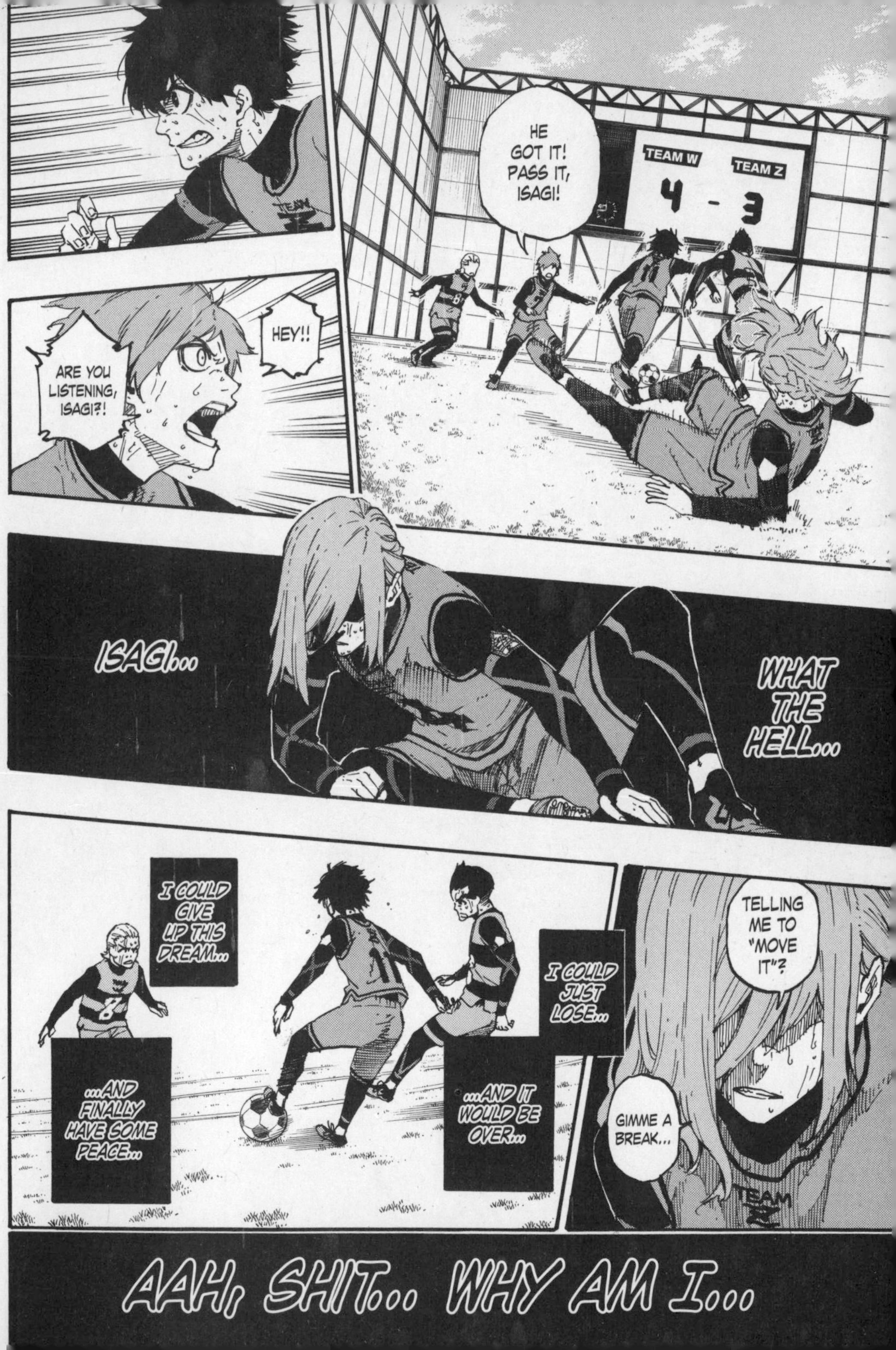
HE GOT IT! PASS IT, ISAGI!
TEAM W
TEAM Z
4 - 3
HEY!!
ARE YOU LISTENING, ISAGI?!
WHAT THE HELL...
ISAGI...
TELLING ME TO "MOVE IT"?
GIMME A BREAK...
TEAM Z
I COULD JUST LOSE...
...AND IT WOULD BE OVER...
I COULD GIVE UP THIS DREAM...
...AND FINALLY HAVE SOME PEACE...
AAH, SHIT... WHY AM I...

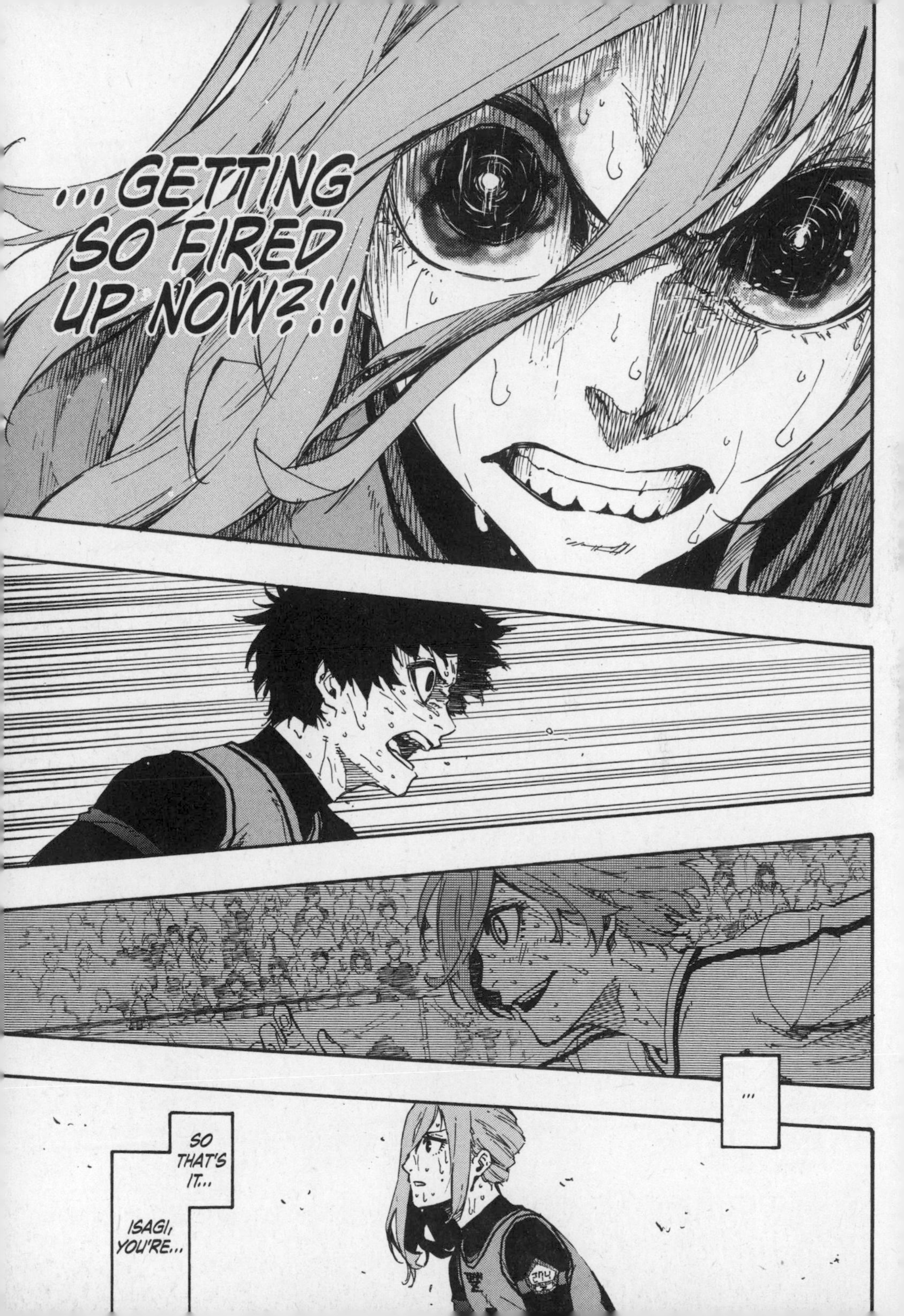
...GETTING SO FIRED UP NOW?!!
...
SO THAT'S IT...
ISAGI, YOU'RE...

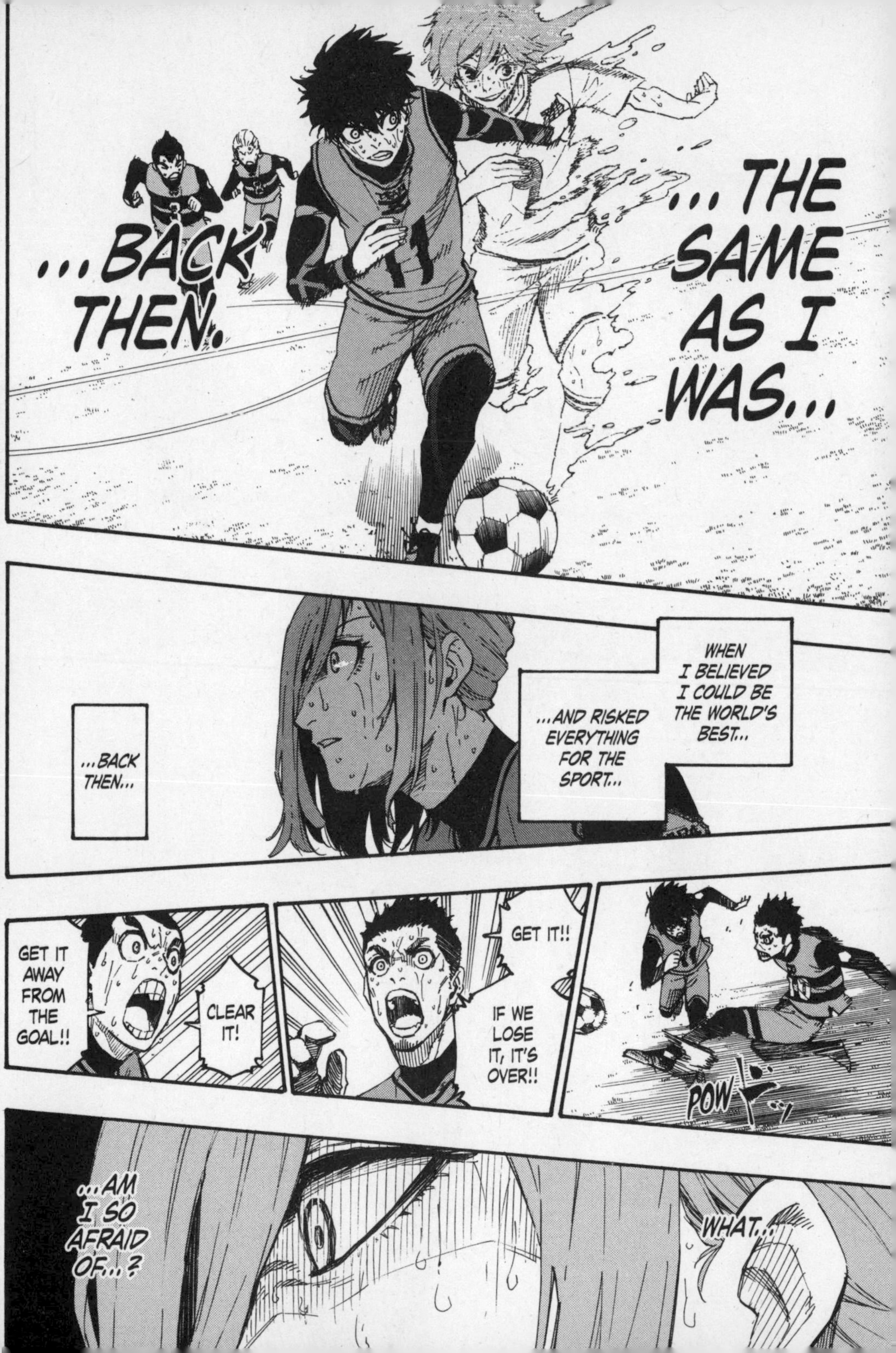
...THE SAME AS I WAS...
...BACK THEN.
WHEN I BELIEVED I COULD BE THE WORLD'S BEST...
...AND RISKED EVERYTHING FOR THE SPORT...
...BACK THEN...
POW
GET IT!!
IF WE LOSE IT, IT'S OVER!!
CLEAR IT!
GET IT AWAY FROM THE GOAL!!
WHAT...
...AM I SO AFRAID OF...?

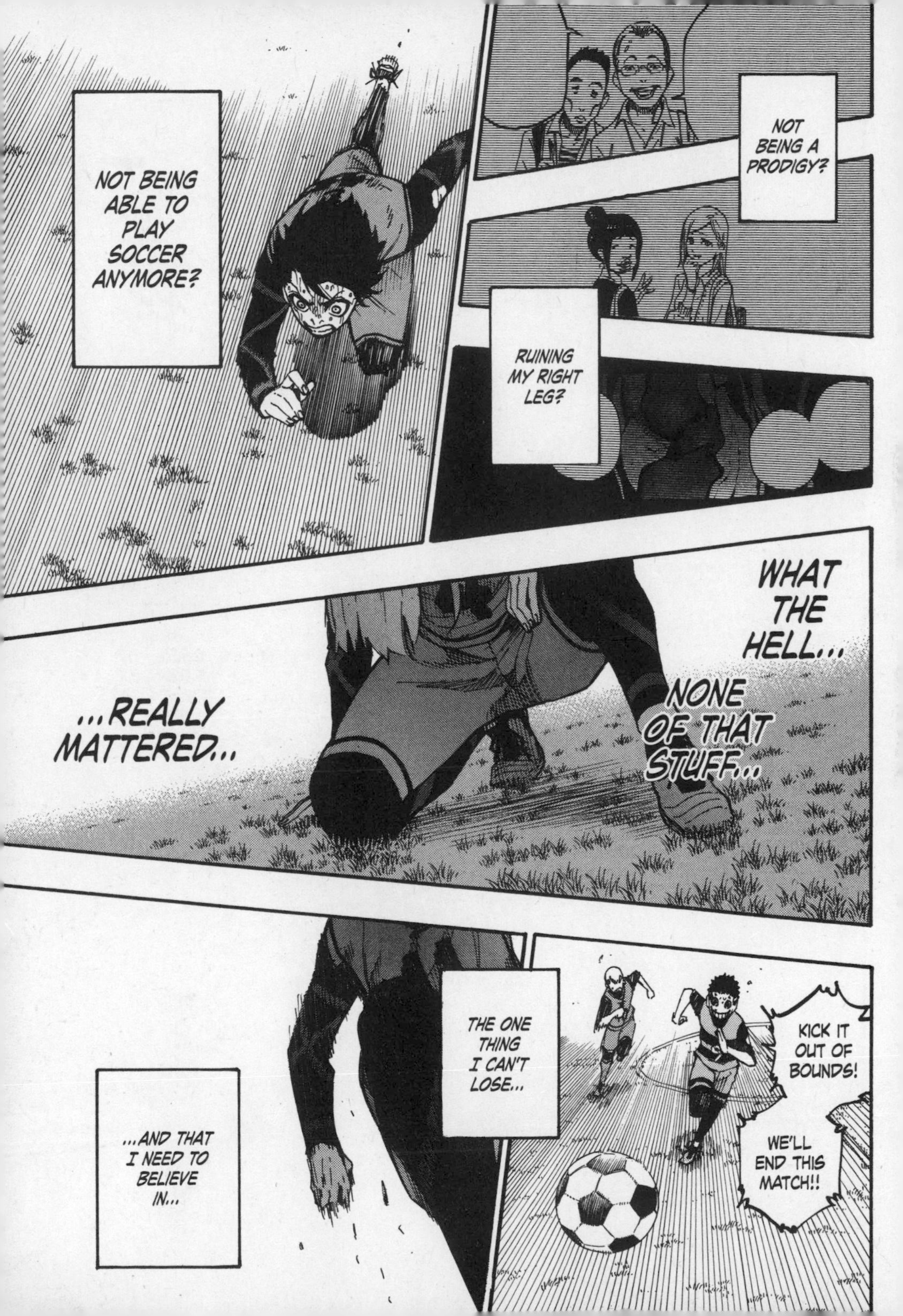
NOT BEING A PRODIGY?
RUINING MY RIGHT LEG?
NOT BEING ABLE TO PLAY SOCCER ANYMORE?
WHAT THE HELL...
NONE OF THAT STUFF...
...REALLY MATTERED...
KICK IT OUT OF BOUNDS!
WE'LL END THIS MATCH!!
THE ONE THING I CAN'T LOSE...
...AND THAT I NEED TO BELIEVE IN...

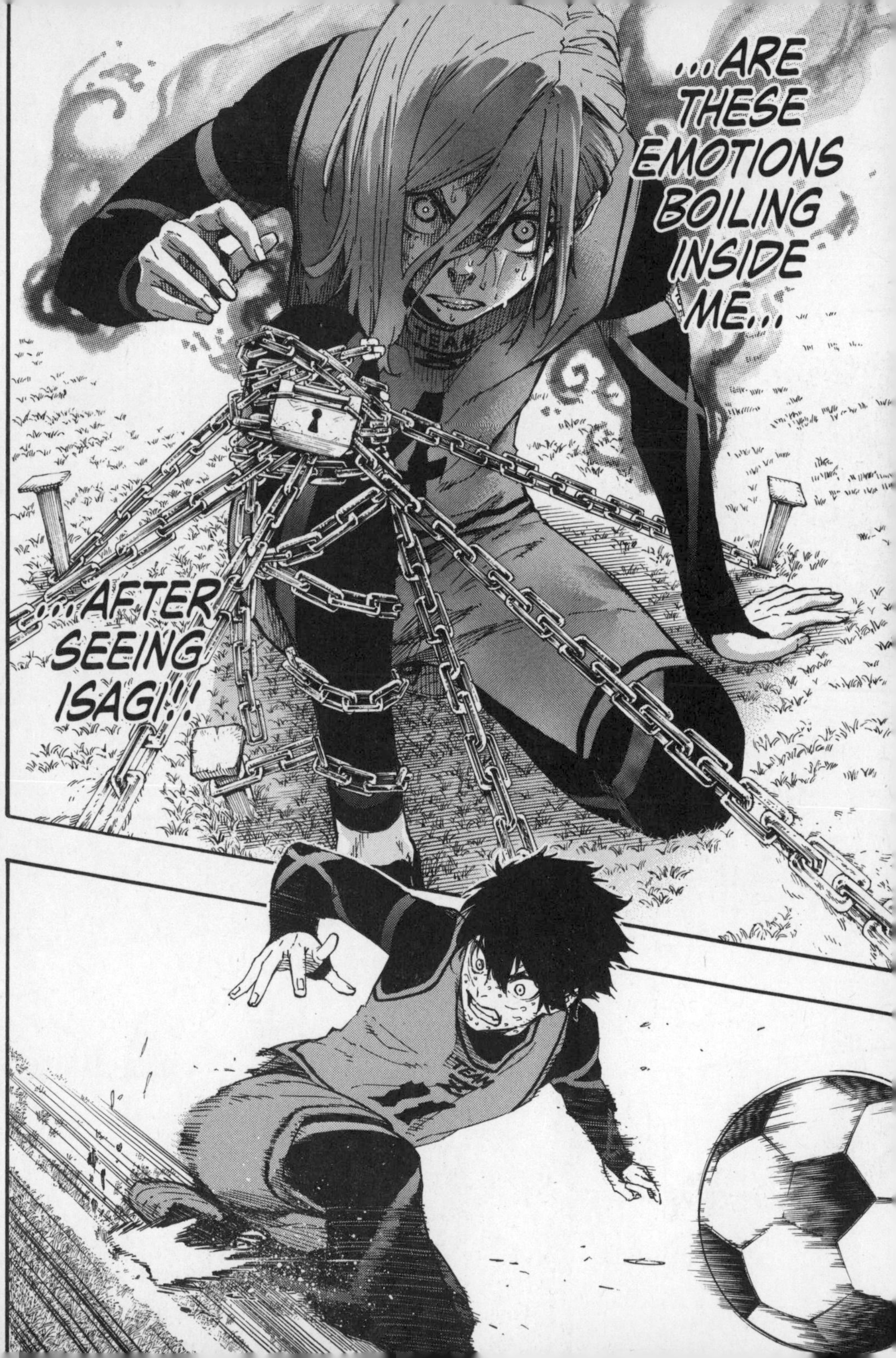
...ARE THESE EMOTIONS BOILING INSIDE ME...
...AFTER SEEING ISAGI!!

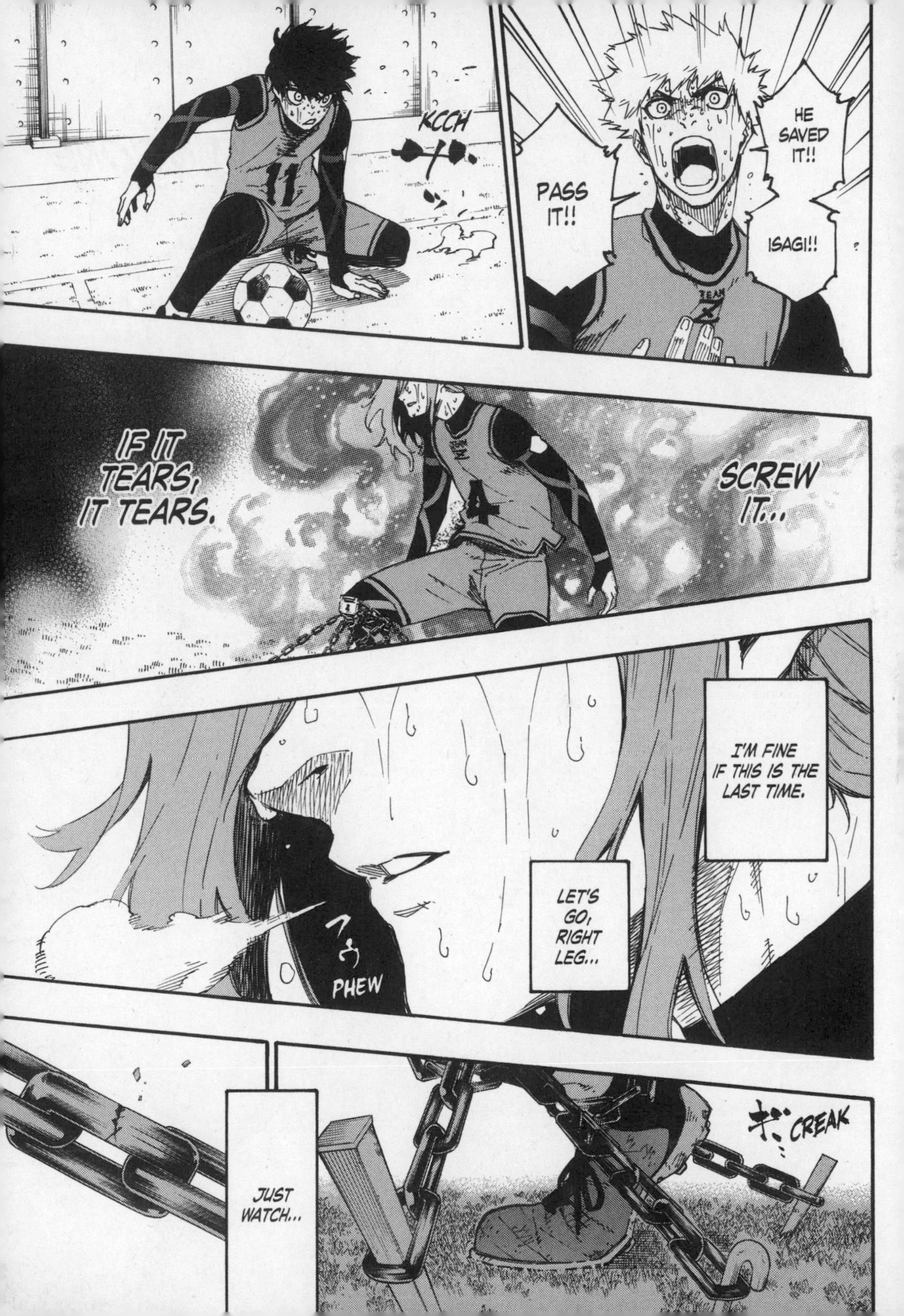
HE SAVED IT!!
ISAGI!!
PASS IT!!
KCCH
SCREW IT...
IF IT TEARS, IT TEARS.
I'M FINE IF THIS IS THE LAST TIME.
LET'S GO, RIGHT LEG...
PHEW
CREAK
JUST WATCH...

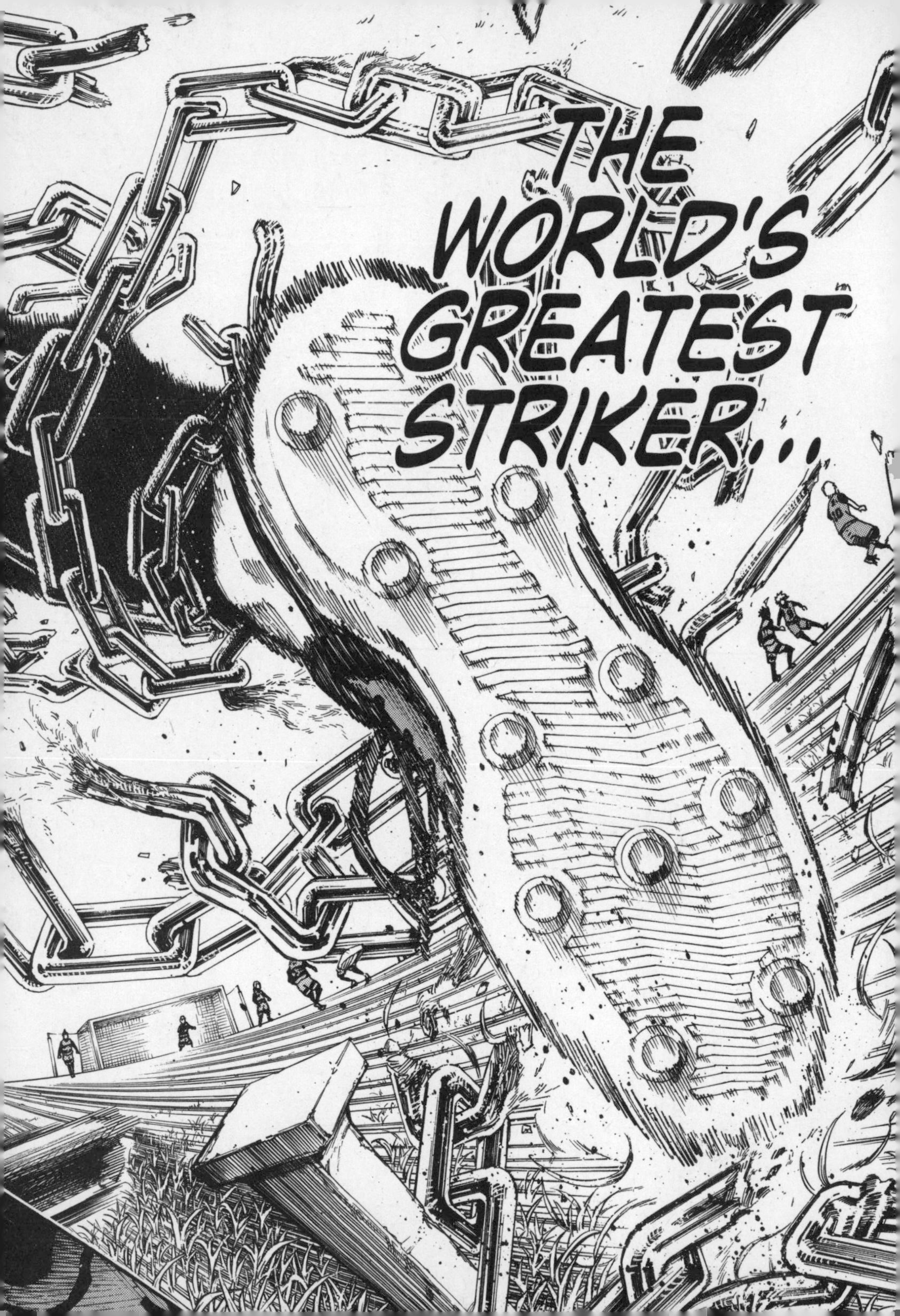
THE WORLD'S GREATEST STRIKER...

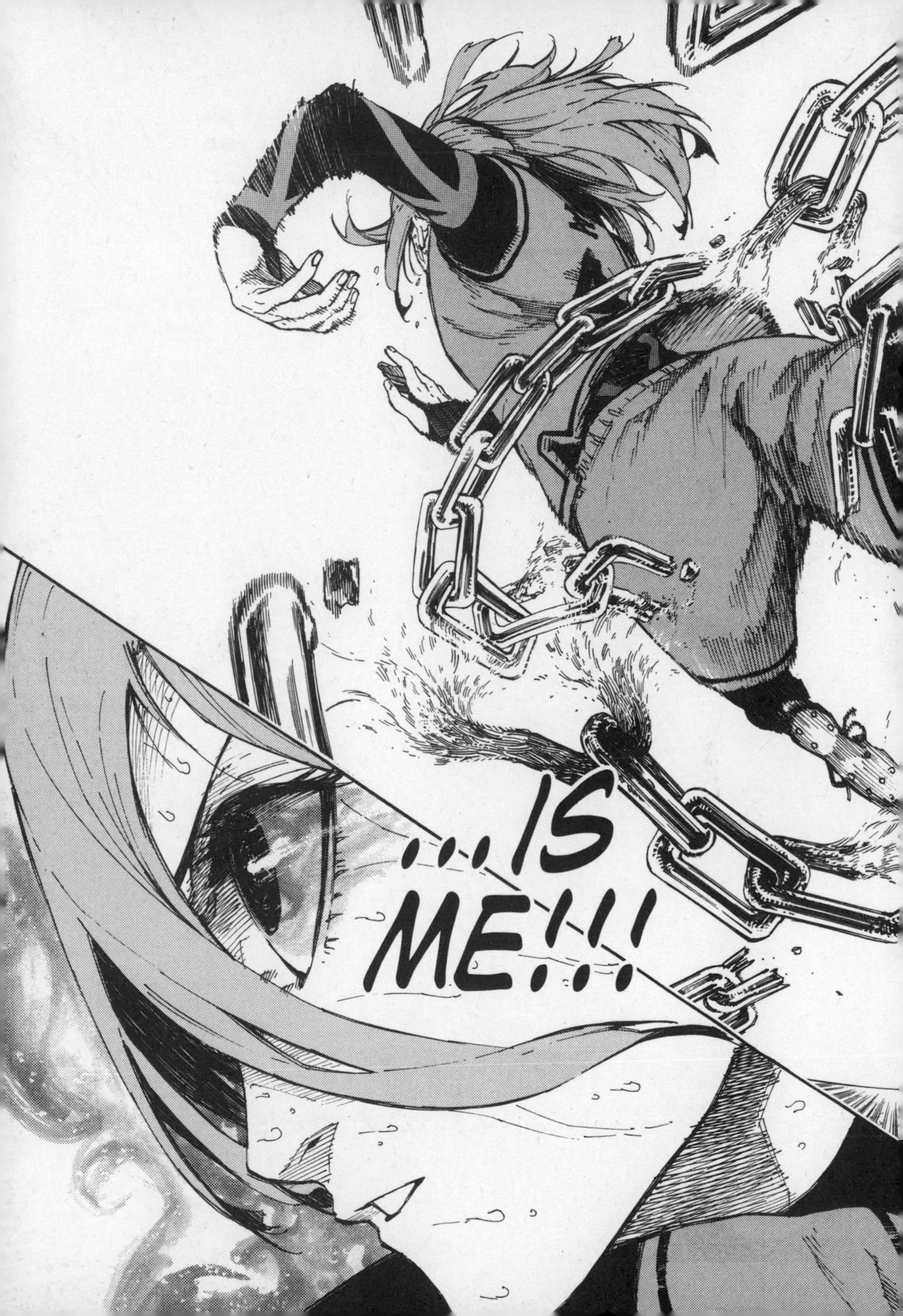
...IS ME!!!

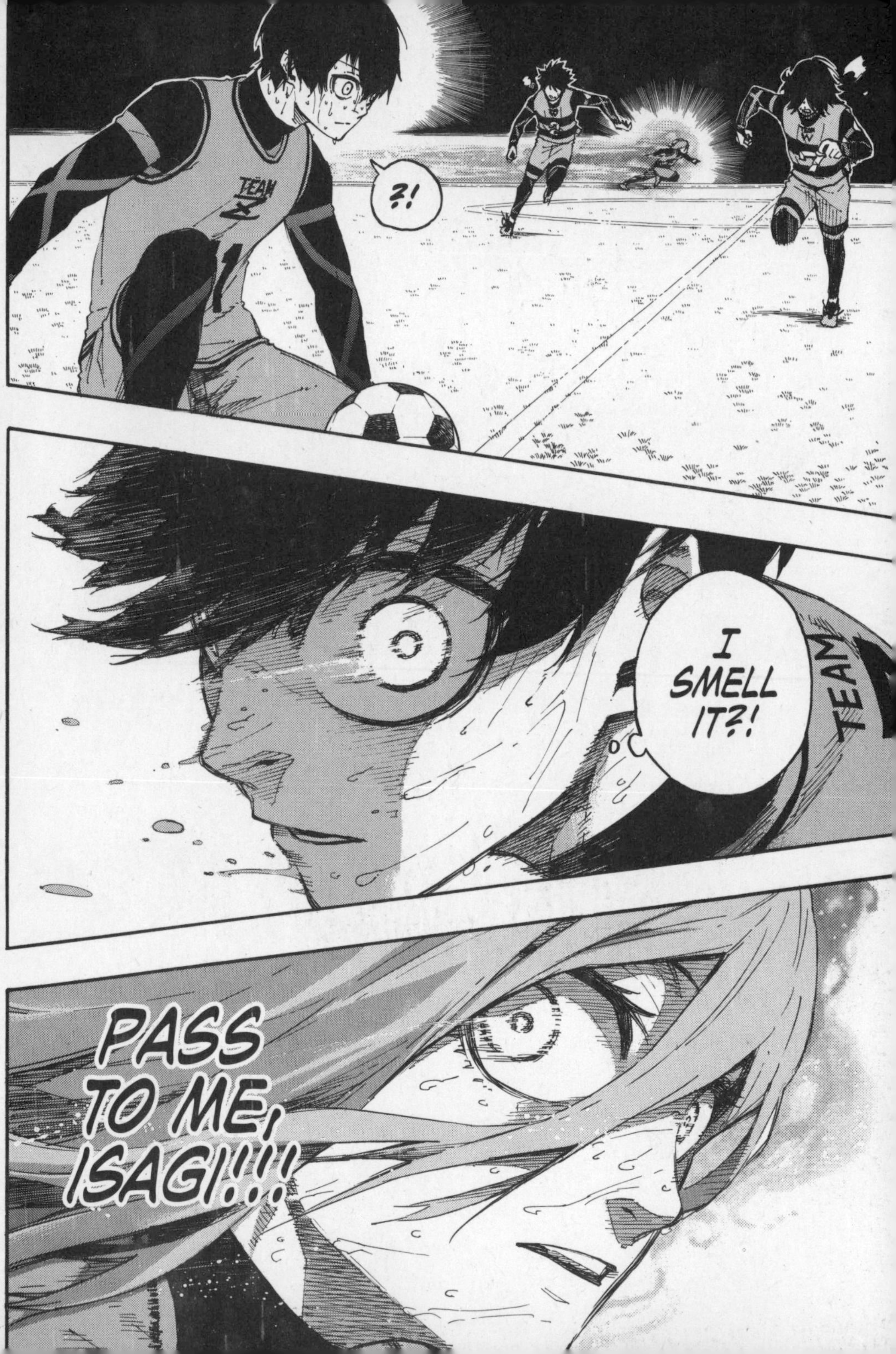
?!
I SMELL IT?!
PASS TO ME, ISAGI!!!

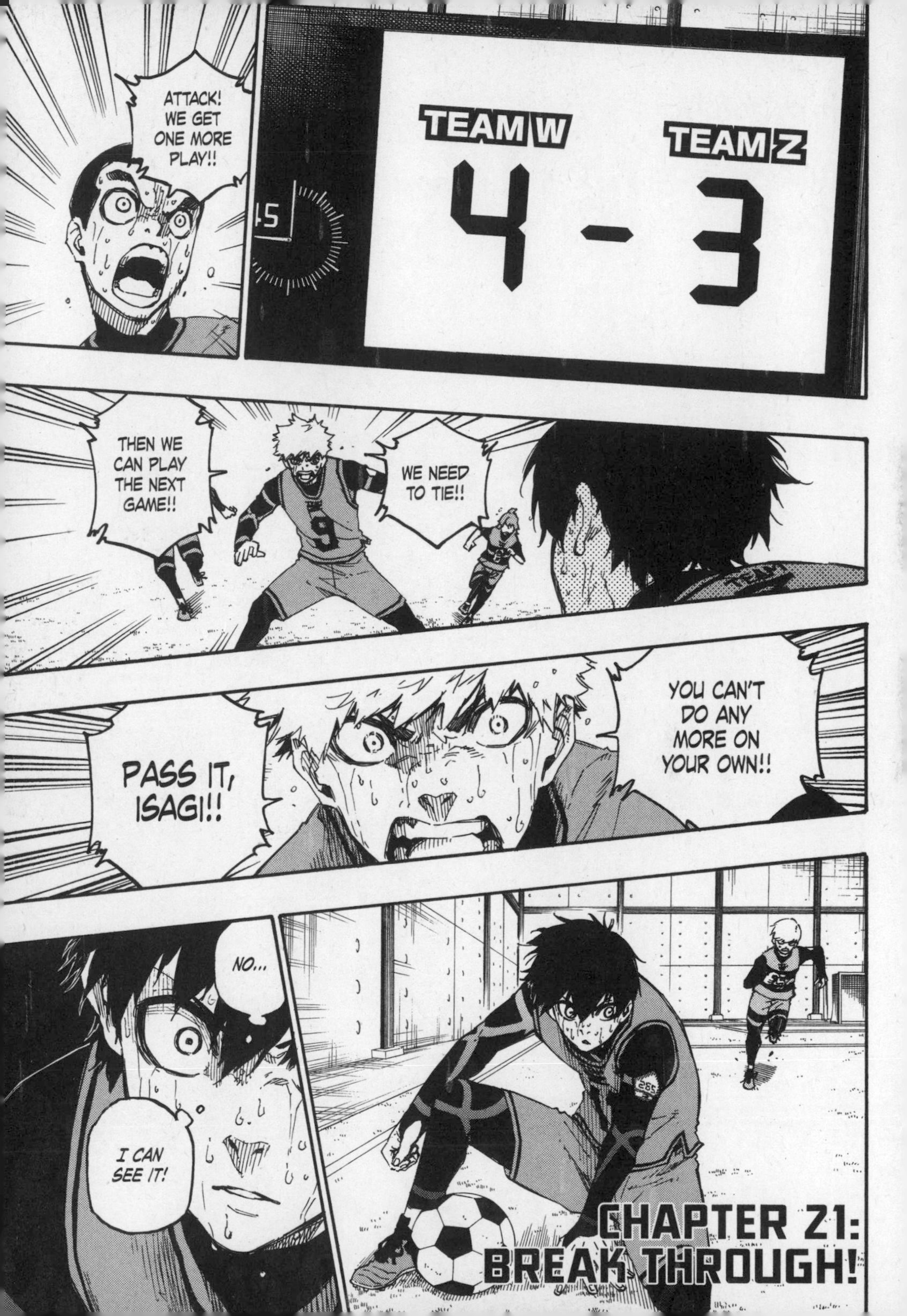
TEAM W
TEAM Z
4 - 3
45
ATTACK! WE GET ONE MORE PLAY!!
WE NEED TO TIE!!
THEN WE CAN PLAY THE NEXT GAME!!
YOU CAN'T DO ANY MORE ON YOUR OWN!!
PASS IT, ISAGI!!
CHAPTER 21: BREAK THROUGH!
NO...
I CAN SEE IT!

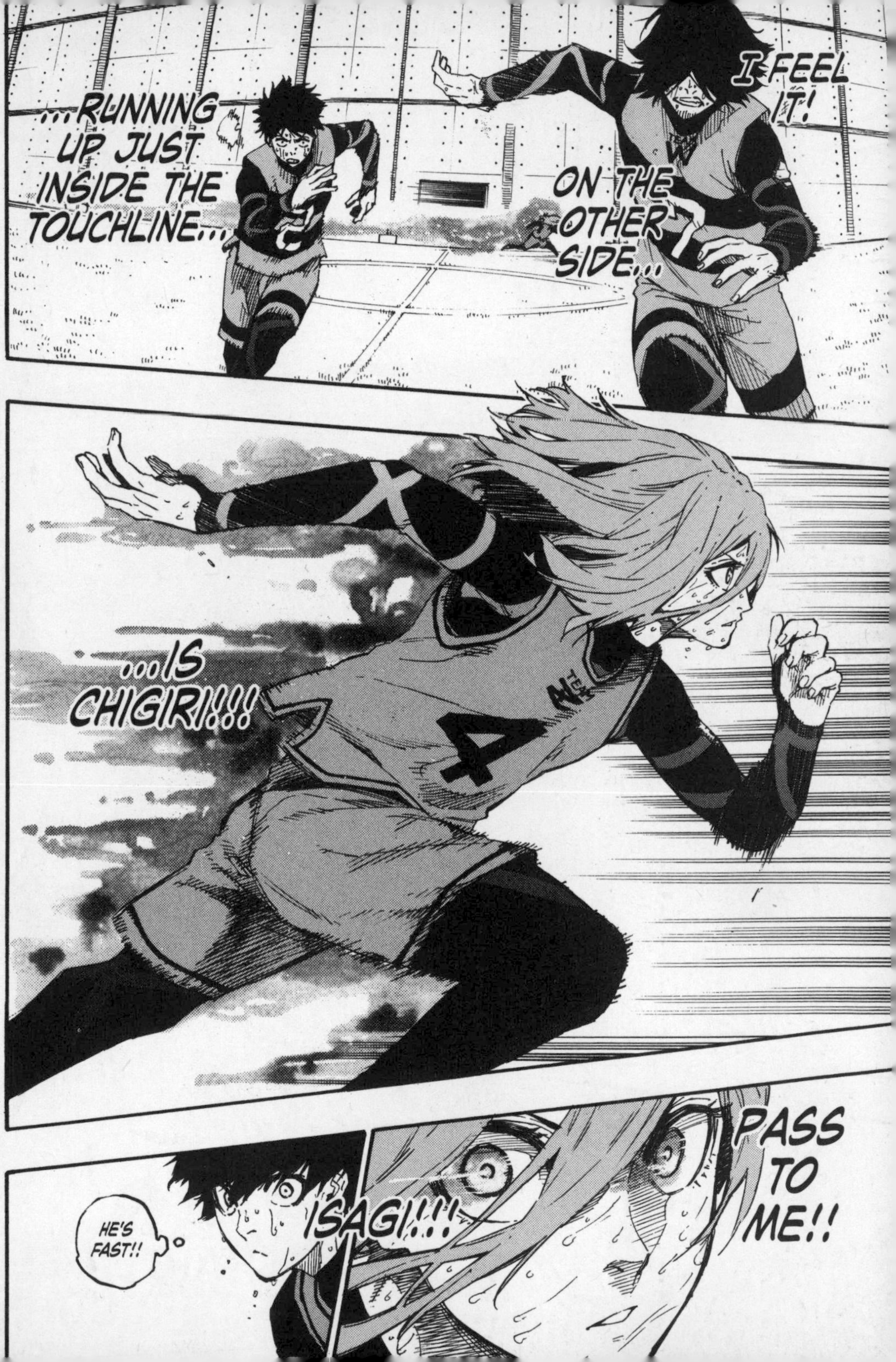
I FEEL IT!
ON THE OTHER SIDE...
...RUNNING UP JUST INSIDE THE TOUCHLINE...
...IS CHIGIRI!!!
PASS TO ME!!
ISAGI!!!
HE'S FAST!!

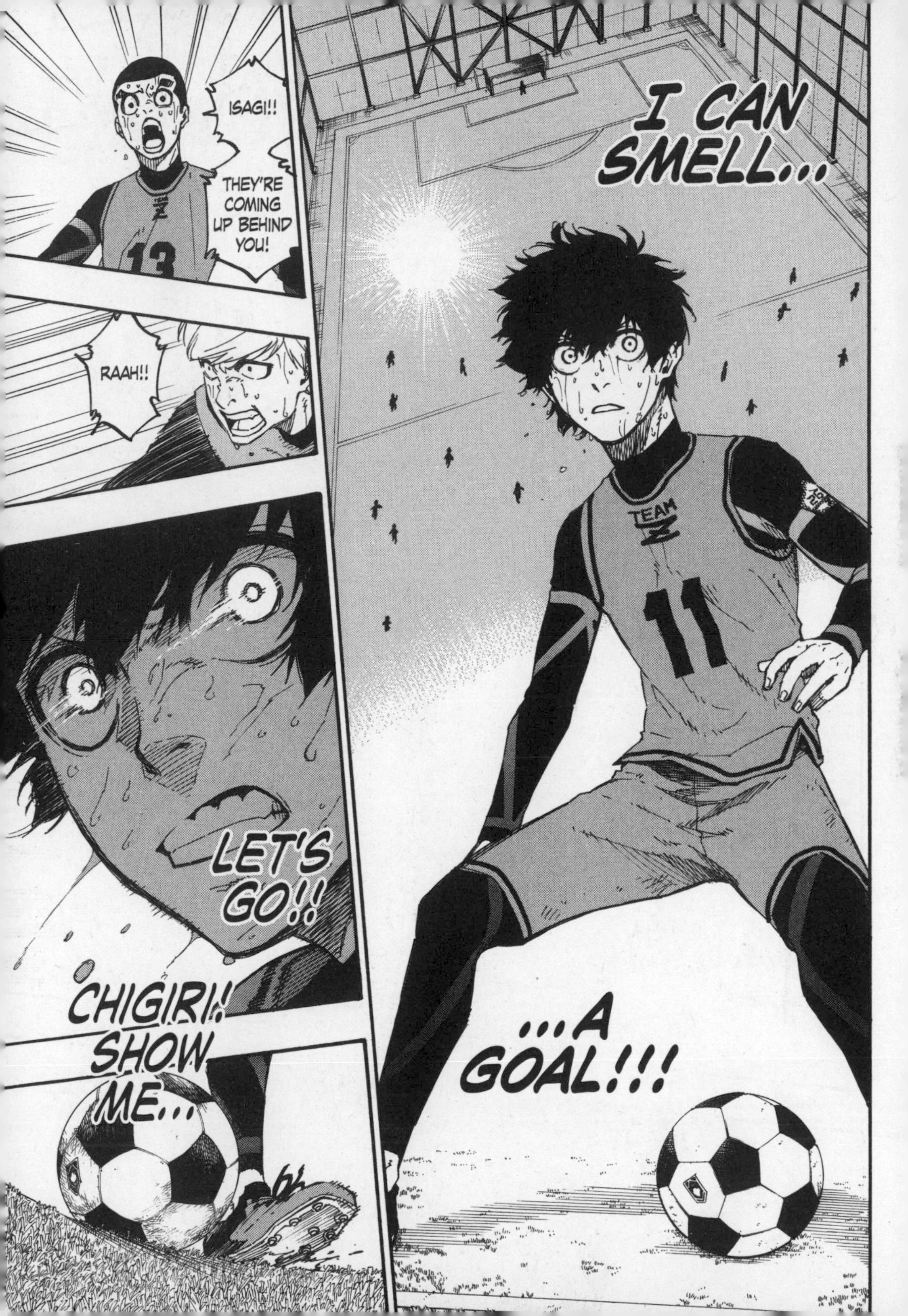

I CAN SMELL...
...A GOAL!!!
ISAGI!!
THEY'RE COMING UP BEHIND YOU!
RAAH!!
LET'S GO!!
CHIGIRI! SHOW ME...

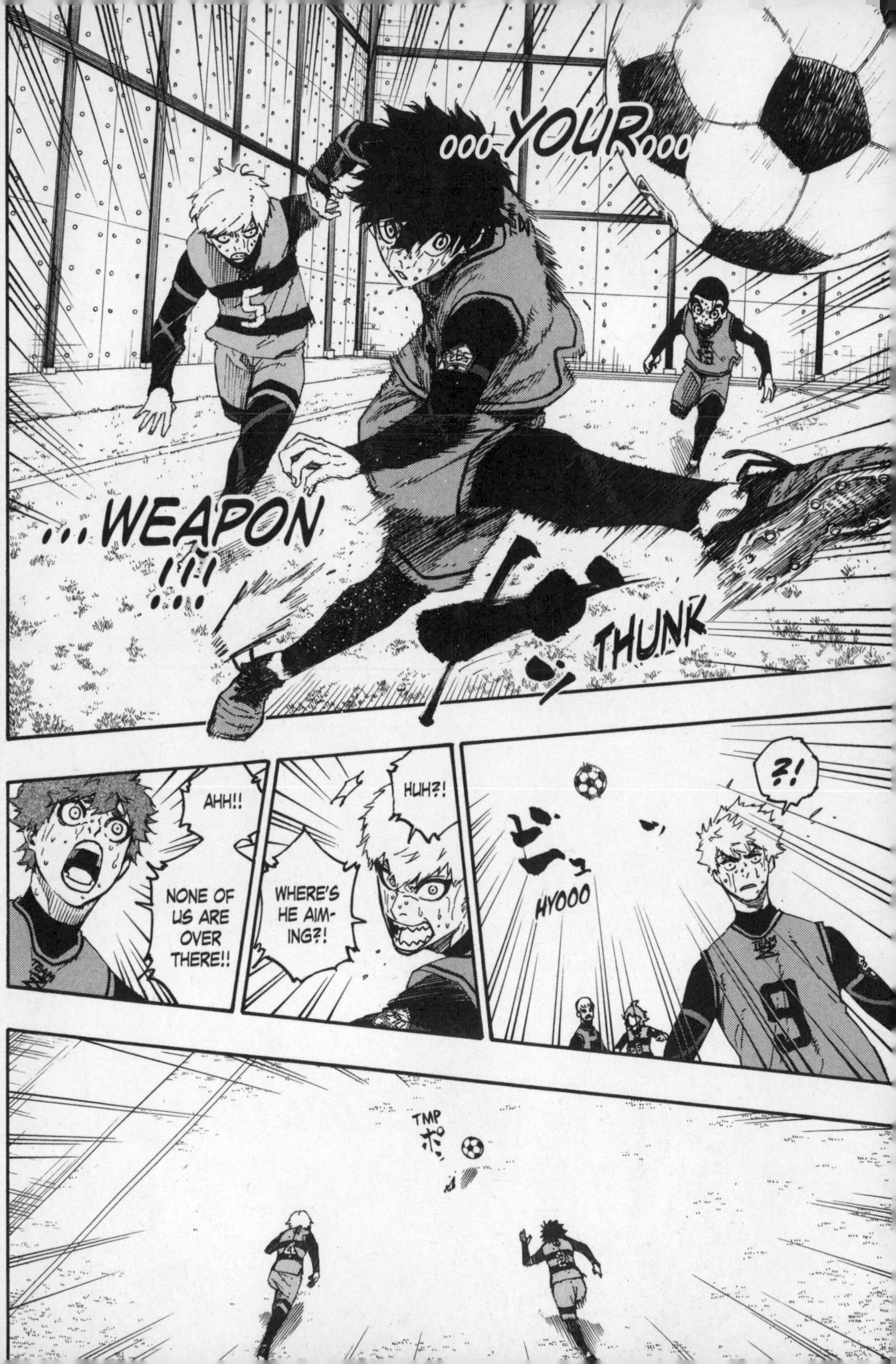
...YOUR...
...WEAPON!!!
THUNK
?!
HYOOO
HUH?!
WHERE'S HE AIM-ING?!
AHH!!
NONE OF US ARE OVER THERE!!
TMP

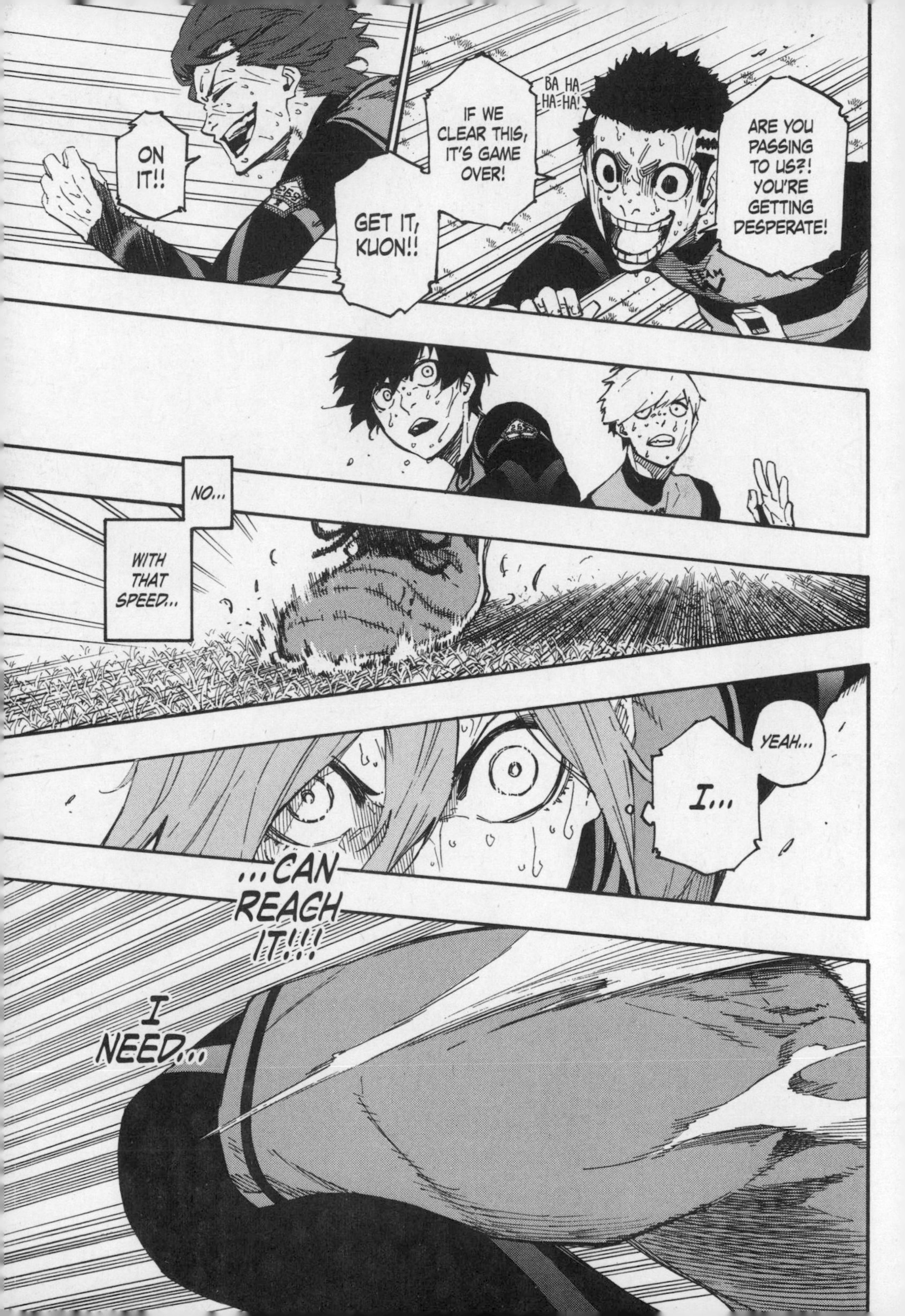
ARE YOU PASSING TO US?! YOU'RE GETTING DESPERATE!
BA HA HA-HA!
IF WE CLEAR THIS, IT'S GAME OVER!
GET IT, KUON!!
ON IT!!
NO...
WITH THAT SPEED...
YEAH...
I...
...CAN REACH IT!!!
I NEED...

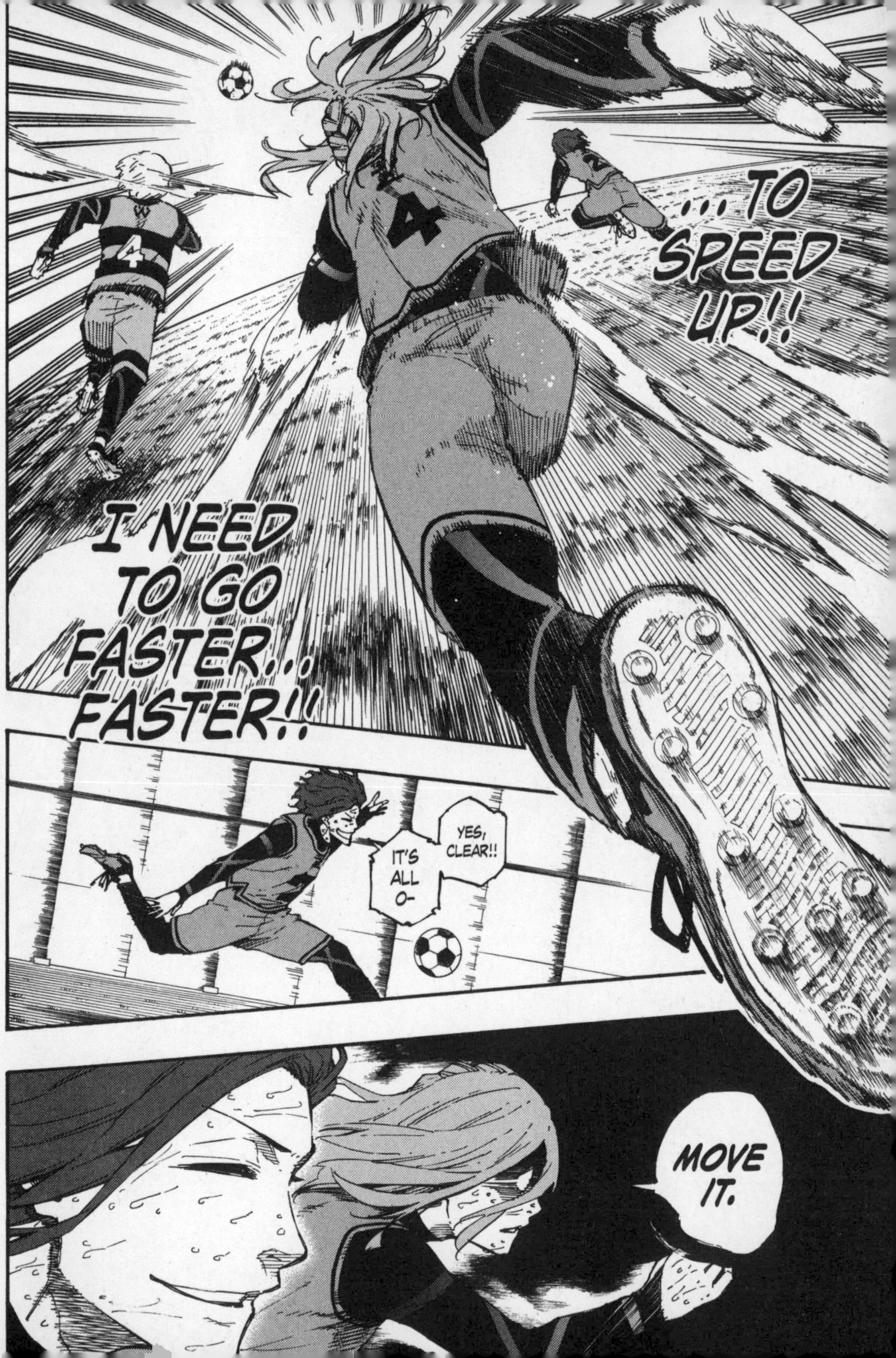
I NEED TO GO FASTER... FASTER!!
...TO SPEED UP!!
YES, CLEAR!!
IT'S ALL O-
MOVE IT.

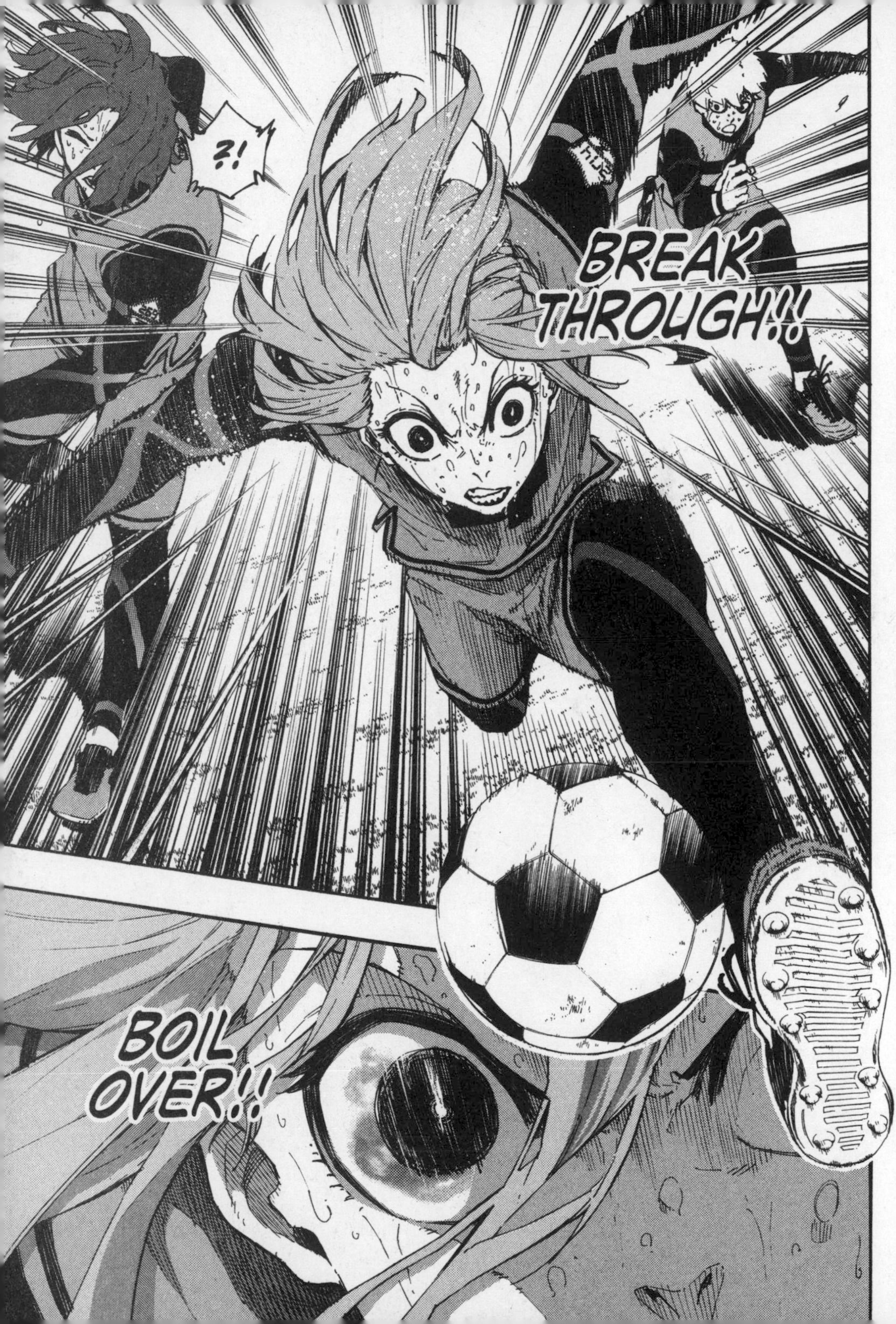
BREAK THROUGH!!
?!
BOIL OVER!!

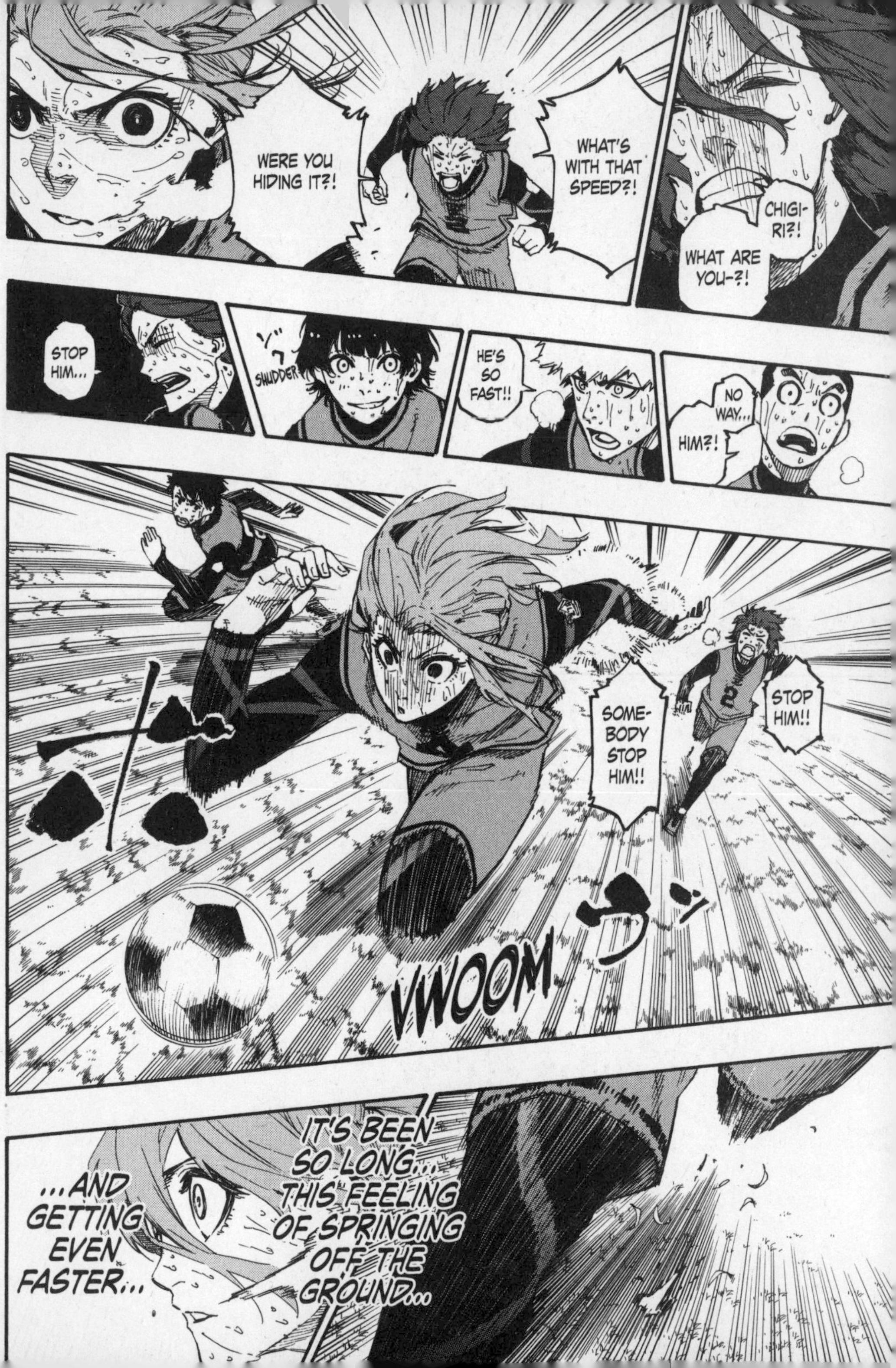
CHIGI-RI?!
WHAT ARE YOU-?!
WHAT'S WITH THAT SPEED?!
WERE YOU HIDING IT?!
NO WAY...
HIM?!
HE'S SO FAST!!
SHUDDER
STOP HIM...
STOP HIM!!
SOME-BODY STOP HIM!!
VWOOM
IT'S BEEN SO LONG... THIS FEELING OF SPRINGING OFF THE GROUND...
...AND GETTING EVEN FASTER...

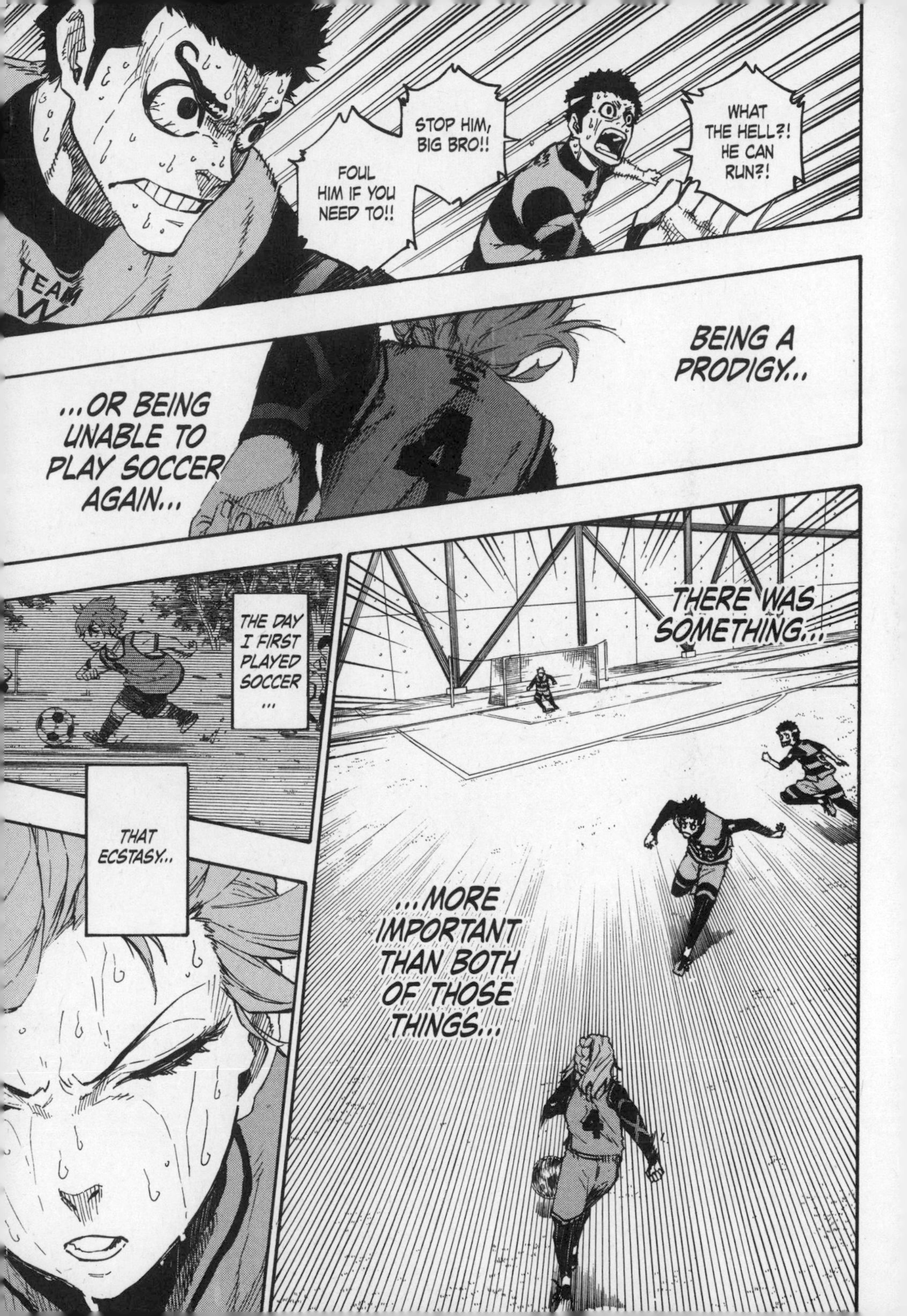
WHAT THE HELL?! HE CAN RUN?!
STOP HIM, BIG BRO!!
FOUL HIM IF YOU NEED TO!!
BEING A PRODIGY...
...OR BEING UNABLE TO PLAY SOCCER AGAIN...
THERE WAS SOMETHING...
...MORE IMPORTANT THAN BOTH OF THOSE THINGS...
THE DAY I FIRST PLAYED SOCCER...
THAT ECSTASY...

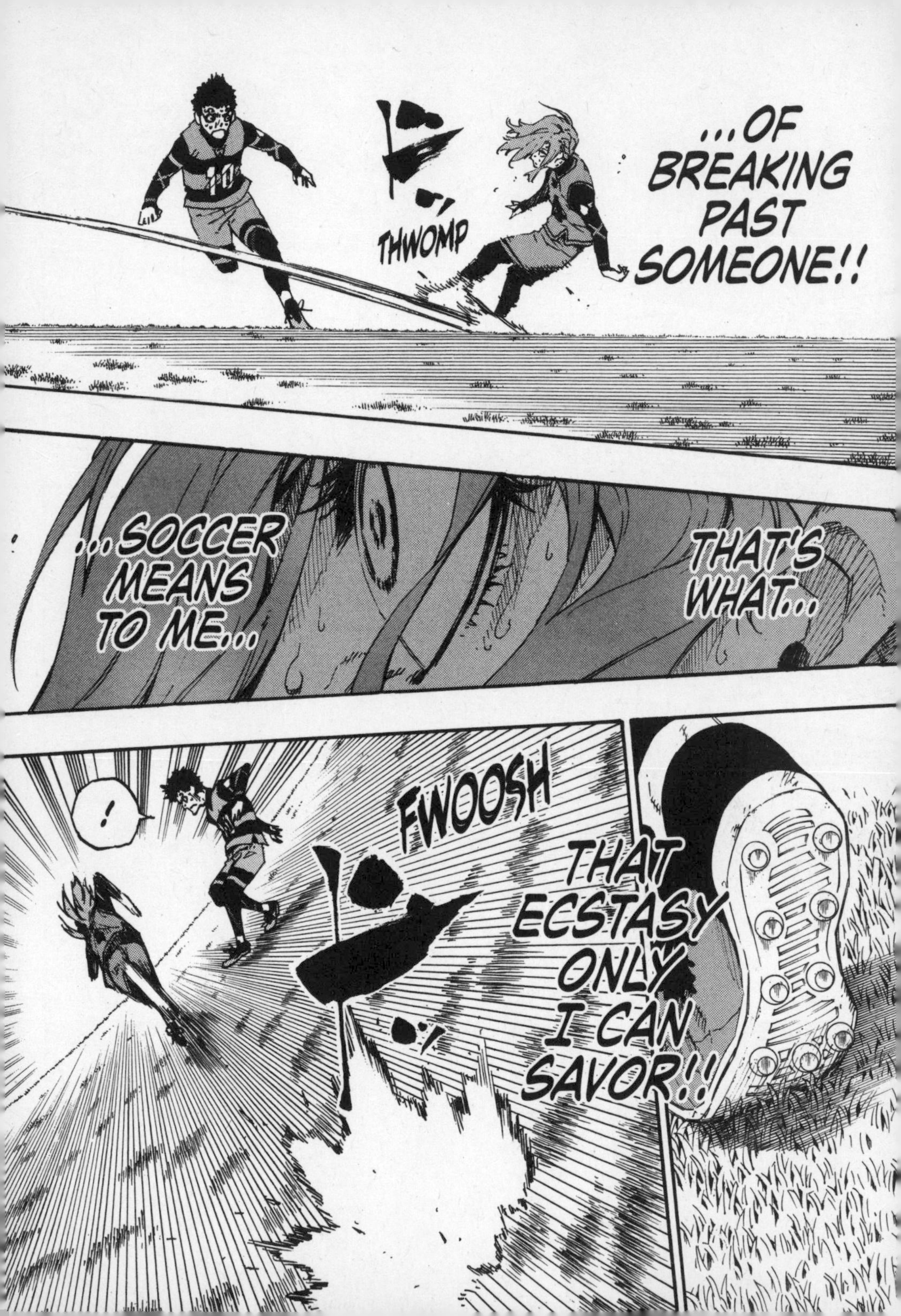
...OF BREAKING PAST SOMEONE!!
THWOMP
THAT'S WHAT...
...SOCCER MEANS TO ME...
THAT ECSTASY ONLY I CAN SAVOR!!
FWOOSH
!

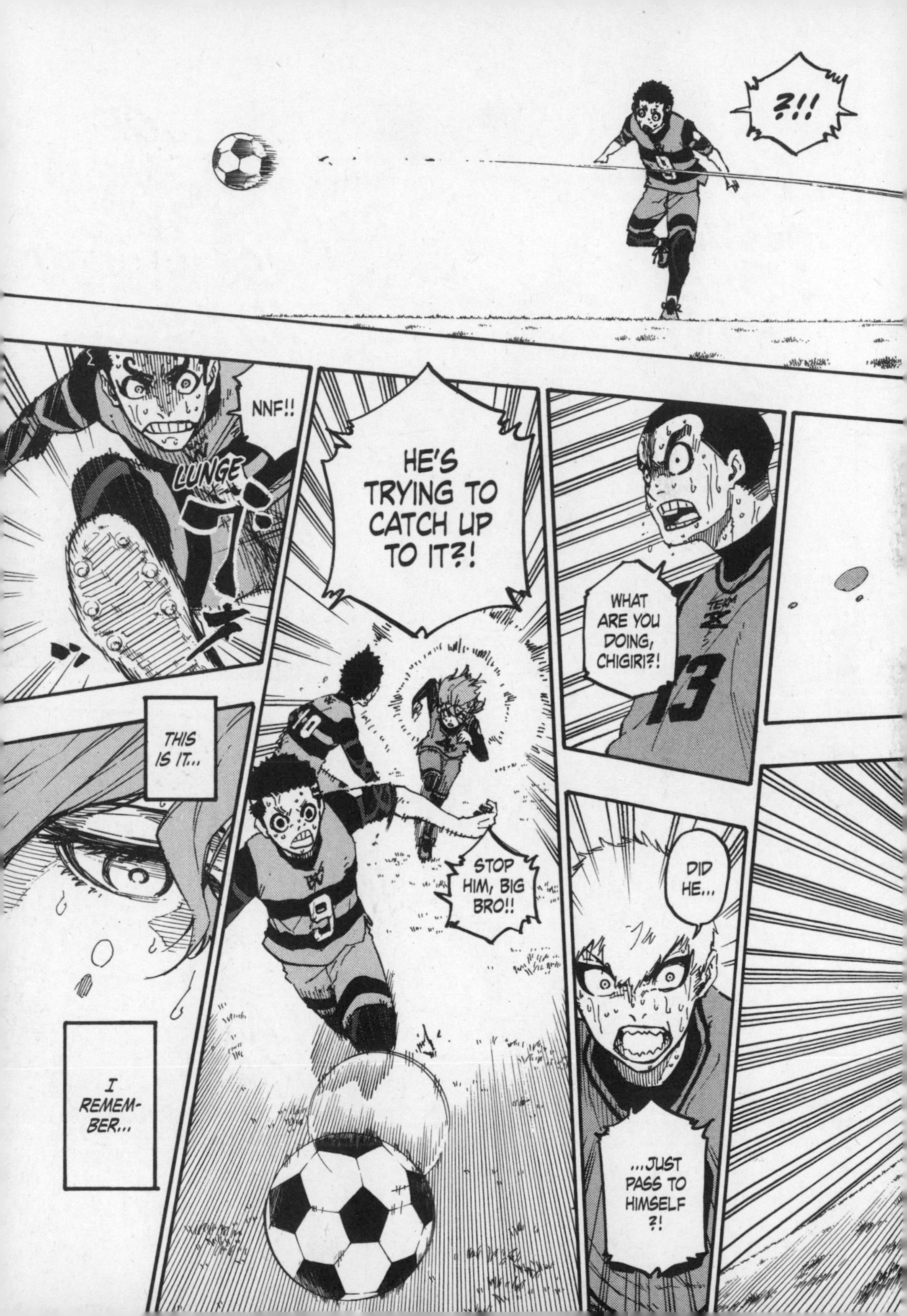
?!!
WHAT ARE YOU DOING, CHIGIRI?!
DID HE...
...JUST PASS TO HIMSELF ?!
HE'S TRYING TO CATCH UP TO IT?!
STOP HIM, BIG BRO!!
NNF!!
LUNGE
THIS IS IT...
I REMEM-BER...

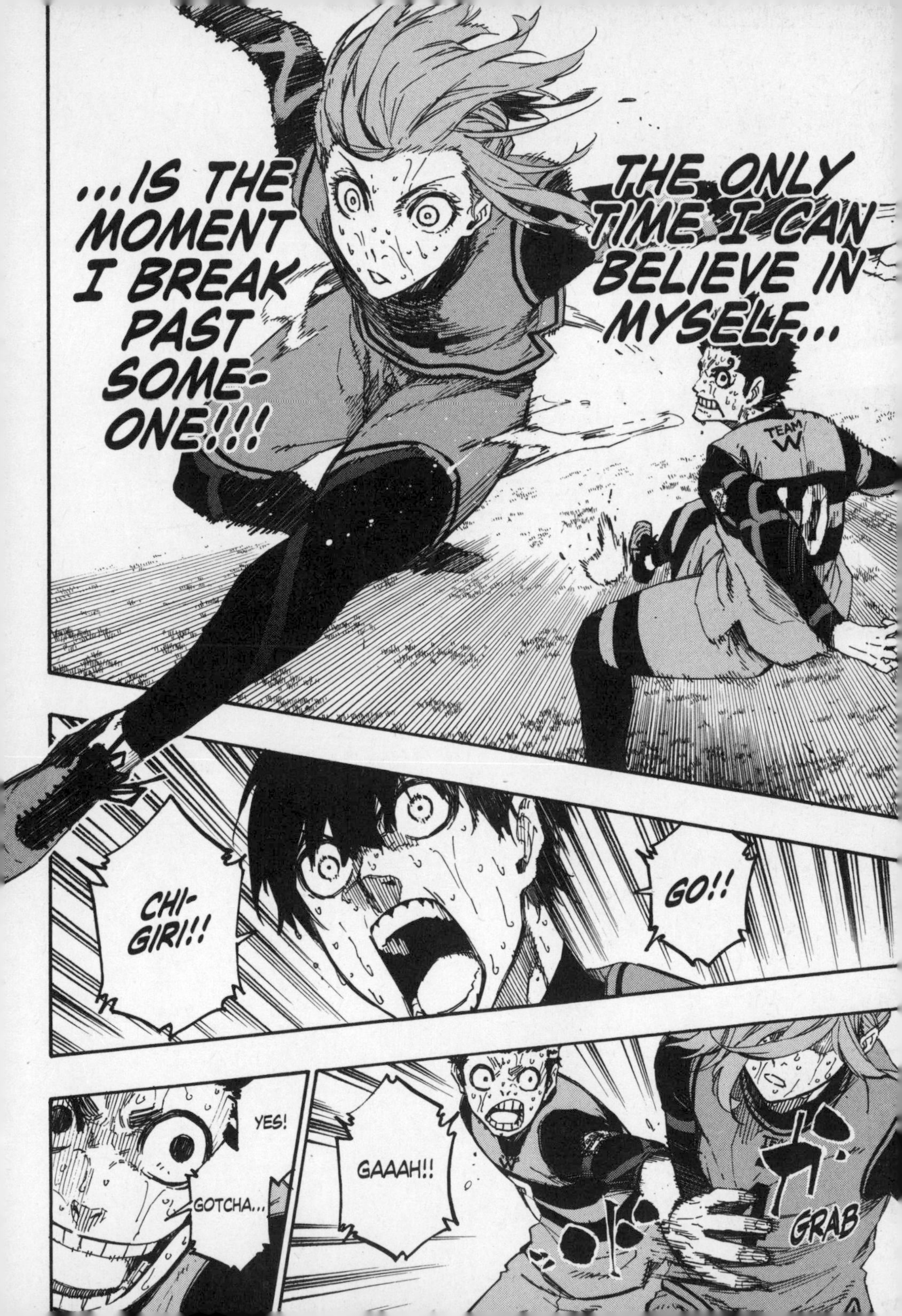
THE ONLY TIME I CAN BELIEVE IN MYSELF...
...IS THE MOMENT I BREAK PAST SOME-ONE!!!
GO!!
CHI-GIRI!!
GRAB
GAAAH!!
YES!
GOTCHA...

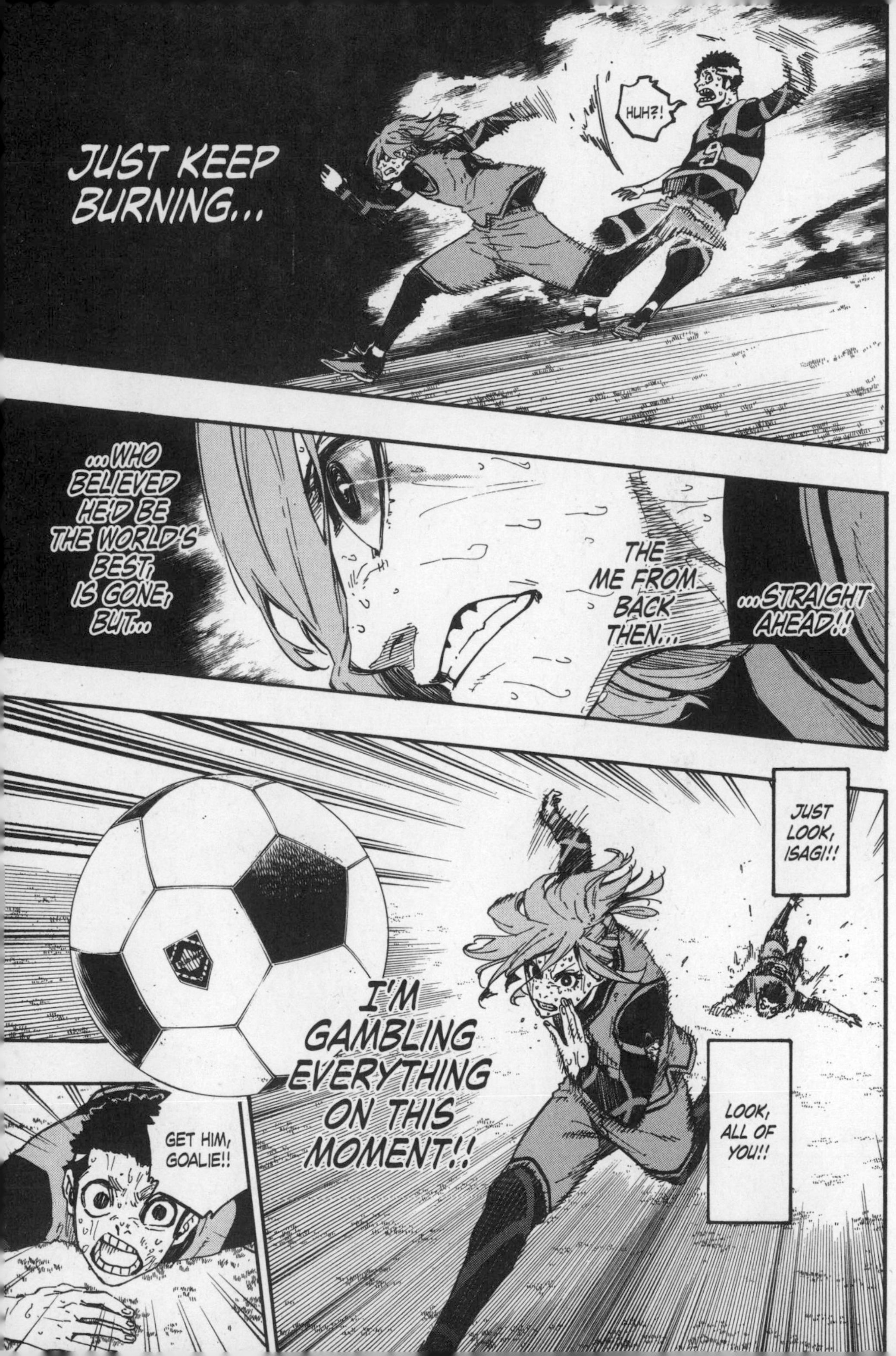
HUH?!
JUST KEEP BURNING...
...STRAIGHT AHEAD!!
THE ME FROM BACK THEN...
...WHO BELIEVED HE'D BE THE WORLD'S BEST, IS GONE, BUT...
JUST LOOK, ISAGI!!
LOOK, ALL OF YOU!!
I'M GAMBLING EVERYTHING ON THIS MOMENT!!
GET HIM, GOALIE!!

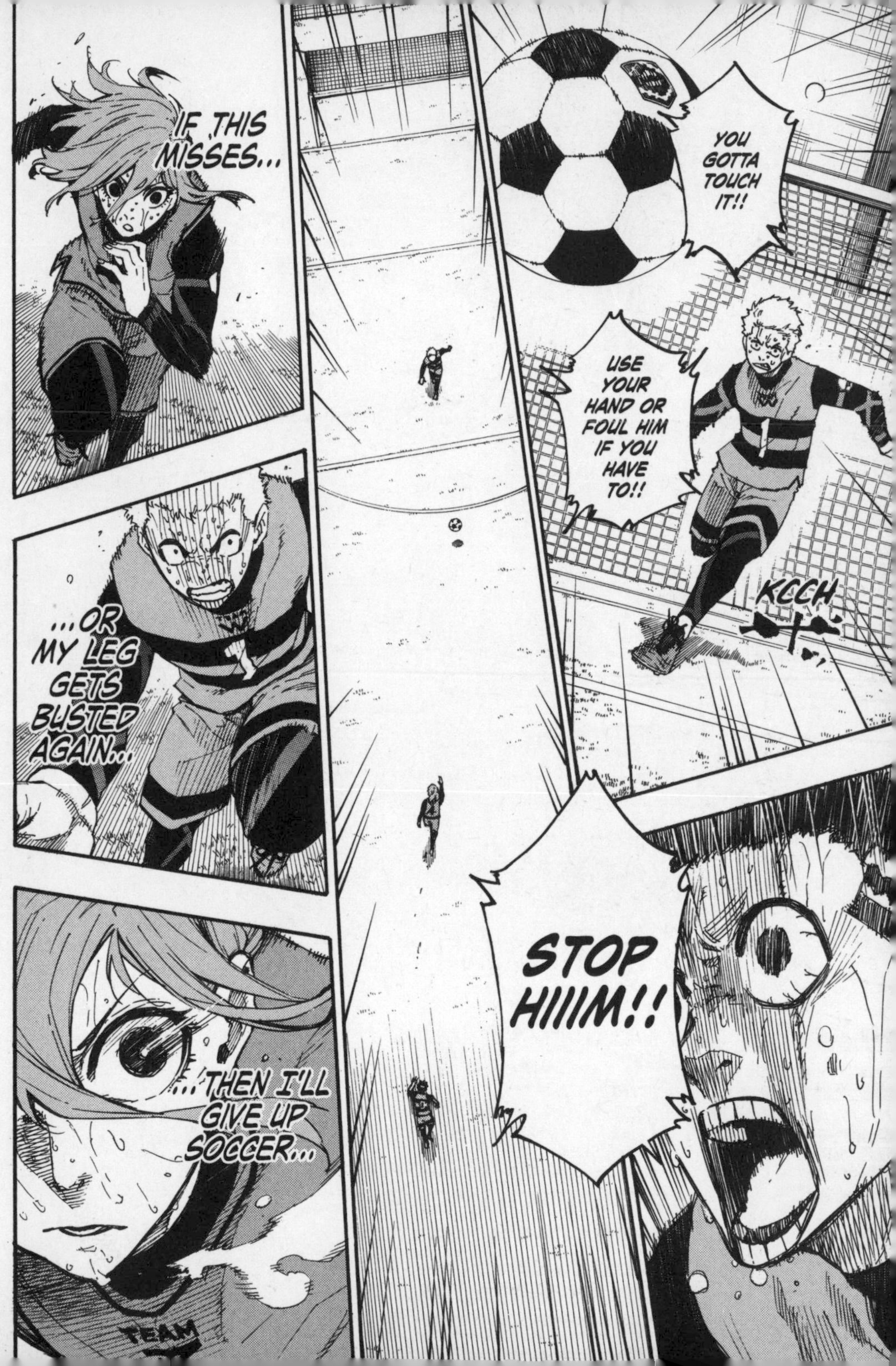
YOU GOTTA TOUCH IT!!
USE YOUR HAND OR FOUL HIM IF YOU HAVE TO!!
KCCH
STOP HIIIM!!
IF THIS MISSES...
...OR MY LEG GETS BUSTED AGAIN...
...THEN I'LL GIVE UP SOCCER...
TEAM

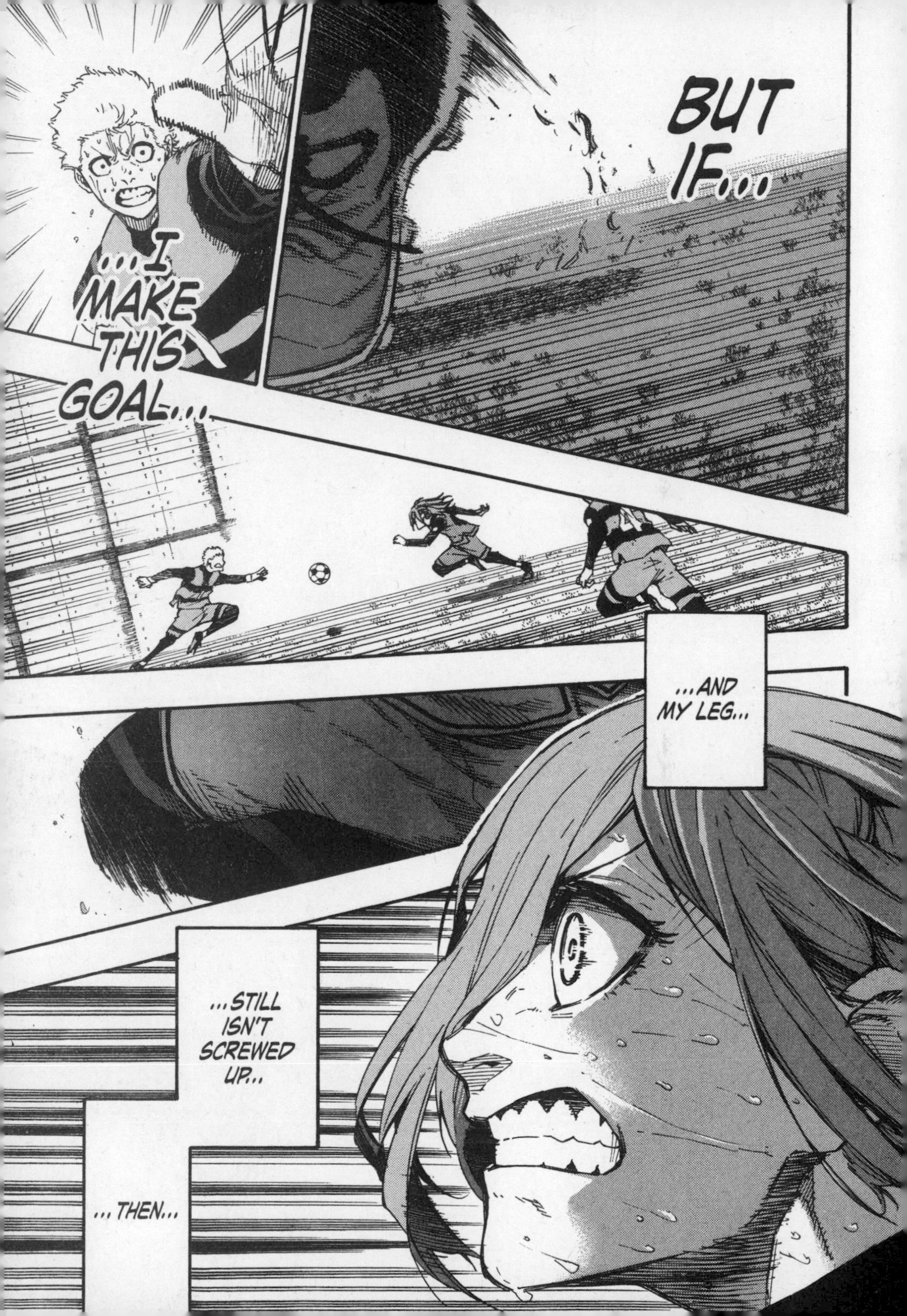
BUT IF...
...I MAKE THIS GOAL...
...AND MY LEG...
...STILL ISN'T SCREWED UP...
...THEN...

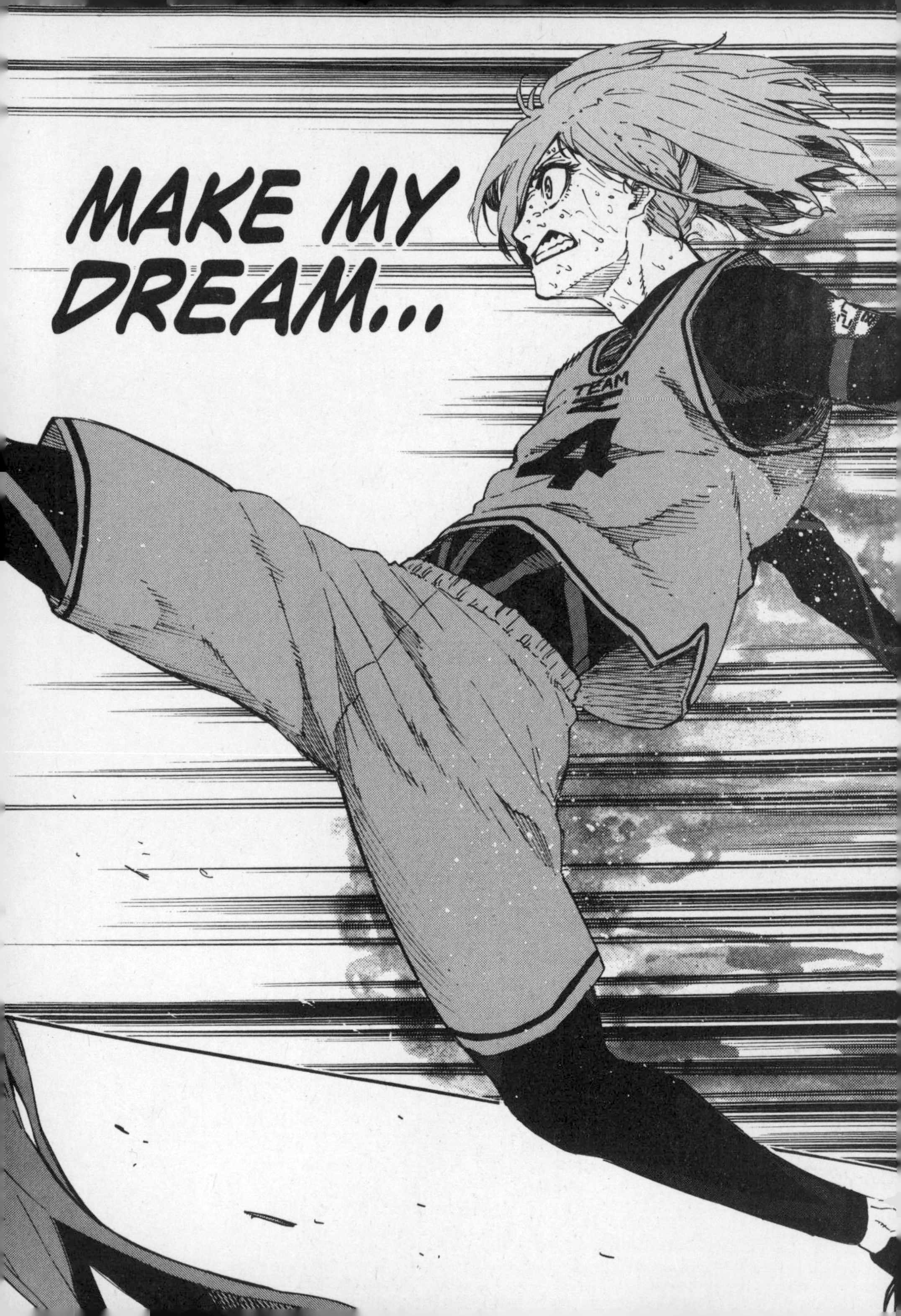
MAKE MY DREAM...
TEAM
4

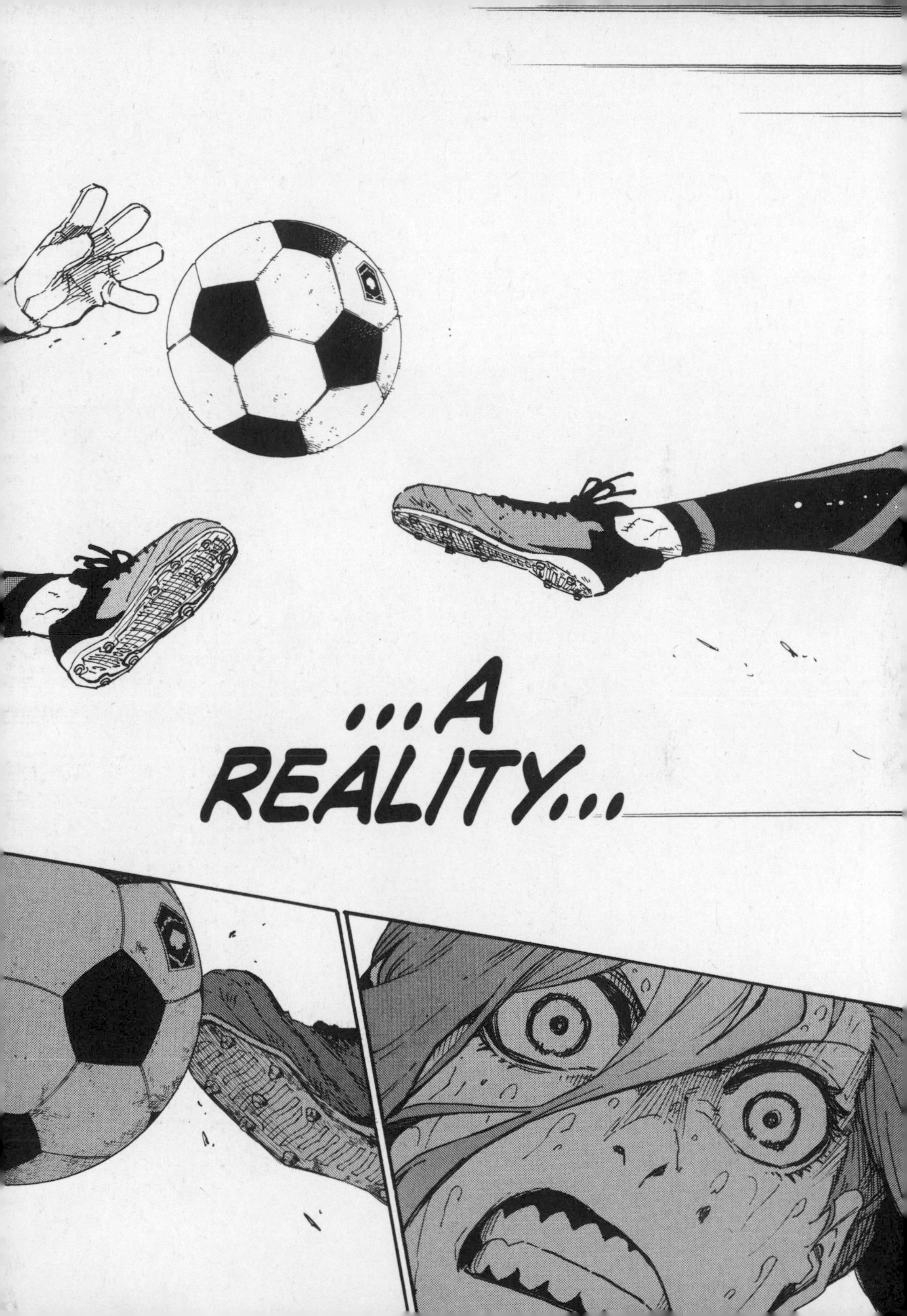
...A REALITY...

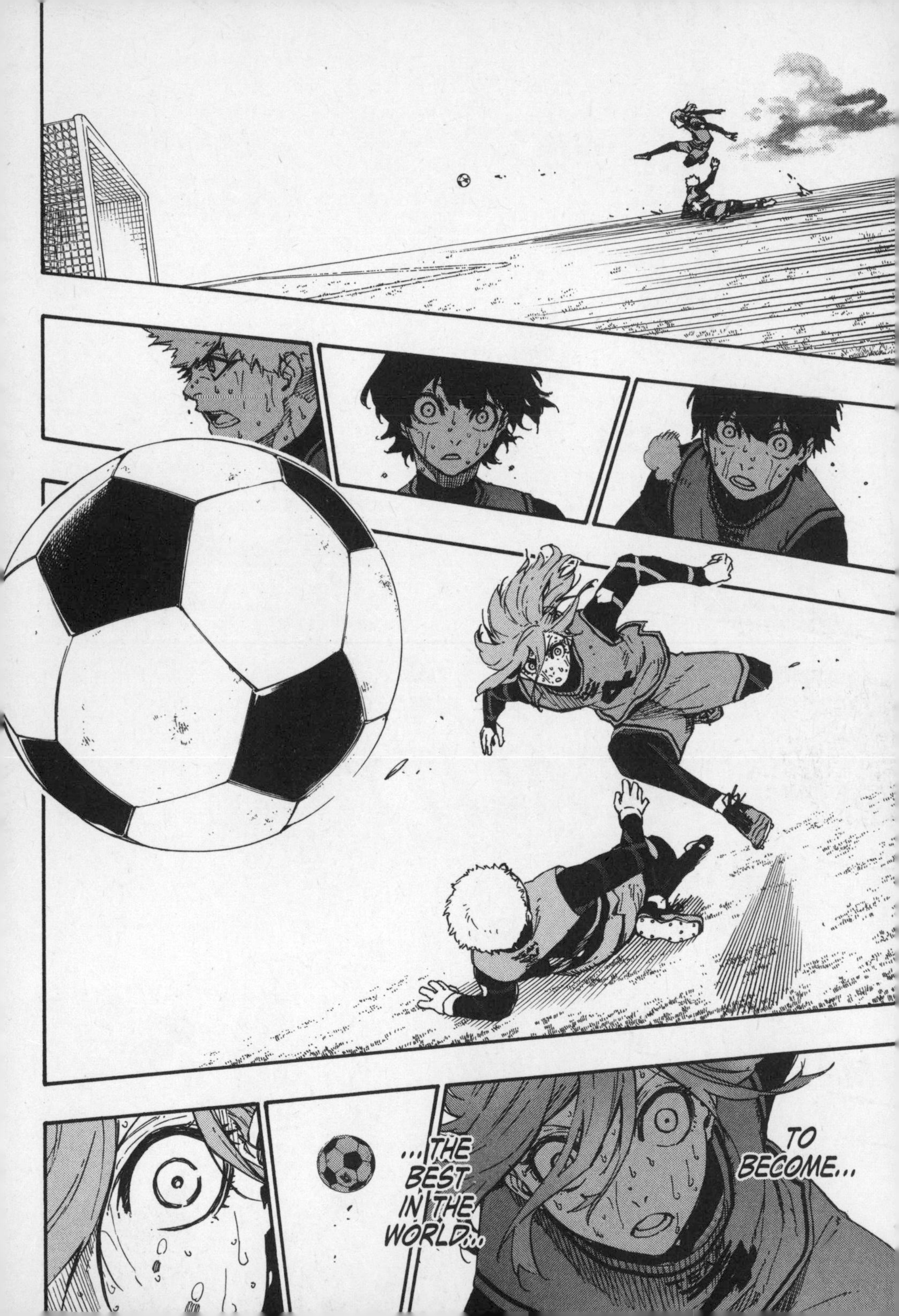
TO BECOME...
...THE BEST IN THE WORLD...

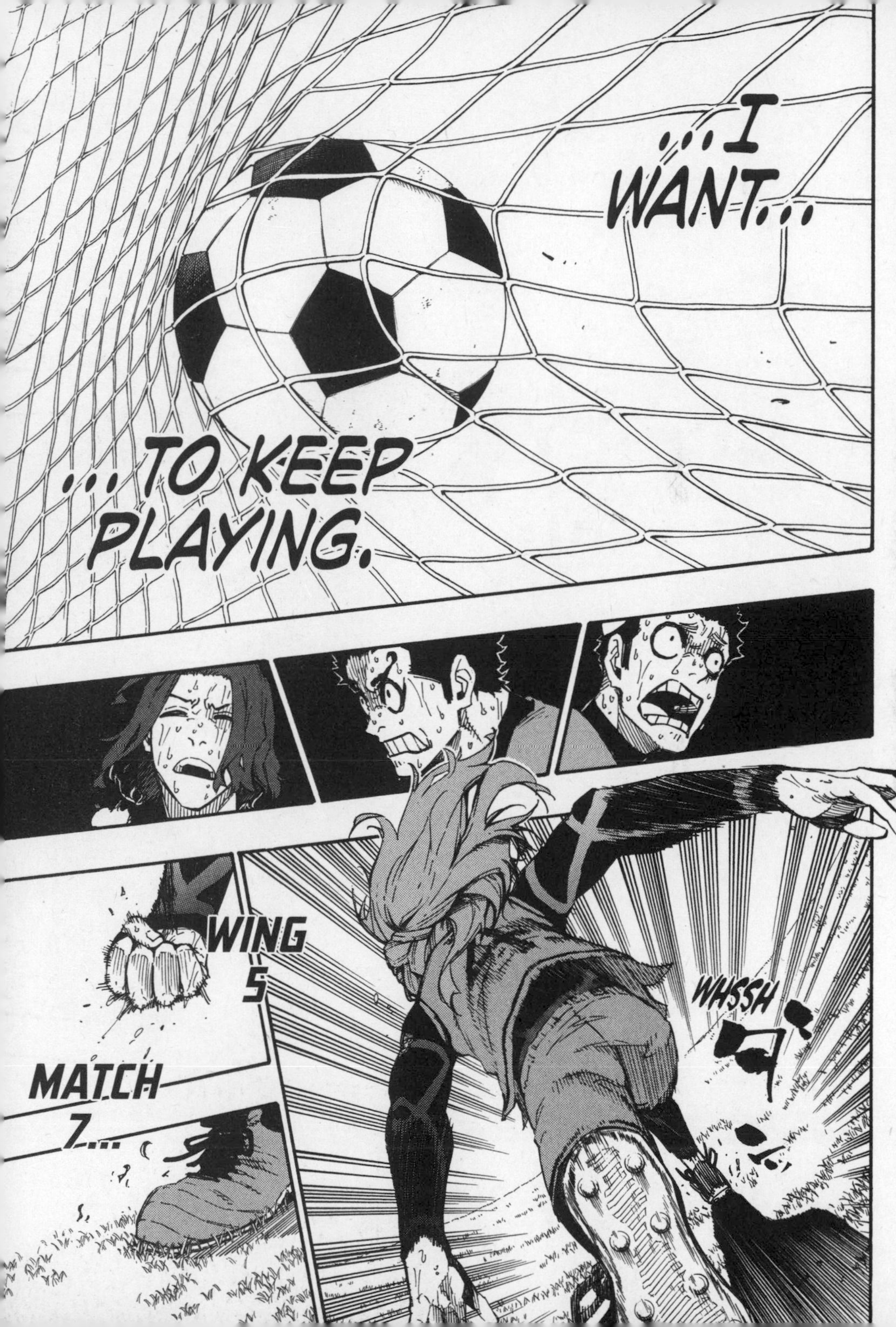
...I WANT...
...TO KEEP PLAYING.
WHSSH
WING 5
MATCH 7...

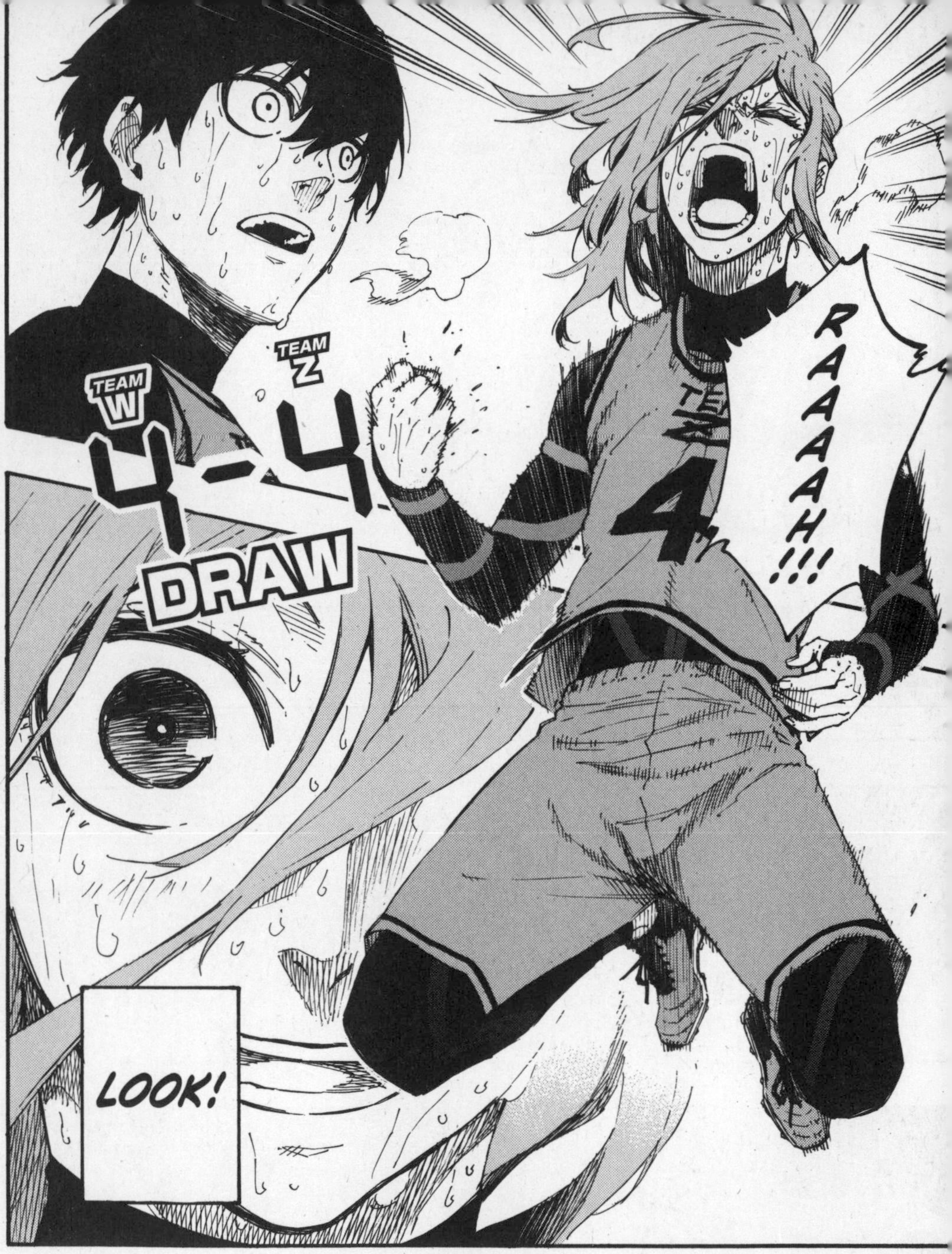
RAAAAAH!!!
TEAM W
4-4
TEAM Z
DRAW
LOOK!

THIS IS HYOMA CHIGIRI!!

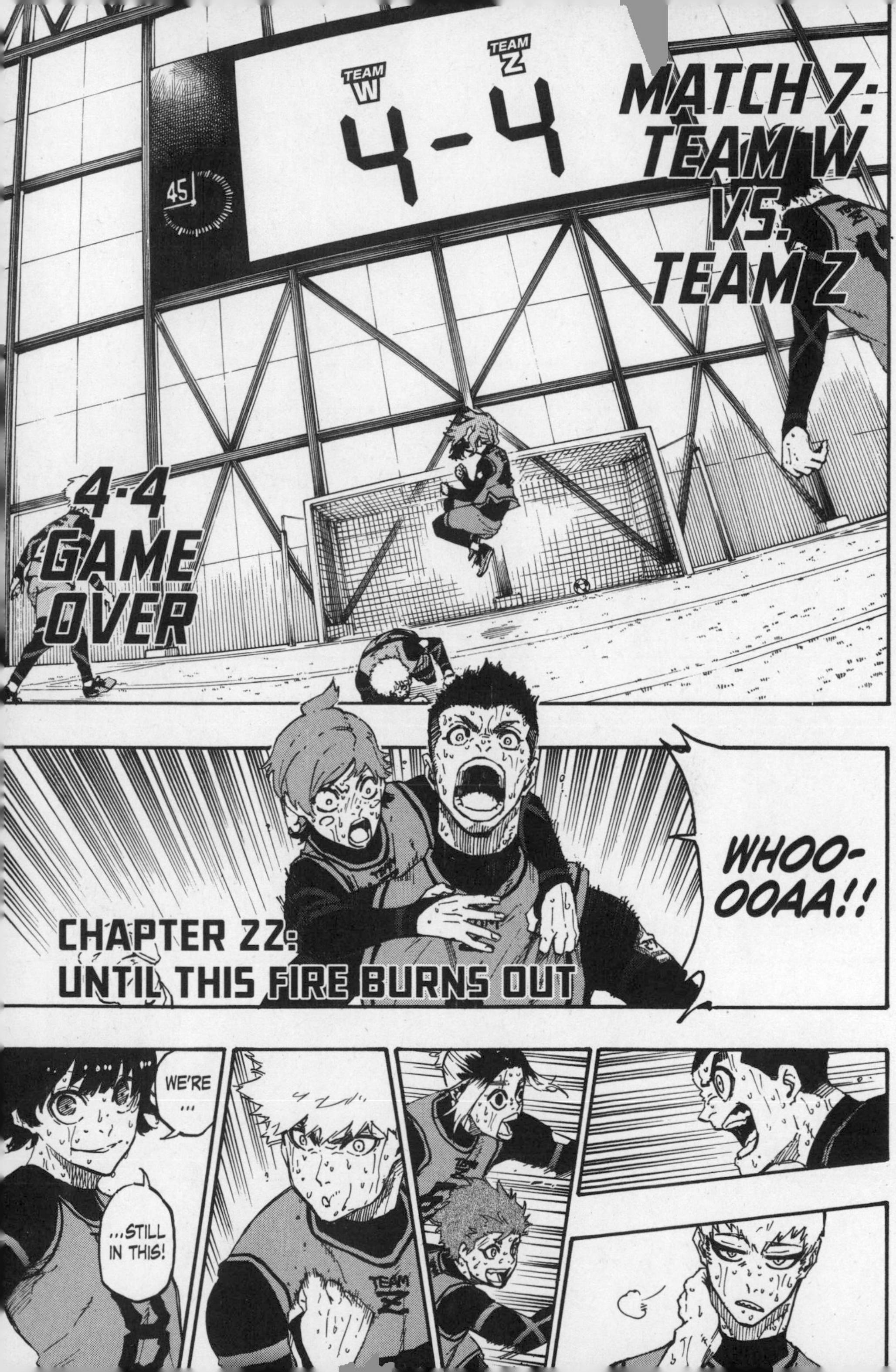
TEAM W
TEAM Z
4-4
45
MATCH 7: TEAM W VS. TEAM Z
4-4 GAME OVER
WHOO-OOAA!!
CHAPTER 22: UNTIL THIS FIRE BURNS OUT
WE'RE ...
...STILL IN THIS!

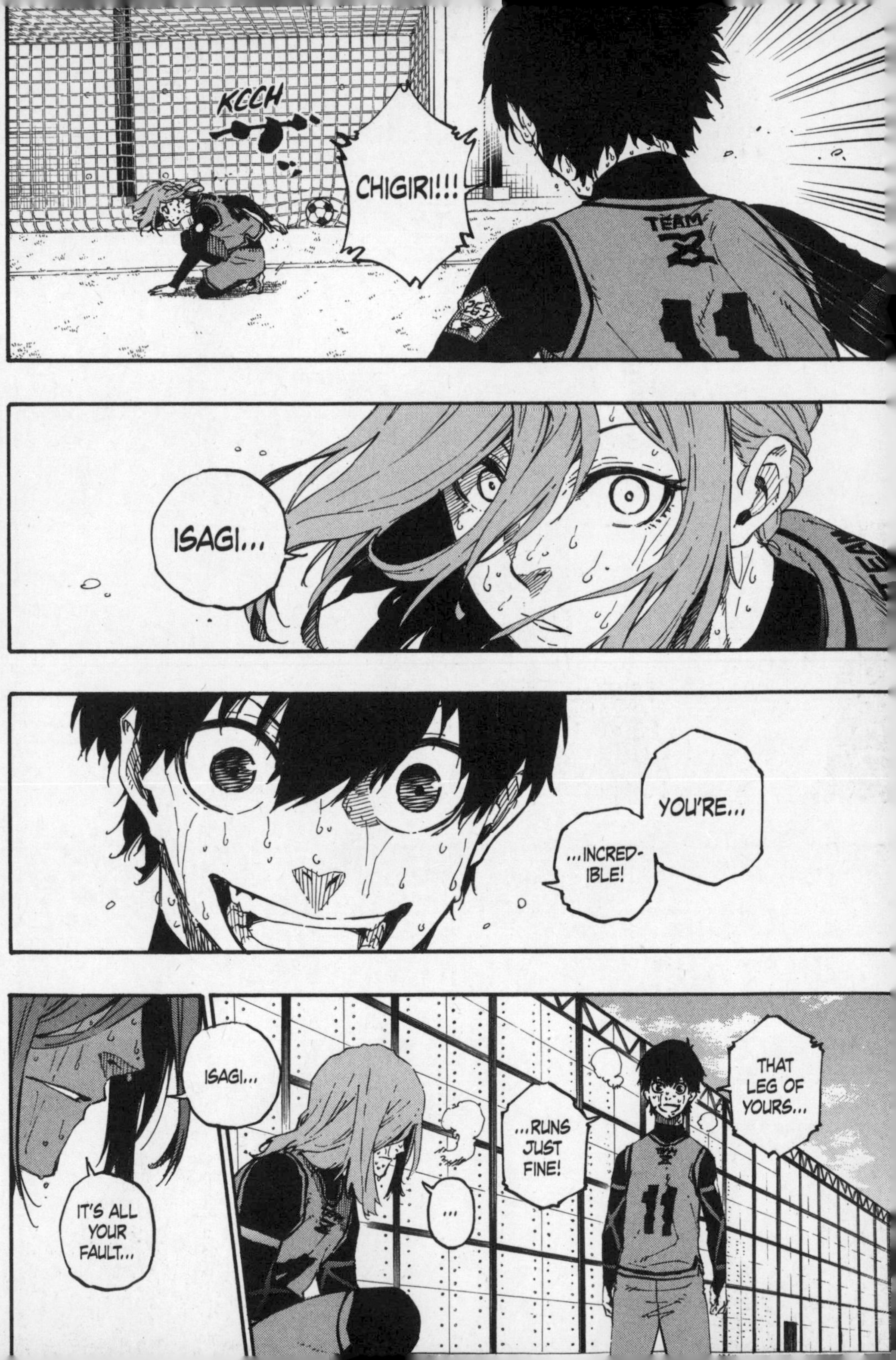
KCCH
CHIGIRI!!!
ISAGI...
YOU'RE...
...INCRED-IBLE!
THAT LEG OF YOURS...
...RUNS JUST FINE!
ISAGI...
...
IT'S ALL YOUR FAULT...

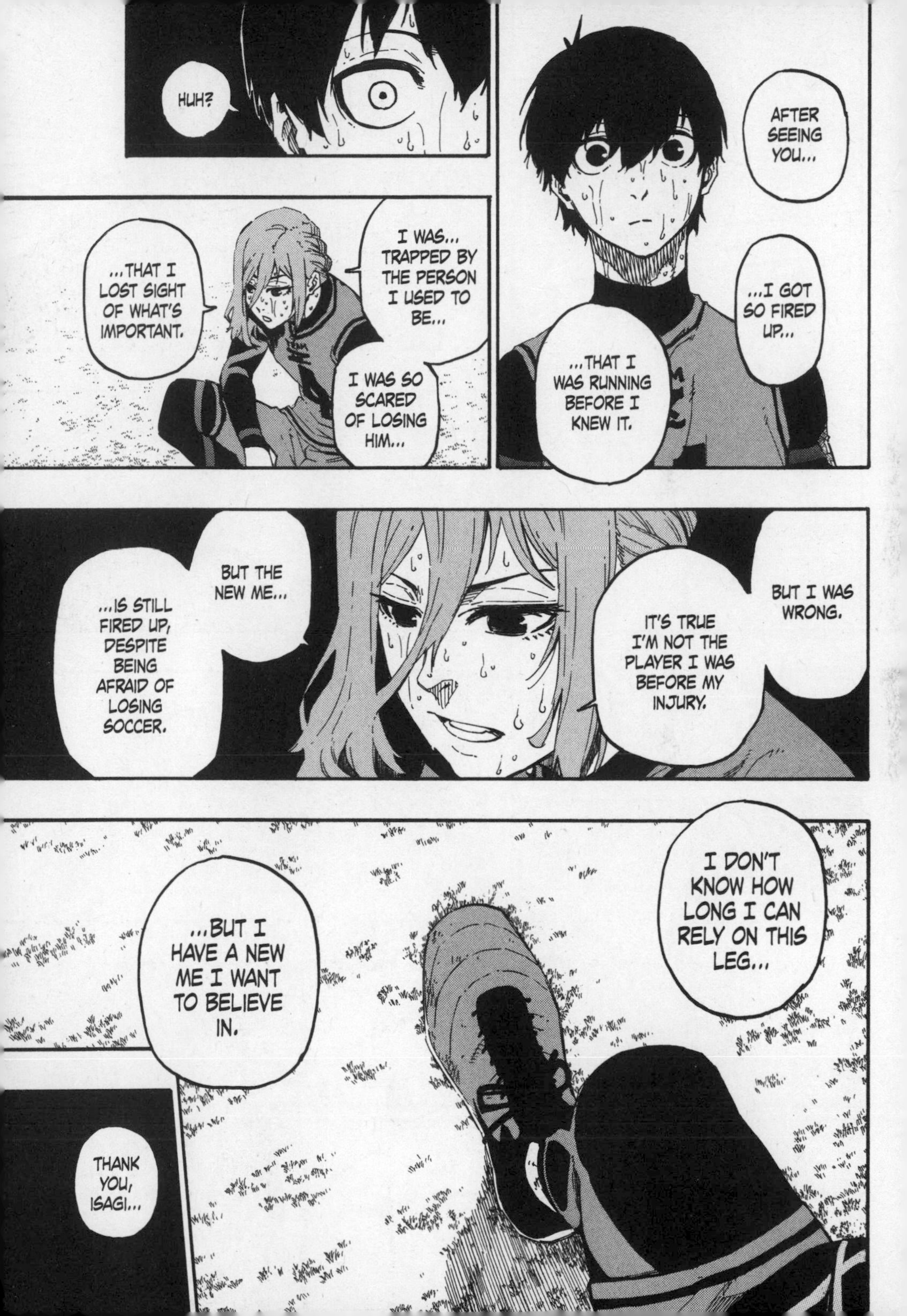
AFTER SEEING YOU...
...I GOT SO FIRED UP...
...THAT I WAS RUNNING BEFORE I KNEW IT.
HUH?
I WAS... TRAPPED BY THE PERSON I USED TO BE...
I WAS SO SCARED OF LOSING HIM...
...THAT I LOST SIGHT OF WHAT'S IMPORTANT.
BUT I WAS WRONG.
IT'S TRUE I'M NOT THE PLAYER I WAS BEFORE MY INJURY.
BUT THE NEW ME...
...IS STILL FIRED UP, DESPITE BEING AFRAID OF LOSING SOCCER.
I DON'T KNOW HOW LONG I CAN RELY ON THIS LEG...
...BUT I HAVE A NEW ME I WANT TO BELIEVE IN.
THANK YOU, ISAGI...

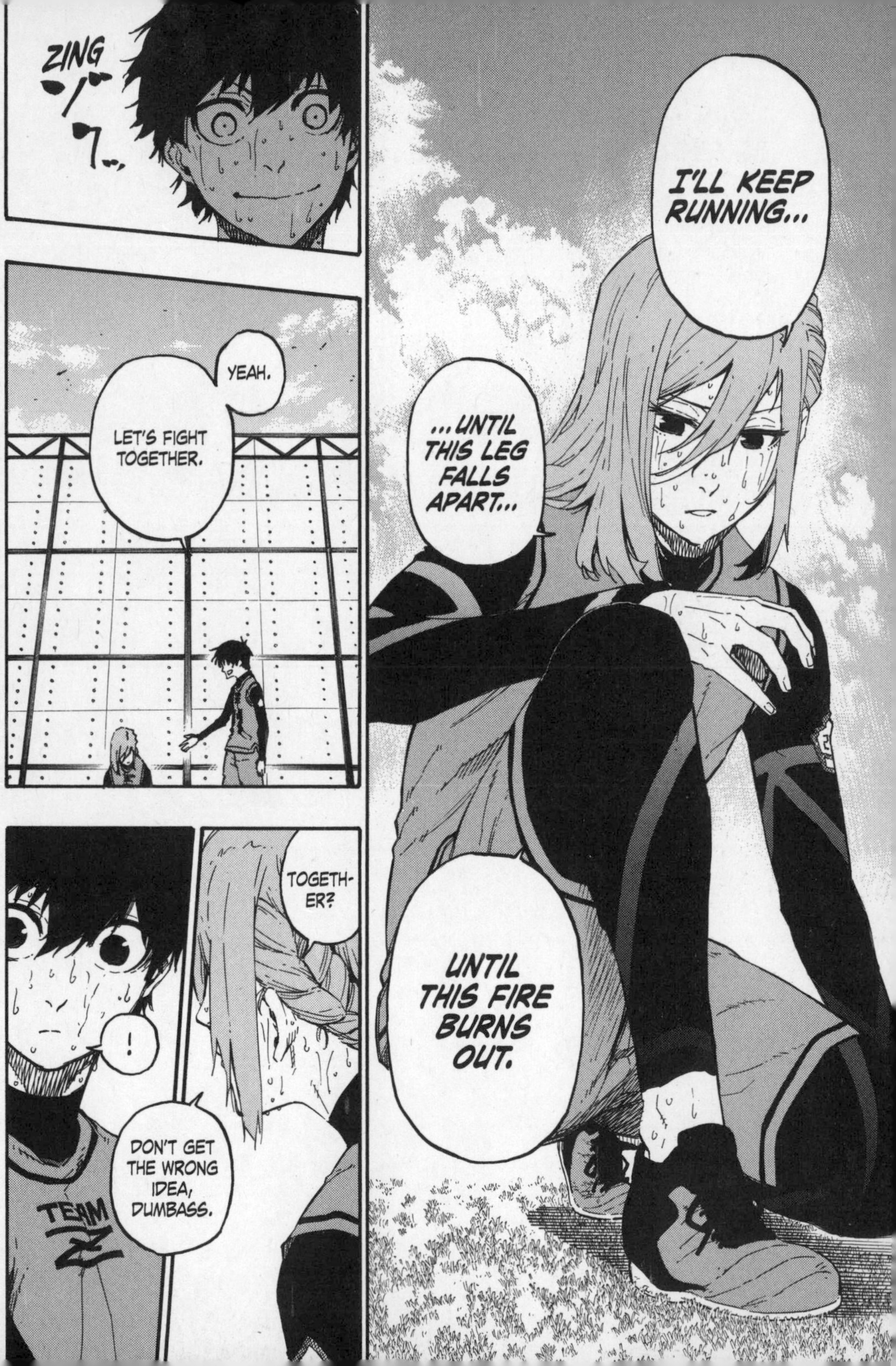
I'LL KEEP RUNNING...
...UNTIL THIS LEG FALLS APART...
UNTIL THIS FIRE BURNS OUT.
ZING
YEAH.
LET'S FIGHT TOGETHER.
TOGETH-ER?
!
DON'T GET THE WRONG IDEA, DUMBASS.
TEAM Z

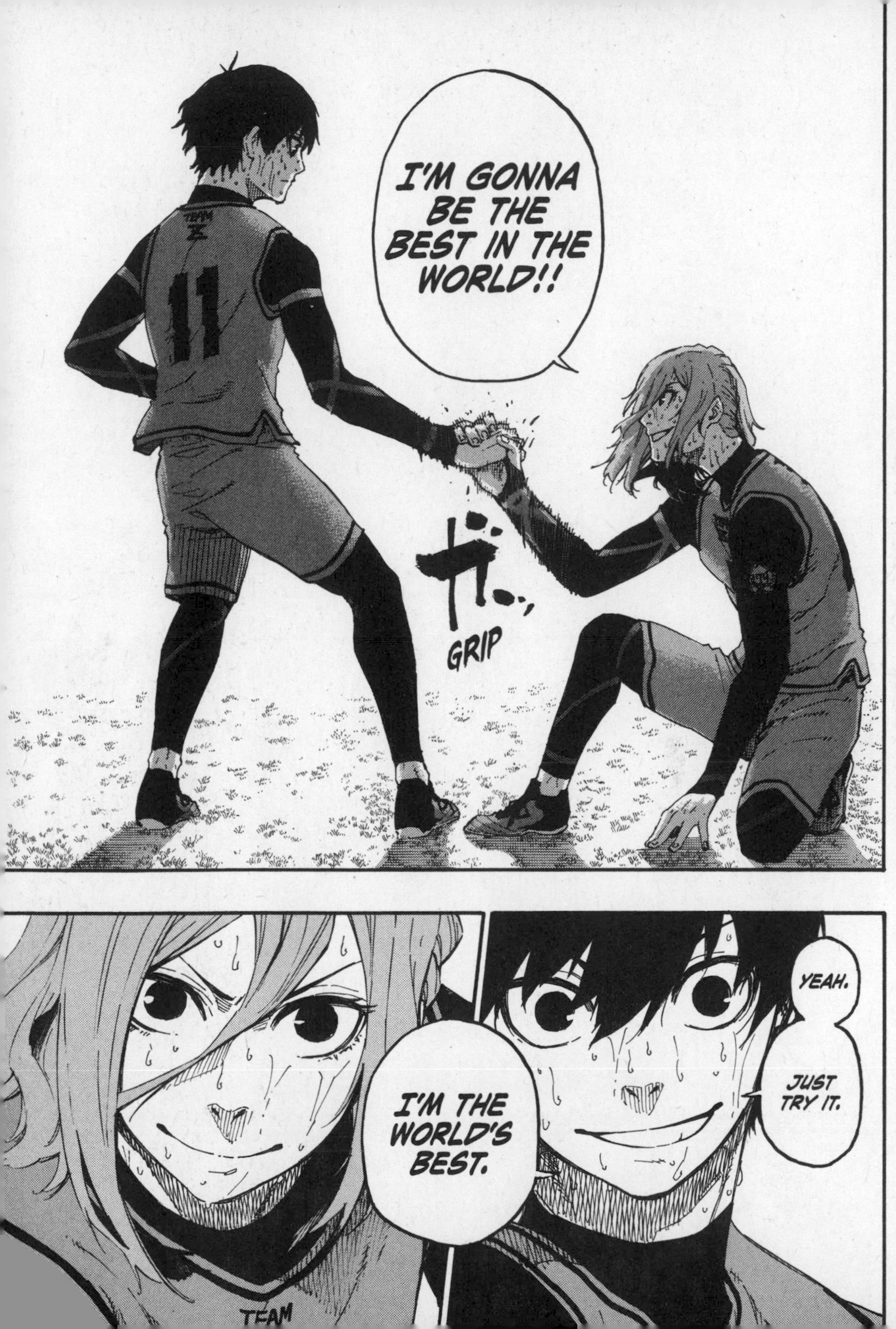
I'M GONNA BE THE BEST IN THE WORLD!!
GRIP
YEAH.
JUST TRY IT.
I'M THE WORLD'S BEST.
TEAM

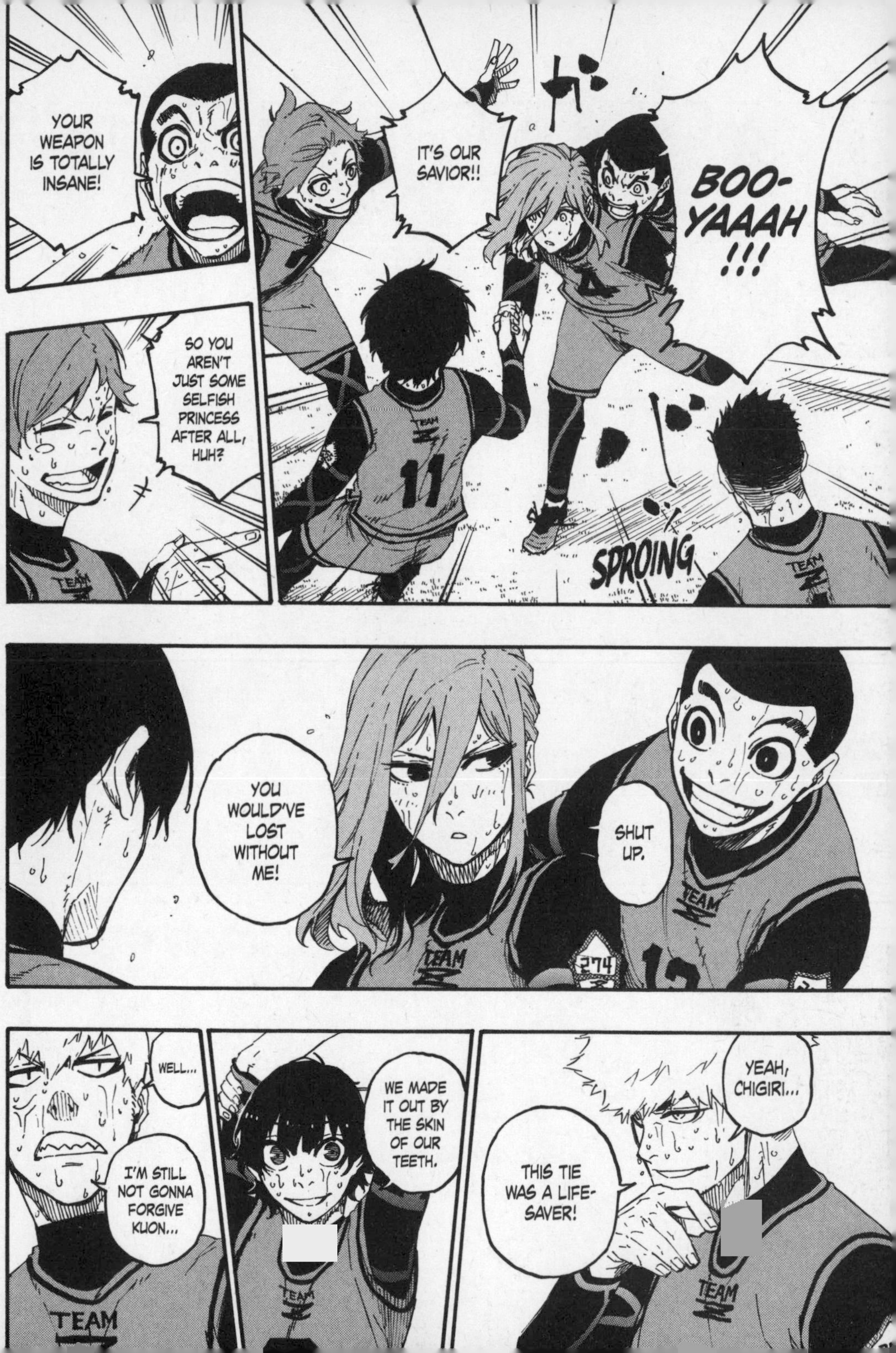
IT'S OUR SAVIOR!!
BOO-YAAAH!!!
SPROING
YOUR WEAPON IS TOTALLY INSANE!
SO YOU AREN'T JUST SOME SELFISH PRINCESS AFTER ALL, HUH?
YOU WOULD'VE LOST WITHOUT ME!
SHUT UP.
YEAH, CHIGIRI...
THIS TIE WAS A LIFE-SAVER!
WE MADE IT OUT BY THE SKIN OF OUR TEETH.
WELL...
I'M STILL NOT GONNA FORGIVE KUON...

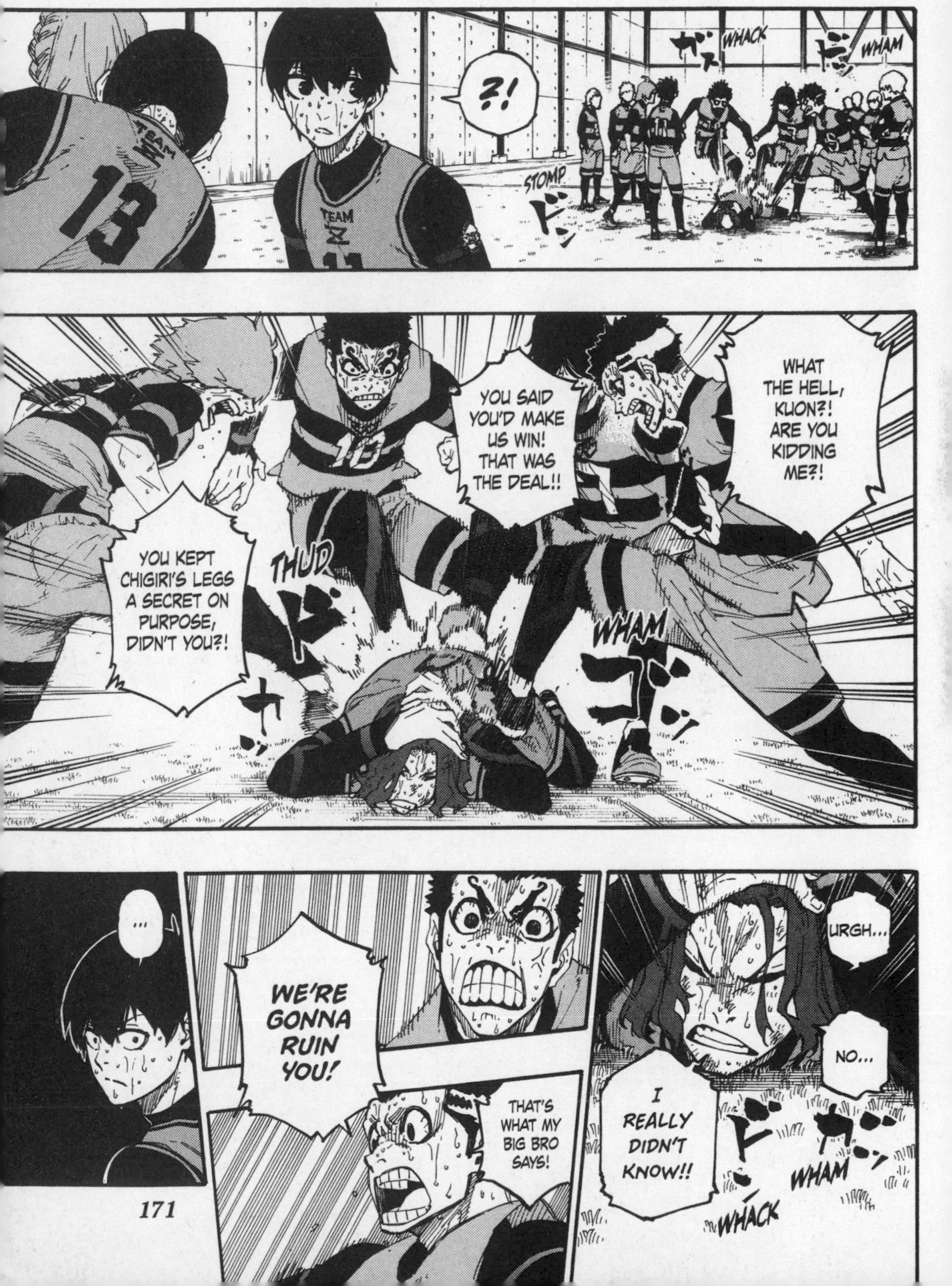
WHAM
WHACK
?!
STOMP
WHAT THE HELL, KUON?! ARE YOU KIDDING ME?!
YOU SAID YOU'D MAKE US WIN! THAT WAS THE DEAL!!
THUD
WHAM
YOU KEPT CHIGIRI'S LEGS A SECRET ON PURPOSE, DIDN'T YOU?!
URGH...
NO...
I REALLY DIDN'T KNOW!!
WHAM
WHACK
WE'RE GONNA RUIN YOU!
THAT'S WHAT MY BIG BRO SAYS!
...

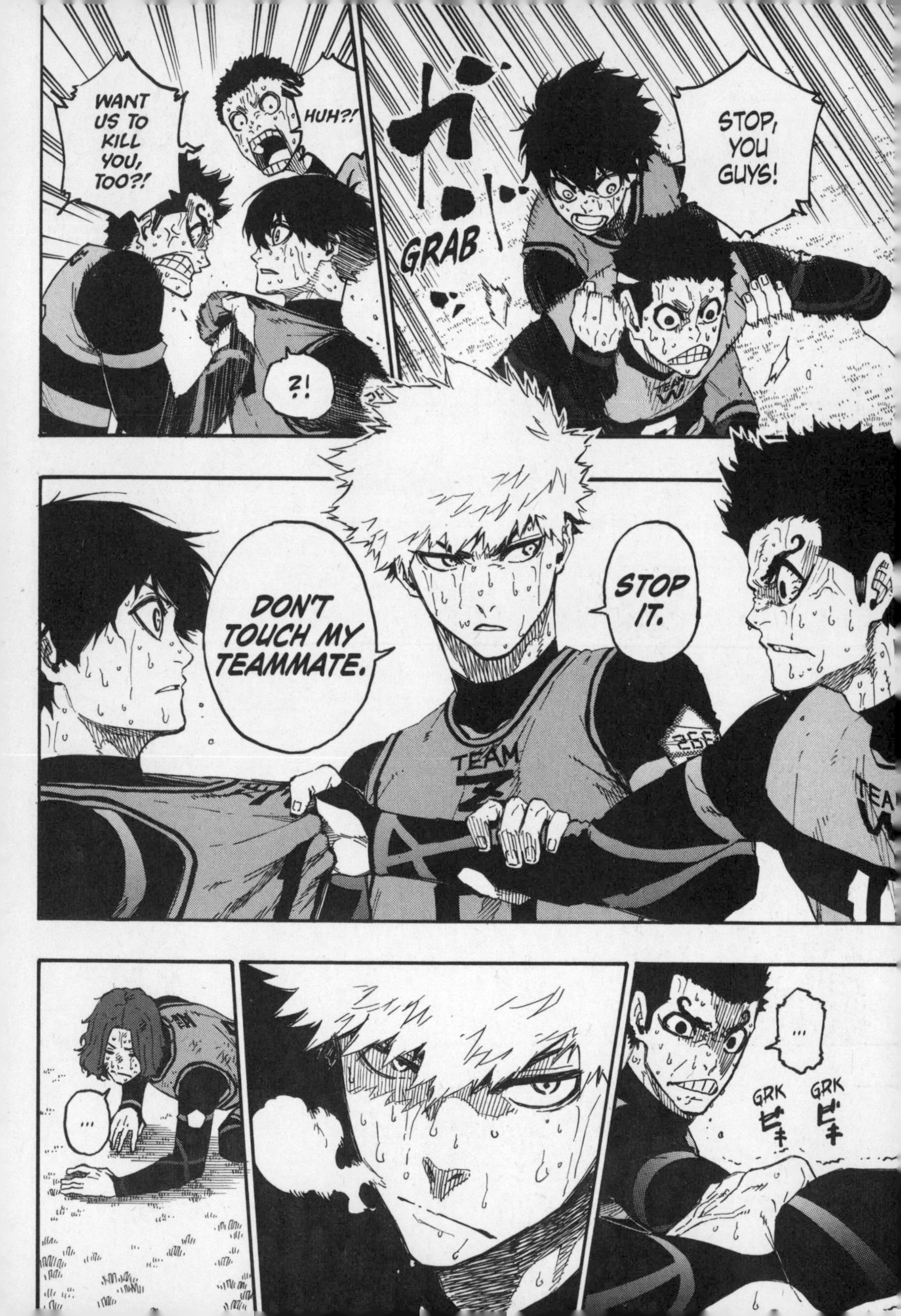
STOP, YOU GUYS!
GRAB
WANT US TO KILL YOU, TOO?!
HUH?!
?!
STOP IT.
DON'T TOUCH MY TEAMMATE.
...
GRK ビキ
GRK ビキ
...

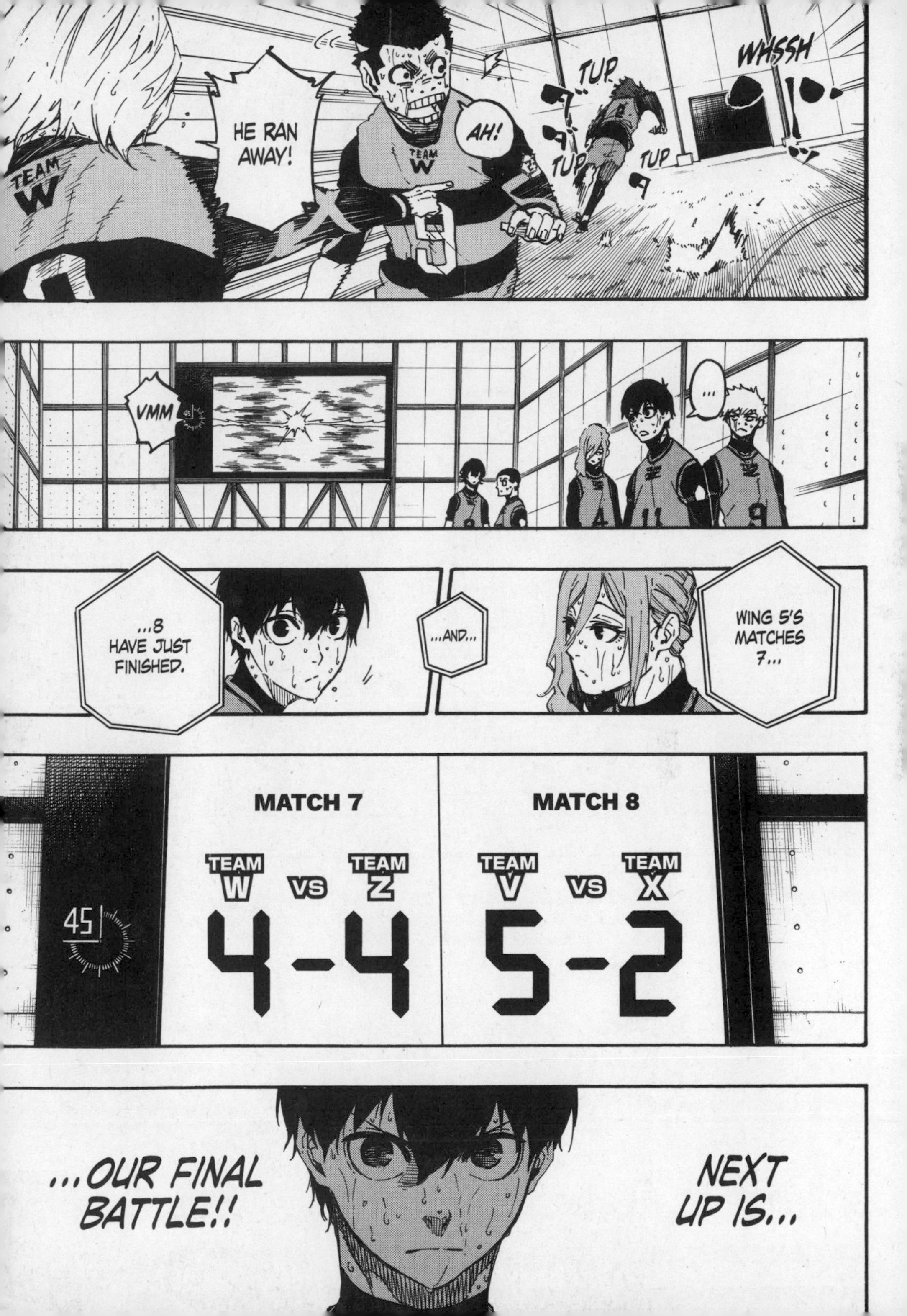
WHSSH
TUP
TUP
TUP
AH!
HE RAN AWAY!
...
VMM
WING 5'S MATCHES 7...
...AND...
...8 HAVE JUST FINISHED.
MATCH 7
TEAM W VS TEAM Z
4-4
MATCH 8
TEAM V VS TEAM X
5-2
45
NEXT UP IS...
...OUR FINAL BATTLE!!

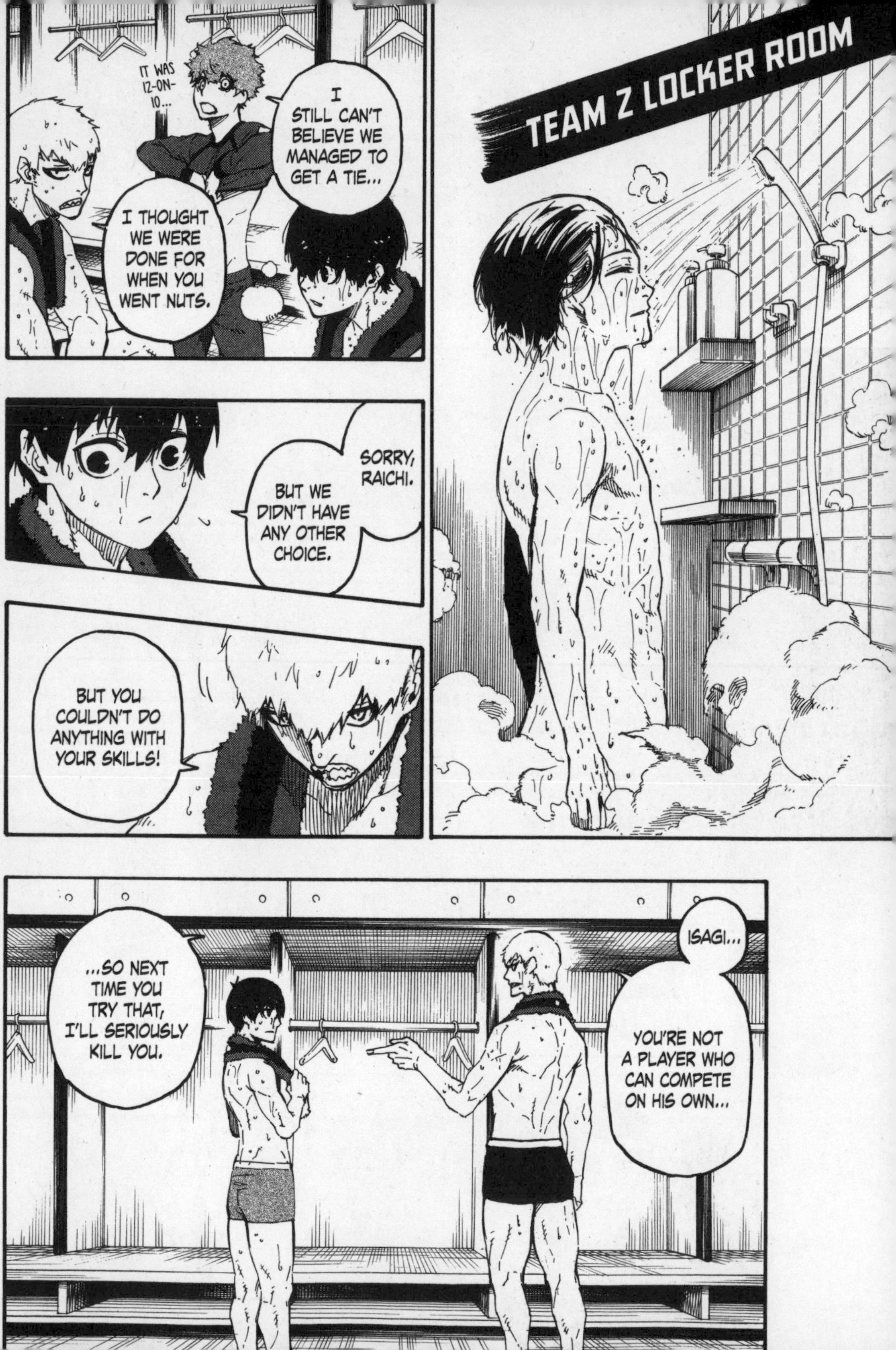
TEAM Z LOCKER ROOM
I STILL CAN'T BELIEVE WE MANAGED TO GET A TIE...
IT WAS 12-ON-10...
I THOUGHT WE WERE DONE FOR WHEN YOU WENT NUTS.
SORRY, RAICHI.
BUT WE DIDN'T HAVE ANY OTHER CHOICE.
BUT YOU COULDN'T DO ANYTHING WITH YOUR SKILLS!
ISAGI...
YOU'RE NOT A PLAYER WHO CAN COMPETE ON HIS OWN...
...SO NEXT TIME YOU TRY THAT, I'LL SERIOUSLY KILL YOU.

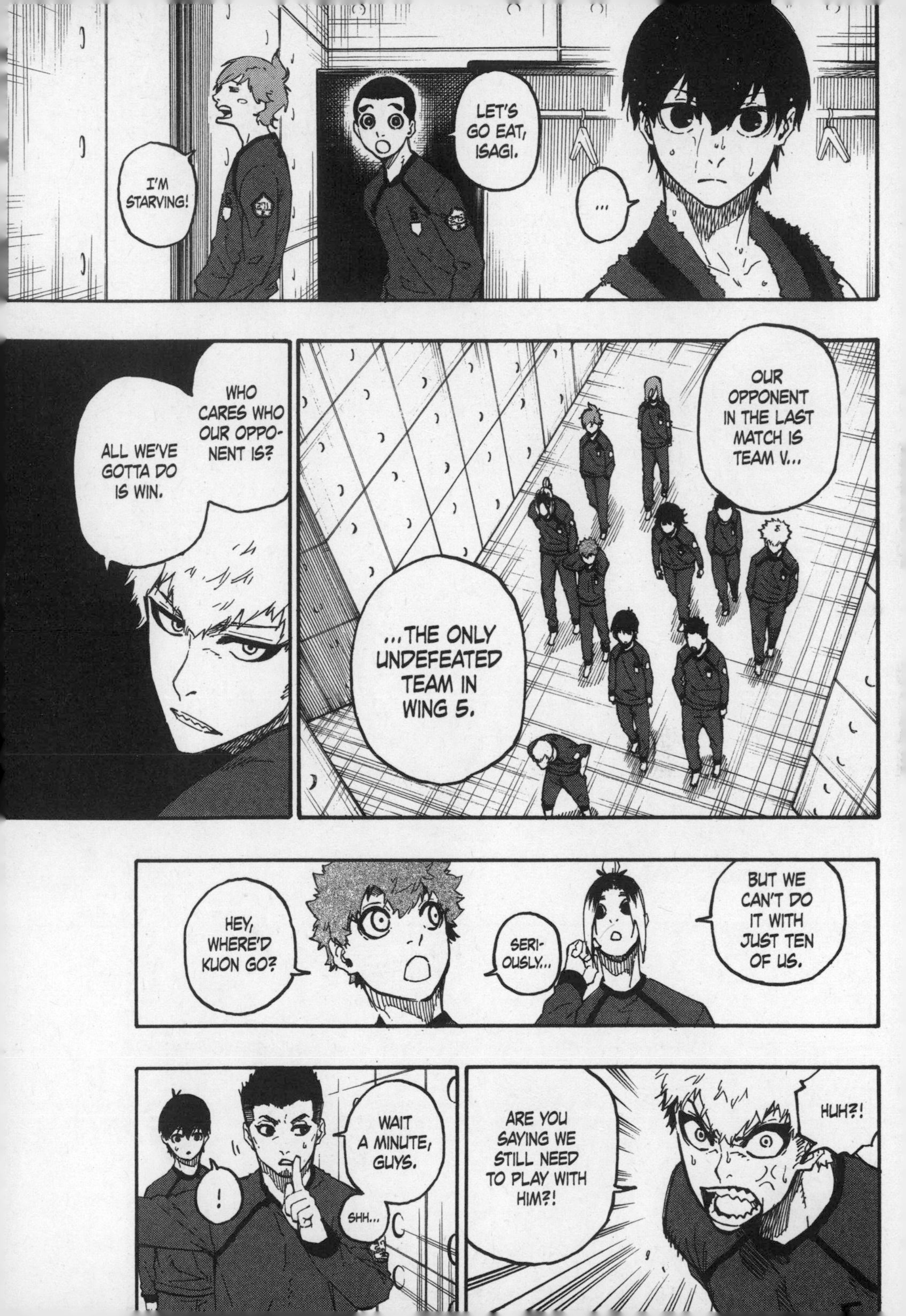
LET'S GO EAT, ISAGI.
...
I'M STARVING!
OUR OPPONENT IN THE LAST MATCH IS TEAM V...
...THE ONLY UNDEFEATED TEAM IN WING 5.
WHO CARES WHO OUR OPPO-NENT IS?
ALL WE'VE GOTTA DO IS WIN.
BUT WE CAN'T DO IT WITH JUST TEN OF US.
SERI-OUSLY...
HEY, WHERE'D KUON GO?
HUH?!
ARE YOU SAYING WE STILL NEED TO PLAY WITH HIM?!
WAIT A MINUTE, GUYS.
!
SHH...

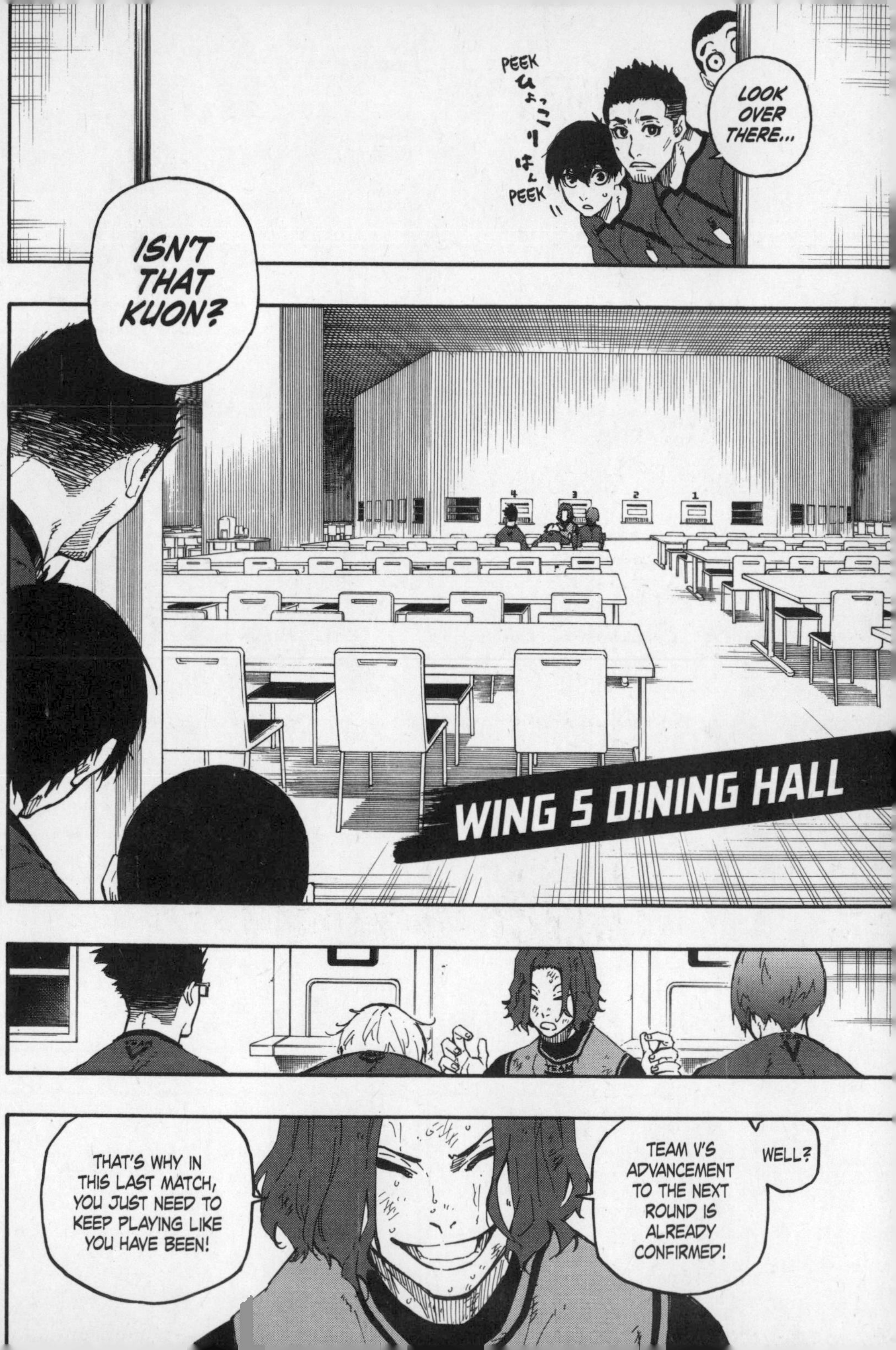
LOOK OVER THERE...
PEEK
ひょっこり
はん
PEEK
ISN'T THAT KUON?
WING 5 DINING HALL
WELL?
TEAM V'S ADVANCEMENT TO THE NEXT ROUND IS ALREADY CONFIRMED!
THAT'S WHY IN THIS LAST MATCH, YOU JUST NEED TO KEEP PLAYING LIKE YOU HAVE BEEN!

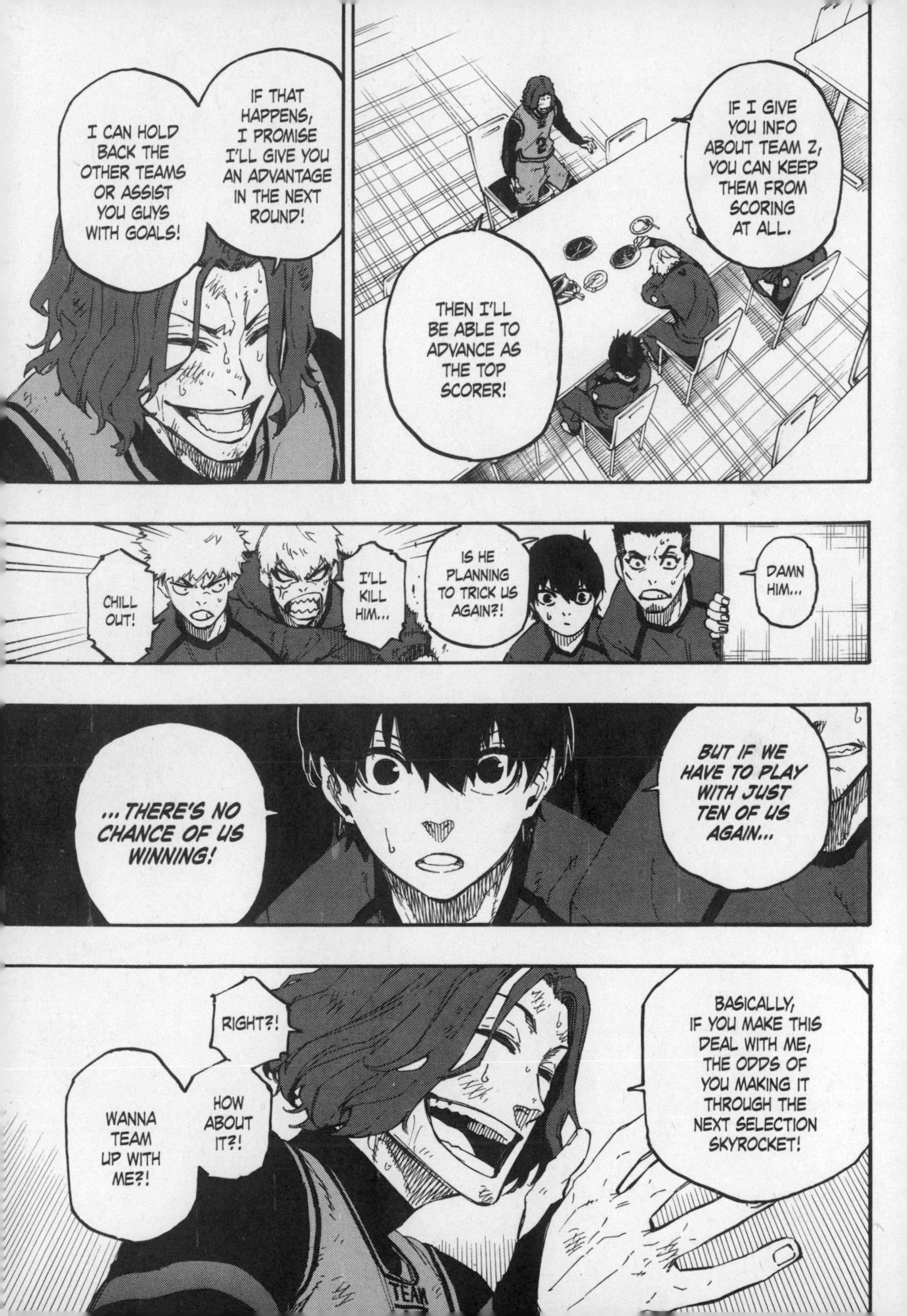
IF I GIVE YOU INFO ABOUT TEAM 2, YOU CAN KEEP THEM FROM SCORING AT ALL.
THEN I'LL BE ABLE TO ADVANCE AS THE TOP SCORER!
IF THAT HAPPENS, I PROMISE I'LL GIVE YOU AN ADVANTAGE IN THE NEXT ROUND!
I CAN HOLD BACK THE OTHER TEAMS OR ASSIST YOU GUYS WITH GOALS!
DAMN HIM...
IS HE PLANNING TO TRICK US AGAIN?!
I'LL KILL HIM...
CHILL OUT!
BUT IF WE HAVE TO PLAY WITH JUST TEN OF US AGAIN...
...THERE'S NO CHANCE OF US WINNING!
BASICALLY, IF YOU MAKE THIS DEAL WITH ME, THE ODDS OF YOU MAKING IT THROUGH THE NEXT SELECTION SKYROCKET!
RIGHT?!
HOW ABOUT IT?!
WANNA TEAM UP WITH ME?!

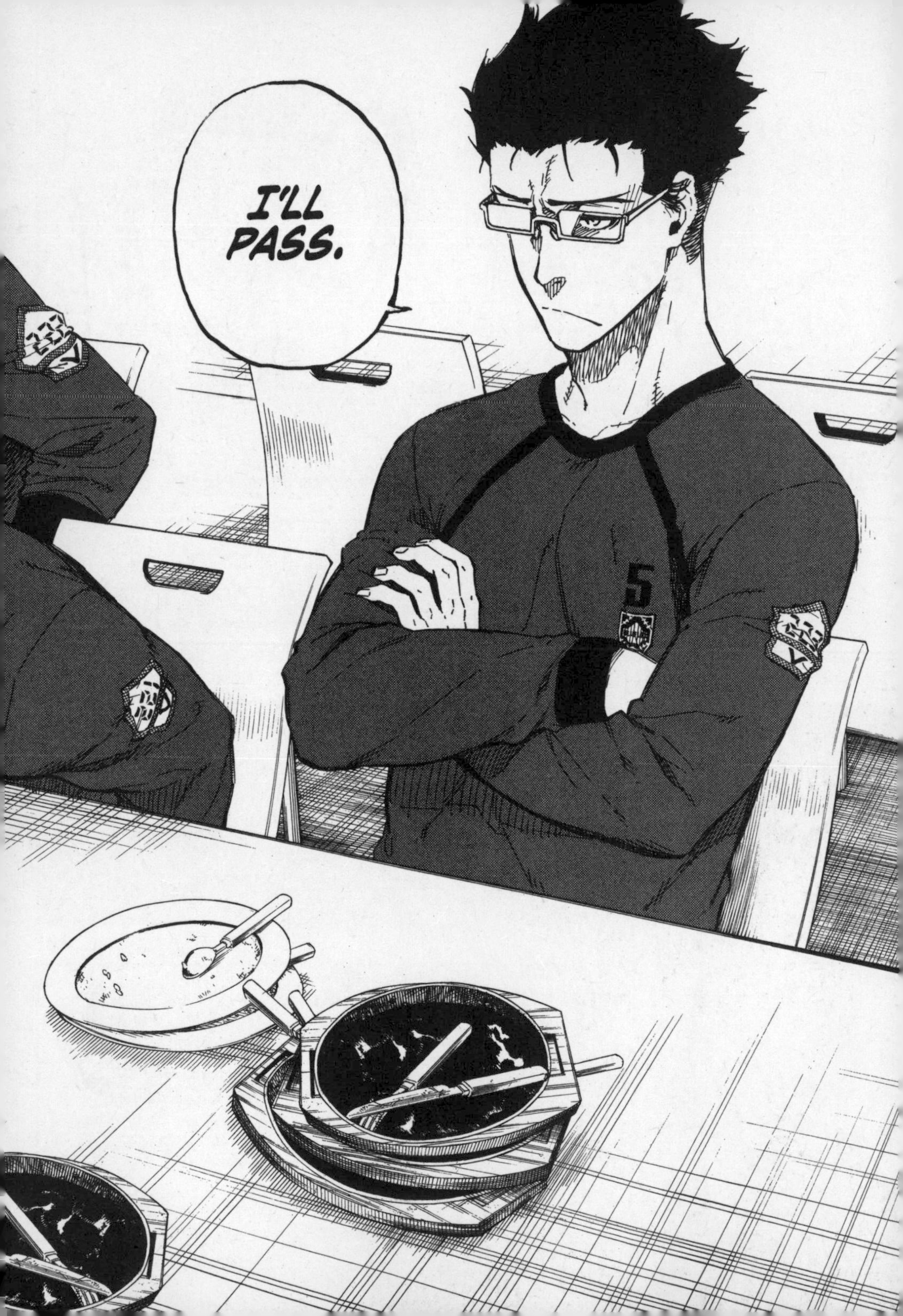
I'LL PASS.

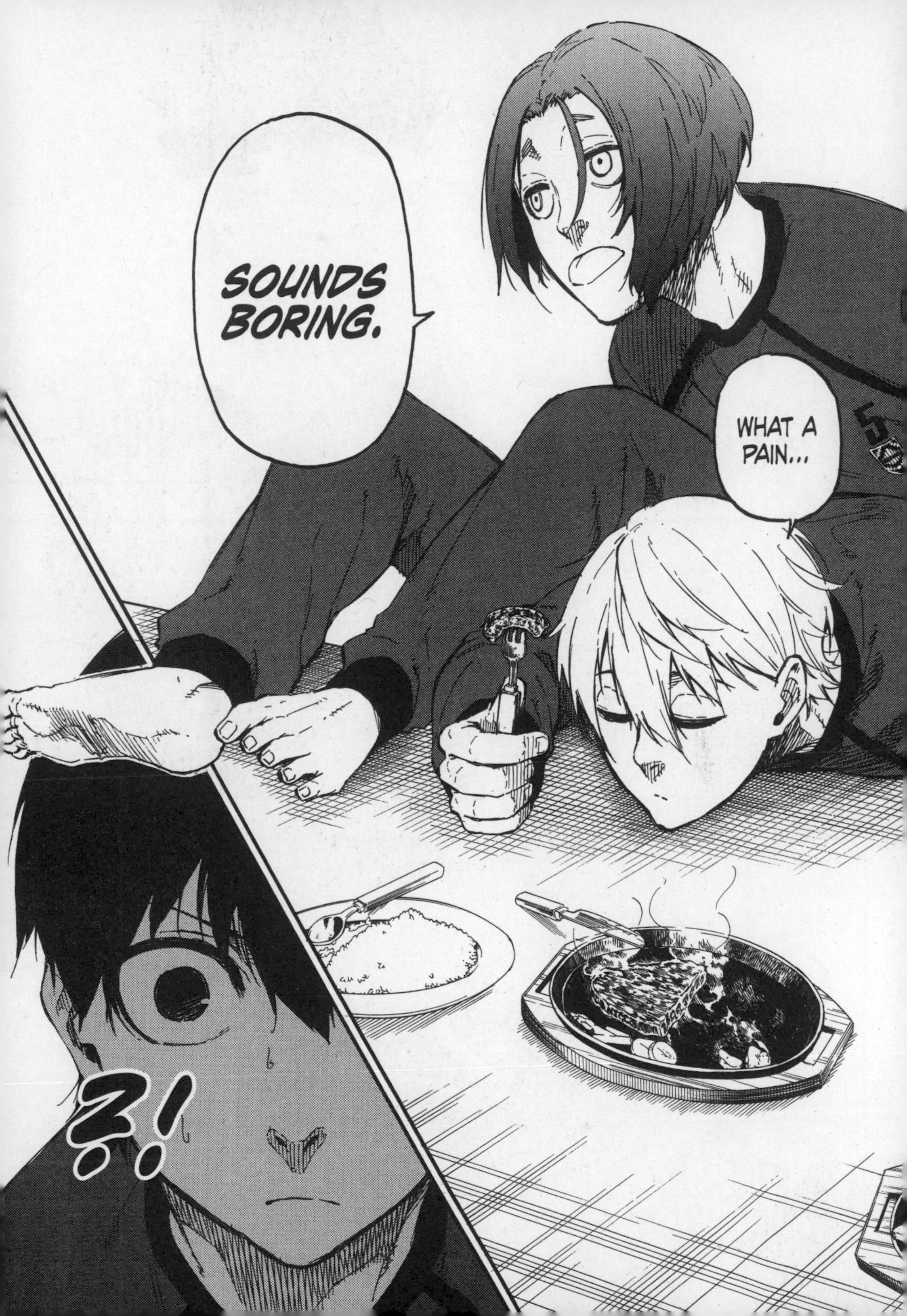
WHAT A PAIN...
SOUNDS BORING.
?!

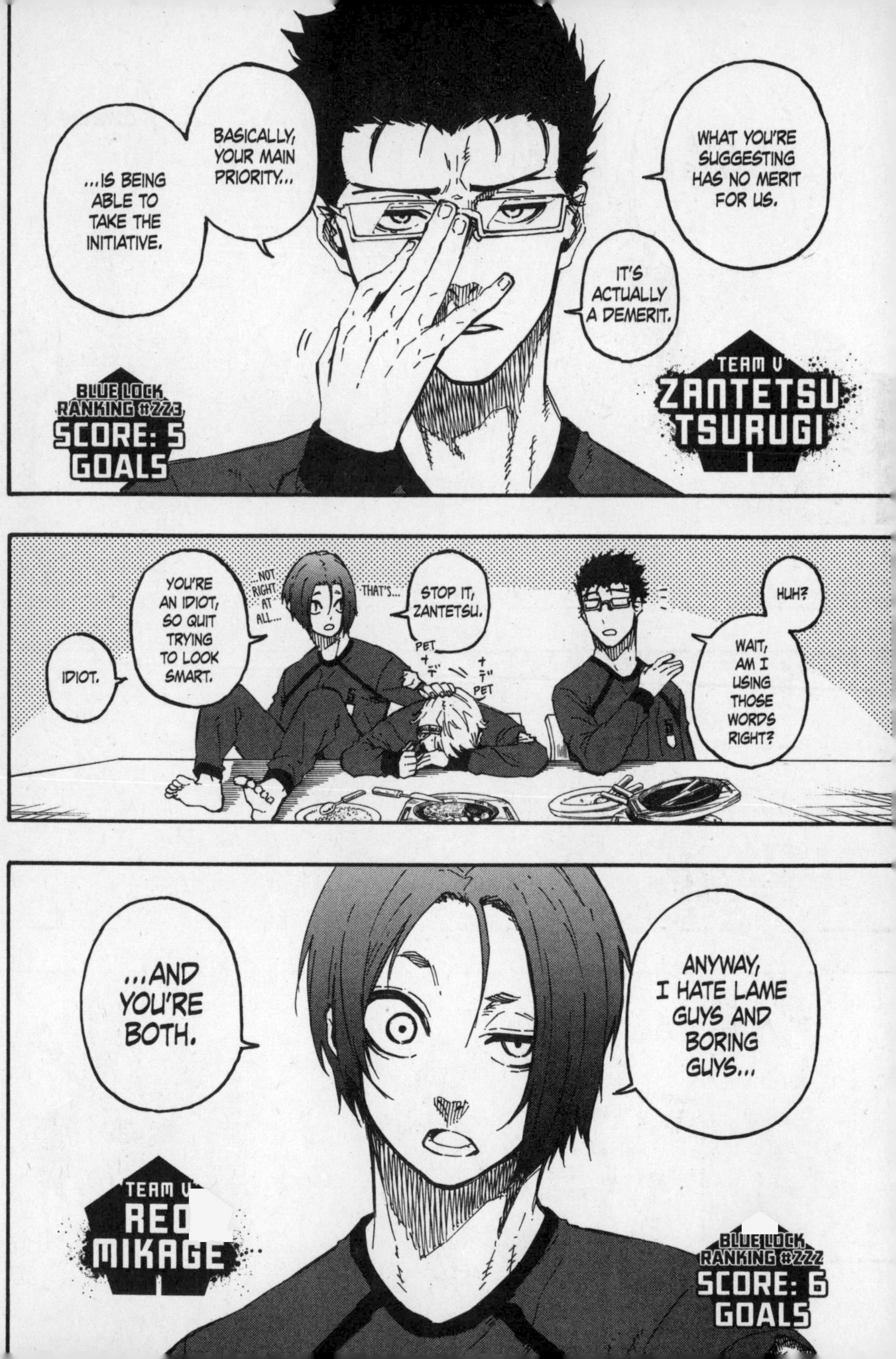
WHAT YOU'RE SUGGESTING HAS NO MERIT FOR US.
IT'S ACTUALLY A DEMERIT.
BASICALLY, YOUR MAIN PRIORITY...
...IS BEING ABLE TO TAKE THE INITIATIVE.
TEAM V
ZANTETSU TSURUGI
BLUE LOCK RANKING #223
SCORE: 5 GOALS
HUH?
WAIT, AM I USING THOSE WORDS RIGHT?
STOP IT, ZANTETSU.
THAT'S...
...NOT RIGHT AT ALL...
PET
PET
YOU'RE AN IDIOT, SO QUIT TRYING TO LOOK SMART.
IDIOT.
ANYWAY, I HATE LAME GUYS AND BORING GUYS...
...AND YOU'RE BOTH.
TEAM V
REO MIKAGE
BLUE LOCK RANKING #222
SCORE: 6 GOALS

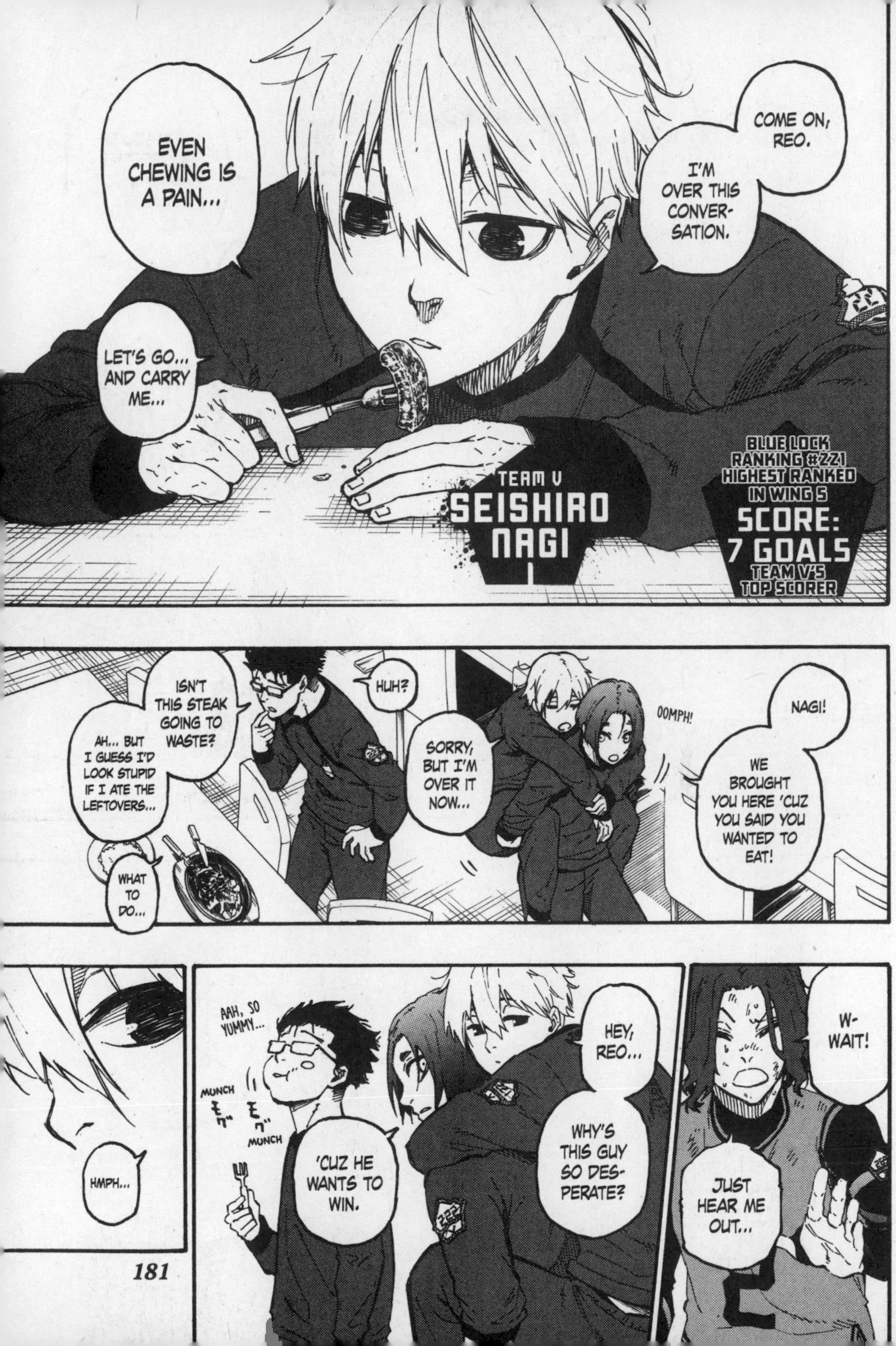
COME ON, REO.
I'M OVER THIS CONVER-SATION.
EVEN CHEWING IS A PAIN...
LET'S GO... AND CARRY ME...
BLUE LOCK RANKING #221 HIGHEST RANKED IN WING 5
SCORE: 7 GOALS
TEAM V'S TOP SCORER
TEAM V
SEISHIRO NAGI
NAGI!
WE BROUGHT YOU HERE 'CUZ YOU SAID YOU WANTED TO EAT!
OOMPH!
SORRY, BUT I'M OVER IT NOW...
HUH?
ISN'T THIS STEAK GOING TO WASTE?
AH... BUT I GUESS I'D LOOK STUPID IF I ATE THE LEFTOVERS...
WHAT TO DO...
W-WAIT!
JUST HEAR ME OUT...
HEY, REO...
WHY'S THIS GUY SO DES-PERATE?
'CUZ HE WANTS TO WIN.
AAH, SO YUMMY...
MUNCH
MUNCH
HMPH...

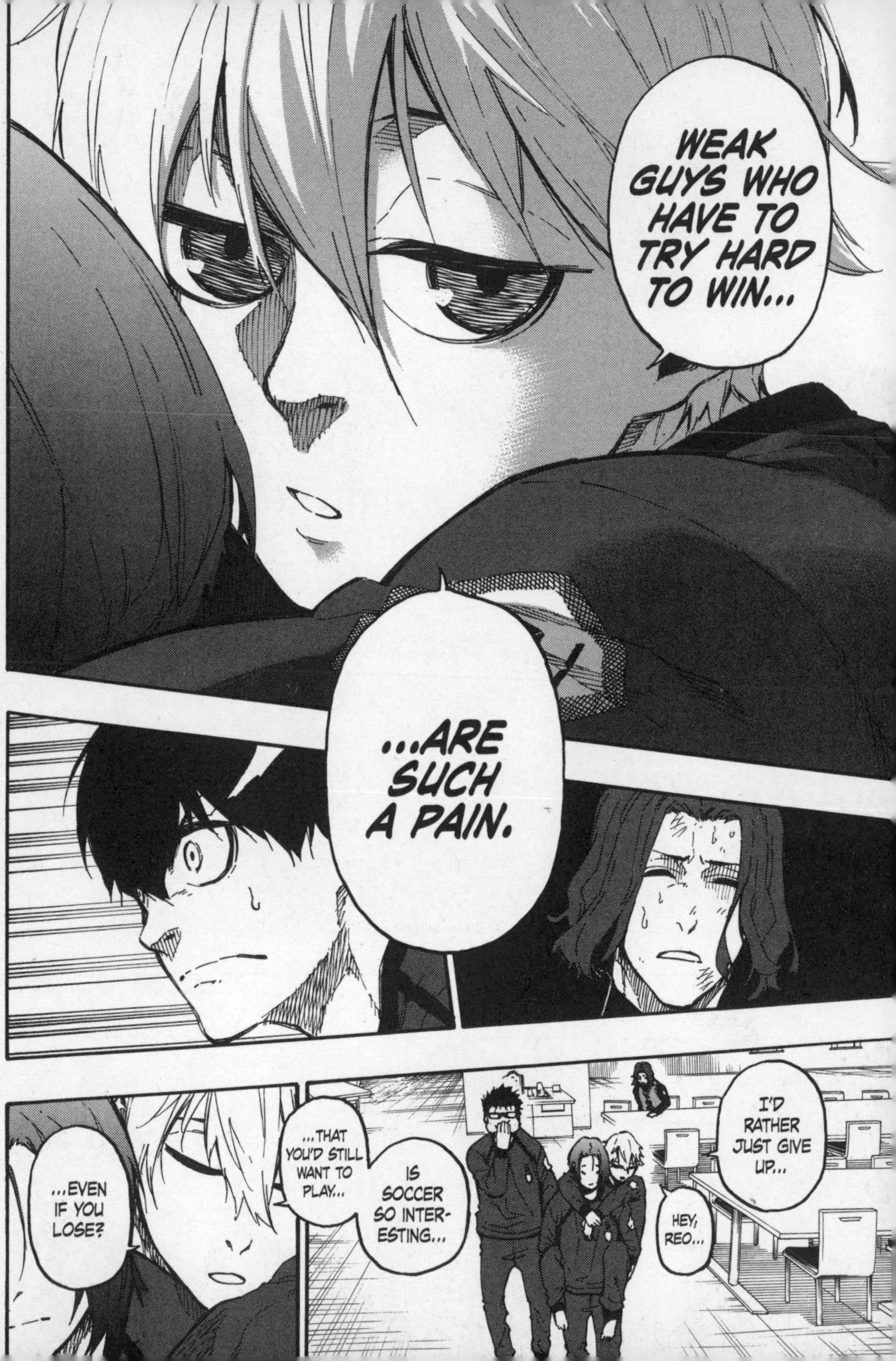
WEAK GUYS WHO HAVE TO TRY HARD TO WIN...
...ARE SUCH A PAIN.
I'D RATHER JUST GIVE UP...
HEY, REO...
IS SOCCER SO INTER-ESTING...
...THAT YOU'D STILL WANT TO PLAY...
...EVEN IF YOU LOSE?

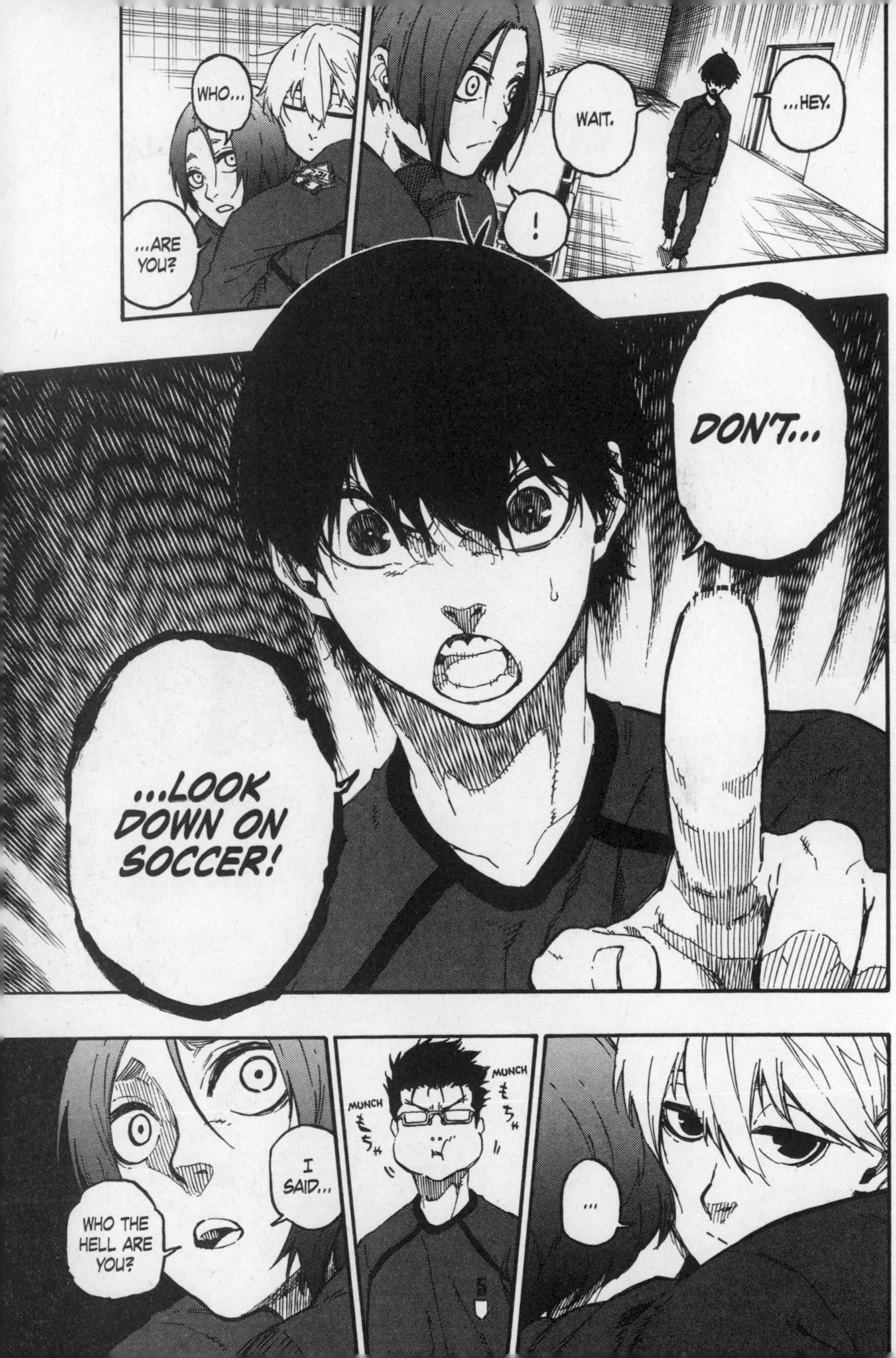
...HEY.
WAIT.
!
WHO...
...ARE YOU?
DON'T...
...LOOK DOWN ON SOCCER!
...
MUNCH
MUNCH
I SAID...
WHO THE HELL ARE YOU?

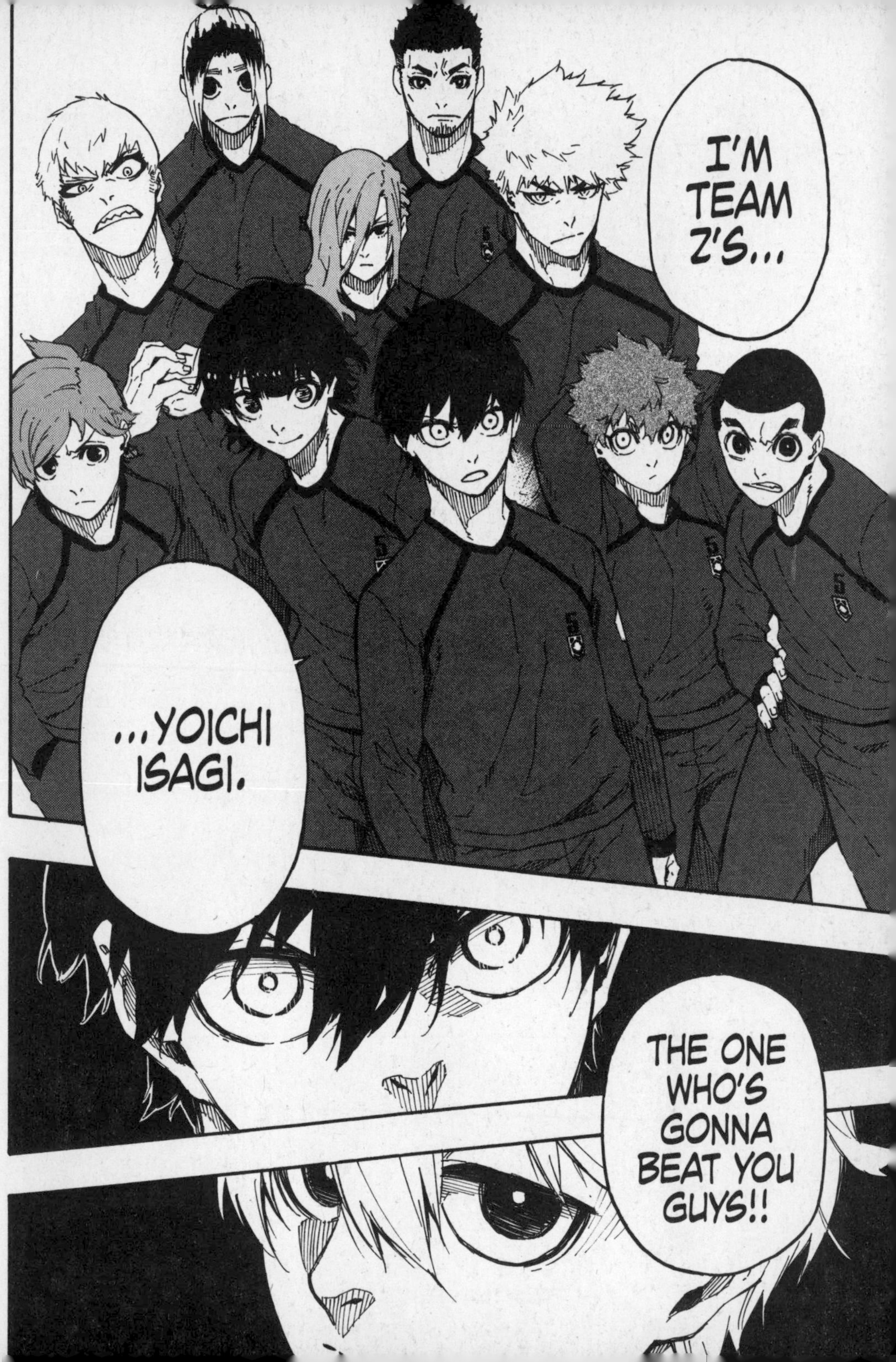
I'M TEAM Z'S...
...YOICHI ISAGI.
THE ONE WHO'S GONNA BEAT YOU GUYS!!

BLUE LOCK

CONTINUED IN VOL. 4

BLUE LOCK DAILY SCHEDULE

DAYS WITHOUT MATCHES

BONUS SECTION

TIME	CONTENTS
07:00	WAKE UP BREAKFAST
08:00	MACHINE TRAINING IN THE TRAINING ROOM
09:00	INDIVIDUAL WARM-UPS RUNNING
10:00	TEAM TRAINING • TACTICAL TRAINING • PRACTICE GAMES
11:00	

BACHIRA OFTEN OVER-SLEEPS, SO ISAGI OR KUON HAS TO WAKE HIM UP

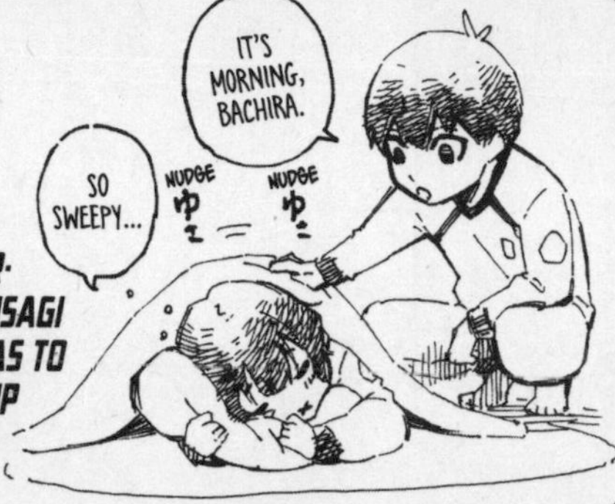
IT'S MORNING, BACHIRA.
SO SWEEPY...
NUDGE
NUDGE

KUNIGAMI STARTS TRAINING BEFORE ANYONE ELSE

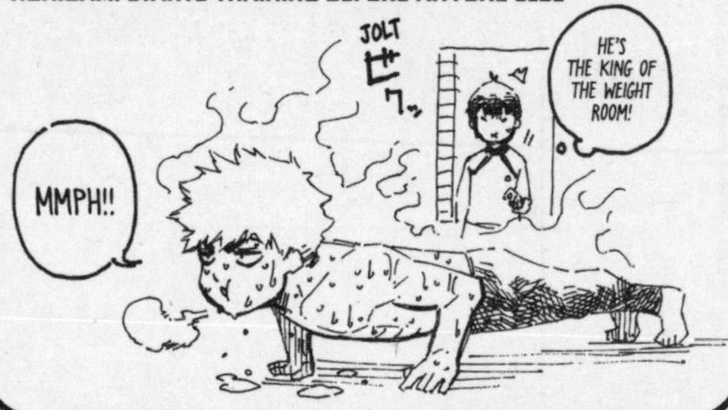
HE'S THE KING OF THE WEIGHT ROOM!
JOLT
MMPH!!

IGA-GURI OFTEN SKIPS THIS

IEMON TAKES THE INITIATIVE TO SHOW UP EARLY TO DO THINGS LIKE SET UP CONES

12:00

LUNCH

~

REST

13:00

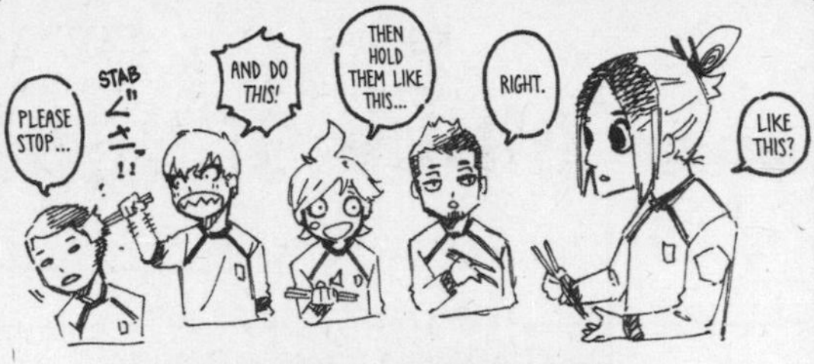
LIKE THIS?
RIGHT.
THEN HOLD THEM LIKE THIS...
AND DO THIS!
STAB
PLEASE STOP...

- BACHIRA OFTEN FALLS ASLEEP WHILE EATING
- RAICHI ALWAYS GETS ANGRY ABOUT HIS SIDE DISH, SO SOMEONE HAS TO SHARE WITH HIM
- GAGAMARU TRIES TO EAT WITH HIS HANDS, SO SOMEONE HAS TO TEACH HIM HOW TO USE CHOPSTICKS

14:00

TEAM TRAINING

- TACTICAL TRAINING
- PRACTICE GAMES

15:00

16:00

INDIVIDUAL TRAINING
↓
AFTERWARDS, SHOWER AND EAT DINNER INDIVIDUALLY

17:00

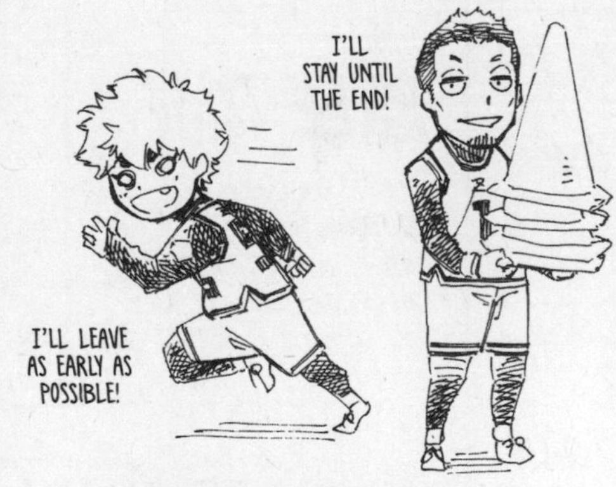
I'LL STAY UNTIL THE END!
I'LL LEAVE AS EARLY AS POSSIBLE!

- ISAGI OFTEN PRACTICES WITH BACHIRA
- NARUHAYA ALWAYS LEAVES PRACTICE EARLY
- IEMON ALWAYS STAYS UNTIL THE END TO PRACTICE WITH THE OTHERS

18:00

DINNER

~

EVERYONE EATS SEPARATELY

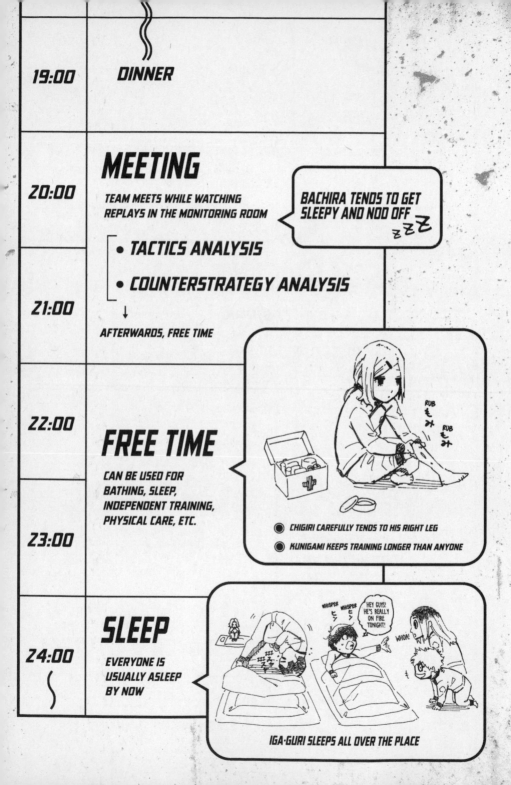

19:00	DINNER
20:00	**MEETING** TEAM MEETS WHILE WATCHING REPLAYS IN THE MONITORING ROOM • TACTICS ANALYSIS • COUNTERSTRATEGY ANALYSIS
21:00	↓ AFTERWARDS, FREE TIME
22:00	**FREE TIME** CAN BE USED FOR BATHING, SLEEP, INDEPENDENT TRAINING, PHYSICAL CARE, ETC.
23:00	
24:00	**SLEEP** EVERYONE IS USUALLY ASLEEP BY NOW

BACHIRA TENDS TO GET SLEEPY AND NOD OFF zzZ

RUB
もみ
RUB
もみ

- CHIGIRI CAREFULLY TENDS TO HIS RIGHT LEG
- KUNIGAMI KEEPS TRAINING LONGER THAN ANYONE

WHISPER
ヒソ
WHISPER
ヒソ
HEY GUYS! HE'S REALLY ON FIRE TONIGHT!
WHOA!
ZZZ
スヤ

IGA-GURI SLEEPS ALL OVER THE PLACE

◉STORY	MUNEYUKI KANESHIRO
◉ART	YUSUKE NOMURA
◉ART ASSISTANTS	SUEHIRO-SAN SATOU-SAN FUJIMAKI-SAN OTAKE-SAN MAEHATA-SAN FURUMOTO-SAN ARATAMA-SAN HARADA-SAN URATANI-SAN NAKAMURA-SAN TAKANIWA-SAN IMANO-SAN (LISTED RANDOMLY)
◉DESIGN	KUMOCHI-SAN OBA-SAN (HIVE)

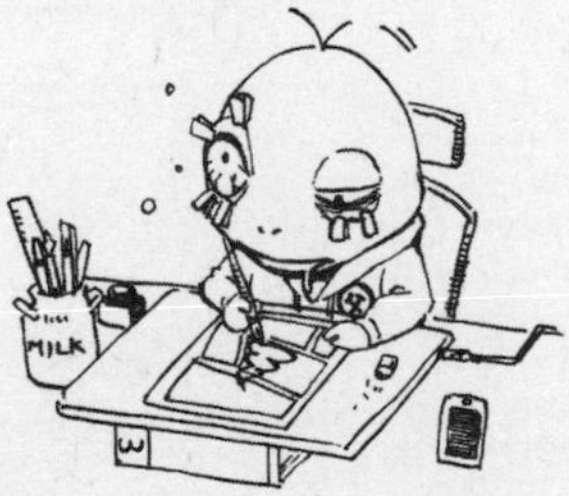
MILK

THANK YOU SO MUCH FOR BUYING VOLUME 3!!

Yusuke Nomura

"It's been half a year since serialization, and we've made it to volume 3! But only volume 3...? When I line up volume 1, 2, and 3, the colors resemble a traffic light. That's totally what I was aiming for. (/s)"

Yusuke Nomura debuted in 2014 with the grotesquely cute cult hit alien invasion story *Dolly Kill Kill*, which was released digitally in English by Kodansha. Nomura is the illustrator behind *Blue Lock*.

Muneyuki Kaneshiro

"When I was a kid, I would break out into tears when watching sports. The sweet taste of victory is still the driving force behind this story."

Muneyuki Kaneshiro broke out as creator of 2011's *As the Gods Will*, a death game story that spawned two sequels and a film adaptation directed by the legendary Takashi Miike. Kaneshiro writes the story of *Blue Lock*.

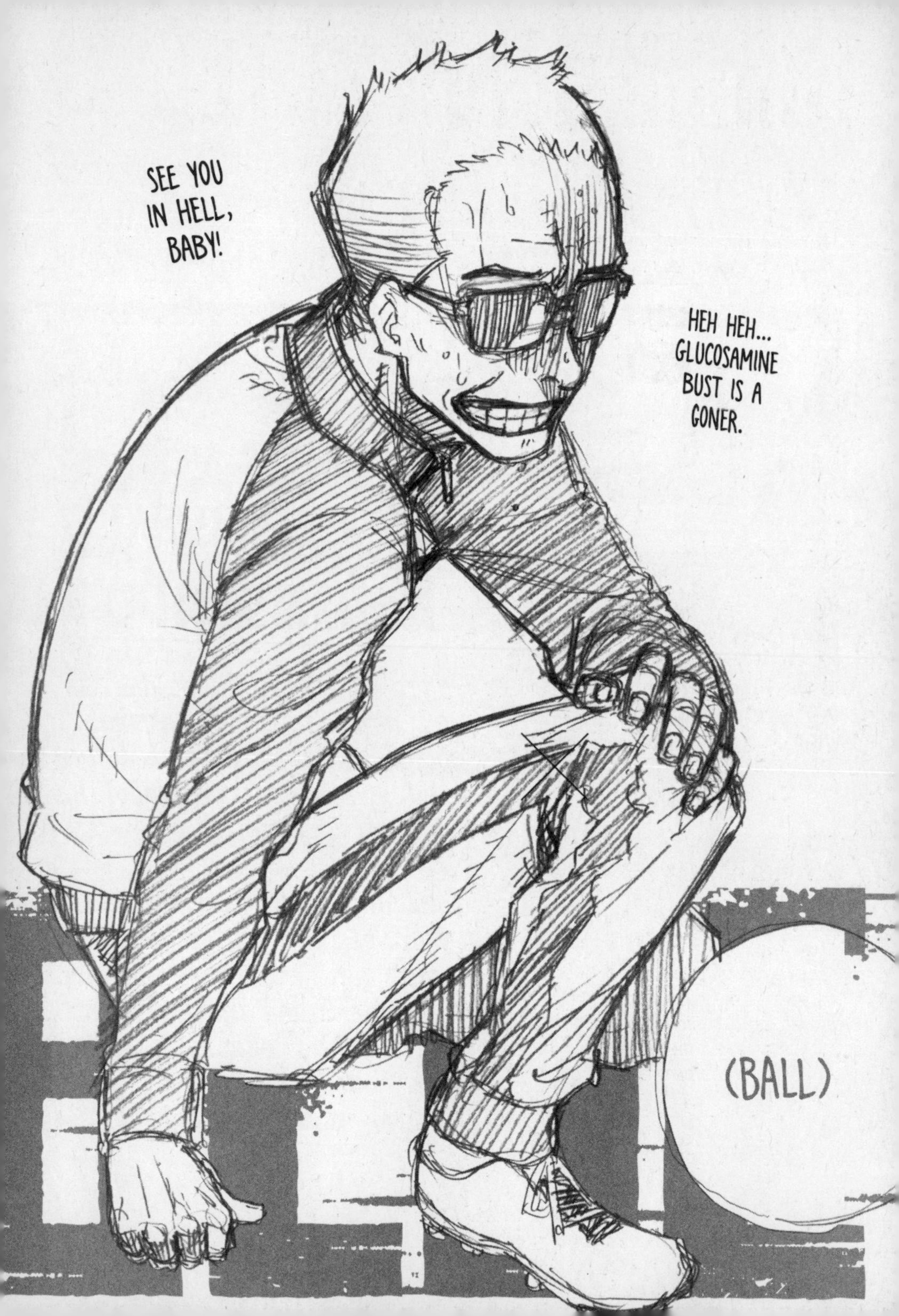
HEH HEH... GLUCOSAMINE BUST IS A GONER.
SEE YOU IN HELL, BABY!
(BALL)

TRANSLATION NOTES

Wanima
page 45

The name "Wanima" has the character "wani" [鰐], which means "crocodile." Junichi's eyebrows look familiar...

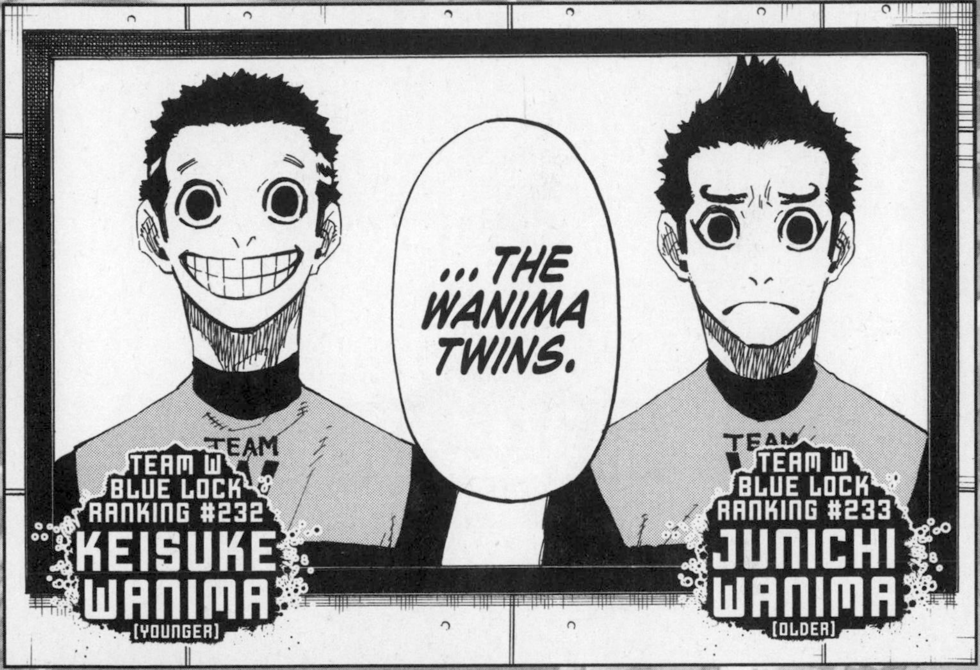

...THE WANIMA TWINS.
TEAM W BLUE LOCK RANKING #233
JUNICHI WANIMA
[OLDER]
TEAM W BLUE LOCK RANKING #232
KEISUKE WANIMA
[YOUNGER]

"3x3 All Stars"
page 49

When Gagamaru notes that Kuon's plan name has a "classic ring to it," Gagamaru is referencing the classic Japanese rock band, "Southern All Stars." In the Japanese, they both are commenting that they are fans of the group, which has been around since 1977.

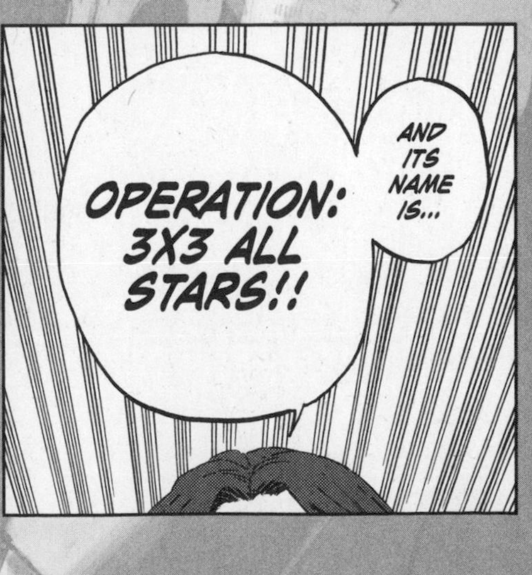

AND ITS NAME IS...
OPERATION: 3X3 ALL STARS!!

BLUELOCK

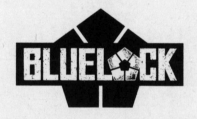

Young characters and steampunk setting, like *Howl's Moving Castle* and *Battle Angel Alita*

Beyond the Clouds © 2018 Nicke / Ki-oon

A boy with a talent for machines and a mysterious girl whose wings he's fixed will take you beyond the clouds! In the tradition of the high-flying, resonant adventure stories of Studio Ghibli comes a gorgeous tale about the longing of young hearts for adventure and friendship!

A SMART, NEW ROMANTIC COMEDY FOR FANS OF *SHORTCAKE CAKE* AND *TERRACE HOUSE!*

A romance manga starring high school girl Meeko, who learns to live on her own in a boarding house whose living room is home to the odd (but handsome) Matsunaga-san. She begins to adjust to her new life away from her parents, but Meeko soon learns that no matter how far away from home she is, she's still a young girl at heart — especially when she finds herself falling for Matsunaga-san.

Perfect World

Rie Aruga

A TOUCHING NEW SERIES ABOUT LOVE AND COPING WITH DISABILITY

An office party reunites Tsugumi with her high school crush Itsuki. He's realized his dream of becoming an architect, but along the way, he experienced a spinal injury that put him in a wheelchair. Now Tsugumi's rekindled feelings will butt up against prejudices she never considered — and Itsuki will have to decide if he's ready to let someone into his heart...

"Depicts with great delicacy and courage the difficulties some with disabilities experience getting involved in romantic relationships... Rie Aruga refuses to romanticize, pushing her heroine to face the reality of disability. She invites her readers to the same tasks of empathy, knowledge and recognition."
—Slate.fr

"An important entry [in manga romance]... The emotional core of both plot and characters indicates thoughtfulness... [Aruga's] research is readily apparent in the text and artwork, making this feel like a real story."
—Anime News Network

KODANSHA COMICS

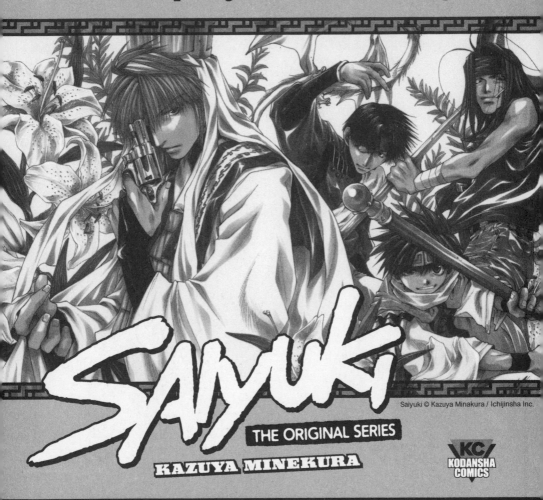

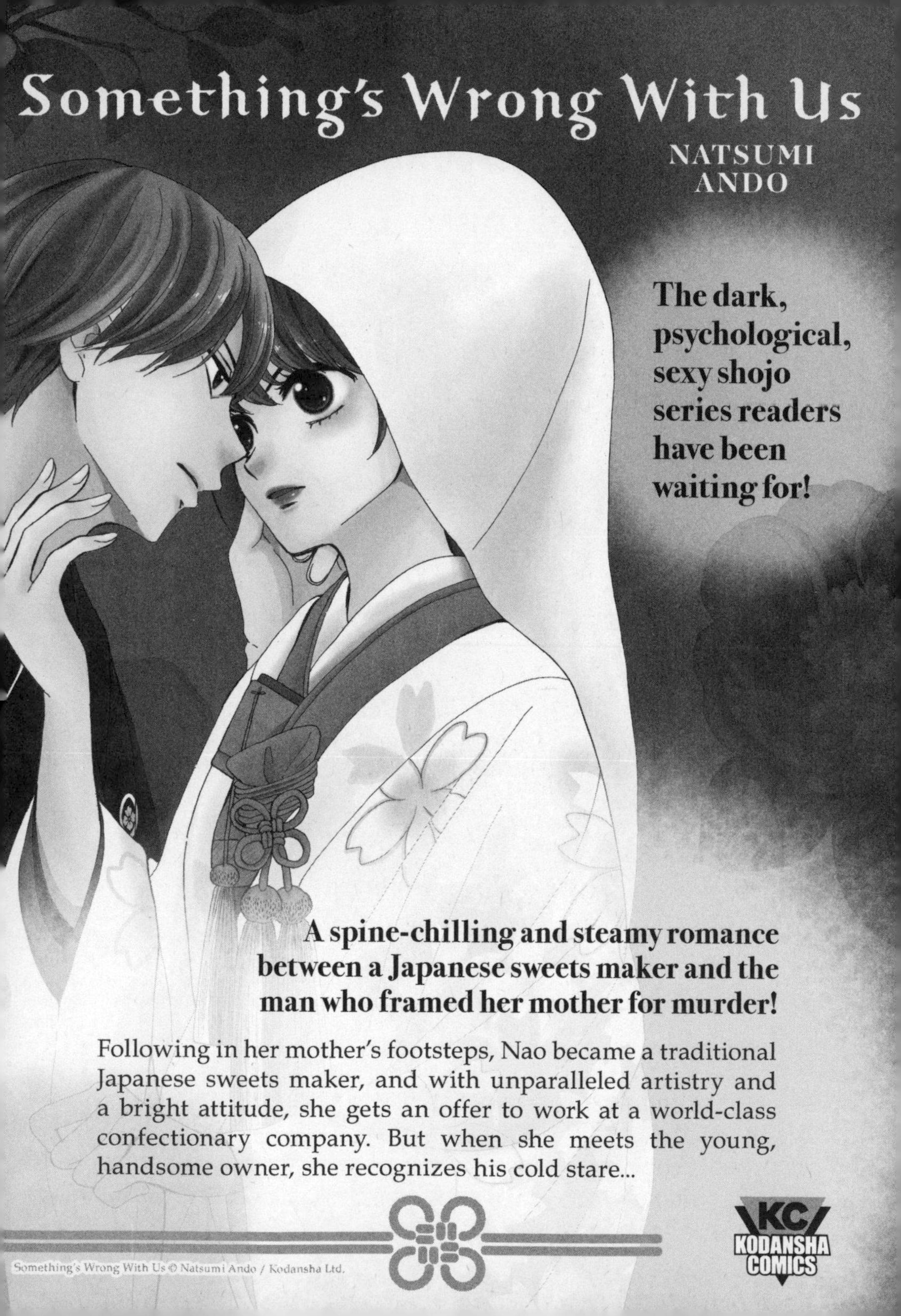
Something's Wrong With Us
NATSUMI ANDO
The dark, psychological, sexy shojo series readers have been waiting for!
A spine-chilling and steamy romance between a Japanese sweets maker and the man who framed her mother for murder!
Following in her mother's footsteps, Nao became a traditional Japanese sweets maker, and with unparalleled artistry and a bright attitude, she gets an offer to work at a world-class confectionary company. But when she meets the young, handsome owner, she recognizes his cold stare...
KC KODANSHA COMICS
Something's Wrong With Us © Natsumi Ando / Kodansha Ltd.

THE SWEET SCENT OF LOVE IS IN THE AIR! FOR FANS OF OFFBEAT ROMANCES LIKE *WOTAKOI*

Sweat and Soap © Kintetsu Yamada / Kodansha Ltd.

In an office romance, there's a fine line between sexy and awkward... and that line is where Asako — a woman who sweats copiously — meets Koutarou — a perfume developer who can't get enough of Asako's, er, scent. Don't miss a romcom manga like no other!

SAINT ☆ YOUNG MEN

A LONG AWAITED ARRIVAL IN PREMIUM 2-IN-1 HARDCOVER

After centuries of hard work, Jesus and Buddha take a break from their heavenly duties to relax among the people of Japan, and their adventures in this lighthearted buddy comedy are sure to bring mirth and merriment to all!

"Brilliant…the physical comedy and facial expressions will make you literally LOL."

—Sam Humphries (host of *DC Daily*; writer, *Green Lanterns*, *Legendary Star-Lord*)

KAMOME SHIRAHAMA

Witch Hat Atelier

A magical manga adventure for fans of Disney and Studio Ghibli!

Witch Hat Atelier © Kamome Shirahama/Kodansha Ltd.

The magical adventure that took Japan by storm is finally here, from acclaimed DC and Marvel cover artist Kamome Shirahama!

In a world where everyone takes wonders like magic spells and dragons for granted, Coco is a girl with a simple dream: She wants to be a witch. But everybody knows magicians are born, not made, and Coco was not born with a gift for magic. Resigned to her un-magical life, Coco is about to give up on her dream to become a witch…until the day she meets Qifrey, a mysterious, traveling magician. After secretly seeing Qifrey perform magic in a way she's never seen before, Coco soon learns what everybody "knows" might not be the truth, and discovers that her magical dream may not be as far away as it may seem…

KC KODANSHA COMICS

The beloved characters from *Cardcaptor Sakura* return in a brand new, reimagined fantasy adventure!

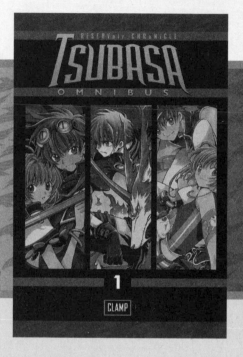

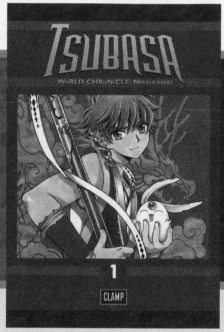

"[*Tsubasa*] takes readers on a fantastic ride that only gets more exhilarating with each successive chapter." —Anime News Network

In the Kingdom of Clow, an archaeological dig unleashes an incredible power, causing Princess Sakura to lose her memories. To save her, her childhood friend Syaoran must follow the orders of the Dimension Witch and travel alongside Kurogane, an unrivaled warrior; Fai, a powerful magician; and Mokona, a curiously strange creature, to retrieve Sakura's dispersed memories!

KC
KODANSHA
COMICS

Beautifully seductive artwork and uniquely Japanese depictions of the supernatural will hypnotize CLAMP fans!

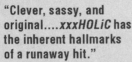

xxxHOLiC © CLAMP ShigatsuTsuitachi CO.,LTD./Kodansha Ltd
xxxHOLiC Rei © CLAMP ShigatsuTsuitachi CO.,LTD./Kodansha Ltd

Kimihiro Watanuki is haunted by visions of ghosts and spirits. He seeks help from a mysterious woman named Yuko, who claims she can help. However, Watanuki must work for Yuko in order to pay for her aid. Soon Watanuki finds himself employed in Yuko's shop, where he sees things and meets customers that are stranger than anything he could have ever imagined.

A Kodansha Trade Paperback Original

Blue Lock 3 copyright © 2019 Muneyuki Kaneshiro/Yusuke Nomura
English translation copyright © 2022 Muneyuki Kaneshiro/Yusuke Nomura

All rights reserved.

Published in the United States by
Kodansha USA Publishing, LLC, New York.

Publication rights for this English edition arranged through
Kodansha Ltd., Tokyo.

First published in Japan in 2019 by Kodansha Ltd., Tokyo
as *Buruu rokku,* volume 3.

ISBN 978-1-64651-656-8

Printed in the United States of America.

2nd Printing

Translation: Nate Derr
Lettering: Chris Burgener
Additional lettering and layout: Scott O. Brown
Editing: Thalia Sutton, Maggie Le
YKS Services LLC/SKY JAPAN, Inc.
Kodansha USA Publishing edition cover design by Matthew Akuginow

Publisher: Kiichiro Sugawara

Director of Publishing Services: Ben Applegate
Director of Publishing Operations: Dave Barrett
Associate Director of Publishing Operations: Stephen Pakula
Publishing Services Managing Editors: Alanna Ruse, Madison Salters,
with Grace Chen
Production Manager: Angela Zurlo

KODANSHA.US

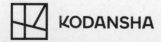